Return to the One

Return to the One

Plotinus's Guide to God-Realization

A Modern Exposition
of an Ancient Classic,
the *Enneads*

Brian Hines

Unlimited Publishing
Bloomington, Indiana

Adrasteia Publishing
Salem, Oregon

Distributing Publisher:
Unlimited Publishing LLC
Bloomington, Indiana

http://www.unlimitedpublishing.com

Contributing Publisher:
Adrasteia Publishing
Salem, Oregon

http://www.adrasteiapublishing.com

First edition.

Copies of this fine book and others
are available to order online at:

http://www.unlimitedpublishing.com/authors

ISBN 1-58832-100-2

Unlimited Publishing
Bloomington, Indiana

Contents

Acknowledgements

MANY THANKS to Gurinder Singh for suggesting that Plotinus would be a suitable subject for my next book, and stimulating my interest in this marvelous mystic philosopher. In the initial stages of my research, Michael Chase, a translator of the *Enneads*, patiently answered many questions via email and pointed me in some fruitful directions. Faith Singh served as an able editorial advisor, helping guide this book through several early drafts.

As my inquiry into the teachings of Plotinus progressed, I relied heavily on the scholarly expertise of Donka Markus (Department of Classical Studies, University of Michigan). *Return to the One* never could have been completed without Donka's help.

Other scholars contributed much to this book. I'm especially appreciative to Dan Dombrowski (Department of Philosophy, Seattle University) and Shimon Malin (Department of Physics and Astronomy, Colgate University) for their detailed reviews and specific suggestions. In addition, hearty appreciation goes to Michael Sells (Department of Religion, Haverford College), Sara Rappe (Department of Classical Studies, University of Michigan), and John Bussanich (Department of Philosophy, University of New Mexico) for their cogent comments.

Jane Humphries copy-edited a pre-publication draft and corrected many typographical/grammatical errors.

After searching long and hard for a suitable publisher, it was a joy to become involved with Dan Snow of Unlimited Publishing and Charles King of Cox-King Multimedia. Their professionalism and dedication to producing quality books made the process of publishing *Return to the One* flow smoothly.

Many people read and commented on the book's various drafts. Kudos to these dedicated reviewers (listed in alphabetical order) for the time and effort they put into making this a better book:

Chris Ashton, Luther Askeland, Frances Chapple, Jane Clarke, Nirmal Singh Dhesi, Mike Dorr, E.M. Easterly, Keith Ecklund, Steve Evans, Richard Geldard, Johann Grove, Molly Hoffer, Linda Loranger, Michael Loranger, Peter Loranger, Maggie McManus, Rita Morey, Ron Morey, Antoine Nohra, Rob Norman, Marjorie Panditji, Iannis Pangakis, Dafni Samara, Scott Sanders, Donald

Sargeant, Sue Sargeant, Vince Savarese, Randy Smith, Frank Vogel, Mary Wallace, Stan White.

If I have neglected to thank anyone who helped with this book, please forgive me. Your contribution is reflected in these pages, even if your name is missing from the acknowledgements. During the several years I put into researching and writing *Return to the One*, I benefited much from many informal dialogues about Plotinus's philosophy with people—some cited above, and some not—who sharpened my thinking, challenged my assumptions, and led me to look more deeply into my self.

Laurel, my wife, supported me wonderfully through all the ups and downs of this challenging project. When I got frustrated, she soothed my concerns; when my mental health suffered, she restored my sanity; when I needed a shoulder to lean on, she was firmly beside me.

A big pat goes to Serena, our canine companion, who would enter my office and cajole me with what can only be called dogged determination to take a break from my writing, allowing fresh Plotinian insights to spring to mind during our walk in the countryside.

Lastly, grateful thanks to the following for permission to reprint passages from their books:

Reprinted by permission of the publishers and the Trustees of the Loeb Classical Library from *Plotinus, Volumes I-VII*, translated by A.H. Armstrong, Cambridge, Mass.: Harvard University Press, Copyright © 1966, 1967, 1984, 1988 by the President and Fellows of Harvard College. The Loeb Classical Library ® is a registered trademark of the President and Fellows of Harvard College.

Reprinted by permission of The University of Chicago Press from *Plotinus or The Simplicity of Vision*, by Pierre Hadot (trans. Michael Chase), © 1993 by The University of Chicago.

Reprinted by permission of Harmony Books, a division of Random House, Inc. from *The Passion of the Western Mind*, by Richard Tarnas, copyright © 1991 by Richard Tarnas.

Reprinted by permission of Routledge from *Plotinus*, by Lloyd P. Gerson, © 1994 Lloyd P. Gerson.

Reprinted with the permission of Cambridge University Press from *Plotinus: The Road to Reality*, by J.M. Rist, © 1967 Cambridge University Press.

Reprinted by permission of Oxford University Press from *Plotinus: An Introduction to the Enneads*, by Dominic J. O'Meara, © 1993 Dominic J. O'Meara.

Introduction

IF SOMETHING has been lost and you're not sure where to look for it, there's good reason to start searching right where you are rather than far afield. Most of us have had the experience of wandering around the house looking for our car keys, only to find that they were sitting unnoticed in our pocket or purse the whole time. Can we apply this lesson to finding meaning and well-being in life? I believe we can.

This book is about the spiritual teachings of Plotinus, a third-century Greek philosopher and mystic. He left a collection of writings known as the *Enneads*, so called because one of his students, Porphyry, edited that collection into six sets of nine treatises each (*enneades* in Greek means "nines").

A central message of the *Enneads* is that what each of us truly longs for, even if we don't consciously realize it, is to return to the One—which may be thought of as "God," if this more familiar term for ultimate reality is stripped of its personal or theistic connotations.

The One, for Plotinus, is unequivocally and indisputably *one*. It is the root of everything in existence, for the One is both the source of being and the ground of being (even though, as we will learn, it also is beyond being). So at a deep, mystical level you are the One, I am the One, this book you are holding is the One, and everything else outside and inside of us is the One.

Sign in the seeking

WHY IS IT, then, that the world appears to be constituted of so many distinct entities? I certainly seem to be separate from you, and you from me. Each of us feels closer to some objects, people, and concepts than to other objects, people, and concepts, but always there remains a gap between one's self and all that is other than one's self.

It is natural to try to bridge this gap because humans have an innate longing for intimacy and union, not isolation and separation. Indeed, every urge—such as to worship, to act rightly, to love, to create, to know—flows from a primal drive for fulfillment. We want to make whole what has been broken, to find what has been lost, to do what demands to be done, to return from where we have come.

Looking at the world, people appear to be going in myriads of different directions. It is difficult to discern much rhyme or reason in the wondrous diversity of human pursuits. Some devote their lives to selfless service, others to egotistical self-aggrandizement. Some avidly pursue scientific knowledge, others spiritual wisdom. Some hold family and friends dear, others find companionship in solitude. Where, in all this chaotic activity, is there any sign of the universal order Plotinus speaks of in the *Enneads*?

The sign is in the seeking, not in what is being sought. Everyone is looking for something—desperately, passionately, ceaselessly. There is no end to the number of different "somethings," but the *looking* is common to all. So we are drawn to ask: What if the seeming multiplicity of the cosmos is an illusion and a clearer vision would see that unity underlies all this manyness? Then the quest for any particular thing would, in truth, be a quest for that single thing.

Perhaps all of the seemingly random motion of life on Earth, with six billion people scurrying here and there, each seeking a unique this and that, actually results from an astoundingly simple and largely unconscious impulse: to return to the One. Here is how Plotinus puts it (see the "Reading the Writings of Plotinus" chapter for a description of the numbering scheme, such as "VI-7-31," used in the *Enneads*):

> *The soul loves the Good* [the One] *because, from the beginning, she has been incited by the Good to love him. And the soul which has this love at hand does not wait to be reminded by the beauties of this lower world, but since she has this love—even if she does not realize it—she is constantly searching.* [VI-7-31][1]

Almost every one of us is looking for meaning and well-being everywhere except the most obvious and closest place: the center of one's consciousness. This is, of course, the place where we are right here and right now, for if you or I were not conscious, we could not be reading or writing these words. The problem is that we are aware not only of a conscious core but also of the many peripheral sensations, thoughts, and emotions scattered throughout the consciousness.

The great Plotinian goal is to discard from consciousness all that is not the One. What remains is, logically, the One—divine reality, plain and simple. In this sense, then, Plotinus is highly religious; the root meaning of "religion" is found in the Latin *religare*, to bind back, or reconnect, the individual with God.

Since Plotinus's teachings clearly point toward a direct experience of the One and other spiritual realities, not merely an intellectual understanding of them, Plotinus is recognized as a mystic as well as a philosopher. There are many connotations of "mystic," but Evelyn Underhill cogently notes there is one essential of mysticism: union between God and the soul.[2]

This is precisely Plotinus's overarching purpose, which he shares with many other mystics, religious believers, and spiritual seekers. Aldous Huxley neatly summed up the essence of this universal mystical metaphysics in his book, *The Perennial Philosophy.*

> *Philosophia perennis*—the phrase was coined by Leibniz; but the thing—the metaphysic that recognizes a divine Reality substantial to the world of things and lives and minds; the psychology that finds in the soul something similar to, or even identical with, divine Reality; the ethic that places man's final end in the knowledge of the immanent and transcendent Ground of all being—the thing is immemorial and universal.[3]

Wisdom for a Western mind

So PLOTINUS ISN'T telling us anything new, nor is he telling us anything complex. The meaning of life (or, we might say, that which gives life meaning) is to be found as close to home as could possibly be imagined: right within, or more accurately *as*, the center of one's consciousness. What makes Plotinus unique is that, as a Greek philosopher, his explication of the perennial philosophy is framed in a thoroughly "Western" fashion.

If someone has a Western mind, he or she is more likely to be convinced by another Western mind that the tenets of the perennial philosophy are true. Such conviction is requisite for believing in those tenets and for making them the foundation of one's life, and indeed one's very being. But what is the Western mind? It's easier to inwardly intuit than to outwardly describe.

I'm quite sure that I have a predominantly Western mind. But since Western ways of thinking and relating to the world are so intimately entwined in my consciousness, I primarily notice my Western-ness when I associate with people thoroughly imbued with an Eastern mentality—who may or may not be Indian, Chinese, Japanese, or such, because "Western" and "Eastern" are internal attitudes, not external attributes. In our increasingly borderless world marked by free-flowing education, information, and technology, an Indian computer scientist may have a Western mind, while her American tai chi instructor may have an Eastern mentality.

I don't have an ironclad definition of the Western and Eastern minds (which implies that my own may not indisputably be of the Occidental variety). But here are a few lighthearted ways to distinguish them experientially.

If you attend a talk on some spiritual subject—a lecture, sermon, discourse—and the people around you are reaching for handkerchiefs to dab their tears of love and devotion, while you are pulling out a notebook and pen to jot down critical questions to ask the speaker, you have a Western mind. If passages in your Bible or other holy book are highlighted in various colors, you have a Western mind (give yourself extra points if objections are penciled in the margin next to pronouncements you disagree with).

I don't mean to imply that the Western mind is entirely detached, rational, skeptical, independent, and analytical. Even those with a strong predilection toward a Western mentality are capable of manifesting the opposite characteristics as well: intimacy, intuition, faithfulness, interdependency, holism. This is because each of us is a mixture of what we might call "masculine" and "feminine" qualities. The challenge, psychologically, spiritually, even societally, is to find the proper blend of masculine and feminine, Western and Eastern, yang and yin, respectively.

Richard Tarnas, author of *The Passion of the Western Mind*, says that the masculinity of the Western mind is a questing force, ceaselessly striving for freedom and progress. Present in both men and women, the rebellious and individualistic Western mind seeks to become differentiated from the cultural matrix that gives it birth.[4]

Yet Tarnas also observes that "this separation necessarily calls forth a longing for a reunion with that which has been lost. . . . I believe this has all along been the underlying goal of Western intellectual and spiritual evolution. *For the deepest passion of the Western mind has been to reunite with the ground of its own being.*"[5] Tarnas implies that there is no conflict between the Western mind and the spiritual goal of divine union, which fits with the fact that Plotinus embraces both.

The roots of Western thought spring from the fertile ground of ancient Greece. So when I discovered the spiritual teachings of

Plotinus, I felt like I had come home. I was instantly comfortable with his approach to spirituality: a blend of rationality and mysticism, of reasonable words and ecstatic contemplation. The culture within which Plotinus studied, taught, and wrote his philosophy is the culture that gave birth to Western civilization. Could there be a better place for a Western mind to look for spiritual inspiration?

Richard Tarnas explains why his book starts off as it does:

> We begin with the Greeks. It was some twenty-five centuries ago that the Hellenic world brought forth that extraordinary flowering of culture that marked the dawn of Western civilization. Endowed with seemingly primeval clarity and creativity, the ancient Greeks provided the Western mind with what has proved to be a perennial source of insight, inspiration, and renewal. Modern science, medieval theology, classical humanism—all stand deeply in their debt.
>
> Greek thought was as fundamental for Copernicus and Kepler, and Augustine and Aquinas, as for Cicero and Petrarch. Our way of thinking is still profoundly Greek in its underlying logic, so much so that before we can begin to grasp the character of our own thought, we must first look closely at that of the Greeks. They remain fundamental for us in other ways as well: Curious, innovative, critical, intensely engaged with life and with death, searching for order and meaning yet skeptical of conventional verities, the Greeks were originators of intellectual values as relevant today as they were in the fifth century B.C.[6]

Alfred North Whitehead famously said that it is a safe generalization that all of Western philosophy is but a series of footnotes to Plato. This is an implied endorsement of Plotinus's importance, since Plato is Plotinus's philosophical forebear. Separated by some 600 years (Plato lived from 427–347 B.C.E., and Plotinus from 205–270 C.E.), modern scholars call Plotinus a Neoplatonist.

I won't go into the details of what distinguishes a Platonist from a Neoplatonist, because this isn't necessary to appreciate Plotinus's teachings. Suffice it to say that, according to Maria Luisa Gatti, Plotinus differs from Plato mainly in the elimination of politics from his philosophy, his more radical assertion that reality is monistic (a unified whole), and the spiritualization of his philosophical system.[7]

Neoplatonism and Christianity

ECHOING WHITEHEAD, can we say that all of Western spirituality is but a series of footnotes to Plotinus? This would be going too far, even though Richard Tarnas says this of Saint Augustine (354–430), who had a great formative influence on Christian theology: "Plotinus's philosophy, in turn, was pivotal in Augustine's gradual conversion to Christianity. Augustine saw Plotinus as one in whom 'Plato lived again,' and regarded Plato's thought itself as 'the most pure and bright in all philosophy,' so profound as to be in almost perfect concordance with the Christian faith."[8]

During the third century, in Plotinus's lifetime, Neoplatonism and Christianity competed for the hearts and minds of those in the Mediterranean world. Nowadays, among Christians at least, this tends to be viewed as a battle between the ethereal teachings of Jesus and a crude paganism.

Indeed, the spiritual message of one of these combatants can be summarized in this fashion: There is only one God, who is all love; every human being has an immortal soul, whose highest destiny is to be united with God; if we live virtuous lives, we will join our heavenly Father after death, but if we do not, justice will be done; we must humbly yield to the divine will, accepting with equanimity whatever life brings us; to be attracted to the sensual pleasures of this world is to be distanced from God, the Good we seek but never find in material pursuits. And then there is the Christian conception of spirituality, which I won't bother to summarize, as it should already be familiar to the reader.

The Neoplatonic metaphysics encapsulated in the paragraph above bear a strong resemblance to Christianity. So just as Plotinus has been pithily described as "Plato without the politics," it can be said, albeit somewhat simplistically, that Christianity is "Neoplatonism with Jesus."

Keith Ward, an Anglican priest and author of *God: A Guide for the Perplexed*, writes: "Why is there no Platonic religion? Well, in a sense there is. It is called Christianity. Or at least Christianity took from Plato many of the most important aspects of his thought, and attached them to its own central teaching that Jesus was the supreme manifestation of God."[9]

What we find in the *Enneads*, in contrast to the *Bible*, is an elevated spirituality almost completely devoid of particulars. Plotinus, along with virtually all of his Greek philosophical brethren, sought universal truths, not individual instances of those verities. Neoplatonic spirituality thus has a scientific tenor that is rarely found in other religious theologies or metaphysical systems, for science similarly seeks knowledge of the fundamental laws of nature, as well as an understanding of the relations between the general laws and particular phenomena.

Resonating with Plotinus

IT SHOULD BE obvious that I resonate with Plotinus, or I wouldn't have devoted so much time and effort to writing *Return to the One*. Up to a few years ago I knew next to nothing about his teachings. But I was strongly drawn to his mystic philosophy once I started to seriously study the *Enneads*. For most of my fifty-five years I've cast my intellectual net widely in the world's ocean of philosophical, religious, mystical, and metaphysical literature. Yet I've never found a spiritual system so simultaneously appealing to the mind and the heart, to reason and intuition, to logic and passion.

So I must unabashedly admit that throughout *Return to the One* you will find a prejudice that colors every aspect of my commentary. Here is that presumption: the general thrust of Plotinus's philosophy is true. I don't mean that it is just true for me, or for Plotinus, but that it is objectively true—an accurate reflection both of the nature of ultimate reality and the means by which it is possible to know this highest truth.

The content and style of my writing follows naturally from this prejudice. My un-hidden agenda is to be an advocate for Plotinus's teachings, not a detached analyzer of them. In taking this stance, I chart a course midway between the extreme objectivist position that it is possible to know exactly what Plotinus taught if we study his language, culture, philosophical influences, and so forth, in sufficient precision and detail, and the extreme subjectivist position that whatever I or anyone else says about Plotinus, it is just a personal opinion to be taken as such.

I do believe that it is possible to know the spiritual truths that Plotinus knew, but only if we inwardly become our true selves, which will be found to be identical with Plotinus's true self. This obviously separates my approach from that of most scholars, for they poke and probe Plotinus's teachings as if they were external objects of knowledge akin to fossils excavated from an ancient riverbed, which is exactly how Plotinus says we should *not* consider his philosophy.

We will not be able to fully understand Plotinus's teachings through a method that isn't in tune with Plotinus's theory of knowledge, which Sara Rappe encapsulates: "For him [Plotinus], the condition sine qua non for knowledge is the unity of the knower and the object of knowledge, a condition that discursive thought of any kind necessarily precludes."[10]

It's much as if you were out on a walk with a friend, and she said, "Come over here and smell this flower. It's got an amazing fragrance." Your friend knew about the fragrance because she had inhaled it and thereby made it part of her (physical) being.

You wouldn't be able to know what she knew if, instead of smelling the flower, you broke it off at the stem, took it to a laboratory, and analyzed its chemical composition. This would give you a certain knowledge but not the knowledge of fragrance. In fact, after you pluck the flower, the fragrance will begin to fade, indicating that an effort to obtain analytical knowledge obviates the intuitive knowledge that comes from simply smelling.

Bringing bones to life

SIMILARLY, we have to embrace Plotinus's philosophy in the fashion in which he himself embraced it if we want to absorb the inner spiritual essence as well as the outer conceptual trappings of his teachings. Plotinus wants to change our whole way of looking at the world and ourselves. This is much different, and considerably more difficult, than perceiving his teachings as we perceive everything else: as something separate and distinct from our own selves. Sara Rappe says:

> For Plotinus, the task of the philosopher will not be to deliver a discursive exposition concerning the principles of reality, but rather to remind the reader to 'turn the act of awareness inward, and insist that it hold attention there.' (*Enneads* V.1.12.15)[11]

Along these lines, Robert Meager, author of *Augustine: An Introduction*, describes the approach he took toward his subject: "Any authentically open inquiry into the thinking of another person must at some point take the form of commentary, of 'minding-with' that person. To mind with someone is to assume a common posture of mind with that person. . . . Indeed, unless we are willing to think Augustine's thoughts we cannot presume to think about them."[12]

Meager says that his commentary on Augustine's writings "strives to resume and to continue the original activity."[13] This also is my goal with *Return to the One*. I don't want you to look on Plotinus's teachings as if they were bleached dinosaur bones from a far-distant time and place reassembled for your inspection in a musty museum. So in this book I have done my best to flesh out the skeleton of Plotinus's often austere exposition of his mystical message, and to describe his philosophy in an informal, modern style. I am hopeful that this will help his teachings come alive for you, as they have for me.

"Return to the One" in a nutshell

FOLLOWING this introduction is a description of Plotinus the person and his thoroughly Greek teaching approach. Then we turn to how the ancient Greeks viewed philosophy: as a way of life, an art of living. As a mystic philosopher, Plotinus taught that life is lived truly not *here* but *there*, on a plane of consciousness closer to ultimate reality than this crude physical existence.

This leads us naturally into a chapter concerned with the mystical connotation of a "leap of faith," which is quite different from how religions generally use this phrase. Mystics such as Plotinus urge us to embrace mystery rather than clinging onto theological or philosophical concepts that claim to explain mystery (but really just push it out of sight of the mind's eye).

I should mention that if the reader wants to jump right into the detailed discussion of Plotinus's teachings that begins with the "God Is the Goal" chapter, he or she should feel free to do so, coming back later, if desired, to the preliminary chapters. But the final chapter in this Preliminaries section, "Reading the Writings of Plotinus," shouldn't be skipped, as it contains information that is critical for appreciating and understanding the many quotations from the *Enneads* in this book. This chapter includes an explanation of how Plotinus's paradoxical use of language supports his mystical philosophy.

We then move into the core of *Return to the One*, the organization of which reflects the grand themes of Plotinus's philosophy: "The One," "And Many," "Soul's Descent," "And Return." The first two sections lay out the design of the cosmos, from the highest unity of the One down to the lowest multiplicity of the physical universe. The last two sections describe the soul's journey through these realms, descending to materiality from spiritual regions and returning, through contemplation, to its original home.

Within each section are short topical chapters with quotations from the *Enneads* and my commentary. The chapter titles reflect my fondness for alliteration: "Reality Is a Radiation," "First Is Formless," "Soul Is the Self," and so on. These short aphorisms are intended to be an aid in remembering the central tenets of Plotinus's teachings.

You'll find that I frequently use examples from everyday life to illustrate a philosophical point, and often try to leaven Plotinus's serious tone with some lighthearted observations. To my mind, humor and spirituality are better thought of as bedfellows than antagonists: a smile points us up, both bodily and spiritually, whereas a frown turns us down.

This book wraps up with a section called, entirely appropriately, "Wrap-Up." Here I begin by considering Plotinus's teachings within the broader purview of exoteric and esoteric spirituality, which are distinguished by their relative emphasis on seeking divinity outwardly and inwardly, respectively (Plotinus is decidedly in the esoteric camp). This leads into a more extensive examination of a subject raised earlier: that mysticism has an affinity of method with science, and an affinity of subject matter with religion, producing the possibility of a true spiritual science.

I argue, in the next chapter, that viewing Plotinus as a spiritual scientist helps to explain why Neoplatonism and Christianity were so much at odds in the period surrounding Plotinus's death in 270. This theme continues into a chapter concerned with the legacy of Plotinus and Plato, which can be recognized in the Neoplatonist sentiments expressed by such great medieval thinkers as Meister Eckhart, Nicolas of Cusa, the anonymous author of *The Cloud of Unknowing*, and Marsilio Ficino.

The wrap-up finishes with a personal summation of how I've come to look upon the rational mysticism of Plotinus: as a great experiment with truth. Then, the book concludes with something completely different from what has come before: a fable. This tale, "Stuck at Lake Partway," is my attempt to relate to the reader, in a non-intellectual fashion, how Plotinus has led me to critically examine the nature of my commitment to spirituality.

Preliminaries

Plotinus, a Rational Mystic

PLOTINUS TIRELESSLY WORKED on personal and cultural levels to find the oneness beyond multiplicity. Within his own consciousness, he sought unity. Within the Greek philosophical tradition, he sought unity. By all accounts, he ably succeeded in accomplishing both ends. As J.V. Luce says:

> Plotinus was an idealistic thinker who believed he could give positive answers to the great philosophical questions about God, the soul, and the world. Looking back over the whole course of Greek philosophy he tried to distill its inherited wisdom into one all-embracing and spiritualistic system.
>
> . . . He inherited and worked within the best traditions of Greek rationalism deriving ultimately from Plato and Pythagoras. But he was also a mystic in the sense that his philosophy was enhanced and deepened in its spirituality by a recurrent experience of mystical union with the divine nature.[1]

Most of what we know about the life of Plotinus comes from a short biography written by one of his students, Porphyry, a noted philosopher in his own right. Porphyry begins by explaining why the biography is brief: "Plotinus resembled someone ashamed of being in a body."[2] Plotinus wouldn't speak about his parents, homeland, or date of birth.

In like fashion, we're told that Plotinus refused a request made by one of his students to have a portrait made of him, explaining: "Isn't it enough that I have to bear this image with which Nature has covered us? Must I also consent to leaving behind me an image of that image—this one even longer-lasting—as if it were an image of something worth seeing?"[3]

Realizations before writing

PLOTINUS PROBABLY was born in Egypt in 205. Even though he may not have been of Greek parentage, scholars agree that his background is thoroughly Greek. Porphyry tells us that in his late twenties Plotinus began studying in Alexandria with a teacher, Ammonius Saccus, and remained with him for eleven years. This was after Plotinus

3

had gone to other teachers who left him unsatisfied. A friend had referred him to Ammonius and at once Plotinus knew that he was the man for whom he had been searching.

After trying (but failing) to journey to Persia and India to investigate Eastern thought, Plotinus went to Rome in 244. For about ten years he taught philosophy, but wouldn't speak about what he had learned from Ammonius. Eventually, though, Plotinus began to base his lectures on Ammonius's teachings. Still, ten more years passed before Plotinus started writing.

Philosophy was a way of life for Plotinus, not an intellectual exercise. He studied for eleven years with Ammonius, a man who wrote nothing. Plotinus taught for ten years in Rome but refused to talk about what he learned from Ammonius. Then, after finally feeling free to speak of Ammonius's wisdom, for another decade Plotinus refrained from setting down his own teachings in writing.

Dialogue over dissertation

PLOTINUS CLEARLY FAVORED dialogue over dissertation. A conversation between a student and teacher is alive, open-ended, full of possibilities, a meeting of soul with soul in the present moment. A writing is dead, closed up, completed, a record of what was thought by someone else in the past. In *The Seventh Letter*, Plato explains why he will never write a treatise on some subject:

> For it does not admit of exposition like other branches of knowledge; but after much converse about the matter itself and a life lived together, suddenly a light, as it were, is kindled in one soul by a flame that leaps to it from another, and thereafter sustains itself.
> . . . For this reason no man of intelligence will venture to express his philosophical views in language, especially not in language that is unchangeable, which is true of that which is set down in written characters.[4]

This doesn't mean that books are useless for the seeker of wisdom, just that the value of genuine inner knowledge is much greater than any attempt to outwardly communicate the knowledge one has attained. Thus, as has already been noted, the rational side of Plotinus's mysticism is aimed not so much at transmitting some bit of philosophical knowledge from teacher to student, but rather at encouraging the student to search out that truth for him- or herself. Questions are more important than answers.

Plotinus didn't force his teachings upon anybody; his students were free to decide for themselves what to accept or reject. Porphyry says, "He used to encourage his listeners to ask questions themselves, and as a result his classes were full of disorder and idle babble."[5] When Porphyry first started studying with Plotinus, he questioned a central aspect of Plotinus's philosophy: that the forms did not exist outside of *nous*, or spirit, (the next highest level of reality after the One).

Porphyry set down his objections in writing. Plotinus had another student, Amelius, read Porphyry's essay to him. Then he smilingly said, "It's up to you, Amelius, to solve the problems into which Porphyry has fallen out of ignorance of our views."[6] According to Porphyry:

> Amelius then wrote a rather lengthy book entitled "Against the Objections of Porphyry." I in turn wrote a response to this, and Amelius replied to my writing. On the third time, I, Porphyry, was able—albeit with difficulty—to understand what was being said, and I changed my views, whereupon I wrote a retraction, which I read before the assembly.[7]

This anecdote captures the spirit of classic Greek philosophy: restrained, courteous, respectful, patient, non-authoritarian. Even though Plotinus was a spiritual guide for his students, he did not preach to them; he did not demand unthinking fealty; he did not set himself up as the only channel of truth. Plotinus's warmth and love pervaded his school's meetings, as Porphyry tells us:

> His intelligence was clearly evident when he spoke; its light used to illuminate his face. He was always pleasant to look at, but in those moments he was even more beautiful. He would break into a light sweat, and his gentleness shone forth. He showed his gentle tolerance for questions as well as his vigor in answering them.[8]

To form, not inform

WHEN PLOTINUS BEGAN writing the *Enneads*, he did not intend them to be a tightly organized description of his philosophy. Instead, Plotinus wrote about subjects and problems that came up in the meetings of his school. Few people ever saw the treatises, as Porphyry says that it wasn't easy to make copies. Living as we do in an age when printed books are cheap and readily available, it is difficult to imagine how precious a hand-copied set of the *Enneads* would have been to Plotinus's students.

Porphyry tells us, "These books were entrusted only to a small number of persons, for it was not yet easy to obtain them; they were given out with a bad conscience, and not simply or recklessly. Rather, every effort was made to choose those who were to receive them."[9]

Today, we tend to look upon philosophical works as informative rather than formative. That is, a philosopher's book is read with the expectation of learning something new, not of becoming someone new. Pierre Hadot speaks of the difficulty of comprehending classical philosophical writings from our present perspective.

> Above all, the work, even if it is apparently theoretical and systematic, is written not so much to inform the reader of a doctrinal content but to form him, to make him traverse a certain itinerary in the course of which he will make spiritual progress. This procedure is clear in the works of Plotinus and Augustine, in which all the detours, starts and stops, and digressions of the work are formative elements. One must always approach a philosophical work of antiquity with this idea of spiritual progress in mind.[10]

The world's worst written book?

THUS I BELIEVE that R. Baine Harris is unduly critical when he says, "Although extremely profound and provocative, the *Enneads* probably deserves to be called the world's worst written book since Plotinus seems to presume that the reader already has a complete knowledge of his system when he discusses any topic."[11]

True, but we need to remember that Plotinus was writing for his innermost circle of students, who were well acquainted with the general thrust of his philosophy. This helps explain why the treatises in the *Enneads* are almost impenetrable if one reads them without any prior knowledge of Plotinus's philosophy.

Plotinus jumps around from subject to subject; he sets up counterarguments to a possible answer to a question and argues each so persuasively that the reader has trouble deciding which side Plotinus truly favors; he uses the same term, such as "soul" or "intellect," in various ways depending on the context, frustrating a literal translation through his unique use of the Greek language; he sprinkles his writing with "as it were" and "so to speak," indicating that even if the reader grasps what he is saying, what he is saying is not the whole truth.

Some of the literary eccentricities evident in the *Enneads* can be attributed to Plotinus's mystical subject matter and some are commensurate with the sophisticated audience for whom he was writing. And then there is the factor of his unusual composition style. His biographer, Porphyry, says that Plotinus never reread what he wrote because his eyesight was so poor. Further, he had bad handwriting and was a terrible speller.

Plotinus composed fluidly, however, "writing down what he had stored up in his soul in such a way that he seemed to be copying straight out of a book."[12] He had a remarkable ability to maintain a focus on his subject matter even while attending to other tasks. Porphyry says that Plotinus could be fully engaged in a conversation and still keep his mind on what he had been writing about. When his guest left, Plotinus would return to composing as if he had never taken a break.

In the world, not of the world

PLOTINUS'S PERSONAL LIFE testifies to his ability to adhere to the oft-heard spiritual adage, "live in the world without being of the world." Porphyry writes:

> Many men and women of the most eminent families, when they were about to die, brought their children to Plotinus—males as well as females—and handed them over to him, along with all their possessions, as if to a kind of holy and divine guardian. This was why his house had become full of boys and girls.
> . . . And yet, although he was responsible for the cares and concerns of the lives of so many people, he never—as long as he was awake—let slacken his constant tension directed towards the Spirit.[13]

This reminds us that philosophy, the love of wisdom, was a full-time pursuit for Plotinus. He ceaselessly sought to unite his consciousness with spirit, the first emanation of the One, knowing it to be the essence of his existence. Yet Plotinus didn't live in a philosophical ivory tower far removed from everyday life. In addition to his teaching duties, caring for the children entrusted to him involved him in many practical affairs.

We're also told that "although he spent twenty-six entire years in Rome, and acted as arbitrator in disputes between many people, he never made a single enemy amongst the politicians,"[14] another indication of his ability to remain inwardly centered in spirit while outwardly acting in the world.

The primary goal of the mystic philosopher, as Plotinus teaches in the *Enneads*, is to bring the movable center of his or her consciousness into alignment with the unmoving center of existence, the One. A person's illusory and shifting sense of individuality thus must be distinguished from a true sense of self. If one traces his or her I-ness back to its source, as one would trace a line (or radius) back to the center of the circle from which it emanates, then the core of one's self will be found to be identical with the core of everything.

Truth trumps tradition

WISDOM LIES WITHIN, not without. The only way to know divine truth is to unite one's consciousness so fully with it as to become it. Since union with anything or anyone outside of one's own self is impossible, this leads the philosopher to be more respectful than reverential of other people, regardless of their seeming spiritual attainments. Though Plotinus had a tremendous respect for his fellow Greek philosophers, alive or dead, we can be sure that he agreed with Plato: "But a man is not to be reverenced more than the truth, and therefore I will speak out."[15]

Hence, Porphyry tells us that Plotinus writes what is in his own mind rather than bowing to tradition. After a student would read a commentary by another philosopher on a text from Plato or Aristotle, "Plotinus borrowed nothing at all from these commentaries; on the contrary, he was personal and original in his theoretical reflection, and brought to his investigations the spirit of Ammonius."[16] In a treatise about time, for example, Plotinus says:

> But, as it is, we must first take the most important statements about it and consider whether our own account will agree with any of them. [III-7-7]

And after observing that the pre-Socratic philosopher Heraclitus has left us guessing about what he really meant, Plotinus makes a telling statement that could apply equally to portions of his own writings:

He has neglected to make clear to us what he is saying, perhaps because we ought to seek by ourselves, as he himself sought and found. [IV-8-1]

It is much more important to actually tread the path that leads to the One, than to have an intellectual understanding of what lies along the path. Spiritual knowledge is gained by direct experience, not second-hand reports. Plotinus urges us to carefully examine the teachings of past philosophers (including him now) to sort out those who appear to have come closest to the truth and then to question how we can attain the same level of understanding.

Now we must consider that some of the blessed philosophers of ancient times have found out the truth; but it is proper to investigate which of them have attained it most completely, and how we too could reach an understanding about these things. [III-7-1]

Plotinus doesn't claim he has climbed to any philosophical heights that were not reached by at least some of his predecessors. What he has done, they did, and we can also do. The door that leads to the chamber of spiritual truth always has been, is now, and always will be wide open. All that changes is how those who have passed through this door attempt to describe the indescribable perennial philosophy.

Our doctrines are not novel, nor do they date from today: they were stated long ago, but not in an explicit way. Our present doctrines are explanations of those older ones, and they use Plato's own words to prove that they are ancient. [V-1-8][17]

Philosophy as a Way of Life

UNDENIABLY, there is an adventurous spirit in Plotinus's philosophy. Bernard McGinn says: "Plotinus's ability to combine abstruse philosophical analysis with a tone of deep personal feeling is unique—reading him is like being invited to embark on a journey of exploration into uncharted territory in search of hidden treasure: a bracing and perhaps dangerous enterprise."[1]

Contrast this with the modern perspective of what philosophy is all about. When people envision a philosopher, a likely image is of a gray-haired intellectual ensconced in a high-backed leather chair surrounded with floor-to-ceiling bookcases filled with musty tomes, holding forth with his or her fellow philosophers on some abstruse question that has little or nothing to do with everyday life.

There is considerable truth in this image, for much of what passes for philosophical inquiry today is little more than word-play, abstract ideas having sport with other abstract ideas in a conceptual arena far removed from everyday life. This is much different from the goal of Greek philosophy during Plotinus's lifetime.

Philosophy, an art of living

IN HIS BOOK, *Philosophy as a Way of Life*, Pierre Hadot says, "Ancient philosophy proposed to mankind an art of living. By contrast, modern philosophy appears above all as the construction of a technical jargon reserved for specialists. . . . In modern university philosophy, philosophy is obviously no longer a way of life or form of life—unless it be the form of life of a professor of philosophy."[2]

As an ancient rather than a modern philosopher, Plotinus isn't asking us to merely intellectually believe in a philosophy of life; he extends a much more significant invitation to embrace philosophy *as* life, inseparable from our very being. This is why Plotinus's mystical philosophy seems so exciting, challenging, and adventurous: so is life.

Hadot notes that for the ancients, "Philosophy . . . took on the form of an exercise of the thought, will, and the totality of one's being, the goal of which was to achieve a state practically inaccessible to mankind: wisdom. Philosophy was a method of spiritual progress which demanded a radical conversion and transformation of the individual's way of being."[3]

In the age of Plotinus, the word "philosophy" had not yet lost its original meaning: love of wisdom. *Philo*, in Greek, means love. *Sophia*, wisdom. Just as philodendrons are climbing plants that love to entwine themselves around trees (*dendron*), so did the ancient Greek philosophers seek to embrace wisdom. For them philosophy wasn't an academic exercise but a way of life that led to the greatest possible well-being, *eudaimonia*.

Wisdom and well-being are intimately connected in Plotinus's philosophy because the highest truth is also the highest good—the One (often termed the Good, with a capital G, indicating its superiority to all lesser goods). Hence, the key to achieving *eudaimonia* is realizing what truly exists. Without a solid foundation of being there is no possibility of achieving well-being.

This is why Plotinus taught that no matter what we're doing with our lives, it's all pretty much worthless if we're not yet in touch with our genuine beings. We are like children playing make-believe who don't realize the princess is really a plastic toy, her castle is a cardboard box, and her precious gems are cheap trinkets. However important this children's play may seem to us when we are young and impressionable, with the coming of maturity these things are seen for what they really are.

Plato's cave

PLOTINUS, following Plato, did not cleanly divide creation into what exists and what doesn't exist, or into being and not-being. Instead, he envisioned a great chain of being connecting everything, all the way from what is most lasting and real down to the things in this physical universe, which possess the least being of anything. Thus, something can exist yet barely be. And this, of course, includes one's own self.

Plato, in *The Republic*, provides a vivid metaphor of our human condition: we are prisoners in a cave. The cave is both without and within us, for we are aware of both external and internal reality. Plato says that we human beings have been living in this cave from birth, chained so that we cannot move, able to look only at the far wall of the cavern.

On this wall we see shadows dancing. A shadow may be our own, that of another person, or of an object that is being carried along a low wall behind us, behind which a fire burns, enabling the shadow of the object to be seen. These substantial objects, the spiritual forms, are real; their shadows are much less real. So the basic message of this metaphor is that what we are aware of now, physical existence, is smoke and mirrors, while the unseen mystery of spiritual existence is the solid truth behind appearances.

What we generally consider to be beautiful and good, then, isn't real. This world is like a dream, illusory and ephemeral. Whatever beauty and goodness it seems to possess is a shadow of true beauty and goodness. Hence, it is supremely important to pursue wisdom above all else. If we don't know what really is, how can we make the correct choice about what to do? Right living flows naturally from knowledge of real being.

Love is wonderful but our love should be directed toward what is most real. Otherwise, our situation is akin to that of a man who embraces his lover's shadow when she enters his bedroom. How senseless it would be for him to cast himself upon the floor, passionately grasping at a vague image of the beautiful woman standing before him. He will never enjoy the delight of her company, nor will he be able to know and love her as she truly is, until he turns from her shadow to the reality.

Nothing in this world can fully satisfy us because nothing here truly is. And the farther away we are from consciousness of the One, the less being we ourselves possess. We are shadows trying to drink from a mirage. We're in love with reflections. We're starving for reality but continue to devour illusion. Not surprisingly, we're never satiated.

From this perspective, it's time to stop trying to squeeze more happiness out of the things, thoughts, and people of this world. We need to recognize that we're living in a desert—our arid consciousness of physical reality alone—that is almost completely devoid of sustenance for the soul, the enduring essence of us that feels spiritual hunger and thirst. We have to start moving toward the One, for this is our source and it alone will satisfy.

Where is the One?

THE PROBLEM, though, is knowing which direction to go. Parts of reality are lying around all over the place in plain view. But the wholeness of reality is well-hidden. If this weren't the case, there would be no need for scientists to labor so mightily to discover a theory of everything that explains the fundamental nature of the universe, nor for mystics to undergo such arduous disciplines to realize God. The soul needs a guide to the realm of ultimate truth and well-being, the One. Plotinus says:

> We must not look, but must, as it were, close our eyes and exchange our faculty of vision for another. We must awaken this faculty which everyone possesses, but few people ever use. [I-6-8][4]

Plotinus taught that anyone in love with wisdom (namely, a philosopher) has to undertake a quest to find his or her beloved, for truth resides at the summit of the spiritual mountain that is the cosmos. The path leads the soul from its current immersion in the depths of materiality and sensual pursuits to the more ethereal heights of mind and intuitive intelligence, and then to the spiritual pinnacle of reality, the One.

Plotinus invites us to enter an unfamiliar domain of consciousness that is beyond matter, sensation, reason, and all that is known now. As was noted earlier, this truly would be "a bracing and perhaps dangerous enterprise," for journeying to an unknown higher level of consciousness obviously is a much more adventurous move than simply rearranging the familiar thoughts that comprise the contents of one's present level of consciousness.

Simply put, actually returning to the One bears no resemblance to merely thinking, "I am returning to the One."

Philosophy is lived, not thought

IN LIKE FASHION, Pierre Hadot observes that there is a distinction between discourse about philosophy and philosophy itself.

> Philosophical theories are in the service of the philosophical life. . . . The act of living in a genuinely philosophical way thus corresponds to an order of reality totally different from that of philosophical discourse.[5]

This gets back to the distinction between a philosophy of life and philosophy *as* life. The former is separable from someone's life, a collection of concepts that mirrors, more or less, his or her understanding of the purpose of earthly existence and the priorities that should be placed on various worldly activities. Since concepts can differ significantly from reality (I can conceive that the earth is flat, but it really is round), a person's philosophy of life usually bears only a passing resemblance to his or her actual life. The face we present to others when we respond to the question "What do you believe in?" generally is a mask that disguises, to a greater or lesser degree, our hidden heartfelt beliefs and desires.

By contrast, the goal of a person who aspires to philosophy *as* life is to significantly narrow, if not eliminate completely, the gap between his philosophy of life and his life. Then there is no need for him to utter a word when queried about what he believes in, because his everyday actions, including his demeanor at the very moment the question is asked, comprise the complete honest answer. The philosophy he espouses then is not something that explains his life; his life explains the philosophy he espouses.

This is how the ancient Greeks, including Plotinus, looked upon philosophy, the love of wisdom. A lover shouldn't have to say, "I love you," to his or her beloved, as lovely as those words are. Actions do the speaking in love, as in philosophy. As Pierre Hadot puts it:

> One could say that what differentiates ancient from modern philosophy is the fact that, in ancient philosophy, it was not only Chrysippus [a founder of Stoicism] or Epicurus [founder of Epicureanism] who, just because they had developed a philosophical discourse, were considered philosophers.
>
> Rather, every person who lived according to the precepts of Chrysippus or Epicurus was every bit as much of a philosopher as they. A politician like Cato of Utica was considered a philosopher and even a sage, even though he wrote and taught nothing, because his life was perfectly Stoic.[6]

The philosophical systems of Stoicism and Epicureanism are poles apart; Stoicism posits that good lies in the virtuous state of the soul, and Epicureanism affirms that matter alone is real and that the good life consists in the pursuit of pleasure. However, Hadot notes, they are united in their embrace of philosophy as a way of life to be pursued at each instant, whatever that life may be, a stance shared by the other Greek philosophical traditions such as Socratism, Platonism, Aristotelianism, Cynicism, and Skepticism.

Plotinus considered himself a Platonist, but modern scholars usually call him a Neoplatonist, largely because his teachings are decidedly more mystical and less worldly than Plato's. Regardless of what term is used to classify Plotinus's philosophy, there is no doubt that he intended it to be the foundation of an experiential way of life rather than an intellectual philosophy of life.

A central message of the *Enneads* is that the basic "itinerary" of our return to the One is to know ourselves first as soul, then as spirit, and finally as the source—God, the One. This steadily leads us from multiplicity to unity. Our goal is to be one, not many. In reality, for each of us there is only one being thinking thoughts and acting out actions. So whenever someone thinks one way and acts another a division is created that is at odds with the true nature of both the self and the cosmos. Truth is One, not multiple.

> *If we come to be at one with our self, and no longer split ourselves into two, we are simultaneously One and All, together with that God who is noiselessly present, and we stay with him as long as we are willing and able.* [V-8-11][7]

Making a Leap of Faith

A PERSON splits himself into two when he professes beliefs that are decidedly at odds with his behavior; that is, when his philosophy differs significantly from his life. To become whole, he has to find a way to make his philosophical thoughts and his worldly experience consonant.

Materialists obviously find this easier to do than people who profess spiritual beliefs. Everyday experience of the physical world confirms the reality of material existence, so a materialistic philosophy of life is appealingly honest: I experience matter and I believe in matter. There is no conflict here between inner belief and outer reality.

A spiritually-inclined person, on the other hand, has thoughts running through his head that are at cross-purposes to the sights, sounds, and other impressions entering his consciousness through the senses. A spiritual philosophy of life is open to being accused—if not actually convicted—of hypocrisy: I experience matter yet I believe in spirit. This produces an unavoidable tension between what is believed to be ultimately true and what is immediately apparent.

The philosophical tension a materialist feels isn't so extreme because he doesn't believe in anything that can't be experienced within the physical world. Naturally he recognizes he doesn't know everything that can be known about materiality; but what he *can* realize as truth is on the same level of reality as the life he is experiencing now. A spiritual believer is in a less comfortable position, having one experiential foot set firmly on Earth and one conceptual foot up in the air, stretched out toward an unknown Heaven he hasn't yet been able to touch.

Believing versus seeing

IT ISN'T SURPRISING, then, that so many religious people come to embrace a rigid fundamentalism that gives them the support spirituality otherwise lacks. A true adherent of fundamentalism holds onto his beliefs so strongly he loses sight of the fact that they aren't grounded in a directly experienced reality.

Religious fundamentalism takes to the extreme the leap of faith that, in most religions, is necessary to bridge the gap between a believer's philosophical concepts (or theology) and a believer's experience of the truth of those concepts (which I'll call salvation). In effect, a religious person is asked to accept a promissory note for truth that reads, "The holder's faith eventually will be exchanged for salvation." Belief is considered to be an essential prerequisite for divine experience.

The problem, though, is that while all sorts of holy books and holy people claim to know the truth about God and the cosmos, generally the claims are self-validating. That is, a skeptic is referred to the very scripture or person making the claim for proof of the claim. Christians often cite a biblical quotation to defend the truth of the Bible, as Muslims do with the Koran, Jews with the Talmud, Sikhs with the Adi Granth, and so on.

In like fashion, even if we heard Jesus speak these words from St. John (14:6) with his own lips, "I am the way, and the truth, and the life. No one comes to the Father except through me," what independent evidence do we have that these sentiments are true?

So we arrive at a classic chicken-and-egg situation that has vociferous adherents on both sides of the question. Do our beliefs about life flow from our actual life experiences or do our actual life experiences flow from our beliefs? This question can be framed as a choice between "I'll believe it when I see it," which assumes the primacy of experience, and "I'll see it when I believe it," which assumes the primacy of belief.

The scientific method, by and large, is founded on the first assumption: what we experience is an objective reality that is independent of human beliefs or cognition. If observation, either perceptual or mathematical, proves the scientist wrong, then his beliefs change to match the actual observational experience.

Observations, of course, are not made in a conceptual vacuum, so there is a continual interplay between believing and observing in both everyday life and scientific inquiry. At the most basic level, a belief that there is something real to be observed lies at the root of every act of observation. Physicist Shimon Malin suggests this is one implication of Einstein's statement "it is the theory which decides what we can observe."[1]

But this is a far cry from the more extreme position that theories, or beliefs, actually bring into being the object of observation. If I'm on a sinking ship, my belief that there may be lifejackets aboard will lead me to look for one in the storage locker. However, that belief won't produce a life jacket if none are on the ship. When I open the locker, what I see doesn't depend on what I subjectively believe is inside; it depends on what is objectively there.

By contrast, most religions assume a person comes to be saved spiritually after believing in salvation. Thus, to experience salvation one has to have a firm faith in the possibility of salvation. This is the flip side of a null hypothesis, which helps explain why science and religion are so frequently at odds. Science sees religion blindly accepting unproven beliefs as truth whereas religion sees science as shutting its eyes to truths proven only to those who believe.

Now, if salvation could occur during a person's earthly life, we would not have such a great conflict between science and religion. For even if salvation was a personal affair, unobservable (and hence unconfirmable) by others, at least the person who had been saved would have convincing proof, the goal of science, that the theological tenets of his or her chosen religion were true. The problem, though, is that religions traditionally teach salvation occurs only after physical death, not before.

Stripped-down spirituality

A RELIGIOUS BELIEVER is expected to accept a philosophy of life that can't be proven to be true until the believer's life is over. From Plotinus's perspective this isn't so much a leap of faith as an irrational dive. Plotinus is a mystic, and a mystic wants to make his spiritual beliefs consonant with his experience by experiencing, in this life, all that his beliefs hold to be true.

What distinguishes Plotinus is that he is a supremely rational mystic whose intense love for God is balanced by a deep appreciation for reason. In the *Enneads* his mystical side passionately urges us to leap across the divide separating our consciousnesses from the One while his rational side urges us to carefully consider, before we leave the ground of our reason behind, what we are leaping from and to. If we don't, we may find that our efforts to traverse the spiritual path are bringing us no closer to divinity.

Plotinus teaches that when the *psyche*, or soul, is cleansed of matter and multiplicity, what is left is the irreducible foundation of being: *nous*, or spirit, the first emanation of the One. In the *Enneads* Plotinus clearly describes, given the limits of language, the nature of spirit, and how consciousness can be united with it. Spirit is the reality that lies behind the illusion of matter, so if our purported spirituality is mixed with materiality, it isn't truly spiritual, no matter how we may conceive of the situation.

Somewhat paradoxically, Plotinus's philosophy is so spiritually pure it doesn't seem spiritual to many people. Today, most of us want our religion or spiritual path to address human concerns, along with providing metaphysical guidance. We expect that our spirituality will help us make friends, feel less lonely, and solve social problems. We want happy gatherings with like-minded people, uplifting talks, communal prayer and music, tasty food and drink in a spirit of brother- and sisterhood.

Plotinus doesn't offer us any of that in the *Enneads*. His sole focus is on uniting one's soul with universal truth. To do this, one must become more than human, and pass beyond everyday human concerns. Refreshingly, he reminds us that spirituality has everything to do with spirit. Nothing else matters, especially matter.

Worshipping in a holy place? If the place is physical, this isn't spiritual. Reading a sacred book? If the book is physical, this isn't spiritual. Being in the presence of a saintly person? If the person is physical, this isn't spiritual. Thinking divine thoughts? If the thoughts are physical, this isn't spiritual. Doing good works? If the works are physical, this isn't spiritual.

"Well, gosh!" one feels like crying out in exasperation. "What do you want, Plotinus? If none of this is spiritual, then what is?"

From the essence of his teachings, an answer comes: "What is spiritual is spirit. Spirit forms matter but isn't part of matter. So spirituality means leaving behind all physical sensations and thoughts of materiality."

> *To be sure, you were already previously the All, but since something other came to be added on to you besides the "All," you were lessened by this addition. For this addition did not come from the All—what could you add to the All?—but from Not-Being.*
>
> *When one comes to be out of Not-Being, he is not the All, not until he rids himself of this Not-Being. Thus you increase yourself when you get rid of everything else, and once you have gotten rid of it, the All is present to you.* [VI-5-12][2]

Subtract, don't add

WE HAVE TO START on the spiritual path from wherever we are now and that place is right here, the material world, relative Not-Being. Here we think many thoughts, emote many emotions, and perceive many perceptions. Plotinus tells us that the best thing we can do is get rid of what we have within our minds now, by stopping what we are habitually doing now.

Hence, the best thought is the concept that leads to no further thoughts, the best emotion is the feeling that leads to no further emotions, and the best perception is the sensation that leads to no further perceptions—at least during the period of contemplation when we seek to experience spirit and the One, the All. In essence, the only belief a spiritual seeker should aim to retain is, "I will see it when I stop believing in, and seeing, what is not it."

Reason, then, guides us to an understanding that spirituality is a process of subtraction, not addition. This is an eminently scientific approach to the investigation of whatever non-material reality may exist apart from the physical universe because it is founded on the ultimate null hypothesis: a mystic, or spiritual scientist, subtracts from his or her consciousness all thoughts, emotions, and perceptions concerning materiality and simply observes what remains. To my mind, the logic of this metaphysical experiment is persuasive. Elimination of what is physical and personal necessarily leaves what (if anything) is non-material and universal.

Where to leap?

SINCE RELIGION generally emphasizes faith over reason, it is commonplace in spiritual circles to downplay or even disparage the value of rationality in one's search for God or the ultimate meaning of life. We're told that all we need to do is to have faith.

Well, fine. But faith in whom, in what? In Jesus? Buddha? Muhammad? Moses? Lao Tzu? Guru Nanak? Angelic guides? Our own souls? God? Nirvana? Tao? Spirit? The Holy Ghost? Even if I accept that I need to make a leap of faith, tell me: why should I leap in *this* direction, rather than in *that* direction?

All manner of faiths—Christianity, Judaism, Islam, Buddhism, New Ageism (if we may use such a term), and many others—vie for our attention and "shelf space" in the world's grand storehouse of spiritual options. When someone feels a strong attraction for one of these faiths he steps forward and buys into its beliefs. Or, as is becoming more and more common, he cobbles together theological bits and pieces from a variety of religious practices and forms his own unique faith: the Religion of Me.

Since there is no objective proof that one religion or philosophy is truer than the others this sort of religiosity often is called a leap of faith. Yet it is more accurately described as a sideways step toward one set of spiritual dogmas and a commensurate distancing from all others. Such a movement is a matter of changing the shell of one's beliefs, not the core of one's being. Hence, conversion can occur almost instantly. Yesterday I was a non-believer, today a believer. Stepping from one set of thoughts to another isn't difficult.

And it does not get us very far. Plotinus, echoing the teachings of many other mystics, holds that spiritual reality lies on the other side of belief, reason, and sense perception. A person enters this reality by a leap like no other leap, a leap of the whole of his or her consciousness across the boundary that separates whatever can be named from the Nameless.

Have faith in nothing

THE NAMELESS is the One, the source of names and forms. The source, teaches Plotinus, is completely separate from its products, in the same sense as consciousness is completely separate from thoughts, emotions, and perceptions. When we cease to think, feel, and sense, we still *are*, just as the One *is*. It isn't anything particular, not even *being*, for *to be* is to be something, and the One is not any thing. Michael Sells says, "After speaking of absolute unity as that which is most powerful in an animal, a soul, or in the all, Plotinus writes of 'the one':"

> But should we grasp the one of authentic beings, their principle, wellspring, and 'dynamis'—will we then lose faith and consider it nothing? It is certainly nothing of the things of which it is the origin, being such, as it were, that nothing can be attributed to it, neither being, nor beings, nor life. It is beyond those. If then by withdrawing being you should grasp it, you will be brought into wonder ['thauma']. [III-8-10][3]

Sells comments on this passage: "After contemplating the world view of his tradition, the mystic then withdraws being from the source. At this moment the soul 'fears that there be nothing' (VI-9-3). . . . At this point Plotinus writes of not losing faith. This faith is not a faith in anything but a willingness to let go of being. Such a letting go results in wonderment (*thauma*)."[4]

I'm struck by how Plotinus and St. John of the Cross, a sixteenth-century Spanish Carmelite, have almost exactly the same attitude toward faith. Many people would be surprised that a "pagan" Greek philosopher and a Catholic friar agree on anything, much less the nature of faith, but they do. Since they are mystics, the strongest bond between Plotinus and St. John of the Cross is not their theological or metaphysical beliefs but their conviction that God, the One, transcends any and all beliefs, including their own.

In *The Ascent of Mount Carmel*, a writing about the soul's ascent to union with God, St. John of the Cross speaks of the secret ladder by which the soul climbs higher:

> The secret ladder represents faith, because all the rungs or articles of faith are secret to and hidden from both the senses and the intellect. Accordingly the soul lived in darkness, without the light of the senses and intellect, and went out beyond every natural and rational boundary to climb the divine ladder of faith that leads up to and penetrates the deep things of God.
>
> . . . Consequently, a person who wants to arrive at union with the Supreme Repose and Good in this life must climb all the steps, which are considerations, forms, and concepts, and leave them behind, since they are dissimilar and unproportioned to the goal toward which they lead. And this goal is God.[5]

Just as Plotinus's faith is not a faith in anything particular that can be encompassed by the limited grasp of the senses and reason (but rather in the existence of the ineffable, unlimited, and incomprehensible One), so is the faith of St. John of the Cross. Both mystics urge us to return to God along the path of the *via negativa*, the negative way. Since this material world is at the opposite pole of the cosmos from the spiritual world, a negation of materiality leads to the most positive spirituality.

St. John of the Cross says, "All the world's wisdom and human ability compared to the infinite wisdom of God is pure and utter ignorance. . . . Accordingly, to reach union with the wisdom of God, a person must advance by unknowing rather than by knowing."[6]

And Plotinus advises, "One must not make it [the One] two even for the sake of forming an idea of it." [VI-8-13]

Confusion—no cause for concern

Now, when a mystic expresses the idea that it is wrong to express ideas about God, we have a contradiction, at least from the point of view of a logician. "Plotinus just demolished his own argument!" such a person would cry. "Yes, that's his intention," another person more attuned to the subtleties of Plotinus's teachings would respond. Reading the *Enneads*, we find Plotinus, like St. John of the Cross, continually blowing up the conceptual structures he has just constructed with such care.

So don't be concerned if you get confused in the course of trying to understand Plotinus's teachings. This is to be expected and, indeed, is to be welcomed.

For at the crossroads of belief and the negation of belief, of sensation and the negation of sensation, of thinking and the negation of thinking, we stand at the juncture of the Known and Mystery. Continue straight on your course down the path of knowledge that got you to the crossroads and you experience more of the same conceptual and sensible scenery. Make an abrupt shift in direction, a genuine leap of faith, and you end up somewhere completely different.

Crossroads are confusing when we aren't sure in which direction our destination lies. There are no clearly marked signs showing the way to the One. In fact, it seems that if you see anything familiar along the path, including a signpost akin to those you've encountered before, you haven't yet taken the fork that leads most directly to the spiritual summit.

Plotinus continually emphasizes that there is a stark distinction between the everyday reality where almost all of us live now and the spiritual reality of higher domains of consciousness. To be genuinely converted, in his view, is to convert our attention from awareness of material thoughts and things to an inward, intuitive perception of spirit. Even the lowest reaches of the spiritual realm bear little resemblance to the physical universe, and when the soul attains to heaven, less will be familiar.

> *There are few things here that are also there* [in the higher world]*; and when it is in heaven it will abandon still more.* [IV-3-32]

If little or nothing here will accompany us on our return to the One, what purpose is there in filling our heads with all the concepts contained in the *Enneads* and reiterated in this book you are reading now? Good question. As someone who enjoys playing with ideas, I have to admit, reluctantly, that an entirely defensible answer is: no purpose at all. This presumes, however, that a spiritual seeker's consciousness is standing directly in front of the passageway that leads to the One, ready and eager to dive in and start the journey. Since usually this isn't the case, the rational side of Plotinus's philosophy is intended to prepare us for true mystical experience.

Reaching the end of the line

STEP BY STEP, reason leads us to the point at which rationality ends. When the spiritual seeker is convinced he truly has reached the end of the line down which the train of thought travels, there is nothing to do but get on board some other means of transport. In a Zen context, Hubert Benoit aptly speaks of the need of the Western mind to be led by reason to the edge of the void dividing expressible and inexpressible truth.

> It seems that, in order to enlighten an Occidental, dissertations are, within a certain measure that is strictly limited, necessary. Doubtless the ultimate, the real point of view, cannot be expressed in words, and the master would injure the pupil if he allowed him to forget that the whole problem lies precisely in jumping the ditch which separates truth which can be expressed from real knowledge. But the Occidental needs a discursive explanation to lead him by the hand to the edge of the ditch.[7]

Plotinus, like every great mystic, uses words to urge us to experience what is beyond words. The *Enneads* reflect his great love for the One and his struggle to convey what is ineffable. Pierre Hadot writes: "Plotinus has only one thing to say, and in order to say it, he has recourse to all the possibilities of the language of his time. And yet, he never will say it."[8]

He does not because he cannot. What Plotinus points us toward is right before our eyes, so close we are unable to see it. How immensely difficult it must have been for one with a vision of divine reality to try to describe it to the spiritually blind. And how grateful we should be that Plotinus made such a great effort.

Have we said enough now, and can we be released? But the soul is still in the pangs of labor, even more now than before. . . . For though the soul goes over all truths, even those in which we participate, yet she still evades us if someone wishes her to speak and think discursively.

In order for discursive thought to say something, it must consider its objects successively, for such is the unfolding of thought. Yet what kind of unfolding can there be, in the case of something which is absolutely simple? [V-3-17][9]

The One is simple because it is one. Nothing is simpler than the One, for there is nothing other than the One. So nothing marks the path by which the soul returns to the One. When everything other than the One is discarded, what is left is the irreducible foundation of existence: God.

This is why Plotinus teaches that emptiness is the key to spiritual attainment, just as St. John of the Cross, echoing Luke 18:19, says that "Nothing is good save God only."[10] What could be simpler than emptiness? Just as we move from one room to another through an open doorway, the soul passes from one realm of consciousness to another through an ineffable connection.

With the best nature, then, which needs no assistance, we must leave aside everything; for whatever you add, you have lessened by the addition the nature which needs nothing. [VI-7-41]

Those who desire to escape from Plato's cave of illusion can feel their way along the reassuringly solid wall of materiality up to the very edge of the cavern opening. Not yet able to perceive the light of reality, groping sightlessly for truth in what a medieval mystic called the "cloud of unknowing," the spiritual seeker reaches out and touches . . . *nothing*—i.e., no thing. That nothing is the way to freedom, the opening that connects what is within and without the cave. But to those who have spent their whole lives trusting in shadows on a rock wall, existing without that support is inconceivable and terrifying.

So they grope their way back into the depths of the cave, muttering "What a waste to come all this way and find nothing at all!" If only they had realized that they were only a few steps away from their goal, needing only to boldly embrace the cave opening's nothingness in a genuine leap of faith rather than shrink away from it. For there is a gulf between the One and Many that cannot be bridged by anything familiar to everyday experience; everything that is known now is a characteristic of our starting place, not our destination.

In spirituality a leap of faith is needed but it is a leap based on true unknowing, not on false knowing. It is a leap to the mystery beyond, not a shuffle-step to the more-of-the-same close at hand. Plotinus urges us to learn how to embrace mystery rather than push it away by premature explanation. This happens when beliefs or concepts about the true nature of life's mysteries are too quickly accepted as facts rather than as hypotheses to be confirmed or denied by direct experience.

In Plato's "Apology," Socrates is reported to have found, after talking with a man who was thought by many to be wise, that actually the man wasn't what he seemed to be. "Well," says Socrates, "although I do not suppose that either of us knows anything really beautiful and good, I am better off than he is,—for he knows nothing, and thinks that he knows; I neither know nor think that I know. In this latter particular, then, I seem to have slightly the advantage of him."[11]

Ignorance, if not bliss, at least borders on knowledge. Take one truthful step and the border is crossed. However, when we are ignorant of our ignorance we stand considerably farther away from the border zone since a wall of illusory understanding must be broken down before truth can be approached. So mysteries should remain mysterious until they are cleared up.

Reading the Writings of Plotinus

BEFORE WE MOVE into the body of this book and start studying the details of Plotinus's philosophy, I want to explain how I went about researching, organizing, and writing *Return to the One* and also present for consideration the spirit in which I believe Plotinus's teachings should be read.

First, I've already stressed that *Return to the One* is not intended to be a scholarly examination of Plotinus's teachings. I am not qualified to write such a book, and even if I was, there were would be little point in duplicating the work of the distinguished Plotinian scholars who are cited throughout these pages. Rather, my purpose is to expose the general reader to the writings of a marvelous mystic philosopher whose teachings have greatly influenced Western thought and spirituality but, unfortunately, are little known by the world at large.

Selling Plotinus

MICHAEL CHASE, a classics scholar and translator of Plotinus, shared with me the "selling points" he would use to try to convince the general public to examine Plotinus's philosophy. To my mind, Chase makes a persuasive argument in favor of reading the writings of Plotinus.

> Since the dawn of time, mankind has sought answers to a certain limited number of questions: Who are we? Why are we here? Why is there something rather than nothing? What happens after we die? Lots of people toss off trashy books in an afternoon that purport to answer these questions, which gnaw at the consciousness of human beings every bit as much today as they did two thousand years ago. It is arguable that ancient Greek philosophy developed as a response to these needs, and Plotinus represents the culmination of hundreds of years of Greek philosophy.
>
> If you, the reader, are looking for answers to life's questions, then why not try the solutions proposed by Plotinus? His answers to these very same questions have been taken seriously for seventeen hundred years by people in the Islamic East, the Medieval Latin West, and in Byzantine Greek Orthodoxy. Why not try to find out what so many

people, from so many different times and cultures, found so deeply satisfying about the teachings of Plotinus?

Choosing translations

YES, why not try? This is what I asked myself when I made my own decision to learn more about Plotinus, having been intrigued by brief mentions of his philosophy that I had come across in several books. I then had to decide which of the available translations of the *Enneads* to study. In 1930 Stephen MacKenna completed the first English translation. It is still in print, and is admirably literary. But scholars acknowledge that MacKenna's work has been superseded by A.H. Armstrong's more definitive translation completed in 1988.

Hence most of the Plotinus quotations in this book have been drawn from Armstrong's translation of the six *Enneads*, or treatises, published in seven volumes by the Loeb Classical Library. These quotations are indicated by a bracketed notation such as [IV-3-12], where the Roman numeral denotes the treatise, the middle number the section in the treatise, and the last number the chapter in the section.

Notwithstanding the strength of Armstrong's translation, this book also includes many quotations from the *Enneads* translated by another well-respected scholar, the aforementioned Michael Chase. There is a certain artistry involved in translating and I feel that Chase wonderfully captures the spirit as well as the letter of Plotinus's writings. When the notation is followed by a endnote, such as [IV-3-12][3], this usually means that the Plotinus quotation is a Chase translation included in Pierre Hadot's book, *Plotinus or The Simplicity of Vision*. Two quotations with endnotes were translated by other scholars.

The nature of nous

NOUS is the second grand realm of reality in Plotinus's metaphysical cosmology, the immaterial World of Forms. Armstrong translated *nous* as "intellect," whereas Chase generally chose "spirit." I am sympathetic to Chase's choice, as "spirit" does seem to come closer than "intellect" to expressing the nature of *nous*; "intellect" has a rational connotation not found in Plotinus's writings. Similarly, I prefer Chase's usual translation of *noêtos* as "spiritual" to Armstrong's "intelligible."

So, in my commentary I generally speak of spirit rather than intellect and of the spiritual rather than the intelligible. To remind the reader that *nous*, spirit, and intellect all refer to the same unitary reality that is beyond words, periodically you will find me writing "spirit or intellect." I have chosen to leave these terms in lower-case, reserving capitalization for the ultimate in Plotinus's metaphysics: God, the One, the Good. Armstrong and Chase, though, capitalize Intellect and Spirit (except when "intellect" refers to the lower state of individual rational consciousness).

When a bracketed explanatory term in a translation has been added by the translator, it is shown in italics: "*He [the One] . . .*" When a bracketed term is shown in plain type, "*He* [the One] . . . ," I have added it.

Concerning Plotinus's use of the masculine "he" in referring to God, I am sure that he would agree with my wife, who never fails to remind me that ultimate reality doesn't have a male sex organ. Plotinus also sometimes uses "man" in the sense of "humanity." Similarly, when readability demands it, you will find me using "he" in the sense of "he or she." I am hopeful that readers sensitive to the sexist use of language will forgive Plotinus and me for bowing to literary tradition in these instances.

Spiritual self-absorption

UNDERSTANDING that Plotinus asks us to become self-absorbed (in the most spiritual fashion) is the key to appreciating the fashion in which his writings should be read. The mystic philosopher seeks to be fully conscious of his own consciousness, completely absorbed in the One that is both the root of himself and the root of the cosmos. So, in the *Enneads* Plotinus continually turns the reader back upon himself, challenging him to discern who he is when he is not busy being someone he is not.

In her book, *Reading Neoplatonism*, Sara Rappe says, "Plotinus demands a kind of ultimate privacy from the person who wishes to gain self-knowledge. He demands an activity of the mind that is entirely self-directed. . . . The appeal to introspection invites a scrutiny of the assumptions that the knower makes about himself."[1]

Whoever I am, I am not an object that I can look upon, separate from the consciousness doing the looking. In Plotinus's philosophy, the highest aspect of *psyche*, or soul, is identical with *nous*, or spirit, the universal consciousness that contains the essential forms of everything in creation.

This is a special sort of containment because spirit *is* the objects contained within itself. By contrast, ordinarily we are not the objects contained within our minds—all those thoughts, feelings, perceptions, and whatnot that ceaselessly occupy our attention. This is why we can forget what we once knew and not know the entire truth about anything external to ourselves.

Sara Rappe notes that when a person stops identifying with the contents of consciousness and tries to experience consciousness apart from its usual contents, his or her customary identity begins to erode. When we aren't thinking, feeling, or perceiving, we are who we really are, pure souls.

Speaking of the unspeakable

I AM HOPEFUL that this discussion has helped the reader better understand that, as a philosopher, Plotinus has much to say. Yet, as a mystic, Plotinus has nothing to say. So how does he resolve the tension that results from having to say what can't be said, to speak of the unspeakable? By using words to point toward what is beyond words, the mystery of the One. The pointing is not the goal; the One is. This largely explains why it is so difficult for scholars to agree about what Plotinus means.

Often Plotinus's goal is to produce in the reader what Michael Sells calls a "meaning event." This event, Sells says, is "the semantic analogue to the experience of mystical union. It does not describe or refer to mystical union but effects a semantic union that re-creates or imitates the mystical union. . . . We might call the event, then, the evocation of a sense of mystery."[2]

I don't know if I really understand what a meaning event is, or if I've ever truly experienced one while reading the *Enneads*. However, I do know that there have been times, many times, when I would read a passage and be left with an ineffable realization that I could only vaguely express as, "Ah, yes; just so." Plotinus's words would lead me to intuit, however dimly, that there is One, lying just beyond my conscious awareness; and I cannot lay hold of it, for it is the very ground of my consciousness, that which makes me aware.

> *But when the soul wishes to see [the One] by itself, it is just by being with it that it sees, and by being one with that it is one, and it is not capable of thinking that it possesses what it seeks, because it is not other than that which is being known.* [VI-9-3][3]

Knowledge is one, not many

THE *ENNEADS* ARE a paradox through and through since all the thoughts Plotinus expresses are ultimately intended to lead the reader to stop thinking. The wisdom the mystic philosopher seeks can't be found with the discursive mind, which thinks one thought after another.

Rather, wisdom is part and parcel of the intuitive intelligence that is spirit. We as souls participate in spirit—and indeed are virtually identical with spirit—when we stop participating in lower activities such as reasoning, emoting, and perceiving sense objects.

In the *Enneads*, Plotinus points us toward the only way of unmasking the deepest mysteries of life: become the mystery you wish to unmask and be nothing else. If you want to know what the essence of life is, simply be alive. If you want to know what the essence of consciousness is, simply be conscious. If you want to know what the essence of the One is, simply be the One.

Sara Rappe says, "What characterizes the faculty of insight is unitive knowing, non-separation of subject and object, or complete assimilation to and identification with the object of knowledge."[4]

Obviously, our everyday lives are far removed from this sort of unitive knowledge. We don't know everything about anything, including our own selves, which is the place where Plotinus advises us to start in accord with the Socratic adage "Know yourself." His goal, then, is to help the reader form his or her consciousness into an empty receptacle for receiving (or becoming) wisdom. This is much more a process of emptying the mind of erroneous conceptions than of filling the mind with accurate information.

From this perspective, if we come to know only one thing, the nature of the One, we are wise; if not, we are ignorant, no matter how many facts about how many separate things we may possess.

A Buddhist sage, Ching K'ung, puts it nicely: "*Prajna* [wisdom] means having a profound and correct understanding of the true nature of all things. It is completely different from what is known in this world as intelligence."[5]

This helps explain why it is normal to feel uncomfortable at times while reading this book. Plotinus challenges us. He forces us to compare what we believe about God and spirituality with what we know as an indisputable fact because it is identical with our very beings. He asks us to consider if what we are confident is true actually is.

Plotinus isn't comfortable

ALONG THESE LINES, when I wrote Michael Chase complimenting him on the tone of his translations, he responded that he tried to bring urgency to his scholarly work, adding, "Whatever else one may say about Plotinus, he is *not comfortable*." I heartily agree. But different readers of the *Enneads* find Plotinus's teachings uncomfortable in different ways.

For example, scholars struggle with the difficulty of making sense of Plotinus's highly idiosyncratic and apophatic use of the Greek language. Chase told me that in 1999 a seminar was held at the Sorbonne that attracted the world's best Plotinus scholars to speak on a single section (V-3) of the *Enneads*. "Scarcely any two experts gave the same interpretation of the same texts," he said. Certain sections of the *Enneads*, Chase added, are "some of the most ragged, jagged, harsh, and just plain difficult philosophical prose ever written, in any language."

I can testify to the truth of this statement. Plainly put, I wouldn't wish reading the *Enneads* straight through on any but my worse enemies. Even though I'm a glutton for intellectual punishment, making my way through the seven volumes of Armstrong's English translation, pen and highlighter in hand, definitely tested my fortitude. Plotinus can write marvelously passionately and simply; he also is capable of writing horribly dryly and complexly.

How I wrote what you're reading

ONE OF MY PURPOSES in writing *Return to the One* was to relieve non-scholars of having to read the *Enneads* directly. I put considerable effort into finding quotations that contain the clearest and most definitive descriptions of Plotinus's teachings. These quotations frequently are brief, because less tends to be more with Plotinus. If lengthier quotations from the *Enneads* had been cited, in most cases it would have diminished the meaning of a passage, since what precedes or follows a quotation included in *Return to the One* often is barely comprehensible.

I used two approaches for selecting quotations. First, I read almost all of the scholarly books in English about Plotinus's teachings. These are cited in the "Bibliography" and "Suggestions for Further Reading" sections at the end of this book. In the course of taking copious notes, I became aware of the passages in the *Enneads* repeatedly cited by scholars as being representative of some aspect of Plotinus's philosophy. These constituted my initial set of "must quote" passages.

Second, in reading Armstrong's translation of the *Enneads* I found some quotations that appeared significant or simply appealed to me, but hadn't been cited by anyone else I had read. It's interesting to ask why. I'm not sure, but often it seems that these passages relate more to the mystical side of Plotinus than to his rational side.

Because Plotinian scholars, not surprisingly, are inclined more to scholarship than to mysticism, some of the mystic musings of Plotinus are given short shrift in comparison to his overtly philosophical proclamations. For example, unless someone is open to the possibility of reincarnation, Plotinus's comment about vegetative people "taking care to turn themselves into trees" isn't going to be taken as seriously as his more elevated statements about the One, spirit, and soul.

Seek the tabletop, not the puzzle

HERE IS SOME ADVICE about how to approach the rest of this book. If something doesn't make sense, just keep reading. It may come clear in the end. Be more concerned with grasping the broad outlines of Plotinus's philosophy than the specifics. It is better to comprehend the treatises in the *Enneads* as a whole, in an almost intuitive fashion, than to try to assemble a logical understanding bit by bit.

Stephen MacKenna, the aforementioned translator of the *Enneads*, says that "Plotinus is often to be understood rather by swift and broad rushes of the mind—the mind trained to his methods—than by laborious word-racking investigation."⁶ Plotinus himself tells us that the valuable part of philosophy "perceives by directing intuition, as sense-perception also does, but it hands over petty precisions of speech to another discipline which finds satisfaction in them." [I-3-5]

Reason (discursive thought) is akin to the piecing together of a jigsaw puzzle. It is satisfying when our logic succeeds in forming a coherent picture of reality, and this indeed is part of what Plotinus sought to accomplish by writing the *Enneads*—but, I believe, it was just a small part. His greater goal was to turn our attention to what supports the multitudinous pieces of creation, the omnipresent ineffable foundation of the One.

Just as a tabletop lies under each piece of a jigsaw puzzle, so is the One beneath every separate sensory perception and mental thought. Neither the tabletop nor the One is far away from what is supported. Delve only a tiny distance, a fraction of an inch for a puzzle, a dimensionless shift in consciousness for the One, and the simple substance of the foundation is reached.

So you and I shouldn't worry if there is a gap in our understanding of Plotinus because this emptiness can serve as the opening that enables us to realize the One lying beneath appearances.

Section I

THE ONE,

And Many—

Soul's Descent,

And Return

God Is the Goal

TOO OFTEN, our lot in life's journey is just to travel around in small circles because most of our goals are trivial or futile. Plotinus urges us to carefully consider what we are seeking and avoid useless wheel-spinning, false starts, and blind alleys. Everyone is looking for something so our problem isn't lack of desire. It is how to direct that desire to assure that what we end up with is truly and permanently fulfilling.

> And we must consider that men have forgotten that which from the beginning until now they want and long for. For all things reach out to that and long for it by necessity of nature, as if divining by instinct that they cannot exist without it. [V-5-12]

Plotinus isn't a world-denying ascetic determined to take all the juicy fun out of life, leaving only a dry rind of abstract thought and spiritual discipline. He can sound that way at times but his asceticism is always a means, not an end. He urges us to turn away from our concern with lesser goods and attain *the* Good. Plotinus is not content with enjoying partial and ephemeral pleasures. His goal is the complete and permanent pleasure that comes through union with the One, also known as the Good, or what many call God.

> So the good life will not belong to those who feel pleasure but to the man who is able to know that pleasure is the good. . . . The Good, therefore, must be desirable, but must not become good by being desirable, but become desirable by being good. [I-4-2, VI-7-25]

Animals are fully capable of feeling pleasure. Observe a cat playing with catnip or a dog savoring a bone. If this is all we aspire to we are missing the point of being human.

All souls—celestial, human, animal, insect, plant—desire the One. For the One, or God, is the goal to which all animate beings aspire. This yearning is built into the structure of creation, since the Good is desired because it is the ultimate reality, whereas other things become good for us because we desire them. Hence, there is one objective highest Good and a multitude of subjective lesser goods. As humans we are capable of recognizing the difference between what is merely pleasurable and what is truly good for us. Other living beings lack this ability.

Because humans have the ability to play such an exalted role in the cosmos, we cannot be truly happy if we merely act out the parts of beings with a much lesser capacity. As a military recruiting slogan put it: "Be all that you can be." A good life is a full life, which means expressing all of our innate capabilities. Unfulfilled potential, like a half-empty balloon, does not allow us to soar to the heights of happiness.

> *Could one say that the good for a thing was anything else than the full natural activity of its life?* [I-7-1]

It is understandable if we fail to realize that the One is our good, since our "full natural activity" seems to be firmly rooted in the familiar pursuits of everyday life: working, raising children, learning new things, enjoying nature, helping others, praying, exercising, relaxing, making love, eating and drinking. Where in all of this activity is there any sign of an urge toward a divine reality that transcends sensation, emotion, and reason?

"Everywhere," we can imagine Plotinus answering. "You are not looking deeply enough. Ignore outward appearances. What common desire lies behind the actions of all living beings and even inanimate objects? To be one."

Consider a large rock. Lodged firmly in the middle of my garden plot, it tries with all its might to remain a rock, notwithstanding the sledgehammer blows with which I attempt to convert it to an unrock. Even if I am able to break the rock into pieces, each piece retains its rockness. Similarly, everything alive strives more actively to maintain its oneness. An ant flees the beetle that wants to destroy its antness. A chicken races to avoid the fox bent on annihilating its chickenness. A soldier fights against the enemy set on obliterating his humanness.

> *For each thing wishes not just for being, but for being together with the good. . . . For all individual things do not strive to get away from each other, but towards each other and towards themselves; and all souls would like to come to unity, following their own nature.* [VI-2-11]

Even suicide, it may be argued, reflects a desire for unity, a hoped-for final rest that seems preferable to a shattered life. And self-sacrifice aims to preserve the unity of the larger family, species, culture, nation, or ideal that is more important to the altruistic individual than his or her personal needs. So Plotinus seems to have it right that people seek both to be one with themselves, by preserving their existence and sense of selfhood, and to be one with others, through all the things they do to feel close to their fellow humans.

Possessions, of course, are another reflection of this innate urge for the One. We are not satisfied with having just the idea of a big-screen television, slinky black dress, umpteen megahertz computer, or turbo-charged sports car. We want to make that idea a reality, to bring the object of our desire right into our living rooms, closets, offices, or garages, and then to make it as much a part of our lives as possible. Until, at least, an even better thing comes along.

Our aspiration is fine, to unite as closely as possible with what is good for us. The problem lies with our understanding of what the ultimate good is, and how it can be possessed.

What is really worth aspiring to for us is our selves, bringing themselves back for themselves to the best of themselves. [VI-7-30]

Plotinus teaches that the best in us is essentially identical with the highest reality of the One. Thus we can never have what we are looking for, happiness and well-being, through becoming one with anything or anyone outside of ourselves. In fact, that is impossible, since there always is a gap between us and what we seek to possess. I watch my television and drive my car; I can't *become* these things. Nor, indeed, would I want to, which makes me wonder why they hold such an attraction.

Could it be that what I am looking for is actually within me, not outside? Is it possible that all the people and objects that hold such a fascination for me are crude, material reflections of a refined, spiritual reality and it is the latter I really long for?

Imagine, says Plotinus, that what you have desired most passionately your whole life finally is within your grasp. The fervently desired object of your secret dreams, your intimate longings, your heartfelt prayers—now it stands before you, fully yours now and forever. Imagine this, and you will have an idea of what it means to return to the One.

As for those unfamiliar with this state, let him imagine after the model of the loves of this world what it must be like to encounter what one loves most of all. Besides, these objects which we love are mortal, harmful images; they are changing, for they are not the true Beloved: they are not our Good, not what we are searching for.

The true Beloved is in that other world, and it is possible to be united with him, if we participate in him and thus possess him truly, and not only from the outside, as would be the case if we only embraced him with our arms of flesh and blood. [VI-9-9][1]

Plotinus does not espouse the extinction of desire, but the channeling of desire. Within us is a spiritual engine, longing, that is always running strong. We lack steering, not power; it is easy to be thrown off course by lower desires and inclinations, wrongly believing that things of this world can fill the emptiness within us. In truth, that hunger can only be satisfied by the One.

Hence, Plotinus advocates what might be called a one-stop shopping approach to finding satisfaction in life. Rather than picking up bits and pieces of well-being here and there, hoping that they will somehow mesh into a satisfying whole, we should concentrate on obtaining from one source that single thing which will satisfy completely.

The One is both the object and the cause of desire, as it is both the origin and the reason for being.

It is the source therefore of being and the why of being, giving both at once. [VI-8-14]

Plotinus asks: Do desire and longing go on forever, always seeking a greater good beyond what already has been attained? If so, life seemingly would be insufferable, a never-ending cycle of "I want, I get; I want more, I get more." Thankfully, he says, wanting will end if we are able to reach the summit of reality beyond which there is nothing more to be desired.

But it will come to a stop at the ultimate, at that after which one cannot grasp anything higher, and this is the First and the really good and the Good in the strictest sense, and the cause also of the other goods. [VI-7-25]

Thus we have in the One what Lloyd Gerson calls the "way to measure achievement, that is, the coincidence of desire and result."[2] "All striving or desire," says Gerson, "aims at achieving an intrinsically satisfying condition not already present or the continuation of such a condition."[3] The One is the ultimate measure of goodness because only in the One is there complete simplicity and unity. Here, and nowhere else, is the absolute confluence of wanting and getting, the final end of desire.

The endpoint of the journey of the soul is not, however, to be entirely absorbed into the One like an ice cube thrown into a warm ocean. Rather, it is to be united as closely as two entities can be while still remaining distinct. Speaking of this blissful condition, Plotinus says:

> *Everything longs for its parent and loves it, especially when parent and offspring are alone; but when the parent is the highest good, the offspring is necessarily with him and separate from him only in otherness.* [V-1-6]

Life sets before us many challenges. It is difficult enough for a person to simply maintain his or her bodily existence by finding food, shelter, and clothing. To also nurture a family, succeed in a profession, gain worldly knowledge, help solve social problems, remain devoted to a marriage partner, and pursue any of the other myriad activities to which we are drawn seems to make us stretched, and often stressed, as much as can be imagined.

Plotinus is not asking us to add one more to-do to our ever expanding list of aspirations: (1) learn to play piano, (2) lose fifteen pounds, (3) smooth out golf swing, (4) return to the One. No, the message of the *Enneads* is much more radical: to look upon everything other than spiritual uplift as a mere pastime unworthy of being taken seriously. If we must shed tears or smile with joy, it should be for the One, not anything else, no matter how important it may appear to worldly eyes.

> *The man who attains this is blessed in seeing that "blessed sight," and he who fails to attain it has failed utterly. . . . For this he should give up the attainment of kingship and of rule over all earth and sea and sky, if only by leaving and overlooking them he can turn to That and see.* [I-6-7]

One Is Overall

SO WHERE IS this wonderful One? Plotinus has gotten us excited about finding it. He says that it is "beauty most of all" and "the best of visions." [I-6-7] A man or woman who deserved such praise would be seen on the cover of newsstand magazines. An uncommonly lovely spot of nature would be featured in travel guides. An extraordinarily beautiful work of art would be reproduced in art books, or displayed in a gallery. How, then, do we see the One?

Plotinus gives us a hint when he says that only by leaving and overlooking earth, sea, and sky will we be able to turn to That which is incomparably more desirable than anything we know now. In the final section of this book we will learn more about how the soul is able to return to the One. The key to making this journey is that the One is both everywhere and nowhere; ultimate reality is both present in all and separate from all.

> *Therefore he must fill all things and make all things, not be all the things he makes.* [III-9-4]

Don't be misled by Plotinus's choice of words here. "He" does not refer to a personal God. Plotinus occasionally refers to the One as "father," but this is literary license and doesn't match with how Plotinus generally describes the nature of the highest Good. John Kenney says, "Personality, extrinsic orientation, purposive planning, volition, even self-consciousness and intellection, are all denied the One, not because the One lacks these theologically positive attributes but because they are deemed inadequate to it."[1]

In other words, whatever we can say about the One doesn't begin to capture the true nature of the One. Nevertheless, Plotinus does his best to point us in the right direction, which eventually will lead to a direct experience of unity that is the only way the One can be known. Here is a simple description of the overall scheme of creation:

> *For from that true universe which is one this universe comes into existence, which is not truly one.* [III-2-2]

The One, then, is the source of physical and spiritual existence. Why? Only the One knows. Obviously, though, if it had remained itself alone we would not be here asking the question. But it is not the creator of what exists within material existence. This is the role of spirit, the first emanation from the One. And neither is it identical with manifold existence, for this would negate the absolute unity of the One.

> *The One is all things and not a single one of them. . . . It is because there is nothing in it that all things come from it: in order that being may exist, the One is not being, but the generator of being.* [V-2-1]

It isn't possible to grasp the source of physical existence through what already exists. This would be like a baby looking at its own body, and trying to figure out what part of itself—fingers, toes, arms, legs?—caused it to be born.

> *But what is above life is cause of life; for the activity of life, which is all things, is not first, but itself flows out, so to speak, as if from a spring. For think of a spring which has no other origin, but gives the whole of itself to rivers, and is not used up by the rivers but remains itself at rest.* [III-8-10]

The One, then, is the cause of both material and spiritual domains of creation, and even of itself. Trace anything in existence back to its ultimate source, and you always will arrive at the One.

How then can it be that this power behind all other powers is so well hidden? Precisely because it is everywhere and everything. But we shouldn't think that this is like a grain of sand hiding out on a beach. The grain of sand is disguised because it is so similar to all its brethren. The One, however, is difficult to discern because it is so utterly unlike anything we know now, and requires a different sort of looking to discern.

I once saw a television moderator on a public affairs program ask a minister, "How can you be sure that God exists?" The reply: "Because I see Him reflected in the face of a newborn baby." Now, this was a sincere answer and certainly has an intuitive appeal. Still, we have to ask: Why didn't the minister see God in a poisonous snake, a nuclear power plant, or an ax murderer? If God is omnipresent, why does this power seem to appear in some places and not in others? And why is it that he sees divinity in a baby's face while others just see a plain baby?

Plotinus indicates that considerable subtlety is required to even begin to understand the answer to the question, "Where is God, or the One?" First, we have to entertain the possibility that the One can simultaneously be everywhere and nowhere, in everything and in nothing.

> *How then does multiplicity come from one? Because it is everywhere, for there is nowhere where it is not. . . . Now if it itself were only everywhere, it would itself be all things; but since it is also nowhere, all things come into being through him, because he is everywhere, but are other than him, because he is nowhere.* [III-9-4]

So the One is neither to be found up in the heavens nor down here on earth. It indeed is overall, yet also is underall. Everything in creation is filled with the One but the One remains separate from every created thing. Without the One we would be nothing. Without the unity that is the hallmark of the One we would not be what we are. Thus every part of creation, including ourselves, stands as indirect evidence of the One.

> *It is by the one that all beings are beings. . . . For what could anything be if it was not one?* [VI-9-1]

Something, Plotinus says, makes everything exist. Without that something there would be no cosmos. Just as a human being and life are inseparable (without life, a human does not exist) so is something holding the cosmos together. For lack of a better term, he calls this "the One."

Why do space and time provide a solid foundation for the universe? From where do the immutable laws of nature originate? What is the source of the energy that keeps the subatomic realm whirling in constant motion, without which all matter would cease to exist? What makes something separate and distinct from everything else? How is it that we are able to point to this one and that one, rather than physical existence being just a featureless blob? There is a single answer to all these questions.

> *For all that is not one is kept in being by the one, and is what it is by this "one."* [V-3-15]

To return to the One, then, doesn't require any precise navigation skills. Pick up a dart, put on a blindfold, spin around, and throw the dart in any direction. Wherever it lands, there is the One. Anywhere in the physical universe you might throw the dart, whether it be right where you are now or a black hole at the center of a galaxy billions of light years away, you still will pinpoint the One. It is impossible to miss your mark. So why is it so difficult to make the journey to our true spiritual home?

Not because the One has left us, but because we have left the One. We could say that God's distance from us is zero, and our distance from God is as far as scattered attention has taken us.

Where is the One? At the heart of everything that exists, whether animate or inanimate. But the One can be realized only by those living beings able to turn back upon themselves and contemplate their own center. I cannot find the One within you, and you cannot find the One within me. Everyone has an equal opportunity to know the highest reality, because it is separate from none and present to all.

> *God is present to all beings, and he is in this world, however we may conceive of this presence; therefore the world participates in God. Or, if God is absent from the world, he is also absent from you, and you can say nothing either about Him or the beings which come after Him.* [II-9-16][2]

There are, however, degrees of separation from conscious awareness of God's presence. For Plotinus this is analogous to the length of a radius extending from the center of a circle. As souls we are free to travel as far as we like or as far as is possible from the center of existence, the One. When we have grown weary of our journeying and long to return to our source, the way back is the way in. The center of each of us is the same as the center of the cosmos.

> *For a god is what is linked to that center, but that which stands far from it is a multiple human being or a beast.* [VI-9-8]

The great Plotinian quest is to realize this common unifying center of being. This is the place where we know ourselves to be at one with the creation. When a person is united both with his true self and with the highest reality, nothing more is left to be done. All our striving, all our longing, all our yearning is for this alone.

First Is Formless

PLOTINUS GIVES US our goal: God, or the One. He has told us where the One can be found: everywhere, which also means nowhere because if the One was in some particular place it could not be in all places. So, how can the One be recognized? How would we know we have reached it?

As might be expected from a mystic philosopher, Plotinus's answer initially appears to be nonsensical.

> *Truly, when you cannot grasp the form or shape of what is longed for, it would be most longed for and most lovable, and love for it would be immeasurable. . . . The nature of the best and the nature of the most lovable is in the altogether formless.* [VI-7-32, 33]

It is difficult for us to imagine having so much love for someone or something that can't be grasped by the senses. Still, when you think about it, isn't love itself ungraspable? Can we put a finger on love or delimit love's boundaries? Perhaps, then, it is not so strange that what is most lovable of all, the One, has no form—even spiritual—just as love is formless.

> *We will not be surprised to see the object which produces such ardent desire completely free of all form, even intelligible.* [VI-7-34][1]

Indeed, how could the wellspring of physical and spiritual existence have any form? The ultimate must not be limited in any fashion. Whenever we say, "This is hot," coldness is denied. "It's over there," means the thing isn't here. If the One possessed any characteristic of its own that would enable it to be described, it could not be infinitely productive.

Every positive attribute implies a simultaneous limiting negation. If the One was to think, it could not be without thought; if it was in motion, it could not be at rest; if it was a certain size, it could not be bigger or smaller; if it was a particular age, it could not be older or younger. Lawrence Hatab observes that Plotinus's perspective added a new dimension to Greek philosophy.

With his distinct vision of the One Plotinus undermines a principle that had apparently been fundamental to Greek thought—that the limited and finite is the perfect, while the unlimited and infinite is the imperfect. In contrast, Plotinus claims infinity, unlimitedness and formlessness to be the One's nature, and then calls this the ultimate ground.[2]

If we are to contact the One, says Pierre Hadot, it will be as "pure, simple, undecomposable presence."[3] As soon as you try to take hold of the One, it slips away. The One hides when called by any name, revealing itself only when beckoned by silence. If we think we know what the One is like, we don't. Nothing created bears any resemblance to the One, for it is the source of form, not a form itself. It cannot even be said to have being, nor is it non-being.

> *Form is only the trace of that which has no form; indeed, it is the latter which engenders form. . . . But if all things are in that which is generated [from the One], which of the things in it are you going to say that the One is? Since it is none of them, it can only be said to be beyond them. But these things are beings, and being: so it is "beyond being."*
> [VI-7-33[4], V-5-6]

As dryly philosophical as these words may sound, the formlessness of the One is central to Plotinus's vision of a spiritual life. God cannot be known by turning to anything God has made, for the creator is beyond all that has been created. Since everything that has being necessarily possesses some form (or there would be no way to distinguish creation from the uncreated) the formless One must be beyond being.

This conception of God is disconcerting because there is nothing in it that can be conceived. Plotinus urges us to expand the boundary of our spirituality beyond the familiar since we spend almost all of our waking hours immersed in sensual perceptions. Such are the foundation of our worldly lives: sights, sounds, smells, tastes, touches. We speak fondly of feeling grounded, implying that we yearn for the reassuring solidity of the earth beneath our feet rather than the empty ethereality of the sky above our heads.

Yet who can say that they haven't been drawn toward the unknown, the mysterious, the darkness beyond light? When I was ten years old I remember going out one night to the backyard of my country home in the foothills of the Sierra Nevada mountains and gazing at the stars. Then I wrote a poem that began:

> Look up the heavens.
> What do you see?
> Tiny pinpoints of light.
> But is that all?
> Look past the stars,
> Into the blackness of the void.

This is what Plotinus asks us to do within ourselves, to look past sensations and thoughts of materiality. One's inner vision then comes to gaze upon the psychic equivalent of deep space, the dark void that remains when familiar material and mental preoccupations are discarded. Find a quiet place, close your eyes, focus your attention within, and this emptiness will be immediately evident.

But not for long. Even if you are able to detach yourself from external sights and sounds, it is almost certain that your mind will quickly dispel the inner darkness and silence. Mental images, memories, and imaginings will pop up. The voice that speaks your thoughts will start chattering away. At the very least, what has been called the emptiness of emptiness soon will be papered over with concepts about nothingness, which obviously are not nothing at all. The idea, "I'm immersed in the void," is five words away from being true.

Plotinus is well aware of this strong and almost universal reluctance to come face-to-face with formlessness because he confronted, and overcame, this fear himself. In Plato's parable of the cave, the escaping prisoner initially can't stand a vision of bright, formless light and turns away to gaze upon familiar shadows. Similarly, when long-incarcerated criminals are released they often find the shock of freedom unbearable. They may commit another crime just to regain the reassuring structure of prison life: four walls and a locked door, but at least a place to call their own.

For Plotinus, perceptions and thoughts are the "crimes" the spiritual seeker commits to avoid embracing the liberating formlessness of the One.

> *But in proportion as the soul goes towards the formless, since it is utterly unable to comprehend it because it is not delimited and, so to speak, stamped by a richly varied stamp, it slides away and is afraid that it may have nothing at all.* [VI-9-3]

There is the One, or God, and then there are our ideas about this supreme reality. Every idea, every thought, every concept is necessarily limited. The One is infinite. Unbounded. Beyond being and not-being. Not constrained in any fashion. So the closer a person's consciousness comes to the utter formlessness of the One, the less able it is to hold onto its rigid, preconceived imaginings. Truth trumps supposition. What is triumphs over what might be.

It is not possible to know the One without absolute surrender. Surrender of what? Of everything that is not one. In Plotinus's mystic philosophy, true knowledge is gained through union of the knower and what is known. Since the One is formless those seeking to know this ultimate reality must become similarly formless. Formless, though, is not the same as nothing. In fact, the All lacks any specific form precisely because it contains all forms.

A vast number of things of all sorts of shapes and sizes could be put into a huge warehouse. But the warehouse couldn't hold a similarly huge warehouse. Construct a building as large as the universe and it still wouldn't be capable of holding another building of the same dimensions. So the One, containing all that could possibly be, must necessarily have no shape or size of its own, or any other sort of quality.

So that no other form is left outside it, the One must be without form.
[V-5-6]

We begin to see, then, the method behind Plotinus's seeming spiritual madness. The soul resists giving up all it presently has and all it considers itself to be because nothingness appears to be a crazy means of attaining the All. We think that if we already are something—not everything, certainly, but at least *something*—isn't tossing all of it aside a step in the wrong direction?

No, because there is an unbridgeable gap between the whole and any of its parts. Union, the goal of divine love, means near-absolute identity. Whatever is other than the One cannot be united with the One. Whatever possesses some form, no matter how elevated or refined, cannot merge with the formless.

Even our worldly loves imperfectly reflect this principle. When I love someone I often try to adjust to his or her needs, not my own. I may go to a movie I don't really want to see and eat at a restaurant that serves food I don't really like because my love will enjoy that film and meal.

The same applies to other sorts of passions. Someone who loves Shakespeare reads the playwright's work with an open mind, allowing the eloquent words to flow freely into his own consciousness. If he also loves Mozart then he listens to the composer's music with rapt attention, completely immersed in the sublime tones and melodies. If the doorbell rings while he is reading or listening with such absorption he may not even notice it. For at that moment it is Shakespeare or Mozart with whom he desires to be united and his normal preoccupations have been supplanted.

Similarly, says Plotinus, love for the One means putting aside all other concerns. Whatever the One is, that also is what we wish to be. Rather than open-minded, we seek to be open-souled. Just as lovers embrace tightly, their desirous bodies separated by as little as possible, so does the soul yearn to unite even more closely with the One. If there is anything between us and the One it must be discarded. Since the One is formless all that possesses any sort of shape—physical, mental, or spiritual—is a barrier between us and what we truly long for.

> *When the soul feels passionate love for him, she puts aside all shape she has, including whatever form of the intelligible may be within her, for it is impossible either to see him or to be adjusted with him while possessing and acting upon anything other than him. Rather, we must keep nothing else at hand—whether good or evil—so that the soul alone may receive him alone.* [VI-7-34][5]

Love Is Limitless

PEOPLE OFTEN SAY "God is love." Plotinus agrees so long as we understand that God is not only love. To ascribe any sort of quality to the One implies a limit. If it is this, then it cannot be that. So whatever words we use in our feeble attempts to describe the indescribable are reflections of our everyday human experiences. Since we are bounded, we put bounds on God. How is it possible to conceive of a love that eternally encompasses all of existence?

> *For love is not limited here* [with the One], *because neither is the beloved, but the love of this would be unbounded.* [VI-7-32]

Normally, love is considered to involve some sort of relationship. A relationship by definition consists of a connection that includes some and excludes others. If I am related to members of my family it means that there are many other people in the world with whom I am not related. Having an intimate relationship with one person implies less than intimate relationships with others. There are shallow acquaintances and deep soul-mates.

It is easy then to project this sort of love onto the One. Some people believe that they have a personal relationship with God. Thinking like Plotinus, we might ask them: "Does this mean that God is a person? Or does it mean that you are a person?" Perhaps it is possible for my relationship with the One to be markedly different from the One's relationship with me, because I am a minute part of creation and the One is the whole of creation.

There is no mention in the *Enneads* of a divine love that waxes and wanes or falls more upon some than others. It is our love that has these changeable and arbitrary qualities, not the One's love. For universal love is founded in absolute unity. When love, the lover, and the beloved are all the same entity, where is there room for any limit or duration?

> *It is, at the same time, the beloved, love, and love of itself, for it is beautiful only in and for itself. . . . In it, being and its desire for itself are one. . . . It is itself that which it loves; which is to say, it brings itself into existence.* [VI-8-15][1]

We would not be wrong to call such all-pervading and never-ending love grace. Yet this is a grace inseparable from existence and thus is present to all living and non-living beings in equal measure. Parts of creation differ only in the extent to which they are capable of discerning and making use of this grace: humans, fully; animals, partly; plants, barely; inanimate objects, not at all.

Only a soul capable of discriminating between the radiance that illuminates materiality and the source of that light is able to return to the One. It is all too easy to be enthralled by lesser and limited material delights and forget that, if the creation is lovely, the creator must be lovelier. And what lies beyond both, the creation and its creator, can only be love beyond love. The wise soul is not content with shadows; only the sun of reality will satisfy her.

> *Since she wants to rise up to the Good, the soul disdains the beauties of this world. When she sees the beautiful things in this universe, she mistrusts them, for she sees that they are in flesh and in bodies, and that they are polluted by their present dwelling place.*
> *. . . When the soul further sees that the beauties of this world flow away, she knows full well that the light which was shimmering upon them comes from elsewhere. Then the soul rises up to the other world, for she is clever at finding what she loves, and she does not give up before she has seized it, unless her love were somehow torn away from her.* [VI-7-31][2]

Whomever or whatever we may love in this world will die or disappear one day. And this naturally includes ourselves. Species become extinct. Pyramids turn to dust. Stars go black. Where do the life and energy that hold these things together come from? And where do that life and energy go when they are held together no more? Wherever that place is, there is the wellspring of love.

I remember sitting by my mother's side and holding her hand as she died in a hospital bed, eyes closed, unconscious from the stroke she had suffered. As her breathing slowed and stopped it seemed that one moment she was there and the next moment she wasn't. My love for her did not change in the instant of her passing but I no longer felt the connection of love to anything in her body. What she truly was, her soul, was gone from it. Our love now was shared on some other plane, not physically.

Some might call it strange that I felt no sadness when my mother died, just relief that she was released from the confines of her worn-out body. I shed no tears; I might have smiled if another person had not been in the room. My reaction was, I'm quite sure, in tune with Plotinus's teachings. Grief is for what passes away. Soul never dies nor does the soul's love. So where is there cause for lamenting the loss of the shell of love, a body, a physical form, when the kernel remains intact? Love grows stronger with no coverings.

To those familiar with only the love of body and body, form and form, the Plotinian love of invisible things may seem like madness. Plautus, a Roman dramatist, succinctly said "Lover, lunatic" (*Amans, amens*).[3] Intense love is always more than a little crazy. Reason bids us to go slow, consider pros and cons, evaluate alternatives, always leave an escape route. Love says, "jump first, think later." It casts us headfirst into a bottomless ocean, where we are only too happy to drown in the embrace of our beloved.

Is it insane to give up all that you have for a chance to have the All? Each person must answer this question for him- or herself. But Plotinus advises that this is the most sensible thing to do.

> *Once the soul receives an "outflow" coming to her from the Good, she is excited and seized with Bacchic madness, and filled with stinging desires: thus love is born.* [VI-7-22][4]

Plenitude Is Power

IT SEEMS DIFFICULT to disagree with the popular adage, "use it or lose it." On the face of it this principle appears universally applicable. Won't intelligence decline when thinking stops? Isn't morality strengthened by doing virtuous deeds? Can one remain artistic without ever creating works of art? Don't we need to exercise our bodies to stay physically fit?

We also tend to believe that more is better. Not just in the sense of quantity, we'd prefer a million dollars to a thousand, but also in the sense of differentiation. Few of us would be content to simply gaze fondly at a bankbook balance that reads "$1,000,000." We'd want to convert that single accounting entry into much other stuff: TVs, clothes, books, donations, however we felt the money could be best put to use.

Similarly, if a skilled carpenter is left alone with a stack of lumber and a set of woodworking tools, he or she would find it difficult not to build something. Or many things. One artist produces many paintings. One farmer grows many crops. One shopkeeper sells many items. It seems natural to make more out of less, complexity out of simplicity, plurality out of unity.

Talented people who remain quiescent often are told: "You aren't living up to your potential." To be fully alive, we assume, is to be lively. Yet Plotinus poses, and answers, this question:

> *And are we evil when we are multiplicity? For a thing is multiple when, unable to tend to itself, it pours out and is extended in scattering. . . . For everything seeks not another, but itself, and the journey to the exterior is foolish or compulsory.* [VI-6-1]

There are two grand flows in creation, teaches Plotinus. From the One proceeds a stream of ever-increasing multiplicity as unity becomes the many. This is the downward flow of emanation: expansive, outward, centrifugal. There also is a current that leads back to the One, in the course of which parts become wholes. This is the upward flow of return: concentrated, inward, centripetal.

Both flows are entirely necessary and natural, so when Plotinus calls manyness evil he doesn't mean that it is ungodly. After all, there is nothing apart from the One, or God. But whatever leads farther away from the Good is, obviously, not desirable.

And this is why Plotinus warns of the peril of "pouring out." It's not so much a moral evil as a navigational evil. Whatever takes us off-course on our return to the One is a senseless distraction. This includes being excessively preoccupied with external, rather than internal, activities and knowledge.

The One is all-powerful precisely because it is perfect unity. A self-contained plenitude of power, the One expends no energy outside of itself. How could it? It is the All, beyond which is no other. Everything that comes after the One, however, is fragmented to some degree and so possesses a lesser productive capacity.

> *But that true All is blessed in such a way that in not making it accomplishes great works and in remaining in itself makes no small things.* [III-2-1]

If our goal is to return to the One, we must become like the One. So whenever Plotinus describes some characteristic of the highest Good, it is intended as a guide to the spiritual seeker: what the One is, we should strive to be.

Thus the One serves as the exemplar of what it means to be a true human being. Just as a person's consciousness should become as universal and formless as possible, filled with unlimited love, so should he strive to preserve his spiritual energy within and not allow it to be drained away through excessive attention to worldly pursuits. The One creates without being affected or lessened by what it has created. So does spirit, or intellect, the initial emanation from the One.

> *It has been said elsewhere that there must be something* [spirit] *after the first* [the One]*, and in a general way that it is power, and overwhelming power.* [V-3-16]

Even so, Plotinus goes so far as to say that it would have been better if spirit had never become differentiated from the One. We might think to ourselves, "How is it possible to second-guess the workings of God?" I believe, though, that the message Plotinus wants us to hear is that if it was unfortunate that the absolute unity of the first became the near-unity of the second, spirit, how vastly more unfortunate is it that we fragmented souls have entered into the multiplicity of the last and lowest: physical existence.

> *But beginning as one it* [spirit] *did not stay as it began, but, without noticing it, became many, as if heavy [with drunken sleep], and unrolled itself because it wanted to possess everything—how much better it would have been for it not to want this, for it became the second! . . . The better is the "whence," the worse the "whither."* [III-8-8]

I'm reminded of an adage: more possessions, more possessed; less possessions, less possessed. This world of "whither" in which we live is filled with so many options. Hundreds of channels to watch on cable television. Thousands of movies to rent at the video store. Millions of books to order over the Internet. Almost whatever we want can be delivered to our doors next day by an express service. Except, it seems, what we really want: simple truth and lasting happiness. For that, we must return to the One, "whence."

For Plotinus, then, it isn't what we do that is most important but who we are. There is no harm in doing so long as all our activity doesn't diffuse our spiritual energy and leave us with less being. What comes before is always a higher good than what comes after. The creator is never less than what is created. Thus our attention should be directed toward the source, not its products.

This holds for ourselves, since the creative power of our souls is the source of many things: ideas, technology, children, art, knowledge, emotions, to name but a few. If we are masters of what we create there is no problem. But all too often these creations usurp our control and come to dominate our energy and attention. The master is enslaved by the servant.

Creation when viewed from above is contemplation. This is Plotinus's vision of the natural order. Whatever is higher contemplates and brings what is lower into being. At this moment my attention is contemplating my train of thoughts, picking and choosing which should be brought to the forefront of consciousness and which should be consigned to the dustbin of useless ideas. When a thought appears promising my attention shifts to typing out the letters that represent the concept and watching them appear on a computer screen.

In an ideal situation, I should be able to toss away the words I write as easily as I create them. But every writer knows how difficult it is to highlight a lengthy passage and hit the "delete" key. Why? Because we are captured by our creations.

I come to think that part of me is in those words and that I somehow will be diminished if they are sent into electronic oblivion. Actually, says Plotinus, this cannot happen, since my true self is soul, eternal and unchangeable. However, we fail to see this and over-identify with what we do or create. And what we make, including what we make of ourselves in life, is beset by limitation. This is why the universal soul, also called the Soul of the All, has the power to create entire universes; in contrast, our individual souls sometimes can barely get our bodies out of bed in the morning.

> *The Soul of the All, then, abiding in itself makes, and the things which it makes come to it, but the particular souls themselves go to the things.* [IV-3-6]

The Soul of the All effortlessly manages the affairs of its "body," the physical universe. Nature always is natural. Everywhere the laws of nature operate seamlessly, flawlessly, incessantly. Never is there any sort of hitch, glitch, fatal error, or breakdown. We don't find nature posting a "Sorry, gravity temporarily unavailable" sign.

The Soul of the All, whose lower contemplation manifests as nature, never becomes confused, depressed, listless, or out-of-sorts. But we, to the extent that we leave our center, lose sight of the perfect harmony of the cosmos. We become deluded by the diversity that surrounds us and seemingly is us. We forget that conflict and contention are products of a limited vision, not the way things really are.

There is a great lesson here for us: look toward what is higher, not lower. Create, but do not lose yourself in what you fashion. Always remain in close communion with what lies above, and inspires, your present state of consciousness. For spirit, this is the One. For the universal soul and particular souls, this is spirit. For nature, this is the universal soul, the Soul of the All. Wisdom and power belong to those who draw their intelligence and energy from a higher source. Their contemplation is of what is greater than themselves, not lesser.

We shouldn't think that if we learn how to abide in ourselves we will attain world-creating powers. For one thing, who really would want such a responsibility? For another, there is scant evidence that humans have ever demonstrated such power regardless of their spiritual attainment. Rare purported miracles, it must be admitted, always are picayune in comparison to what nature produces all the time. No saint or prophet ever has placed a star in the sky or established a new law of physics.

It is much more important to attain inward freedom and wisdom than outward power and knowledge. There is a rhyme and reason to creation and our role as individual souls isn't to play Master of the Universe. That function is being carried out by another.

> *Who, then, could capture its* [the One's] *power all together as a whole? For if one did capture it all together as a whole, why would one be different from it?* [V-5-10]

Our goal, says Plotinus, should not merely be to remain as limited human beings with slightly increased capabilities. No, it is to return to the One and enjoy a form of consciousness that is vastly different from what we experience now. But because we are always busy with the world, we never make this grand spiritual journey, a mystical voyage like Ulysses'. We are attached to materiality. We are mesmerized by matter.

> *For everything which is directed to something else is enchanted by something else. . . . For this reason all practical action is under enchantment, and the whole life of the practical man: for he is moved to that which charms him.* [IV-4-43]

When we are motivated by anything outside ourselves, we are reacting to that thing. It is in control of us. Neither a man lusting after a fast car nor a woman pining for a pretty dress is in control of his or her desire. The car and the dress are fully in command of the situation, lifeless objects dominating conscious beings. What a strange state of affairs. On the other hand, when action truly comes from within ourselves there is no question of it being a reaction. This is genuine contemplation, making real, or realizing, that which is within us.

> *Contemplation alone remains incapable of enchantment because no one who is self-directed is subject to enchantment.* [IV-4-44]

So the mystic philosopher is self-contained. He or she realizes that the One is overall and thus is at the core of every atom of creation, including the consciousness of every soul. It is senseless to look for treasure outside a dwelling when it is known to lie within. The energy wasted in digging for happiness out in the world would be put to much better use by exploring the mine of well-being that is inside us.

The great Plotinian message is exceedingly simple: contemplate and become what truly is—genuine being, not shadows and reflections. Look within yourself and turn to a new way of knowing. Learn to be what you truly are.

Infinity Is Ineffable

IMAGINE A WORLD without words, images, or thoughts.

You can't, because imagination involves words, images, or thoughts. As soon as we try to capture this sort of world in a concept such as "all would be so flowing and connected there," our thoughts about thoughtlessness cut ourselves off from actually experiencing that reality. Our imagining destroys what we wish to imagine. This is the great conundrum of mystical spirituality: is it possible to describe the indescribable?

Plotinus, though he spends thousands of words saying so, answers: No. The One is the highest, beyond all description in terms of lower things.

> It is, therefore, truly ineffable: for whatever you say about it, you will always be speaking of a "something." But "beyond all things and beyond the supreme majesty of Intellect" is the only one of all the ways of speaking of it which is true. [V-3-13]

It is easy to understand intellectually why the One is ineffable. When something is unity, wholly and completely, it possesses no qualities that could be described. Even to say that the One is love implies that there is the One, and there also is an attribute that it possesses called love. Now we have two, not one. Yet:

> [The One] is only itself and really itself, while every other thing is itself and something else. [VI-8-21]

What is difficult (so amazingly, stupendously, overwhelmingly difficult) is to break the habit of "is-ing." Obviously I am a good example of this, having just used "is" twice in the previous sentence. I am addicted to "is" and "am." I constantly evaluate and quantify. And almost everyone else does the same. Descriptions permeate the consciousness of humans around the world, no matter in what language they are expressed.

This is because we have no experience of anything other than duality and relativity. Nothing we are familiar with, as Plotinus pointed out, is only itself, a pure existence. And once again we come face-to-face with the limits of language, for to even say that something is itself is to assume a separation between the thing and itself that is bridged somehow by an impalpable is-ness.

The One exists beyond duality, beyond reason, beyond mind and words. In the *Enneads*, Plotinus continually warns about the danger of mistaking words for reality, especially when speaking of the One. He recognizes that words are necessary if we are to say anything about the One. Yet there is an unstated footnote attached to every such expression.

> *But one should understand "as if" with each of them.* [VI-8-13]

What we are after in our search for the One is not a thought or a thing but the source of thoughts and things. So the One is far removed from the sorts of mental machinations that unceasingly course through normal human consciousness, which we carelessly and anthropomorphically ascribe to God as well.

> *If he was thought he would not think, just as movement is not in motion. . . . He is higher than speech and thought and awareness; he gives us these, but he is not these himself.* [VI-7-37, V-3-14]

We talk of God in human terms, as He or She, or with attributes like us, because we know no better. We personify the divine and the mysterious because our experience is limited to the personal and physical. We assume, consciously or unconsciously, that ultimate reality is marked by diversity and variety because we have no experience of anything else. Hence, we believe that the words we use to describe things in our earthly world can be used to describe God.

Our problem, then, is how to avoid making murky what is absolutely clear, how to avoid adding complexity to what is completely simple. In our eagerness to comprehend the One we must be careful not to let our imaginations run away with us. If someone is pressed to try to describe his understanding of God, it is better to admit "I have no clue" than to introduce a fictitious duality into the One. As we read earlier:

> *One must not make it two even for the sake of forming an idea of it.* [VI-8-13]

Plotinus, a mystic as well as a rational philosopher, teaches that the higher reaches of the path that leads to the One are wordless. This is not the same as saying that the path is undefined. A highway may or may not be marked with a name, but if it leads in the right direction, a traveler will get to his or her destination all the same. Traveling by car, bicycle, or foot is accomplished neither through words nor through wordlessness, but by wheels turning or feet walking.

The mystic's mode of transport, however, is consciousness, and the territory to be traversed also is consciousness. So while you can think about whatever you want while driving a car (mind doesn't affect machinery), incorrect thinking slows or stops travelers on their way to the One, or even sends them in the opposite direction. Plotinus explains that attention first has to be shifted from spoken words to unspoken words, and thence to what can only be called wordless words, unitary intelligence without divided thought.

As the spoken word is an imitation of that in the soul, so the word in the soul is an imitation of that in something else. [I-2-3]

Our whole approach to the One will be thrown off course if we believe we can travel to enlightenment through words or thoughts. It isn't a matter of, say, pondering the Buddhist *Dhammapada* for my whole life and then realizing that the Christian *Bible* contains a more correct depiction of divine reality. This would be like me believing that God is square and then finding out that God actually is a circle. Since I was looking for some sort of spiritual shape, I wasn't far off the mark and might simply observe, "Oops, I made a slight mistake; now I know better."

But if God is formless and nameless, far removed from any shape or word, then a much more radical change of direction is needed. A person's entire consciousness must be transformed if he or she is to experience God. A way has to be found of experiencing emptiness, of entering into the nothingness that is the threshold to the One.

The *via negativa* of spirituality, the negative way, is a difficult path to follow because we are so accustomed to experiencing the positive side of life. Teachers, coaches, and bosses encourage us to "think positively." Bare shelves in our homes soon are covered with bric-a-brac. Quiet is disconcerting; we are happier when radios and televisions permeate the air with sound waves. If our minds somehow stop thinking for a moment, a gushing stream of thoughts rapidly fills the void in consciousness.

If we want to return to the One, Plotinus urges us to value negativity more highly, since for him it is the negation of illusion. Our present state of existence is all shadows, Plato's cave. What we think is real and positive actually is unreal. It is better to remain silent than to say anything about the One.

This helps explain why mystic philosophers such as Plotinus and Meister Eckhart so often take away thoughts about God and divine reality immediately after they have offered them. Such verbal behavior is called apophasis, which Michael Sells describes as unsaying or speaking-away. You say something, and then you unsay it.

According to Sells, "An overview of Western apophasis would begin with Plotinus. Though elements of apophasis existed earlier, it was Plotinus who wove these elements and his own original philosophical and mystical insights into a discourse of sustained apophatic intensity."[1] Here's an example.

> *But if the One—name and reality expressed—was to be taken positively it would be less clear than if we did not give it a name at all. . . . Therefore, when you have said "The Good" do not add anything to it in your mind, for if you add anything, you will make it deficient by whatever you have added.* [V-5-6, III-8-11]

Watching a beautiful sunset in the company of others, there always seems to be someone who has to say: "That's a beautiful sunset." Or, relaxing by a mountain stream, a companion breaks the silence: "It's wonderful to just listen to the sound of rushing water." "Well, it *was*, until you opened your mouth!" we may think, rather uncharitably. Do we add anything to reality by naming it? In the case of spiritual realities, Plotinus teaches that this sort of addition is always a subtraction.

Who could draw a picture, sing a song, or compose a poem about infinity? What image, melody, or words could possibly capture the ground and source of all being? It is exceedingly difficult for humans to comprehend even the very small or the very large, the infinitesimal sub-atomic world or the vastness of intergalactic space. It is absolutely impossible to fathom infinity. Not because it is nothing but because it is everything—small, large, and in-between.

And it [the One] *must be understood as infinite not because its size and number cannot be measured or counted but because its power cannot be comprehended. For when you think of him as Intellect or God, he is more; and when you unify him in your thought, here also the degree of unity by which he transcends your thought is more than you imagined it to be.* [VI-9-6]

So the great Plotinian quest is for unity of soul, not of thought. The One is to be found in the seeming emptiness that remains when all images and ideas of material or spiritual reality have been cast out. This vacuum of consciousness is actually a plenum, for it is the boundless spring from which all else flows. What we seek is the source of matter and thought.

All that surrounds us, inside our minds and outside in the world, is merely the crude sediment of creation, what remains when unity becomes multiplicity and spirit becomes matter. Thus it is essential to leave aside knowledge of created things if we are to know the creator.

One must depart from knowledge and things known, and from every other, even beautiful, object of vision. [VI-9-4]

Return to the One is union, pure presence of soul and source, drop and ocean.

For this reason the vision is hard to put into words. For how could one announce that as another when he did not see, there when he had the vision, another, but one with himself? [VI-9-10]

Beauty Is Beyond

AFTER ALL THIS TALK about the One being formless, limitless, and ineffable, the reader may be getting an impression that the One is some sort of amorphous blob of pure existence without any qualities: shapeless, featureless, colorless. In a sense this is correct, since the highest encompasses all that is below and so is not any particular thing, but all things. Yet Plotinus leaves no doubt that the One is the source of all beauty.

> *Therefore the productive power of all is the flower of beauty, a beauty which makes beauty.* [VI-7-32]

Thus the spiritual seeker desiring to return to the One needs only a simple direction. Follow beauty. It is natural to be attracted to earthly sorts of beauty. Handsome men, gorgeous women, visions of nature, alluring artwork—all these and so much more beg for attention. "Look at me; delight in me; long for me."

But Plotinus tells us that what we dimly recognize in every beautiful object is the beauty beyond. We dart from one delight to another yet remain unsatisfied. For we never are able to gaze upon pure spiritual Beauty, only its shadowy material reflection.

> *The lover . . . has a kind of memory of beauty. But he cannot grasp it in its separateness, but he is overwhelmingly amazed and excited by visible beauties. . . . Then all these beauties must be reduced to unity, and he must be shown their origin.* [I-3-2]

This is, I have to say, a beautiful bit of philosophy, at once world-denying and beauty-affirming. So often mysticism is considered to be self-absorbed asceticism, closed-eye introverts contemplating their own navels or foreheads rather than the glories of nature and other human beings. There is indeed this side to Plotinus, yet his only reason for denying physical beauty is to gain a greater spiritual beauty. To empty one's pockets of pennies so they may be filled with dollars isn't the act of a miser, but of a lover of wealth.

Over and over, in many ways, the *Enneads* proclaim the wisdom of what was referred to before as one-stop happiness shopping. Most of us search for well-being hither and yon, here and there, in this person and that thing, in cherished beliefs and comfortable values. We sift through life like prospectors intently searching through huge piles of dirt for small flecks of gold, discarding most of the matter and ideas we come across, carefully clinging to what precious little seems to produce a glimmer of happiness in us.

Plotinus says that it is we who are made of gold, and all our sifting and searching is distracting us from finding the vast treasure of beauty that lies within.

When we know ourselves we are beautiful, but ugly when we are ignorant of ourselves. [V-8-13]

Someone who truly knows him- or herself stands out from the crowd. Porphyry describes Plotinus as a "god-like man . . . mild and kind, most gentle and attractive," who "sleeplessly kept his soul pure and ever strove toward the divine which he loved with all his soul."[1] Through him the divine shone clearly, as sunlight beams brightly through a clear spot on a soot-covered window.

The beauty in both us and the world generally is masked by matter. We can't do anything about the world; that's the province of the Soul of the All, or World Soul. We can, however, transform the ugliness of our own souls through a spiritual makeover. This is accomplished by turning away from every sort of beauty that can be perceived by the senses, for the supposed beauty of matter actually is ugly. Not because it is ugly in itself but because it masks what is true.

It's as if a woman thought she was applying lipstick and eye shadow, and found out that a lump of coal, not makeup, was in her hand. First she would need to drop what she was holding. Then she would need to clean herself up and learn what truly produces beauty. For Plotinus, every addition to the natural beauty of the One is a subtraction. Our consciousnesses, says Plotinus, presently are in a sorry state.

We've become enthralled by images, shadows on the cave wall. What we consider to be substance, seemingly solid matter, actually is a flimsy gossamer covering over the enduring reality of spirit. Physical bodies and forms reveal only the merest hint of the true beauty beyond, just as a close-fitting mask conveys the shape of a face but hides the features that make it so attractive. If we love the ephemeral and derivative beauty of this world then we will be enraptured by the wellspring of beauty.

Even in this world, we must say that beauty consists less in symmetry than in the light that shines upon the symmetry, and this light is what is desirable. After all, why is it that the splendor of beauty shines more brightly upon a living face while only a trace of beauty appears on the face of a dead man? . . . Why is an ugly man, as long as he is alive, more beautiful than the beauty of a statue? [VI-7-22][2]

Great question. Often a good-looking person is observed enjoying the company of someone quite plain. A comment is whispered: "What does she see in him?" (or he in her). Well, a beauty beyond sight—inward beauty.

Men, I have to admit, generally are less able to discern such hidden radiance. My sex is more attuned to lusting after the female form than loving the feminine soul. Women, though certainly not immune to carnal desire, generally are closer to understanding Plotinus's message: when we long for someone, what we really are after is the subtle inner beauty that shines through the body, not the person's plainly visible bodily form. What is it that makes a "real woman" or a "real man"? Something difficult to describe, yet easily recognized by those with the eye to see it.

Just as with the bodies here below our desire is not for the underlying material things but for the beauty imaged upon them. [VI-7-22]

Our return to the One is furthered by looking beyond the physical and acquiring a taste for invisible beauties. Whatever delights us here will also delight us there, in the world beyond. And more so, since here our enjoyment of beauty is constrained by the coarseness of materiality. This is akin to only feeling our lover's skin through thick gloves; the promise of pleasure is all around us, but our fulfillment is continually frustrated. Deeper and deeper we dive into sensuality, desperately trying to get the happiness we feel we deserve, not realizing that what we seek lies in the opposite direction.

So long as we believe that we are our outer selves we will be cut off from the beauties within. We have to experience the beauty of our souls. Our first and most important task is to realize this beauty. A beautiful soul sees beauty everywhere just as a person carrying a bright lantern is continually immersed in light, even during the darkness of night. How does a soul do this? By not gazing upon visible matter with the physical body during spiritual contemplation.

For it is certainly not by running around outside that the soul "sees self-control and justice," but itself by itself in its understanding of itself and what it formerly was, seeing them standing in itself like splendid statues all rusted with time which it has cleaned: as if gold had a soul, and knocked off all that was earthy in it. [IV-7-10]

Every material form—dogs, dirt, daisies, diamonds, whatever—springs from the spiritual realm and is seen much more clearly there. The immaterial forms or concepts in our minds—justice, judgment, joy, jealousy—also are dim reflections of substantial spiritual realities. Matter has cast a veil over simple truth, including the truth about ourselves. The beauty we seek, whether in things or thoughts, is wonderfully close at hand. We just need to look within rather than without.

So all of us are sculptors, regardless of our ability to wield a chisel and mallet. Each person can choose to create the most beautiful *objet d'art* imaginable, his own self. Actually this is not so much a matter of creation as one of discovery and cleansing. Pierre Hadot says, "For the ancients, sculpture was an art which 'took away,' as opposed to painting, an art which 'added on.' The statue pre-existed in the marble block and it was enough to take away what was superfluous in order to cause it to appear."[3]

This is the soul's ugliness, not being pure and unmixed, like gold, but full of earthiness; if anyone takes the earthy stuff away the gold is left, and is beautiful, when it is singled out from other things and is alone by itself. [I-6-5]

Virtue, wisdom, beauty, love—all these divine qualities already exist within us, just as the statue already exists within the stone. This is why spirituality is so natural when practiced correctly. Nothing needs to be forced. No need to pretend to be anything other than what we are. Our artistry is to chip away and toss aside from our awareness all the physical sensations and personal preoccupations that obscure the soul's original glory.

Go back inside yourself and look: if you do not yet see yourself as beautiful, then do as the sculptor does with a statue he wants to make beautiful; he chisels away one part, and levels off another, makes one spot smooth and another clear, until he shows forth a beautiful face on the statue.

Like him, remove what is superfluous, straighten what is crooked, clean up what is dark and make it bright, and never stop sculpting your own statue, until the godlike splendor of virtue shines forth to you. [I-6-9][4]

Our great mistake is believing that beauty and ugliness exist out there in the world somewhere. We spend much time and effort beautifying our homes, our gardens, our bodies, our cars. No one plans a vacation in an ugly place. We love beautiful music, beautiful art, beautiful movies, beautiful books, and do our best to avoid what clashes with our aesthetic sensibilities.

And now Plotinus comes along asking a simple question: Is it possible that we are always and everywhere surrounded by beauty, and don't recognize it?

How then can anyone be in beauty without seeing it? If he sees it as something different, he is not yet in beauty, but he is in it most perfectly when he becomes it. [V-8-11]

An intelligent person carries his intelligence with him everywhere he goes. Ditto with an athletic person or a musical person. Knowledge, physical activity and song accompany these people not because they are picked up in the course of their travels through life but because intelligence, athleticism and musicality are a part of their being. Similarly, says Plotinus, a beautiful soul sees beauty in every nook and cranny of creation. He also attracts and enchants all who come in his presence, for in and through himself he radiates godlike qualities.

There is nothing wrong with creating and admiring external beauty. But our senses can only convey transmitted news of beauty that is now, and will always be, separate from ourselves. We should strive for more than merely enjoying beauty, as it is possible to become beauty.

In the One there is no separation, only union. So it might seem that here is where the soul will unite with true beauty along with all else we could possibly desire. However, in absolute unity there are no qualities. Hence it really is not proper to term the highest Good beautiful or best, but rather, beyond beauty and beyond the best.

Up to it [the Good] *all things are beautiful. But he is beautiful beyond all beauty, and is king in the intelligible realm, transcending the best.* [I-8-2]

It is in spirit, the first emanation from the One, where beauty per se, intrinsic beauty, will be found. Not the beauty of something, but Beauty alone in its fullness. If the One is king, beyond beauty, then spirit is queen, the epitome of beauty. When we are immersed in spirit, we are immersed in beauty.

The Intellect is beautiful; indeed it is the most beautiful of all things. Situated in pure light and pure radiance, it includes within itself the nature of all beings. This beautiful world of ours is but a shadow and an image of its beauty. . . . It lives a blessed life, and whoever were to see it, and—as is fitting—submerge himself within it, and become One with it, would be seized by awe. [III-8-11][5]

Reality Is a Radiation

IF THE ONE had remained wholly itself, unimaginable unity, obviously there would be nobody around to ponder the One, or anything else. Each of us is proof that oneness somehow has turned into many-ness. Additional concrete evidence surrounds us in every direction. Outside my window I see a profusion of trees and bushes, each bearing numerous leaves, each leaf composed of a multitude of cells, each cell a miniature universe of countless atoms.

And so it goes, levels upon levels of fecund multiplicity. Nature, it is said, abhors a vacuum. Every speck of physical reality is filled with energy or matter. Even empty space, physicists tell us, is seething with activity. Virtual particles unceasingly spring in and out of existence, flecks of quantum foam cast up by an invisible, energetic ocean.

What is the ultimate source of all this? The One, from which emanates the Many.

> *Those other than the First have come into being in the sense that they are derived from other, higher, principles. . . . But Parmenides in Plato speaks more accurately, and distinguishes from each other the first One, which is more properly called One, and the second which he calls "One-Many," and the third, "One and Many."* [II-9-3, V-1-8]

Here is Plotinus's grand scheme of creation in a nutshell: the One is, naturally, simply One; the second, spirit, is so much a unity that it is properly called a One-Many; the third, soul, is more divided—hence, a One and Many. And then there is what comes after immaterial soul. Physical existence. The ground floor. Earth. The end of the line. Unity depleted to the utmost.

"Last stop! Everyone out!"

"Where are we?"

"Read the sign: *Many*."

"Oh, God," the soul says. "I didn't mean to go this far."

Yes, but there is a way to turn around and return to the One. This is the central ever-so-optimistic message of Plotinus. And even though we souls have ventured farther from our homeland than is desirable (if we desire happiness and well-being, that is) it isn't the One that is at fault. What has been created is just fine, exactly as it should be. What's gone awry is how we've used creation, not creation itself. The One couldn't help but make what has been made.

> *And all things when they come to perfection produce; the One is always perfect and therefore produces everlastingly; and its product is less than itself.* [V-1-6]

There's our problem: what is produced is necessarily less than the producer. We're at the end of reality's production line, occupied with what are, speaking bluntly, the dregs of creation. What starts off in the divine heights as crystal clear being is unavoidably muddied by form and matter in the course of its flow to the physical universe. There isn't any sort of cosmic conspiracy to make us suffer or tempt us with sordidness. This is just the way it is. Plotinus tries to help us understand with a helpful but limited analogy.

> *The First, then, should be compared to light, the next* [spirit] *to the sun, and the third* [soul] *to the celestial body of the moon, which gets its light from the sun.* [V-6-4]

There is only one entity, the One, underlying all of the apparent diversity in both the spiritual and material realms. It's easy to overlook this, of course, just as someone gazing at a beautiful full moon generally fails to remember that he or she is admiring reflected light. Without the sun, the moon would be dark. And without light, so would the sun.

Plotinus, however, describes a view modern science has disproved: that light radiates from the sun without changing the sun. We know now, of course, that the energetic processes causing photons to leave the sun will, far in the future, cause it to burn out. The One, though, is not comprised of material substance. Nor is spirit (intellect). So neither is affected in any way by the creative energies continuously radiating from them to form the lower realities. Creation did not happen somewhere in the past. It is happening now, everywhere, within and without us.

> *But he* [the One] *irradiates for ever, abiding unchanged over the intelligible. . . . Resembling the One thus, Intellect produces in the same way, pouring forth a multiple power—this is a likeness of it—just as that which was before it poured it forth.* [V-3-12, V-2-1]

To indulge in a little philosophical jargon, Plotinus teaches that existence emanates from the One while essence emanates from spirit and soul (roughly speaking, essence makes something *what* it is while existence produces the actuality *that* it is).

So, spirit, through the intermediary of soul, is the direct creator of all the thoughts and things with which we presently are familiar. If this doesn't make sense, particularly the distinction between spirit and soul, don't despair. Plotinus often fails to clearly differentiate these creative powers and we'll be delving more deeply into the nature of spirit and soul later on.

In the end, it is fruitless to try to comprehend what lies beyond our usual means of understanding: sense perception and reason. As Plotinus told us before, to return to the One we need to "wake another way of seeing, which everyone has but few use." Again and again the *Enneads* caution against reducing spirituality to something physical out of a desire to get a firmer grip on what otherwise seems so ephemeral.

> For the things which one thinks are most real, are least real; and the [materially] large has less genuine existence. . . . So reverse your way of thinking, or you will be left deprived of God. [V-5-11]

How easy it is to read these words and how difficult to take them to heart. Plotinus warns that we are enmeshed in a gigantic illusion that encompasses the entire physical universe, a hall of mirrors that inverts reality so that what is most true, spirit, appears insubstantial and uncertain while what is least true, matter, captures our attention by virtue of its seeming substance.

What we need to do is look more clearly into the nature of things, and try to trace creation back to its divine source. We, of course, are part of creation. So if we can figure out what our essence consists of and where it resides, the mystery of the outward creation also will be resolved.

Plotinus often uses light as an example of how to approach this process of swimming upstream to find the source of creation's flow. Consider all the moonstruck poets who have been inspired to compose flowery odes about earth's nighttime companion. The sun, it seems, inspires less fervent romantic inspiration. Light itself, almost none at all. Light suffuses the air within which we live and breathe so we generally overlook it. What we notice is a source of light: a star, lamp, fire, lantern. Even the moon, a mere reflector of the sun's beams, captures more of our attention than light itself.

There is a spiritual lesson here: dematerialize your vision and you will see more of substantial reality. Though the moon appears lovely, its glory radiates from the sun. And the essence of the sun, the spiritual sun at least, is pure light.

Imagine, says Plotinus, something small and luminous. Next, put a larger transparent sphere around this source of light. Observe: light now shines throughout the sphere, and all this luminosity comes from the central source. Now, here comes the important part. Take away the source's bulk, and leave its power.

> *Would you still say that the light was somewhere, or would it be equally present over the whole outer sphere? You will no longer rest in your thought on the place where it was before, and you will not any more say where it comes from or where it is going, but you will be puzzled and put in amazement when, fixing your gaze now here and now there in the spherical body, you yourself perceive the light.* [VI-4-7]

Here is an example of how Plotinus uses a material metaphor as a crutch to prop up our rational understanding of some aspect of spiritual reality. At first we lean upon the metaphor, comfortably visualizing something familiar: a source of light surrounded by a sphere. "Ah, like a light bulb shining within a circular glass globe," we think. He asks us to picture the light filling all of the sphere, perhaps even spilling over to brighten the room outside. This is still easy to imagine, as we see a similar phenomenon each time a light switch is flicked.

But then Plotinus takes away our crutch and asks us to stand without material support. The light bulb has disappeared, yet there still is light. How can this be? Indeed, it would be puzzling to walk into an absolutely bare room with no windows, close the door, and find the room illuminated bright as day. Our experience has always been that light comes from something. Here, though, it seemingly springs from nothing.

Amazement and puzzlement, these are signs that one has truly seen spirit or the One. It could not be otherwise. Beholding the power behind all other powers, the maker of all that could ever be made, could we be in the presence of anything but wonder beyond wonder?

Universe Is a Unity

A JOURNEY NECESSARILY is across a distance. Otherwise, we would already be at the place that is both our starting point and our destination, *here*. In addition, this distance must be bridgeable; if not, we will never reach our goal, *there*. When here and there span the vastness of intergalactic space or the equally vast expanse of the time since creation began, it is natural to throw up one's hands and say, "Never to be reached, never to be known."

Such is the fate of much of modern science, which has extended theoretical explanations of the universe to places and times, such as the center of a black hole or the first instant of the big bang, which never can be experienced directly. Man seemingly is able to firmly grasp only what little of the cosmos is presently close at hand.

Similarly, for the religiously-minded the unmistakable presence of God is almost always a far-off goal, not an immediate reality. Death, many religions promise, will bridge the gap between spiritual aspiration and realization. The implication is that wherever God or heaven is, this isn't anywhere that we can travel to now. Plotinus disagrees.

> *Our world is not separated from the spiritual world. . . . We deny that God is in one place but not in another.* [II-9-16¹ ,VI-5-4]

Here, in a nutshell, is the reason why it is possible to return to God in this very lifetime. The One has never left us; it is we who have left the One. The distance we have to cross is precisely zero from God's point of view, while from our perspective it is as far as our diverse mental and material cravings have taken us from the central still point of spiritual unity.

> *For nothing is a long way off or far from anything else. . . . But if there is neither far nor near, it* [the All] *must be present whole if it is present at all. And it is wholly present to each and every one of those for which it is neither far nor near, but they are able to receive it.* [IV-3-11, VI-4-2]

This message is wonderfully reassuring yet also rather disturbing. The One is right here, right now, both inside of me and outside of me. Great! But this takes away any excuses I may have been using to explain my lack of spiritual realization: "God is too far away for me to experience him"; "I must wait until God makes his presence known on earth"; "Only after death will I be able to rise up to heaven and meet God." Plotinus tells us that the One is wholly present to those who are able to receive it. And it isn't present to those who are not.

Not so great! For now the responsibility is on my shoulders to experience God. It's much as if I was waiting comfortably at my home for a delivery truck to bring me a long-awaited gift I thought was being sent from a far-distant location. Then a message comes: "Start digging. The gift lies under the ground right in front of your door." Well, while it's nice to know my present is relatively close by, previously I had faith that it would be delivered right into my hands and now I'm told I have to put in some sweat and toil before I can enjoy it.

Spiritual realization is available to all, that's grace, but only obtained by those who work for it, hence the need for effort. In addition to challenging the primacy of grace over effort, or faith over good works, Plotinus's vision of an undivided cosmos leads to a conclusion that is at odds with another central tenet of many theologies: God misses us, and wants us back.

When you think about it, it is indeed a rather strange notion that the almighty lacks anything at all. It's nice to feel needed: "I have to return to God so he can be truly content." But when we speak this way we're saying that even though God created the universe, he placed it so far away from himself that now he's lost touch with us and is sad about the situation. "Come back!" many people imagine God is crying.

Perhaps Plotinus's teaching is closer to the truth.

> *That One, therefore, since it has no otherness is always present, and we are present to it when we have no otherness; and the One does not desire us, so as to be around us, but we desire it, so that we are around it. . . . He does not need the things which have come into being from him, but leaves what has come into being altogether alone, because he needs nothing of it, but is the same as he was before he brought it into being.* [VI-9-8, V-5-12]

In other words, we need God; God doesn't need us. The One is not lessened by creation's emanation, nor would the One gain if creation ceased to exist. It is infinite and unchanging, the All that never can be less or more. So it is a mistake to conceive our relationship with the One in any sort of human terms.

As was noted before, I can only have a genuine personal relationship with someone if that entity is also a person. If that entity happens to be the One, and the One is unity, present in every place (including me), then whatever my relationship is with this power, it isn't personal. In fact, my very personhood is the primary barrier to knowing the One. When I am truly myself, says Plotinus, I will realize I am not separate from all else. Whatever I am in my deepest being isn't different from what you are.

> *Since we look towards the outside, away from the point at which we are all joined together, we are unaware of the fact that we are one. We are like faces turned towards the outside, but attached on the inside to one single head. If we could turn around—either spontaneously or if we were lucky enough to "have Athena pull us by the hair"—then, all at once, we would see God, ourselves, and the All.* [VI-5-7][2]

In the Iliad (I, 197-8) Minerva comes down from heaven and, seen only by Achilles, pulls him by his hair. If we're lucky, Plotinus implies, perhaps a divine being will do us the same favor and jolt us out of our fascination with material multiplicity so that we may behold spiritual unity. Still, there isn't much of a hint elsewhere in the *Enneads* that we should count on a celestial whim for salvation.

Plotinus's mystical philosophy may seem uncomfortably detached to those who turn to angels, spirit guides, and other personalized metaphysical entities for support and guidance. However, we must remember that his teachings are based on nothing other than love. This love, though, is not personal but universal. Its endpoint is unity, or at least the almost complete unity of soul and spirit, rather than a relationship.

In everyday life we are unfamiliar with anything other than relations between parts of creation. Man and woman, mind and thoughts, nature and technology, writers and readers, energy and matter—almost everything we have ever experienced, inside or outside of us, has involved a relationship between something and something else. Even when I say "I think" or "I feel," I'm describing a relation between two different parts of me, the "I" that experiences and the thinking or feeling being experienced.

What if, though, the spiritual essence of outward reality is exactly the same as my own inward spiritual essence, or soul? Could everything out there somehow also be in here? If so, what difference would there be between me, or you, and everything else?

If then we have a part in true knowledge, we are those [spiritual realities]. . . . *So then, being together with all things, we are those: so then, we are all and one.* [VI-5-7]

Here Plotinus points toward the equal opportunity for spiritual realization that a unified cosmos offers. No person, no culture, no country, no religion is any closer to or farther from divine truth than is any other. Spirituality is an individual affair and every human soul is capable of experiencing the great Plotinian truth that all spiritual realities are within the essence of his or her consciousness. Since this is true for every person on earth, not just a favored few, "we are all and one." Though each soul is separate, a drop of the spiritual ocean, the ocean somehow is wondrously contained within each drop.

This sounds marvelous. Yet it isn't reality for most of us. Yes, we may think or believe that we are all one, but this is a far cry from the actual experience of unity. And there are those, perhaps a majority, who don't find oneness all that appealing. "Individuality is the hallmark of being human," they proclaim. "We are meant to be more than a featureless drop in a limitless ocean."

Plotinus found a pleasing middle ground in his mystic philosophy that should appeal to both the unifiers and the individualists. Yes, he taught, each soul is separate. And yes, all souls are one. Logically, this may be confusing. Experientially, it is what Plotinus found in the course of his personal voyage of spiritual discovery.

So then the soul must be in this way both one and many and divided and indivisible. [IV-1-2]

Logic takes us only so far in our quest to know reality as it is, for nature deigns to operate by its own largely inscrutable rules, notwithstanding man's attempts to systematize those rules and package them in tidy analytical bundles. Our angle of vision determines how reality appears. This is why spirit and soul can be both one and many, and the One both everywhere and nowhere.

Consider a candle placed inside a metallic cylinder with variously shaped and sized cutouts: stars, triangles, circles, ovals, hexagons.

When placed in a dark room, the candlelight will cast all sorts of images upon the walls. The light is one, while its projected images are many. The light emanates from a single place, while its radiation is all around the room. As crude as this metaphor is, perhaps it helps us understand how the radiance of the One can appear so diffused and variegated.

> *All these things are the One and not the One: they are he because they come from him; they are not he, because it is in abiding by himself that he gives them.* [V-2-2]

Doodling with a pencil, someone idly sprinkles dots across a blank page. Then each dot is connected with more dots, forming a continuous serpentine sequence. Eventually all the dots will merge into what looks like a solid line. The line then can be said to be both one and many. The individual dots remain under the surface of the line, so to speak, but are as much a whole as they are parts. Each dot, if it was conscious, could say "I am me! A single dot, proudly myself!" Yet a broader vision would see a line with no divisions.

Is it better to know the self as a restricted part, or a boundless whole? For Plotinus, the choice is obvious. My spiritual goal should be to bring together what has been separated, to narrow if not completely eliminate the difference between my limited personal consciousness and the One's universal super consciousness. Presently the One and I are like two concentric circles that have drifted apart (with me, of course, having done the drifting).

> *For here too when the centers have come together they are one, but there is duality when they are separate.* [VI-9-10]

Souls have a choice: to face toward oneness, or manyness. There is no such choice for bodies made of matter, nor is there a choice for the One. Matter is always many and the One is always one. Since presently we find ourselves existing in a material world, the challenge is to turn away from the multiplicity of matter if we have a desire to return to our source, unity.

Certainly there is some vestige of unity within matter or it could not remain what it is. But it is so dim and indistinct as to be almost unrecognizable. This is why it is so easy to distinguish this from that, and here from there, in the physical world. Only at the most basic subatomic level are parts absolutely identical. Every electron is the same, while each person is unique.

The soul's uniqueness always will remain, says Plotinus, but will be greatly reduced after leaving the material realm. He observes that it would be absurd for someone, such as Socrates, to engage in so much strenuous spiritual seeking only to be completely dissolved in oneness when what has been sought is found. Why strive so mightily to be immersed in the One if there will be no consciousness of the immersion?

> *Are they the souls of particular individuals in the lower order, but belong in the higher order to that higher unity? But this will mean that Socrates, and the soul of Socrates, will exist as long as he is in the body; but he will cease to be precisely when he attains to the very best. Now no real being ever ceases to be . . . but each remains distinct in otherness, having the same essential being.* [IV-3-5]

So this is good news. Who would relish the thought of being themselves, just as they are now, for eternity? I frequently get tired of myself—same old thoughts, same old feelings, same old beliefs, same old habits—and I've spent only fifty-five years with my body and mind. The idea of being me forever sounds like some sort of existentialist nightmare.

Yet the prospect of being nothing at all certainly isn't appealing either. Being everything does have a better ring to it. Still, if I turn out to be everything it seems likely that I won't know it. Who will be around to enjoy all that omnipresence? Perhaps being the entire All would be wonderfully pleasant, but I prefer the idea of being a contented piece of the All that has been stripped of impermanence and illusion. And this is just what Plotinus promises.

> *The soul's being one, then, does not do away with the many souls, any more than being does away with beings, nor does the multiplicity there in the true All fight with the one.* [VI-4-4]

Multiplicity and unity are not at war with each other. How could they be? Both are emanations from the One, branches from the same tree, waves from the same ocean.

All the tension, pain, suffering, and anxiety we feel comes from us, not the cosmos. There always is complete harmony in the whole of the universe, for it is unity. Any grating sense of wrongness we may have ("This shouldn't be happening") is, we can be sure, the result of an excessive partness that has set itself at odds with the greater order.

I love the image Plotinus gives us in the following quotation. Who hasn't felt trampled by life? Maybe, he suggests, we need to learn how to dance along with the rest of the universe.

> *As if when a great company of dancers was moving in order a tortoise was caught in the middle of its advance and trampled because it was not able to get out of the way of the ordered movement of the dancers: yet if it had ranged itself with that movement, even it would have taken no harm from them.* [II-9-7]

Whether man or woman, almost every person feels, consciously or unconsciously, that he or she should be the one doing the leading in the dance of life. We all expect that the people and things that surround us, the whole of which Plotinus speaks, will adjust to our needs, desires, and actions. The problem of course is that nearly everyone else feels the same way. And any couple that has taken dancing lessons knows what happens when both parties try to do the leading: chaos. Yet here we are with billions of human souls attempting the same impossible task.

When all are one, in truth there are no leaders and no followers. When we consciously live as parts of the whole we dance through life happily and gracefully, not caring who seems to be doing the leading and who the following at any particular moment. The universe is a unity. With the dawning of spiritual wisdom we realize that all are dancing to the same tune.

Section II

The One
AND MANY—
Soul's Descent,
And Return

Spirit Is Substance

THE CORNERSTONE of Plotinus's spiritual philosophy is, not surprisingly, spirit. This makes complete sense. How can we aspire to spirituality, much less lay claim to actually being spiritual, if we don't understand the nature of spirit? A prospective mountain climber should at least be able to recognize a mountain, even if he doesn't yet know how to scale one.

Strangely, though, one rarely comes across explicit descriptions of spirit in religious literature or philosophical writings. We hear much talk of being filled with spirit or embraced by spirit but little mention of what this mysterious entity we are to be filled with or embraced by actually *is*. Plotinus, thankfully, gives us as good an understanding as will be found anywhere in Western mystic philosophy.

The One, we are told, is beyond being, beyond form, beyond knowledge, beyond time, beyond space, beyond everything we can possibly conceive. So we would not be far off the mark to call the One ineffable existence, the mystery of all mysteries. The first emanation of the One, spirit (intellect) is all being within existence. Spirit is the actual creator of the cosmos. The One creates the creator and endows its offspring with its own power.

> *For Intellect also has of itself a kind of intimate perception of its power, that it has power to produce substantial reality. . . . And because its substance is a kind of single part of what belongs to the One and comes from the One, it is strengthened by the One and made perfect in substantial existence by and from it.* [V-1-7]

According to Plotinus, there is little difference between the One and spirit, other than the fact that spirit is a one-many, containing the entire reality of the cosmos within itself. Spirit may be thought of as all-pervading intelligent energy with unlimited creative power.

Here again, as so often in the *Enneads*, we need to reverse our usual way of thinking. Most people consider spirit to be some sort of wispy, ethereal divinity that episodically makes its presence subtly known on this earthly plane. This is the sense in which spirits, angelic or otherwise, are viewed: occasional visitors from a higher dimension. Similarly, most religions hold that a small number (maybe only one) of humans have been privileged to be embraced by spirit.

Here too, spirit seems highly selective, warmly greeting a few and roundly ignoring everyone else.

By contrast, Plotinus teaches that other than the One, spirit is the most substantial of all substances, the most real of all realities, the most intelligent of all intelligences, the most lovable of all loves. What is wispy and ethereal is this world not the domain of spirit. Matter is a bit of fluff barely worth our consideration.

> *The true substance has stripped off these things* [matter and sense-perception] *and is a power standing on itself, no feeble shadowy thing but the most living and intelligent of all, than which nothing is livelier or more intelligent or more substantial.* [VI-6-8]

Spirit is so wonderful for a simple reason: in truth, there is nothing else in creation. All that is, is spirit. There is nothing material that is not also spiritual. So we need have no fear we will be leaving behind anything important as we return to the One. At first it may seem more is being lost than gained. Plotinus tells us to shun our senses, silence our emotions, and shut down our thinking. "What's going to be left of me?" Well, what's going to be left is reality minus materiality, creation without a covering.

> *Intellect and being are one and the same thing. . . . The knowledge of things without matter is its objects.* [V-4-2]

Spirit, as will be discussed more fully later, is true intelligence. Spirit, or intellect, possesses knowledge of all things because it is all things in much the same sense that I know what I am experiencing because my experience is me. The difference between us, of course, is that the content of my experience is personal and subjective, while the content of spirit's experience is universal and objective.

The ancient Greeks asked the same question that modern scientists struggle to answer: Where does everything in the universe come from? I'm not speaking here of basic matter or energy, which can be thought of as the raw material of physical existence. This too is a mystery, since no one presently can say what energy is, just what it does. The greatest wonder, though, is that the universe began as a formless blob of energy (in the big bang, so physicists tell us) and has ended up so amazingly well-structured.

Galaxies, stars, planets, plants, animals, people—everything is put together so well. DNA, atoms, elements, electricity, gravity, language, music, culture—all that surrounds us and is us and has been created by us is so nicely formed. Not that all this is pleasant, wise, or beautiful. The value placed on creation is a different matter. The mystery I'm pointing toward is twofold: that anything exists at all, and, now existing, that it isn't just a whirlpool of primal chaos.

Plotinus has an answer.

> So Intellect, by giving something of itself to matter, made all things in unperturbed quietness; this something of itself is the rational formative principle flowing from Intellect. [III-2-2]

It is this rational formative principle, or *logos*, that accounts for the structure of both the physical universe and the lower reaches of the spiritual universe, the domain of the Soul of the All. *Logos* is the source of all laws of nature, which generally can be framed in rational mathematical terms. But Plotinus warns against confusing the intelligence that flows from spirit with the limited human intellect. The rationality of *logos* and the Soul of the All isn't thinking as we know it but an intuitive knowledge which translates directly into action.

> Being and Intellect are therefore one nature. . . . And the thoughts of this kind are the form and shape of being and its active actuality. But they are thought of by us as one before the other because they are divided by our thinking. [V-9-8]

Intelligence tends to be associated with complex activity, the dividing intellect Plotinus speaks of. If a movie wants to show an advanced scientist at work, it often depicts him or her filling a blackboard with row after row of indecipherable mathematical equations. Then, with a flourish, this scientist scribbles out the solution and proclaims something like, "So, the comet will hit earth in fifty-six days!"

Yet wouldn't an undivided intellect be even more impressive? The scientist is asked the same difficult question and without any hesitation he or she responds: "fifty-six days." Why do we consider that an answer arrived at with difficulty reflects greater intelligence than one produced with ease?

Nature, which has no apparent brain, clearly is much smarter than all the high-IQ scientists who are trying to figure out her mysteries.

Mathematician John Casti notes how the proteins that make up every living organism fold up into specific three-dimensional structures that determine their function in the organism. It takes merely a second or two for a protein with several thousand amino acids to fold into its final configuration.

Yet Casti says, "When we try to simulate this folding process on a computer, it has been estimated that it would take 10^{127} *years* of supercomputer time to find the final folded form for even a very short protein consisting of just 100 amino acids."[1] He asks, "How does nature do it?" Plotinus's answer likely would be: "Through the intuitive intelligence of spirit, which encompasses all knowledge of everything in creation."

In spirit this knowledge isn't divided, as scientific understanding is, into (1) a thing, and (2) what is known about that thing. Recall the earlier mention of the lively debate between Porphyry and Amelius over the question of whether the forms existed outside of spirit, or *nous*. Porphyry at first believed they did, which meant that spirit would create from a sort of blueprint separate from itself.

But this way of thinking leads to an infinite regress. Where does that blueprint or collection of forms come from? From another blueprint? The cosmos then becomes, in effect, an endless series of plans with no architect in sight. Porphyry became convinced of the wisdom of Plotinus's teaching: that intellect possesses the forms much as we possess our knowledge of ourselves—intimately, immediately, intuitively.

> *Let it be granted then, that Intellect is the real beings, possessing them all not as if [they were in it] as in a place, but as possessing itself and being one with them.* [V-9-6]

Spirit, then, faces no obstacles as it creates the cosmos. For what is created is nothing other than itself. Even though our thoughts seem to be separate from ourselves (each of us says, "I think such-and-such"), we have no difficulty thinking those thoughts. The universe is spirit's thought, brought into being with vastly more ease, just as fire naturally forms heat and a mirror naturally reflects light. What is below comes from above, flowing ceaselessly and effortlessly from the infinitely productive power of the One, or Good.

> *The life of Intellect, then, is all power, and the seeing which came from the Good is the power to become all things, and the Intellect which came*

to be is manifest as the very totality of things. . . . It is, then, thought; that is, all movement filling all substance. [VI-7-17, VI-7-13]

Since we are part of the substance of the universe, spirit is active within us as well. All is ensouled, animate and inanimate alike, but Plotinus teaches that living beings have a special connection with spirit that non-living objects lack. Entities with individual souls such as plants, animals, and humans are directly linked to spirit in the same fashion as a ray of light is linked to the sun.

The souls are like rays, so that it [spirit] *is set firm in itself but the soul-rays sent out come now to one living thing and now to another.* [VI-4-3]

The One produces spirit and spirit produces soul. This means that it is possible to return to spirit, and thence to the One, by retracing the path we took on our earthly descent. The soul turns away from material preoccupations and says, "Whatever I once was I will be again: pure spirit." This, in fact, is the only way to truly be spiritual, or to know spirit. For spirit does not divide itself into parts; it is realized as a unity or not at all. We can possess half a loaf of bread or one-fourth of a gallon of milk but spirit always comes in whole portions.

Intellectual knowledge necessarily is fragmented. Little by little, bit by bit, fact by fact, reason attempts to fit together an understanding of reality. This is a noble but undeniably quixotic undertaking. For no matter how much is learned about the pieces that appear to comprise the totality of the cosmos, a primal enigma remains: Why does all this exist? The unfathomable mystery lying at the heart of a hundred billion galaxies is the same unfathomable mystery lying at the heart of a single atom: existence, plain and simple.

If we ever are to know the deepest mysteries of creation, it will not be by studying what has been created. Instead, Plotinus teaches, we should seek to know the creator, spirit, which as a one-many contains all the myriad forms of creation. Miraculously, when purified, our own souls are identical with the substance of the cosmos.

But how are we related to the Intellect? . . . We have it either as common to all or particular to ourselves, or both common and particular; common because it is without parts and one and everywhere the same, particular to ourselves because each has the whole of it in the primary part of his soul. . . . It is probable, then, that he who intends to know what Intellect really is must know soul, and the most divine part of soul. [I-1-8, V-3-9]

Here Plotinus indicates the central difference between spirit and soul. Spirit is not particularized. It is "without parts and one and everywhere the same." In the *Enneads* there is no individuality associated with spirit, as there is with the Soul of the All, even though both are universal. Yet somehow it is possible for a particular soul to possess the whole of spirit in its primary part. This, then, is how it is possible to know spirit: through "the most divine part of soul."

The grand Plotinian quest is to explore reality from the inside out, as it were. The mystic philosopher finds immense, world-shattering truth in a most unexpected place—the intimate confines of his or her innermost consciousness.

As strange as this may seem, it is no stranger than a central tenet of modern science: that billions upon billions of galaxies were once contained in an infinitesimal bit of seed-energy smaller than a subatomic particle. If physics tells us that a universe can exist in a grain of sand, with lots of room to spare, why should not the seemingly limited consciousness of an individual soul be similarly capable of possessing unlimited truth?

As for soul, the part of it directed to Intellect is, so to speak, within, and the part outside Intellect directed to the outside. . . . But we too are kings, when we are in accord with it; we can be in accord with it in two ways, either by having something like its writing written in us like laws, or by being as if filled with it and able to see it and be aware of it as present. [V-3-7, V-3-4]

Since spirit is a one-many, unlimited multiplicity enfolded within simple unity, Plotinus implies that we can know it in two ways: as one, or many. It seems to come down to a matter of emptiness. So long as we remain filled with our illusory ego-selves, absorbed in what we mistakenly consider ourselves to be, spirit can only "write its laws" in us on whatever blank pages of *psyche* exist. In this way we become more spiritual, but not spirit itself.

But if a person's soul is, as it were, a blank slate then spirit fills him completely. Spirit is present immediately and intuitively. He becomes aware that spirit is the substance of his life, just as spirit is the substance of the universe. Instead of knowing the laws of the cosmos, he comes to know the lawgiver.

Above Is Astonishment

WHAT A WONDER! What a surprise!

What we think is most real, this physical world, actually possesses precious little substance. We've got things completely backward. So it isn't surprising that when reality is realized as it is, not as how it is believed to be, there is going to be some wide-eyed astonishment, and not a little hilarity.

What a relief! What a joke!

What we are so terribly, horribly, sincerely concerned about isn't worth a single tear. "Oh my difficult life. Oh the wretched state of the world. Oh the sad suffering so many have to endure." For Plotinus, both delight and despair flow from ignorance of spiritual truth. Underneath the ugly thin crust of ephemeral matter flows a never-ending clear stream of being, real life. We smile and sob at shadows dancing on the cave wall, while the sun shines brightly just beyond our awareness.

What joy to have a vision of boundless life without any material covering.

> For here below most of our attention is directed to lifeless things, and when it is directed to living beings what is lifeless in them stands in the way, and the life within them is mixed. But there all are living beings, living as wholes and pure. [VI-6-18]

Earthly life, for Plotinus, is akin to a masquerade where the guests dress and act in a fashion that limits their natural beauty and wisdom, sort of an Ugly Idiot's Ball. In the dressing room of materiality, crude coverings—a physical body and brain—are placed over the soul's naked glory and intelligence. If we could see what lies beneath the costume each of us has put on, we would realize that inert coverings come and go while the living substance of soul and spirit abides unchanged.

But what does this vision consist of? Take away what is lifeless (matter) and what would remain to make us "laugh at the lower nature for its pretension to substantiality"? [VI-6-18] Could Plotinus be speaking of pure thought here? If so, what substance is there to thinking?

There are no easy answers to these questions. Plotinus's experience is his own. If we want to know what he has realized we must realize it for ourselves. Still, Plotinus is quite explicit about what spiritual reality is like. There in the spiritual world, as here on earth, one sees, hears, smells, tastes, and touches. Forms impress themselves upon matter both here and there: divided forms upon lifeless material matter here, unified forms upon living spiritual matter there.

> *And if form comes to matter, the composite being will be a body; so that there will be body in the intelligible world too.* [II-4-2]

So what is perceived in the spiritual realms is not ethereal thoughts, but substantial things. Our physical sense organs mirror the soul's immaterial organs of perception. What is sensed here is mirror images of what is sensed there. The spiritual world, though, is the original, and this physical universe is the copy. Thus it isn't surprising that the *Enneads* describe earthly sights as akin to an out-of-focus snapshot of Niagara Falls: somewhat like the real thing, but without the original's clarity, depth, or grandeur.

> *How, then, is there a power of sense-perception in the better soul? It would be a power of perceiving the sense-objects there, and would correspond to the sense-objects there.* [VI-7-6]

It is fair to say, then, that what surrounds us at this very moment is indeed heaven on earth. The reason we don't presently feel embraced by divinity is that much necessarily gets lost in the translation from the immaterial realm of spirit to the physical world of matter. Missing in the earthly copy is the unity that seamlessly connects all spiritual beings and forms, and the undiluted creative power of spirit.

Most of us have the feeling that life truly would be wonderful if we just could get rid of all those nasty "buts." "Our garden is really doing well this year *but* we've been having a problem with moles." "Johnny is getting good grades *but* his teacher says that he needs to develop better social skills." "I like my new job *but* it takes me twice as long to get to work as before." And so on, and so on.

The spiritual world, we're told, basically is this world without the buts. It is all the good stuff without any of the bad, a fine place to return to and enjoy on our way back home to the One.

And nothing there wears out or wearies. . . . Life holds no weariness for anyone when it is pure: and how should that which leads the best life grow weary? [V-8-4]

Many people believe that spirituality and sensuality are contraries. You must choose one or the other; you can't have both. Desires aroused by the senses, they say, glue us to materiality. Our eyes attach us to beautiful sights, our ears to sweet sounds, our mouth to pleasant tastes, our nostrils to fragrant smells, our skin to enjoyable touches. Knowing only bodily delights, not surprisingly our souls are reluctant to let loose of certain physical pleasure for the promise of spiritual bliss.

Plotinus, in large part, agrees with this way of thinking. But as we have noted before, his stern admonition, "Leave this world behind," must be coupled with his equally adamant assurance, "And gain a better one." Plotinus's form of asceticism is more akin to a sensual savings plan: we spend less on material sensation now, so we will have more spiritual sensation later.

There [in the spiritual world], *all things are filled, and, as it were, boiling over with life. It is as though they flowed like a stream, from one source—not from one breath or warmth. Rather, it is as though there were one quality, containing within itself and preserving all the other qualities: that of sweetness along with fragrance; the quality of wine along with the powers of every juice, with visions of colors, and with all that is known by the sense of touch. Let there also be all that the ear can hear; each melody and every rhythm.* [VI-7-12][1]

Amazingly, Plotinus tells us, all of this incomparable life and beauty is within each one of us. No, the truth is even grander than that: it *is* us, part and parcel of every person's essential being. Here we touch upon a great mystery, not just of classic Greek philosophy, but of the human condition throughout the ages. How is it possible that we feel pleasure and pain, or anything at all for that matter? Why does a beautiful person or thing produce feelings of beauty in us, and an ugly thing feelings of ugliness?

The answer, says Plotinus, is that whatever forms exist in the world out there—beautiful or ugly, loving or hateful, bright or dark, colorful or bland, light or heavy—also exist in the world in here, innermost consciousness. So if we are astonished by Plotinus's

descriptions of the marvels in the spiritual realm, we will be flab-
bergasted when we discover that all of this is not only for us to
behold, but to become.

> *If one were to compare [the world of Forms] to a living, variegated sphere,*
> *or to something made up only of faces, shining with living faces . . .*
> *then one would see it, but as it were from the outside, as one being sees*
> *another; in fact, however, one must oneself become Spirit, and oneself*
> *become vision.* [VI-7-15][2]

Still, the spiritual traveler must not remain content with even the
most intimate vision of higher truth and the beauties beyond. Above
every form of creation is the creator; transcending every object of
beauty is the source of beauty; on the further edge of all that exists
is existence itself. Plotinus urges us to keep treading the spiritual
path until there is no more path to be tread and we reach the One,
where all traveling and all questioning come to an end.

> *But we must not remain always in that manifold beauty but go on*
> *still darting upwards, leaving even this behind, not out of this sky here*
> *below, but out of that, in our wondering about who generated it and*
> *how.* [VI-7-16]

All Is Alive

MANY PEOPLE would consider this bold statement "all is alive" implausible. Admittedly, it sounds suspiciously animistic. Are we to believe along with the primitives that earth, water, and sky are as alive as plants and animals? That a boulder somehow shares kinship with a baby, as do a lake and a lizard, a star and a sunflower? Isn't there an unbridgeable difference between animate and inanimate objects that is real and enduring?

Before rejecting Plotinus's perspective as a relic of ancient mythology, let's consider some modern science. No one knows for sure how life appeared on earth. Some scientists believe that life arrived here from space, perhaps in the form of a tiny spore carried by an asteroid. But this begs the question of how that extra-terrestrial life started.

Whether life sprang up on earth or was brought here from beyond, science sees no need for a miraculous explanation of life's beginnings. Neither does Plotinus. Biologists have no problem believing that matter somehow became complex enough to develop the qualities associated with life, such as being highly organized, carbon-based, adaptive, capable of reproduction, and chemically different from the environment.

So if living things are merely a special sort of matter and matter/energy is everywhere in the universe, why is it so strange to hold that life is omnipresent, yet not always recognized?

> *The First Nature is present to all things. Present? But how? Like one single Life which is within all things. In a living being, Life does not penetrate as far as a certain point and then stop, as if it could not spread to the entire being; rather, it is present in every part of it.*
> *. . . If you can grasp the inexhaustible infinity of Life—its tireless, unwearied, unfailing nature, as if boiling over with life—it will do you no good to fix your gaze on one spot, or concentrate your attention on any given object: you will not find it there. Rather, the exact opposite would happen to you.* [VI-5-12][1]

For Plotinus life in the cosmos is much like life in our own bodies. If I try to pinpoint the location of the life that resides within me, I will fail. Life obviously isn't present in some parts of my body and mind while absent from other parts. Life is experienced as a whole.

I can't focus on a particular aspect of me and say, "Ah, *here* is my life." Indeed, the more I try to analyze and dissect myself the more I distance myself from the wholeness that is my self.

Still, while there is no spot in my body where life is not, life manifests in various ways. For example, my toenails and brain are both alive but the life of my innermost consciousness certainly is quite different from the life on the end of my big toe.

It's a humbling thought, but our normal human experience may be as conscious of the larger life that surrounds us as is my big toe. Plotinus teaches that the cosmos is a single living entity, yet awareness of its unified aliveness is greater in the spiritual domains apart from matter. Here on earth, beauty seems to be impressed upon us from the outside. There, beauty is part and parcel of every being, as is life, love, wisdom, and every other spiritual form.

> *[Beauty] shines brightly upon all things, and fills whomever arrives there, so that they too become beautiful. Likewise, people often climb to lofty places, where the earth is colored golden-brown, and are filled with that color, and made similar to that upon which they are walking. In that other world, however, the color which blooms on the surface is beauty itself; or rather, each thing is color and beauty, right from its very depths.* [V-8-10][2]

The realm of spirit is the first life and the best life, where One becomes many, yet all are intimately connected.

> *Indeed, each has everything within it, and again sees all things in any other, so that all things are everywhere, everything is everything, each individual is all things, and the splendor is without end.* [V-8-4][3]

Pierre Hadot says, "In this universe of pure Forms, where each Form is nothing other than itself, there is complete interpenetration."[4] So there is no hint in the *Enneads* that life takes on any sort of personality or personhood in the domain of spirit. Spirit certainly is conscious. It is the intelligence behind all other intelligences. Yet it is too unified, too whole, for the individuality normally associated with a living being. We could say that the One is beyond life and that spirit is undivided life.

The realm of soul, which follows spirit in Plotinus's metaphysical cosmology, is where life begins to differentiate. Yet the Soul of the All still is far beyond everyday comprehension. Wondrously, the entire universe and much that lies beyond is none other than the "body" of a soul, which is similar in kind to the personal human soul but possesses tremendously greater power and wisdom.

> *First of all we must posit that this All is a "single living being which encompasses all the living beings that are within it"; it has one soul which extends to all its parts.* [IV-4-32]

Thus all that we call inanimate—earthly matter, as well as other planets, stars, galaxies, and intergalactic space—actually is the unimaginably vast body of the Soul of the All. As such, all is alive, just as our own bodies are enlivened by our personal souls.

Each of us governs, albeit with considerable difficulty, a body ("Stop gaining weight!" I tell my subject, but he generally fails to obey me). With infinitely greater ease, the Soul of the All guides the affairs of its body, which includes the entire physical universe. Not from without (as a doctor diagnoses and treats people), says Plotinus, but from within.

> *But the administration of the universe is much simpler, in that all things with which it deals are included as parts of a single living being.* [IV-4-11]

We have such difficulty coming to grips with the central mysteries of life—How did it begin? What are its boundaries? Does it ever end?—because life isn't something that can be grasped. To grasp an object one needs to be separate from it. If life isn't just part of creation, but the whole of creation, then these mysteries are ungraspable. They can be understood, perhaps, by becoming the whole, but not otherwise. The pursuit of highest truth necessarily leads beyond the confines of material science. Shimon Malin, a physicist, says:

> The scientific claim that so-called inanimate entities are really lifeless is a statement about the scientific method and not about the entities. In reality there is nothing in the current scientific knowledge that disproves the proposition that putatively inanimate entities are alive.
>
> This proposition can only be verified or disproved through experiences and modes of knowledge that lie outside of the methodology of present-day science. . . . If the universe is indeed alive, or "ensouled" as the ancient Greeks put it, this aliveness will not show up in a scientific context.[5]

The search goes on for extraterrestrial life. Scientists listen for faint signals from distant star systems and probe rocks from Mars for microscopic signs that humans are not alone. Yet the *Enneads* imply that we are unable to recognize life beyond our present ken not because it is too distant or too small, but because it is too close and too large. Everything that we can sense and all that is insensible is alive, teaches Plotinus. Life is everywhere we look, but we are looking for it in the wrong fashion.

> *This one universe is all bound together in shared experience and is like one living creature, and that which is far is really near.* [IV-4-32]

Everything in the universe is connected to everything else. No part stands alone. Whatever we do or think affects other parts of the whole, because the drops of our souls are immersed in the living ocean of the Soul of the All. J.M. Rist says, "The whole cosmos must be regarded as a living being with a body and soul. There is therefore a kind of nervous system, as we might put it, between the different parts."[6]

If too much alcohol passes through my stomach, it will damage my liver; if I'm deathly afraid, my whole body trembles; an infection in my finger summons white blood cells from distant limbs; an intention of my will causes my arms and legs to be put in motion. I readily accept that my body and mind form a single living being, causes here leading to effects there. And if I come to believe that the cosmos is similarly constituted then I will realize that whatever I do, this necessarily will affect other parts of the living All.

> *One principle must make the universe a single complex living creature, one from all; and just as in individual organisms each member undertakes its own particular task, so the members of the All, each individual one of them, have their individual work to do.* [II-3-7]

If one wants a powerful philosophical rationale for environmentalism, here it is. Preserving the earth and all upon it is nothing other than keeping the larger body of the All, within which we live out our smaller bodily lives, in good health. Thus when we despoil the oceans, we despoil ourselves. When we poison the earth, we poison ourselves. When we pollute the air, we pollute ourselves. Some of the connections between humans and the environment are obvious and some are subtle but all are inescapable, the order of nature.

Here it is appropriate to point out that while diet is never explicitly mentioned in the *Enneads,* Porphyry tells us that Plotinus didn't approve of eating animal flesh. How could he? Plotinus's life was devoted to experiencing the reality of limitless love, not the illusion of restricted self-aggrandizement.

> *This All is visibly not only one living creature, but many; so that in so far as it is one, each individual part is preserved by the whole, but in so far as it is many, when the many encounter each other they often injure each other because they are different.* [IV-4-32]

The ecological sciences teach that the continued existence of every species and each individual within a species is dependent on many other life forms. Thus in one sense it is natural to kill and eat other living beings since life necessarily feeds on life. Yet Plotinus draws our attention to the unnaturalness of injuring others simply because they are different from us. This behavior is fitting for an irrational animal but out of sync for humans aspiring to spiritual wisdom.

Plotinus refused to countenance the oft-heard rationale for meat-eating: "Animals are not like us." He considered this to be a shoddy bit of philosophizing. If humans are entitled to pursue happiness, one of the inalienable rights enshrined in the United States Declaration of Independence, then why should other living things be denied their own right to seek well-being, insofar as it is possible? Humans differ from animals in what we are capable of doing and experiencing, but all life is able to do and experience something. So one should be cautious about denying the good life to any form of life.

> *Why will it not seem absurd of him to deny that other living things live well just because he does not think them important? . . . If pleasure is the end and the good life is determined by pleasure, it is absurd of anyone to deny the good life to other living things.* [I-4-1]

Creation Is Contemplation

By NOW I HOPE the reader is beginning to feel familiar with the basic structure of Plotinus's cosmos, an ever-flowing emanation of energy and consciousness with no sharp boundaries, just general demarcations. Accordingly, the descriptions in the *Enneads* of these realms tend to blur into each other so that it often is difficult to tell what level of creation Plotinus is talking about. Still, the basic structure is clear.

Above all is the One, the wellspring of creation. From the One emanates spirit, the unified realm of forms. From spirit emanates soul, a more differentiated domain that includes both individual souls and the all-encompassing Soul of the All. The lowest aspect of soul is nature, which brings into being the physical universe, the last and lowest emanation of the One. The physical universe arguably can be considered a fourth region of creation because of the dominance of matter here.

This is, so to speak, the geography that must be traversed to return to the One. Remember, of course, that the One, spirit, soul, and nature are not separated by time or space, but by degrees of consciousness. The soul's journey is to take place right here, right now. But how? What is the means of transport from one realm to another? And what do we do when we leave the confines of earthly experience? What sort of "culture" can we expect to find in the spiritual regions?

Plotinus makes it simple for us. There is one answer to all of these questions: *contemplation.* Contemplation is how the spiritual seeker rises up and it is how creation came down. Contemplation is the primary activity, perhaps the sole activity, in higher regions of consciousness. Contemplation is what spiritual beings do. If we learn how to contemplate, we'll experience no culture shock during our journey to the One. We'll fit right in wherever we find ourselves.

All things are a by-product of contemplation. . . . Every soul is, and becomes, that which she contemplates. [III-8-8, IV-3-8[1]]

But it is not only souls that contemplate, says Plotinus. Everything contemplates. Even earth, bare topsoil, is a contemplator, along with the plants that spring up from the ground. Plotinus recognizes the seeming absurdity of this point of view, and in one of his rare attempts at levity in the *Enneads* he starts off his arguments about the primacy of contemplation with a self-deprecating, soft-sell approach.

> *Suppose we said, playing at first before we set out to be serious, that all things aspire to contemplation, and direct their gaze to this end—not only rational but irrational living things, and the power of growth in plants, and the earth which brings them forth. . . . Could anyone endure the oddity of this line of thought?* [III-8-1]

It certainly is an odd notion that plants and earth engage in what contemplation normally is considered to be. "Should we lease or buy our next car?" your spouse asks. "I don't know," you reply, "I've got to contemplate the matter."

Usually this means that you'll compare the short- and long-term costs of leasing versus buying, assess how much money you have available for car payments, and arrive at a well-reasoned conclusion. Contemplation, in this sense, is a means to an end. It may not be entirely rational (maybe the facts point toward leasing but your intuition says buy), yet, like reason, this sort of contemplation is an attempt to know something you are presently uncertain of.

This isn't what Plotinus means by contemplation (in Greek, *theoria*). And herein lies the key to understanding that his view of contemplation is not odd at all, but supremely natural. John Deck says:

> For Plotinus as for Aristotle, any contemplation is knowledge. Plotinus does not view it as consideration, or mulling over. For this reason it is a mistake to take "contemplation," as he uses it, to be "thought," if by "thought" we mean a mental process or act which is not in firm possession of its object. . . . In discursive reasoning [*dianoia* or *logismos*], the object is not yet possessed, it is being sought. Thus discursive reasoning is not yet knowledge.[2]

So how is it possible to say that nature does not contemplate? Isn't it a truism that all of nature obeys the laws of nature? Don't all atomic particles know exactly what to do when gravity, electromagnetism, or a nuclear force beckons them into action? Doesn't the silent contemplation of nature know much more about physical reality than all the noisy reasoning of scientists? The cosmos effortlessly creates supernovas, galaxies beyond counting, and black holes. Can we?

> *If she* [Nature] *were asked why she creates, she would reply—if that is, she were willing to listen to the questioner and to speak—*
> "*You should not have questioned me, but understood in silence, just as I myself keep silent, for I am not accustomed to talk. What is there to understand? That what comes into being is the object of my silent contemplation, and that the product of my contemplation comes into being in a natural way. I myself was born of such contemplation; this is why I have a natural love of contemplation.*" [III-8-4][3]

As Pierre Hadot puts it, nature is like a painter who is able to form an image on canvas merely by looking at a model.[4] What does nature look at? What does she contemplate? Spirit, the world of forms. Nature, like almost all contemplators, thus looks Janus-like in two directions: upward toward its prior in the grand scheme of emanation from the One, and downward toward what comes after it, the physical universe (the exceptions are at the extremes: the One, for which there is nothing prior to contemplate, and matter, for which there is nothing after that can come into being).

Creation thus is a continuous flow of contemplation, a never-ending stream of conscious energy that is simultaneously in ceaseless flux and eternal rest. At rest, because spirit, or intellect, eternally possesses all forms as a manyness that still remains undivided. In flux, because here in the physical realm the forms unfold within time and space and we say, with excessive confidence, "This caused that" or "I created such-and-such."

> *Intellect gives to the Soul of the All, and Soul (the one which comes next after Intellect) gives from itself to the soul next after it, enlightening it and impressing form on it, and this last soul immediately makes, as if under orders.* [II-3-17]

Plotinus is saying that normally we individual human souls are almost at the bottom of the cosmos's organizational chart. We've got some powerful bosses above us—the Soul of the All, which takes orders from spirit, which is governed by the One—and there isn't much left after us to order around. Just matter/energy and other souls, whom we do our best to manipulate to our ends with decidedly mixed success. And even these efforts are "under orders," as we shall find in a later section ("Providence Is Pervasive").

As was noted previously, the *Enneads* advise us to shun the role most people long to play, albeit unconsciously, but are terribly unqualified for: Master of the Universe. That position, teaches Plotinus, is already filled and it never will open up for our advancement. All the same, we do our best to be mini-masters of our mini-universes, an exhausting, frustrating, unfulfilling, and ultimately impossible task. We try to create order in our lives but messiness always seeps in around the edges of the little personal islands of peace and harmony we keep trying to construct in the midst of a larger cruel world.

The problem, in Plotinus's view, is twofold. First, we're facing in the wrong direction if we want to move toward lasting happiness and well-being. We should be looking up toward spirit, rather than down toward matter. If our attention is directed toward our source, our creator, we will become that. If our attention is directed toward what comes after us, what we attempt to create, then we will become that. The choice is ours.

Second, even when we try to create something good and beautiful in the world, in our relationships, or within ourselves, we generally make a mess of things. Effective creation requires concentrated contemplation. The most successful people in any area—work, family, romance, athletics, art, science, spirituality—devote themselves wholeheartedly and single-pointedly to their goals. Most of us, unfortunately, lack the willpower to focus so attentively on what we desire to achieve or create.

> *And failures, too, both in what comes into being and what is done, are failures of contemplators who are distracted from their object of contemplation.* [III-8-7]

Along these lines, it's understandable that we usually approach spirituality as we do most everything else in life: as something to be possessed. If, with enough effort, I can get a good job, a loving spouse, a fit body, and a nice home, then why shouldn't I be able to reach out and also bring spirit into my soul?

Because spirit is, so to speak, much bigger than we are. A mouse doesn't hold up an elephant; any holding is going to be accomplished by the larger being. Not only is spirit exceedingly vaster in power and consciousness than we are, it being the creator and we the created, but spirit also is more unified and formless than our divided physicality. So with spirit we not only lack the ability to grasp what might otherwise be an object of contemplation, there also is nothing familiar to lay hold of.

This makes spiritual contemplation exceedingly difficult, at least as long as the contemplator tries to make spirit something to be known. Recall that for Plotinus true contemplation is knowledge, not an attempt at knowing. It seems that we must go directly from ignorance to knowledge, from darkness to light, without passing through the intermediate stages so familiar in everyday life of "I'm starting to understand. Things are getting clearer. Ah, now I know!"

On the journey to the One, it isn't seeing that we want, but sight. Not what has been created, but the creator. Not signs of spirit, but spirit itself. Not thoughts of unity, but actual oneness.

As we return to the One from our sojourn in the depths of manyness, we shouldn't be surprised to find in the course of our ascent that what is experienced becomes more and more akin to the experiencer. As duality is replaced by unity, differences of all sorts become increasingly blurred. And this includes the difference between the seer and what is seen, the hearer and what is heard, the knower and what is known.

> *But, as contemplation ascends from nature to soul, and soul to intellect, and the contemplations become always more intimate and united to the contemplators . . . it is clear that in intellect both are one.* [III-8-8]

In a sense, then, we can indeed become masters of the universe. If we are able to contemplate spirit deeply enough, we will essentially become spirit. Whatever spirit knows, which is everything, we will know. Whatever spirit can do, which is anything, we will be able to do. What a wonder, to be released from the confines of the pitifully limited knowing and doing of everyday life, to be able to enter into the mysteries of the universe not as a detached observer but as an intimate part of Mystery itself.

There is, however, a catch to all this. We can't remain ourselves, at least as we presently know ourselves to be, and also become the creator of the cosmos. This, it must be admitted, would be a ridiculous contradiction. After all, if I'm really on the way to becoming a divine being why can't I find the leftovers in the refrigerator? Hmmm. Maybe it's because I'm so busily occupied with contemplating and creating material things outside of myself instead of the spiritual reality inside myself.

If the form which makes things here below was our real being, our crafts-manship would have the mastery without toil and trouble. [V-8-7]

The key to effortless and potent creating is to unite form and be-ing. The reason I stand in front of the open refrigerator for so long, staring blankly into its recesses, is that the form of the leftovers I'm seeking is separate from my own being. The seeker and the sought are different things, which is why finding the leftovers takes such a long time. By contrast, I have no difficulty creating a thought or an image in my mind because my creation is part of my being, not separate from myself.

In the same fashion, Plotinus teaches that spirit contemplates the forms within itself, and instantly physical reality manifests, just as I am able to contemplate an object, "Volvo," and instantly a men-tal image of a car arises in my mind. The reason a real car doesn't manifest in my garage, saving me from having to go out and buy one, is that my contemplation is of an object outside of myself. Spirit produces real reality because the forms spirit contemplates are part and parcel of itself.

Here Plotinus describes the immediacy and ease of physical cre-ation, making some jibes at those who believe the creator thinks and acts like we do. It's a lengthy quotation, but worth studying for the insights it provides into Plotinus's worldview.

> Since we concede that this world has its being and its qualities from elsewhere, are we to imagine that its creator thought it up by himself, as well as the fact that it ought to be placed in the center; then he thought up water, and that it ought to be placed on top of the earth; and then everything else in order as far as the heavens?
>
> He thought up the animals next, I suppose, and assigned specific forms to each one of them, just as they have today, and for each of them he thought up their guts on the inside and their limbs on the outside? And then, once each thing had been properly arranged within his mind, only then did he set about his task?
>
> Nonsense; in the first place, such a conception is impossible—whence would it have come to him, when he had not yet seen anything? Secondly, even if he had received it from someone else, he could not have put it into action, like craftsmen do now by using their hands or their instruments: hands and feet did not come into being until later!
>
> The only alternative is that everything existed elsewhere [in the spiritual world], but since there was nothing in between them, there suddenly

appeared, as it were, by virtue of their proximity to each other within
Being, an image and icon of the spiritual world. [V-8-7][5]

Creation thus is continuous contemplation in much the same way
that a mirror continuously contemplates the image of that which
stands before it. Instantly and naturally, without effort, a reflection
appears. This physical universe, says Plotinus, is the reflection of
forms within spirit. Matter is the mirror that permits such materi-
alization of spiritual realities to occur.

John Deck explains, "If a mirror is within range of a man, a
reflection of the man simply appears in the mirror. There is nothing apparent leaving the man to go to the mirror. He seems to lose
nothing, yet he *causes* his reflection. No man—no reflection of a
man. The reflection is 'real' because of the man. . . . For Plotinus,
the case a step higher is parallel to this. . . . If there were no true
beings there would be no sensible things."[6]

The mystic philosopher seeks reality rather than reflection. So he
or she aims to contemplate the original forms of creation, not their
copies evident in the physical world. The Platonic and Plotinian view
is that there is a Flower in the spiritual world which isn't a particular
flower such as the rose or buttercup we see in nature. Rather, it is
the immaterial essence of flowerness itself, the Flower from which
all other flowers flow, we might say. And the same goes for every
other form in creation.

Thus someone who longs for beauty, truth, love, power, or anything else he might desire, will not find it in this world as it truly
is. What he will attain, at best, is a relatively crude material image
of that spiritual form. The form itself cannot and does not reside
anywhere but in the spiritual realm. Only the spiritualized soul is
able to contact the forms directly, which is the sole way a longing
for reality, true and simple, can be satisfied.

This leads Plotinus to present us with an astounding conclusion.
In a single sweeping generalization, he turns upside-down one of the
most widely accepted tenets of modern culture: that action is the key
to success in life. Often we are told by advice columnists, personal
development speakers, business school professors, psychotherapists,
and a host of others, that unless we follow our dreams we will never
be able to live life to the fullest. An athletic shoe company summed
up this pop philosophy in a pithy slogan known around the world:
"Just Do It."

Plotinus might well answer: "Do it if you can't contemplate it." Consider: Isn't it true that we do whatever we do because we believe it will bring us something we lack? Why else would we do anything at all?

Stress leads us to go on vacation and get relaxed. Romantic or sexual deprivation causes us to look for a man or woman who will satisfy our needs. Ignorance of something causes us to go to the library or connect to the Internet, seeking information that will fill the void in our knowledge. A yearning to display musical talent impels us to pick up an instrument and play some tunes.

But what if we weren't desirous of anything? What if we possessed within us much or all that we currently seek without? Would we then need to keep acting as we do now?

> *When people are too weak for contemplation, they switch to action, which is a mere shadow of contemplation and of reason. Since, owing to the weakness of their souls, their faculty of contemplation is insufficient, they cannot grasp the object of their contemplation and be fulfilled by it.*
>
> *Yet they still want to see it; and so they switch to action, in order to see with their eyes what they could not see with their spirit. In any case, when they create something, it is because they themselves want to see it and to contemplate it; and when they propose to act, insofar as they are able, it is because they want their act to be perceived by others.* [III-8-4][7]

It certainly is true that much of what I do is intended to fill a spiritual void rather than a material void. I like cars with lots of horsepower—yet if I felt genuinely powerful myself, would I have the same desire? I enjoy going to movies and being entertained—yet if I was really comfortable with myself, would I need to sit in a dark theater and become absorbed in an imaginary depiction of someone else's life?

Plotinus is suggesting that perhaps we already have the ability to possess directly through contemplation what we so assiduously attempt to create in a circuitous way through action.

> *Action, then, is for the sake of contemplation and vision, so that for men of action, too, contemplation is the goal, and what they cannot get by going straight to it, so to speak, they seek to obtain by going round about. . . . For who, if he is able to contemplate what is truly real will deliberately go after its image?* [III-8-6, III-8-4]

Truth Is Transparent

MOST OF US have mixed feelings about truth. On the one hand, we value truth highly. We want true friends, reliable companions who stick with us through thick and thin. We respect truth-tellers whose words are commensurate with the way things are. We strive to be true to ourselves by linking inner being with outer action. We puncture pretenses with a pithy, "Get real."

At the same time, the pursuit of truth can be exhausting. A never-ending existential battle continually rages between what is and what seems to be. Just as true-or-false questions bedevil test-taking students, every person alive is confronted with a constant and ever-changing stream of problems that demand correct answers. What sort of food is best for my health? Which investment strategy is going to make me financially secure? Where did I put my car keys? When is the proper time to plant my vegetable garden?

If there were no right answer to such questions we wouldn't worry about being wrong. So the very existence of truth (or at least its assumed existence) creates a continual tension between what I know and what can be known. It's difficult to ever completely relax. Doubts never disappear completely. Can I truly trust my spouse, my accountant, my spiritual advisor, my lawmakers? Can I really be secure in my philosophy of life, my religion, my code of ethics, my accumulated store of knowledge?

In this world, truth always seems to be concealed under some sort of cover, like a giggling child hiding under a bedspread: we're sure it's there, but we can't see it directly. We do our best to rip off the coverings of ignorance and misunderstanding, yet somehow the fullness of reality always manages to wriggle away and stay just out of reach. Actually, we can't say about anything, "Concerning this, I know all there is to be known."

What about the higher world, the spiritual realm? There, says Plotinus, we can be absolutely certain of what is true because falsehood is an impossibility. In the unitary domain of spirit, there is no other to obscure the truth.

All things are transparent, and there is nothing dark or resistant, but each Form is clear for all others right down to its innermost parts, for light is clear to light. [V-8-4][1]

Philosophers have argued interminably about whether truth is objective or subjective and, if objective truth exists, whether it ever can be known completely. Plotinus's position is wonderfully simple: "Yes, there is objective truth. And yes, it can be known." Yet this answer applies only to spiritual reality. Here in the physical universe, our capacity to experience things as they are is limited by inescapable gaps between the senses and what is sensed, knowing and what is known, reality and what is realized.

But when contemplation is complete and our souls are attuned to the oneness of the spiritual world, we are able to experience reality as it is—with no covers of conceptions, thoughts, emotions, or physical sensations.

> *So that the real truth is also there, which does not agree with something else, but with itself, and says nothing other than itself, but it is what it says and it says what it is. . . . For you could not find anything truer than the truth.* [V-5-2]

Here on earth, our attempts at understanding something tend to be circular, fingers pointing at other fingers pointing. But where and what is the thing itself? For example, Arthur Eddington, a pioneering twentieth-century physicist, noted: "Electric force is defined as something which causes motion of an electric charge; an electric charge is something which exerts electric force. So that an electric charge is something that exerts something that produces motion of something that exerts something that produces . . . *ad infinitum.*"[2]

Whether we study the world inside or outside of ourselves, we end up with precise descriptions of how things are constructed, interrelate, and function, but precious little understanding of what anything is all by itself. Consider yourself. String together as many truthful statements as you like: "I'm a man (or woman); I'm old (or young); I'm tall (or short); I'm a believer in God (or a non-believer)." No matter how many words, pictures, or mathematical equations you use to describe yourself, can these ever manage to encompass you as you truly are?

Through a variety of powerful arguments, the Greek philosophers known as Skeptics asserted that it is impossible to possess true knowledge. Since what we seek to know is always separate from ourselves, in our quest for truth we either have to trust our sense perceptions, which are subjective and unreliable, or our thoughts, which are necessarily founded on premises that are themselves based on other thoughts or sense perceptions.

Like Eddington, the Skeptic finds a world where hunters of truth are doomed, like hyperactive falcons, to forever circle around their prey and never grasp it firmly in the talons of their consciousness.

Plotinus, however, teaches that there is a way for the mystic philosopher to swoop right in and realize truth fully and completely. He agrees with the Skeptics that perceptions and thoughts are inadequate means of bagging reality. Bits and pieces of truth, some large and some small, always end up escaping. But Dominic O'Meara says, "The possibility of true knowledge can be realized if the object known is the same as the subject that knows."[3]

> *It is a kind of understanding and perception of our Self, in which we must be very careful lest, wishing to perceive more, we do not stray away from our Self.* [V-8-11][4]

A spiritual seeker thus is advised to cultivate an inner attitude of not-knowing that is at odds with our habitual way of gaining knowledge of the physical world. Since truth is transparent in the realm of spirit, to have a vision of it takes no special effort of thought or perception. All one has to do is be fully there, as soul conformed to spirit, and wisdom will flow into his or her consciousness as sunlight streams through a clean windowpane. Our goal is to be nothing other than what we truly are; only then will we know everything that truly is.

In the higher spiritual realms, all is effortless. This includes gaining knowledge of truth, real reality. One simply sees. And what is seen is true.

> *Even in this world, we know a great deal about people even when they are silent, through their eyes. There [i.e. in the intelligible world], however, the whole body is pure, and each person is like an eye; there is nothing hidden or fabricated, but before one person speaks to another, the latter has already understood just by looking at him.* [IV-3-18][5]

Not only does communication of spiritual verities take place wordlessly and instantly, it is so natural as to be unnoticed. Here, we rejoice ("Eureka!") when we learn something significant because truth is so elusive and falsehood so evident. On the physical plane, it takes a lot of effort to overcome the barriers to knowledge. The crudity of matter serves as a heavy lid on the strongbox of reality; rational thought, expressive emotion, and sensible perception are not strong enough to toss aside that cover.

What Plotinus advises is to use the right tool for the job. So long as we reside in materiality, truth is never going to be found lying around in the open, begging to be picked up by us. It is going to dart and hide, play peek-a-boo, taunt us with cries of "Thought you had me? Now you don't!" We can choose to continue playing these endless earthly games of maybe-it-is-maybe-it-isn't or we can form consciousness into a means of knowing reality in its fullness.

This is accomplished not by poking and prodding the outer skin of reality, cajoling truth to reveal its secrets from without, but rather by ourselves becoming the very essence of reality, spirit. Since spirit contains the forms of everything in existence, we come to realize truth from the inside, not the outside. Truth becomes not just a familiar companion—a friend who never lets us down—it becomes even more: our very being.

Then, who is there to know? What is there to be known?

> *For truth ought not to be the truth of something else, but to be what it says. . . . The quiet companionship of health gives us a better understanding of it; for it comes and sits by us as something which belongs to us, and is united to us. Illness is alien and not our own, and therefore particularly obvious because it appears so very different from us.* [V-3-5, V-8-11]

When we know something intimately, there is no space between ourselves and our knowing that thoughts or perceptions can creep into. Thus, says Plotinus, we understand the most when we aren't consciously aware of our understanding. Our health usually is so much a part of us that we don't give it a second thought and usually not even a first thought. It is only when someone asks "How are you?" that we engage in some self-examination and say, "Fine."

The most transparent truth is the least recognizable because there is no contrast to make it stand out. It is sickness that makes us notice health, just as pollution draws our attention to normally clear air. So the highest spiritual wisdom isn't a matter of conscious perception ("Now I know the One!") but of a divine union that is so complete there is no discernible difference between the knower, the knowing, and the known.

Form Is Foundation

IF WE TRIED to reduce life's manifold mysteries to two central enigmas, they could well be these: Why does existence exist at all? And how is it that particular things exist within existence?

Both questions lead to the edge of a conceptual abyss. In these depths lie hidden from man's cogitation all that is real but imponderable. When we attempt to imagine the source of everything that is, we may succeed for a moment. Possible answers come: "God," "original potential energy," "the One." But then we must ask, "From what did that source spring?"

It seems, then, that existence must be accepted as an eternally present given. For if at some point nothing existed, not even existence itself, it seems impossible that our present reality could have come from that absolute nothingness. There must be some irreducible, immutable, rock-solid foundation to the cosmos. This is raw existence, unexplained and unexplainable.

In everyday life, however, we are not conscious of existence pure and simple. Instead, the foundation of each person's being is the wondrous variety of forms that have somehow manifested within existence. Everywhere we see distinct objects. Some are natural, others man-made; some are living, others inanimate. Regardless of their nature, we understandably cling to these entities as if our lives depended on them (for so they do).

"No man," the saying goes, "is an island." Every individual is a form that needs the support of other forms to survive. Our physical survival depends on our ability to find food, water, and shelter; our emotional survival depends on the love and nurturance of other living beings; our psychological survival (a capacity to derive meaning from life) depends upon a web of beliefs and concepts, mental forms, about how the world works and what, if anything, lies beyond appearances.

Our trust is fully in forms, for we know no other support. This includes our spiritual or philosophical conceptions, for conceptions almost always enter our minds in the form of written or spoken words. Even if an image is the foundation of faith (a divine vision, for example), it clearly is a form, not nothing at all. But Plotinus warns that the forms appearing in matter are not to be counted on.

Now, first of all, matter does not hold or grasp form as its life or its ac-
tivity, but form comes upon it from elsewhere and is not one of matter's
possessions. [VI-3-2]

Isn't it true that the amount of pleasure derived from something
material—a possession, a person, a pet, a place—usually turns out
to be less than expected rather than more? And when that thing
does provide us with lasting satisfaction, is it the outward materiality that is so enjoyable or some inner form that is utterly real yet
physically insensible?

From what source did the beauty of that Helen shine forth, over whom
men fought so much, or of those women who rival Aphrodite in beauty? . . .
Isn't it always a Form which moves us? . . . Beauty influences us once
it comes to be inside us, but it comes in through the eyes as Form alone.
[V-8-2][1]

Form, in other words, is what we truly love in someone or something, not the physical matter in which the form is reflected. Matter
is just a means of imperfectly communicating a spiritual form to
the physical senses.

Recall Plato's parable of the cave. The unseen objects being carried along the wall that the prisoners have their backs to are forms.
A fire casts the shadows of these objects onto the cave wall that the
prisoners can see. The firelight is the radiant power of spirit and the
Soul of the All; the shadows are everything in this physical universe;
we are the prisoners.

When we try to fully possess something that appears beautiful,
good, or true, we can't. This is impossible because the form we're
attempting to grasp isn't here on earth. It's there in the spiritual
world. This is why nothing material satisfies for long. When the
foundation of our satisfaction is a shadow, it isn't surprising that
well-being continually slips away just when we think we've made
it our own.

So Plotinus teaches that our aim should be to experience the
reality of form unmixed with matter. If you're unclear about what
this reality consists of, don't worry. It is difficult, if not impossible,
to rationally understand the nature of the Platonic forms. For we
are used to describing things, whether material or immaterial, in
terms of something else.

Take the statements, "The dog is brown" and "Love is good." For Plotinus and Plato, "Dog," "Brown," "Love," and "Good" are each forms. The form "Dog" isn't any more brown than it is white; it is simply itself, "Dog." The same applies to the form "Love," which isn't good or beauty or truth, or anything else. It is just "Love," neither more nor less.

J.M. Rist says, "When Plato talks about a Form of Justice, he does not mean a concept of Justice, nor does he regard Justice as a universal which can only exist in the mind of a thinker, nor does he mean the essence of Justice; he means Justice and nothing else, Justice regarded as an actually existent thing. . . . The Forms are the only permanent existents because they are not liable to change and destruction."[2] We can't imagine what the forms could be like, because all that we know is changeable and particularized.

What we observe in this world is the result of spiritual forms impressing themselves upon matter, much as a seal makes an impression upon wax. Just as one seal can make many separate impressions, so can a universal form appear in many particular instances.

The form of Dog can manifest as a white toy poodle or a brown mastiff. These animals look very different but share the form of dogness that is as indefinable as it is readily apparent. It is *this*, Plotinus tells us, that dog lovers truly love. If they find dogs so adorable in their earthly guises with their dogness all mixed up with other forms (such as color and shape), then what a delight it would be for a canine connoisseur to encounter the pure form of Dog, the universal Dog that underlies every particular dog.

> All that is here below comes from there, and exists in greater beauty there. For here it is adulterated, but there it is pure. [V-8-7]

The adulteration of truth, goodness, and beauty in this physical universe is partly the result of the number of separate forms needed to produce all but the simplest objects. Reality here is layered, form upon form, so that everything is a mixture rather than being one thing only. This means that it is impossible to be a pure materialist, because visible matter too is a form covered by other forms.

> All this universe is held fast by forms from beginning to end: matter first of all by the forms of the elements, and then other forms upon these, and then again others. [V-8-7]

Matter, we might say, is the most formless of forms. Interestingly, the top and bottom of the cosmos, the One and matter, are both formless. The One's formlessness is founded in an excess of existence; as All, it cannot be any particular thing. Matter, on the other hand, is the ultimate cipher; since it is as much a nothing as anything existent can be, it can take on the impression of any form. And these impressions, as Plotinus points out, can be layered in amazingly complex and variegated patterns.

The hundreds of known atomic and subatomic particles can be reduced to a handful of fundamental building blocks: three quarks and three antiquarks, leptons (such as the electron and neutrino), and photons. From various combinations of quarks (which form neutrons and protons) and electrons arise the ninety-two natural elements; from this small number of elements come the myriad chemical compounds; and from such compounds all else is made.

Forms upon forms upon forms upon forms, forms without end. The innumerable combinations of all these forms produce the wondrous abundance of life and non-life that surrounds us. Whether we speak in terms of evolution or divine design, clearly the tree of the universe never ceases growing new limbs and buds, flowering in many marvelous ways. All of this complex, creative fervor flows from a single source: spirit.

Plotinus teaches that spirit is an unselfish giver. Spirit, or *nous,* continuously gives to matter all that matter is capable of receiving: the *logos,* or forming principle, that gives matter form and definition. Many non-material forms, *logoi,* exist within the *logos.*

If it were not for this intelligent forming principle, physical creation would be simply primordial unformed matter, a sort of misty chaos. Just as Plotinus has told us that spirit emanates from the One because "all things when they come to perfection produce," so is there a certain necessity to spirit's production of the lower realms of creation from the higher spiritual realities, or intelligibles.

> *Those intelligibles existed and these things here necessarily followed upon them; for it was not possible to stop at the intelligibles there. For who could bring to a stop a power able both to abide and to go forward?* [VI-7-8]

As has already been observed, the forms appear in matter as a person's reflection appears when he stands in front of a mirror: instantly, naturally, effortlessly. Form, then, is the true foundation of the material world. Without spirit's forms, no reflection could be seen in matter's mirror, nor would there be anyone to observe "there is nothing here." For Plotinus taught that every soul is also a form, sometimes called an idea of an individual.

Is there an idea of each particular thing? Yes, if I and each one of us have a way of ascent and return to the intelligible, the principle of each of us is there. [V-7-1]

Now, this subject may seem to be rather dry and abstract but it is actually as vibrant and immediate as our present experiences. For Plotinus's question "Is there an idea of each individual thing?" is the same as each of us asking "Do I exist as me?"; that is, not just as a particular instance of a man or a woman (or more broadly, a human) but as a unique being whose essence is shared by none else.

In the quotation above, Plotinus says that when a person is able to return to the spiritual realm, his or her true self will be discovered as eternal form, a self that always exists. This will not be the person's present body and personality, but an enduring soul-essence that has inhabited many bodies and many personalities during its lengthy sojourn in the physical universe. In the spiritual world we cast off these coverings, all the layers of superfluous form, and know ourselves as we truly are.

As is stressed over and over in the *Enneads*, spiritual realities always are more substantial than material realities. So we need to clearly understand what Plotinus means by an idea of each particular thing, which includes you and me. This doesn't mean that each of us is merely a thought in spirit's consciousness—at least not a thought that bears any resemblance to our own thinking. Our thoughts come and go and are not part of our essential selves, while spirit's forms are part and parcel of its being.

The forms are as eternal and changeless as spirit itself because they are not separate from spirit. This means, of course, that you and I are eternal and changeless, since the true nature of the soul that is reading or writing these words is a form within spirit.

Right now, don't you feel absolutely real? I'm not speaking of the changeable bodily or mental part of you but the "you" that is the center of your consciousness. This sensation of "Yes, I am" is not an illusion, regardless of claims by neuroscientists that our feelings of selfhood are a chimera produced by purely physical goings-on in the brain.

In truth, each of us is much more than just "I," since Plotinus teaches that all forms are unified in the spiritual realm. The simple yet astounding conclusion is that since every individual is a form, and all forms are one, everything in creation is within each of us.

And we do say that each soul possesses all the forming principles in the universe. [V-7-1]

Why, then, do we feel so limited, separate, and alone? Because at the moment we are not solely ourselves. In Plotinus's mystical philosophy, I am most intimately connected to the cosmos when I am most intimately in touch with my true self, the form of "me" that contains all the other forms. So, in an apparent paradox, the more I am immersed within myself, the self beyond matter and mind, the greater is my connection with all that is not my self.

Thus we find that Plotinus's seemingly intellectual doctrine of the forms is central to appreciating the grandeur of his spiritual vision. His mysticism is aimed at removing the barriers that prevent us from knowing ourselves as pure soul, one with all of creation.

The main obstacle that must be surmounted is our infatuation with matter. If material things are beautiful and desirable, it is due to the forms that impress themselves upon matter. If we love the beauty of a shadowy reflection, imagine what it would be like to behold the pristine glory of the original.

Intelligence Is Intuitive

FORTUNATELY, to understand Plotinus's teaching about the nature of intelligence we need only think clearly, not complexly. In fact, perhaps it is not necessary to think at all, as Plotinus taught that genuine intelligence is beyond thought.

He wouldn't have agreed with a noted biologist I saw on television recently who said there is only one intelligent species on earth, *Homo sapiens*, because we are the only animals capable of communicating sophisticated concepts through language, and of engaging in self-referential intellection (thinking about our thinking).

However, this scientist did admit that his conception of intelligence isn't related to a species' survival, since cockroaches (as one example among many) have been around much longer than people. If I was asked to bet on which species is more likely to inhabit our planet 10,000 years from now, I'd place my money on the insect.

So there is an intelligence involved in knowing how to exist that is separate from the abstract reasoning normally associated with being smart. Other forms of intelligence—emotional, creative, interpersonal, and so on—also have been identified by researchers. Thus intelligence must be something that manifests in many ways, a common ground that unites phenomena as disparate as the weaving of a spider web and the solving of a mathematical equation.

What, then, is the essence of intelligence?

Plotinus answers: simply knowing.

Faith and reason often are considered to be different ways of realizing truth. True enough, but neither faith nor reason is simply knowing. We might say that faith is an unconfirmed belief that such and such is true, while reason believes that the truth of such and such can be confirmed. Intelligence lies at the end of the road on which believers travel. It is the destination, actually knowing the truth about something.

> But perhaps someone might say that . . . the intelligence which is in the All should have calculations and memories. This is a statement of men who assume that unintelligence is intelligence, and have come to the conclusion that to seek to be intelligent is the same thing as being intelligent. [IV-4-12]

Reasoning is to intelligence as driving a car is to having a vision of the Grand Canyon. By driving a car we indeed can get to the rim of the Grand Canyon. And once there we can enjoy the vision that was the purpose of the drive. But it also is possible to walk, bike, or take a helicopter to the Grand Canyon. And no matter how we get there, the means of travel has nothing to do with the final destination.

Both of these statements are equally nonsensical: "I'm driving to the Grand Canyon; I see its splendor" and "I'm trying to figure something out; I know it." Just as it is only when we actually are at the Grand Canyon that we perceive its grandeur, so it is only when we have succeeded in knowing something that we are intelligent. Genuine intelligence, says Plotinus, possesses a truth directly and entirely. And the highest intelligence, spiritual intelligence, eternally possesses wisdom in the same fashion:

> *. . . not acquired by calculations, since it has always been present as a whole; because it lacks nothing, it does not need to be sought after.* [V-8-4][1]

Imagine two people being asked what 3^3 ($3 \times 3 \times 3$) equals. One person takes a few seconds to reason out the answer: "Three times three is nine, and nine times three is twenty-seven." The other person immediately says, "Twenty-seven." Even though one took longer than the other to solve the problem, each arrived at the same conclusion. Thus Plotinus observes that someone engages in calculations to find the right answer. When the answer is obtained, the calculations end; reason is motion, and intelligence is rest.

> *For the man who is calculating seeks to learn that which if someone already possesses, he is intelligent: so that intelligence is in one who has come to rest.* [IV-4-12]

Qualitatively, there is no difference between our intelligence and spirit's intelligence. Each is an immediate and intuitive knowing. But there is a quantitative difference in that our knowing proceeds sequentially. Bits and pieces of reality unfold before us in the present moment, then recede into memory. In contrast, Plotinus teaches that spirit is always perfectly intelligent, for the forms that comprise all of creation are inseparable from spirit's very being. Nothing is hidden; nothing remains to be revealed.

Our efforts to act intelligently necessarily involve a struggle to fill some void in our knowledge. We are always laboring to make our mental maps of the world conform, more or less, to the actual geography of reality. This is hard work. Like an explorer trying to get through a thick jungle, we're incessantly hacking at briars of ignorance and tendrils of illusion with our machetes of reason. Spiritual intelligence, by contrast, doesn't have to exert any effort to know what can be known.

A common modern view, says Raoul Mortley, is that "thought somehow runs parallel to reality, responding to it in its own entirely separate way, following its own path, but somehow mimeographing reality in its own terms. Thought is seen as reality in code. For Plotinus, however, the true way is 'to be, our very selves, that we are to see.' Intellect and its objects are therefore held to merge in some way."[2]

As we've already learned, spirit and the Soul of the All are in complete control of the lower regions of creation because what they know and do is not separate from what they are. This is obviously different from what we experience in everyday life. Few people are in firm control of even their own bodies and minds, much less the body and mind of anyone else. Our mastery of the non-living material world is even less certain. This is why higher beings, and especially spirit itself, don't encounter the same sorts of problems in managing their affairs as we do.

> So the maker is in no way compelled to be in doubt or perplexity or to have difficulties, as some people have thought who considered the administration of the universe to be a burden. . . . So a being like this needs nothing for its making, since its intelligence does not belong to someone else but is itself, using nothing brought in from outside. [IV-4-12]

Plotinus presents us with a compelling view of intelligence: a completely natural and unforced quality of those whose being, knowing, and doing is a harmonious union. What they are and know, they do; what they are and do, they know; what they know and do, they are.

If only we could say this about ourselves, we whose actions are so often out of sync with what we purport to know, and who frequently observe "I can't believe I did that." It is difficult to imagine living without calculation or memory but wouldn't it be wonderful if we could, still remaining intelligent? For whenever we strain to think about or recall something, we introduce an unnatural duality into what is in truth a unified world. Reality is not what it is reasoned out to be or remembered to be, but what truly is—separate from the artificial constructs of thought and memory.

If the foundation of a person's consciousness wasn't the personal subjective self, but the universal objective cosmos, then he or she would spontaneously react to every situation with just the right response, saying, doing, or thinking precisely what should be said, done, or thought. In every age there have been some men and women who have exhibited this capacity for living so harmoniously. We call them saints, enlightened ones, realized souls. What they have realized, it seems, is the intuitive intelligence that is natural to spirit and the Soul of the All but which we must labor to reclaim.

> *In the soul of the good and wise man the objects known tend to become identical with the knowing subject, since they are pressing on towards intellect.* [III-8-8]

This applies to knowing the world outside and inside of us. We are better able to attain unity in self-knowledge since there is no material barrier standing between us and what we want to know. I can contemplate a flower until the sun goes down and there always will remain two entities: the flower and me. This is not the case with spirit, where the form of Flower is part of spirit's very being. And this is not the case when I properly contemplate myself, for I am, quite obviously, me. We thus are able to know ourselves by emulating spirit's intuitive intelligence.

> *When [the Intellect] sees being, it sees itself. . . . It does not see one part of itself with another part of itself, but all of itself by means of the totality of itself.* [V-3-6][3]

Here Plotinus zeros in on the central distinction between true intelligence and all other forms of knowledge. When we have an "intelligent" understanding of something that is one, whether this be God, spirit, soul, or anything else, there is no division of the intellectual vision into parts. For if I see as *many* an entity that is *single*, I haven't seen it truly. And if I see my own self with another part of my self, then I will only know the part that is seen, not the part that is doing the seeing.

Complete self-knowledge thus is impossible so long as we try to analyze or delve into ourselves as if we were cadavers on a dissecting table. We may learn something about what we are not—matter, memories, imagination, and such—but not what we are—conscious soul—for consciousness is what is doing the probing, and so cannot be probed by itself.

> *Does he then see himself with another part of himself? But in this way one would be the seer, and the other the seen; but this is not "self-knowledge."* [V-3-5]

We are advised, then, to cultivate a sort of un-self-consciousness so that we may better know ourselves. This may seem paradoxical but it makes sense if our goal is to unify the splintered pieces of ourselves. If I truly am a single being, not many, then how could it ever be possible to know myself as I know other things?

I can know the square root of 16 or the date of D-day because these objects of knowledge are outside of my essential being. But if I am to know myself, then the part of me seeking that knowledge and the part of me that is the knowledge being sought somehow have to be brought into the grasp of an intuitive intelligence that is me, not part of me.

Plotinus suggests that both the activities of everyday life and the pursuit of spiritual wisdom will go better when we are conscious, but not unnecessarily self-conscious. To a mystic, one is always better than two, especially inside our own heads.

> *Even when we are awake, we can find a great many fine activities, meditations, and actions which are not accompanied by consciousness at the very moment when we are meditating or acting.*
> *A person who is reading, for example, is not necessarily aware that he is reading, especially if he is reading attentively. Likewise, a person who performs a courageous act is not aware, at the moment that he performs the act, that he is acting courageously.* [I-4-10][4]

This is the mystery of the wisdom of not-knowing. Since intelligence is intuitive, the height of wisdom is to know but not to know that we know. When we introduce a duality into our knowing and think to ourselves, "I'm reading" or "I'm brave," it doesn't help us read or make us more brave. Quite the opposite. As we move from being conscious to self-conscious, a split develops between our doing and our being that makes us weaker, not stronger.

The pure intelligence of spiritual contemplation, says Plotinus, is what really satisfies. So we need to learn how to bring this un-reasoning intuitive intelligence into play, both in the stillness of meditation and the activity of everyday life. Reasoning, a form of self-consciousness, is necessary only when we are confused by a lack of intelligence. Those who know the most, think the least.

Does the soul use discursive reasoning before it comes and again after it goes out of the body? No, discursive reasoning comes into it here below, when it is already in perplexity and full of care, and in a state of greater weakness. [IV-3-18]

Time Is Temporary

IS THERE ANYONE who hasn't uttered the clarion cry of the modern age? "I need more time."

Time is a commodity that always seems in limited supply. No matter how much of it we have, and everyone has the same amount, it never is enough. At the end of the day there always seems to be a task undone, a goal unaccomplished, a dream unfulfilled.

"If I had more time," most of us think, "I'd be so much happier." That is, we assume that if a few more items could be checked off on our life's to-do list—which may include, of course, "relax and do nothing"—*then* we would finally enjoy the happiness that *now* always seems to be just around the corner.

Plotinus asks us to consider whether it is this very sensation of now-and-then, time itself, at the root of our dissatisfaction. The great illusion is that we presently lack something that, if obtained in the future, will bring us true happiness. The grand reality is that time is temporary: nothing that exists within time lasts forever, so lasting wisdom and well-being will not be found in the realm of now-and-then.

The One and spirit everlastingly possess all that we seek, with such limited success, within time. So it isn't more time that we need. It is less time. More accurately, no time at all: eternity.

> *What would "one thing after another" mean when all things remained in unity? What sense would "before" still have, and what "after" or "future"? Where could the soul now fix its gaze on something other than that in which it is?* [III-7-12]

Here in our universe, material things (including thoughts produced by the physical brain) always are separated by time and space. Since time continually brings about changes and only one thing can occupy a certain space at a particular time, there is a constant push and pull within materiality.

Life on earth bears an unsettling resemblance to a crowded parking lot at a popular shopping mall the weekend before Christmas: there is incessant circling around and jockeying for position, some leaving and some arriving, people frantically striving to be somewhere other than where they are now. Such is the way of this material world, says Plotinus, but not of the spiritual world.

> *The matter, too, of the things that came into being is always receiving different forms, but the matter of eternal things is always the same and always has the same form.* [II-4-3]

Time, then, is a necessary consequence of physical creation. If there is to be anything other (and lower) than the spiritual world where all the forms are eternally the same, there must be some alternative means of manifesting reality. And this is time.

A.H. Armstrong says, "The life of Intellect [spirit] is a life at rest in eternity, a life of thought in eternal, immediate and simultaneous possession of all possible objects. So the only way of being different which is left for Soul is to pass from eternal life to a life in which, instead of all things being present at once, one thing comes after another, and there is a succession, a continuous series, of thoughts and actions."[1]

Soul, teaches Plotinus, is unwisely individualistic. This applies on both a universal level to the all-encompassing Soul of the All, and on a personal level to the separate souls. As will be discussed more fully in another section, an element of *tolma* (self-assertion) is involved in the creation of the lower realms of the cosmos. Plotinus says that soul was not content to be eternally united with spirit and desired to manifest its own creative power.

Since everything that can possibly exist already does, within the one-many of spirit, the only option for further creation is to fold up within time and space what is unfolded in the boundlessness of the spiritual world. Then the Soul of the All, along with the individual souls, can reveal, bit by bit within time, what is hidden. We might say that the cosmos is playing hide-and-seek with itself.

> *For because soul had an unquiet power, which wanted to keep on transferring what it saw there to something else, it did not want the whole to be present to it all together. . . . In general extension of time means the dispersal of a single present. That is why it is properly called "the image of eternity," since it intends to bring about the disappearance of what is permanent in eternity by its own dispersion.* [III-7-11, I-5-7]

Plotinus says that if soul is to transfer the knowledge and power eternally contained within spirit to "something else" (matter), the permanence of unity must be fractured by time. This allows the spiritual forms to seep out, so to speak, in the ever-flowing current of time: little by little, moment by moment, something different is revealed.

In our own lives as in the universe as a whole, everything is constantly changing whether we realize it or not. Even apparently changeless matter, such as a stone resting placidly on a mountain-side for eons, is composed of atoms in ceaseless energetic motion, whizzing around at speeds of thousands of miles per second. Over vast spans of time, earthly rocks crumble into powder while, else-where in the galaxy, new stars and planets are being formed out of interstellar gases and dust.

This is what Plotinus means by an image of eternity. Presently we souls exist in a wavering reflection of unchanging truth. Whether voluntarily, by our *tolma*, or involuntarily, by divine design, we have traded the certain constant bliss of spiritual unity for the uncertain changing anxiety that comes with living in materiality. The lower life of soul is nothing but "insteads."

> And, instead of sameness and self-identity and abiding, that which does not abide in the same but does one act after another, and instead of that which is one without distance or separation, an image of unity, that which is one in continuity; and instead of a complete unbounded whole, a continuous unbounded succession, and instead of a whole all together a whole which is, and always will be, going to come into being part by part. [III-7-11]

We may glibly speak of living in one world, of feeling one with creation, of loving another to such a degree that we become one heart and one soul. But this is just talk, not reality. If we truly were one with the world, or with creation, or with another, there wouldn't be anything to talk about or anyone to do the talking. Because we are only able to experience an image of unity our oneness is necessarily limited by inescapable divisions of time and space.

No lasting wholeness is possible when time keeps on bringing one part of creation after another onto the stage of our attention. "Look at me." "No, forget that, now attend to *me*!" And so it goes, a continuous parade of sights and sounds, thoughts and feelings, imaginings and desires. Instead of enjoying the eternal embrace of the Good we get brief hugs (or slaps) from one thing after another.

Once in a while we meet up with an experience that is so won-derful we can only describe it as a timeless moment. If only this were true. For time takes that moment and shoves it into the past, replacing it with another moment that almost always is less to our liking. So we end up with only pale remembrances of a moment that was once a vibrant living presence.

We are slaves to time, says Plotinus. Time gives us a taste of well-being then snatches away our plate of happiness. Then again a taste, followed by a snatch. Is this any way to live?

> *In the same way, Soul, making the world of sense in imitation of that other world . . . first of all put itself into time, which it made instead of eternity, and then handed over that which came into being as a slave to time, by making the whole of it exist in time and encompassing all its ways with time.* [III-7-11]

How then is it possible to free ourselves from the confines of time? First, it is necessary to understand that such a liberation cannot take place at a particular time. This would be like thinking a thought that stops me from thinking. Impossible. One doesn't leave a prison by staying in the prison.

So long as we are within time, we are, simply put, within time. It doesn't make sense to ask, "When am I going to arrive in eternity?" For *when* is an attribute of our starting place, not our destination.

In the quotation above, Plotinus has given us the key to solving this conundrum. He says that soul put itself into time. Thus soul was not always in time. If, recognizing ourselves as soul, we are able to return to our original state, we will be outside of time—really outside of time.

Every soul exists outside of time, whether it be the Soul of the All that created our universe or the individual soul that is one's true self. But whatever is made by soul does exist within time, which includes everything material outside of ourselves and everything mental or emotional within ourselves. Thus it is not far off the mark to say, "I feel that time is slipping by," for our thoughts and feelings indeed are caught in the flow of time. However, the pure consciousness of soul is within eternity.

> *Since even the [individual] souls are not in time, but such affections as they have are, and the things they make. For the souls are eternal, and time is posterior to them, and that which is in time is less than time; for time must encompass what is in time.* [IV-4-15]

This means that it is possible for a soul to leap across the line that divides time from eternity. Such a leap, of course, will not take any time, nor will it happen at some time. This passage from the domain of time to the realm of eternity is essentially creation in reverse. The soul walks backward, so to speak, along the path that connects the eternal world of spirit and the ephemeral world of matter. How we came down is how we go back. Plotinus's teachings about how time came to be are a helpful guide to the spiritual traveler seeking to retrace his or her steps.

Interestingly, those teachings are paralleled in the writings of a noted modern physicist, Stephen Hawking. In *A Brief History of Time*, Hawking says, "As we shall see, the concept of time has no meaning before the beginning of the universe. . . . One may say that time had a beginning at the big bang, in the sense that earlier times simply would not be defined."[2] In like fashion, Plotinus says that time is created along with the universe, and the soul abolishes time when it leaves physical reality.

> *If, then, when soul leaves this activity* [outside eternity] *and returns to unity time is abolished, it is clear that the beginning of this movement in this direction, and this form of the life of soul, generates time. This is why it is said that time came into existence simultaneously with this universe, because soul generated it along with this universe.* [III-7-12]

So spiritual travelers desiring to return to the One need no itinerary. In fact, they should discard any notion of a schedule they may be carrying around in their minds.

"Today (or tomorrow, or next month, or next year) I'll make this much spiritual progress." Thoughts like this assume that the journey back to God somehow is a matter of speed, a measure of distance traveled over time. But there is no distance between the soul and the One, for the One is omnipresent. And time exists only in the realm of nature and the Soul of the All, not in the domain of spirit and the One.

> *For around Soul things come one after another: now Socrates, now a horse, always some one particular reality; but Intellect is all things. It has therefore everything at rest in the same place, and it only is, and its "is" is for ever.* [V-1-4]

Here Plotinus points toward the paradox of spiritual progress. How is it possible to change into something unchangeable, or become what always is?

We sit and wait for spirit to make an appearance. Our toes tap impatiently. Our eyes glance frequently at the clock. We pass the time by imagining how wonderful the moment of meeting will be. But the moment doesn't arrive. And then it doesn't arrive some more.

We continue to worry and wonder: "What time will it be when the eternal spirit finally comes?" Then more sitting, waiting, tapping, glancing, and imagining.

There's plenty of time to ponder this question. All the time in the world. Which is precisely the problem. For spirit is in eternity, and this world is in time. So long as the world is present to us, spirit and the One are absent. Time and motion are here; eternity and rest are there. So long as the soul is busily engaged seeking spirit here, we are not there.

Marsilio Ficino, a fifteenth-century devotee of Plato, put it nicely when he wrote about the folly of men who seek to find rest through motion: "Because of their ceaseless longing for what is to come, they do not enjoy what is present. Although movement has to be stilled for there to be rest; yet those men are forever beginning new and different movements, in order that they may one day come to rest."[3]

World-Soul Is a Weaver

SPIRIT IS the eternal tapestry of reality. Spirit is dynamic, intelligent energy (*energeia*) so it is not motionless. But spirit's activity is outside of time and space. The spiritual forms are part and parcel of spirit's very being, so there is no place for the forms to move to or from. Yet they are alive, much more alive than the life we experience. Spirit's tapestry is vibrant, the most beautiful of realities other than the One. The forms within spirit are pure and transparent, each being part of the All and the All being part of each.

The Soul of the All, or World-Soul, uses the loom of providence (our subject in the next chapter) to weave these spiritual forms into the warp and weft of material space and time.

Not every form appears in the design at a given moment. Forms come and go as the weaving proceeds. Dinosaurs appear here and disappear there; stars start to shine now and fade away then; a baby makes an entrance and an elder an exit. The intelligence that guides the weaving of the Soul of the All comes from spirit, and the Soul of the All transfers the design to matter. Getting and giving, ceaseless weaving. This is the role of soul.

> But if soul was not present in the Whole these bodies would be nothing, and certainly not in order. [IV-7-3]

Thus soul is spirit's emissary to the material realm. Soul enables matter to receive the forms which otherwise would eternally remain in the spiritual world. Spirit, or intellect, is the king and soul is the messenger. The king does not descend from the throne. If the townspeople, everything in this physical universe, are to realize something of the king's wisdom and majesty, the knowledge will be transmitted through the messenger of the soul.

> But Intellect as a whole is always above, and could never be outside its own world, but is settled as a whole above and communicates with things here through soul. [IV-3-12]

When Plotinus speaks about soul (*psyche*), he may be using the term in any of three meanings. First, there is the domain of soul,

130

the region of creation that comes after the spiritual world. The lower part of this domain is nature, the physical universe. The upper part is a non-material realm of soul that is neither physical nor truly spiritual but a sort of difficult-to-describe in-between state. Scholars call this entire domain the hypostasis of soul, meaning that region of the cosmos where soul is the primary substance.

Second, there is the Soul of the All, also called the World Soul or universal soul. This is the being that rules, so to speak, the domain of soul in the same sense as an individual soul rules its body.

Thus A.H. Armstrong says, "We are not parts or products of the World-Soul, but it and our souls and all other souls are parts of the hypostasis Soul, beings, that is, on essentially the same level. The World-Soul is our elder sister, not our mother, and we can rise as high as it and become its fellow-contemplatives and collaborators."[1] Here Plotinus notes that we and the Soul of the All have the same form (but not, obviously, the same powers):

> But why has the Soul of the All, which has the same form as ours, made the universe, but the soul of each individual has not, though it too has all things in itself? [IV-3-6]

Third, then, are the individual souls such as you and me, and the souls that animate every other animal, plant, and variety of living being. Here we come to an overlap, as Lloyd Gerson puts it, between the Soul of the All and separate souls, for "the bodies of individuals are also parts of the body of the universe. . . . But the universal soul is also prior to individual souls because it 'prepares the way' for them by producing nature which includes the organic bodies that individual souls inhabit."[2]

The Soul of the All has such power and we do not, because the World Soul eternally contemplates the universal intelligence of spirit, while we individual souls generally contemplate our limited partial intellects. Further, the Soul of the All governs its body, the physical universe, in calm detachment. As was previously discussed, Plotinus compares the frazzled state of divided fallen souls with the carefree state of partless souls, such as the Soul of the All, which have not descended into materiality.

The universe, Plotinus tells us, is like a "beautiful and richly various house which was not cut off from its builder, but he did not give it a share in himself either." [IV-3-9] In other words, the builder of the house—the Soul of the All, or World Soul—continues to manage the universe even after it has become inhabited by the separate souls. Yet the builder doesn't get involved in the goings-on within the house. He is akin to an eminently fair and wise landlord who arbitrates disputes and keeps the plumbing in good working order but lives his own life unaffected by what the tenants do.

> *For he rules it* [the universe] *while abiding above. It is in this sort of way that it is ensouled; it has a soul which does not belong to it, but is present to it; it is mastered, not the master, possessed, not possessor.* [IV-3-9]

So the ideal relation between body and soul, nobly manifested by the Soul of the All, is for the two to be interwoven but not interrelated. Plotinus teaches that it is preferable for a soul to remain above in the realm of spirit and have nothing at all to do with a body. However, if a person as soul is involved with a body (and all humans are), then it is best to be unaffected by the body with which the soul is so intimately connected.

To most of us, this seems impossible. "If I have a migraine headache, I'm supposed to be *unaffected*?" Admittedly, Plotinus presents us with an ideal that is difficult to realize completely. Still, he is emphatic that the interweaving of body and soul does not affect the soul's unchanging spiritual essence. This is true whether the weaving is of the Soul of the All with the body of the universe, or of our individual souls with our particular physical bodies.

> *It is possible for the principle interwoven to be unaffected and for the soul to pass and repass through the body without being touched by its affections.* [I-1-4]

The interweaving of body and soul, says Plotinus, is like a line being mixed with a color. It is simple to demonstrate this notion on a computer's word processor. Draw a line and then select various colors for it. Red, green, yellow, white, black, blue. No matter what color the line is, it remains the same line. We may say, "That's a yellow line." But the yellow and the line are completely separate things, just like the soul and the body.

Plotinus provides another image to help us understand the relationship of body and soul: the universe is like a net floating on the ocean of soul. The net is supported by the ocean at every point, but the ocean is not the net and the net is not the ocean.

> *And soul's nature is so great, just because it has no size, as to contain the whole of body in one and the same grasp.* [IV-3-9]

Plotinus points toward several interesting spiritual truths in this quotation. One truth is that the soul isn't in a body; it is a body that is in the soul. So we misspeak when we say that the soul leaves the body at death, for the soul was never in the body. This is easier to understand if we realize the special meaning that "in" has in the Greek language.

Dominic O'Meara says, "In Greek, 'in' can mean to be 'in' someone's or something's power, to be dependent on this power. In this sense immaterial being is 'in' nothing as not depending on any body for its existence. On the other hand body, as dependent on soul, can be said to be 'in' soul, just as material reality depends on, or is 'in,' immaterial being."[3] So this is how the universe is in the Soul of the All just as our bodies are in our own souls: not spatially, because soul has no size or shape, but dependently.

Another truth, related to the first, is that body cannot exist without soul but soul can and does exist without body. This leads Plotinus to view body as being essentially irrelevant to soul. It is fine for a soul not to have a body and it is almost equally fine for a soul to have a body. We must say "almost," because the interweaving of soul and body carries with it a serious potential danger that is, in practice, almost always actualized.

This danger is that the soul will lose sight of the fact that it is soul and see itself as body. The weaver loses control, becomes enmeshed in the weaving, and comes to believe that he is part of the fabric of materiality.

However, this is the weaver's fault. If he could remain detached as does the Soul of the All, his involvement with physical creation would do him no harm. Thus Plotinus teaches that this universe is just as it should be and we shouldn't criticize its creator for defects caused by the inhabitants.

> *He who finds fault with the nature of the universe does not know what he is doing, nor how far his arrogance is taking him. . . . But it is as if two people were living in the same well-built house: one of them*

criticizes its structure and its builder, although he keeps on living in it all the same.

The other, however, does not criticize; in fact, he affirms the builder has constructed the house with consummate skill, and he awaits the time when he will move on, and no longer have need of a house. [II-9-13, II-9-18][4]

We are free to move to the spiritual world from our present dwelling place here on Earth. But we should have a positive motivation for moving: to return to the One. Those who want to leave physical existence because they don't like the conditions here are, in effect, insulting the creator of this universe.

"You should have made things differently" is the unspoken statement that underlies every criticism of earthly life. This is unjustified arrogance, says Plotinus. We can't even properly fashion our own lives, much less an entire universe, so who are we to second-guess the workings of the Soul of the All and spirit? Referring to the Gnostics, who despised materiality, he asked:

Who amongst these insanely conceived people is as well-ordered or wise as the All? [II-9-16][5]

The physical world is limited not by its design, which is an accurate reflection of the spiritual forms, but by the very fact that it is a reflection, not the original. Matter reflects spirit's *logoi*, or forms, just as a mirror reflects an image of whatever is placed before it. If the image isn't as clear and substantial as the original, this is no fault of the mirror. That's simply the nature of images.

We cannot grant, either, that this universe had an evil origin because there are many unpleasant things in it: this is a judgment of people who rate it too highly, if they claim that it ought to be the same as the intelligible world and not only an image of it. [II-9-4]

Many people seem to feel that they should be enjoying heaven on earth. When things go amiss with their lives, they are angry and disappointed. Inside their heads is a voice that tells them: "Everything should be perfect all of the time!" But this is the cry of an ignorant ego, not a wise soul. Plotinus asks us to think clearly for a moment.

If the design of the cosmos is to include material existence, then this obviously must differ from spiritual, or intelligible, existence. Otherwise earth and heaven would be the same, not separate realms.

> *If, being an image, it* [the universe] *is not that intelligible world, this is precisely what is natural to it; if it was the intelligible world, it would not be an image of it. But it is false to say that the image is unlike the original; for nothing has been left out which it was possible for a fine natural image to have. . . . We must not abuse those things which are lower than the first, but gently acquiesce in the nature of all things.* [II-9-8, II-9-13⁶]

The Soul of the All has faithfully transmitted the spiritual forms to our world of matter. Everything good and beautiful that can be here is here. *Logos*, the spiritual intelligence of the Soul of the All, weaves wonderful patterns out of the fabric of physical matter and energy. These patterns are thus ensouled and must be reverenced. You, me, all other people, animals, plants, inanimate matter—Plotinus teaches that everything either has a soul, or is a soul. The stars and planets, for example, have souls.

> *And there are souls in these* [the heavenly bodies] *too, and intelligent and good ones, much more closely in touch with the beings of the higher world than our souls are.* [II-9-16]

So there is no room in Plotinus's philosophy for any complaining about the conditions of earthly life. From the One, or God, emanates the cosmos. So this world and all the souls within it are children of the same father. To hate any part of creation is to hate the creator, for the One, through the intermediaries of spirit and the Soul of the All, is the ultimate source of all that exists. In the light of spiritual wisdom, it isn't possible to hate the weaving and love the weaver.

> *For anyone who feels affection for anything at all shows kindness to all that is akin to the object of his affection, and to the children of the father he loves. But every soul is a child of That Father.* [II-9-16]

Providence Is Pervasive

IN THE GRAND DESIGN of the cosmos, from the One comes many. Yet unity is evident at every level of emanation because the One is overall, even when disguised by multiplicity.

Unity is present in the realm of spirit, for the immaterial forms are inseparable from spirit's very being. Unity is present in the realm of soul, for the Soul of the All contemplates these transcendent forms and weaves them seamlessly into matter, forming the continuous space and time of the physical universe. So even though earthly life may often seem mixed up and unmanaged, Plotinus assures us that actually everything and everyone is being guided by an all-pervasive providence.

For those higher principles are not separated from these here but the better illuminate the worse, and this is perfect providence. [III-3-4]

Providence, then, is a connection between the higher and the lower, between spirit and matter, heaven and earth, God and man. Providence binds together the manyness of materiality into a wholeness that is the best possible reflection of the absolute unity of the One.

Signs of providence are evident everywhere: in the tightly organized laws of nature, in the ecological interdependence of species, in the connectedness we feel with kith and kin, in the mystical experience of contact with a higher power, and many other places within and without ourselves.

But Plotinus indicates that while providence is pervasive it is not dictatorial. Souls still possess a certain power of independent choice or free will. This is why providence is necessary. If everything happened in accord with the perfect unitary intelligence of spirit there would be no need for providence.

Providence binds together what has been separated from divinity. A mother doesn't need to do anything special to provide for her baby while it is still connected to her in her womb. Only after the baby is born and becomes a separate person is her providential care—feeding, bathing, diapering, protecting—needed.

Providence must not be such that it makes nothings out of us. If Providence alone were all there were, it would no longer be Providence, for upon whom would it exert providential action? [III-2-9][1]

Providence doesn't determine our fates but it does assure that we are fated to experience the rational consequences of whatever we determine to do as beings separate from spirit and the One. In the womb a baby is automatically nourished. But as every parent knows, feeding an infant can be a chancy affair. Sometimes the child refuses to eat the food that is offered. Then hunger pangs make her cry in her crib. Such is providence. Those who eat are satiated, just as Plotinus tells us that those who are good enjoy well-being.

But it [providence] *says that those who have become good shall have a good life, now, and laid up for them hereafter as well, and the wicked the opposite.* [III-2-9]

Providence is inseparable from *logos*, which R.T. Wallis says "normally denotes the 'ground-plan' or 'formative principle' from which lower realities evolve and which subsequently governs their development."[2] Plotinus explains that the rational forming principle is not so much a cause as a "knowing." That is, the providential power of *logos* knows how the various parts of creation fit together and what must happen when one part affects another. Providence thus is a universal principle that unfailingly connects causes and effects in a harmonious order.

When the same things come together, the same circumstances arise, then it is altogether appropriate that the same results should follow. Soul takes over or foresees these antecedent conditions and taking account of them accomplishes what follows and links up the chain of consequences, bringing antecedents and consequents into complete connection. [II-3-16]

All this talk of antecedents and consequents sounds rather abstract, but the workings of providence are as immediately present as your next thought or action. Are you free to think or do whatever you like? "No," I believe Plotinus would say. At least, whatever free will we have isn't free for long.

For providence assures that whenever we do something, that cause (or antecedent) is connected with an effect (or consequence).

Thus a freely-willed action necessarily causes a non-freely-willed effect. Further, this effect might be of quite a different order than the cause. Mental causes can have physical effects, and physical causes can have mental effects. The causes and effects also can be far removed in space and time from each other.

For example, if I throw a rock from behind some bushes and hit someone on the head, escaping unnoticed, one would think that the only effect of my action would be a painful bump on the other person's cranium. I could keep on hitting people with rocks with impunity so long as I was never caught. However, since Plotinus teaches that providence is rooted in the all-pervasive realm of the Soul of the All, there is no place to hide from the long arm of this universal law.

> It is fitting to attribute the punishments which fall with justice on the wicked to the [universal] order in that it directs the world according to what is right. [IV-3-16]

This is why free will cannot remain free. Even if I was free to throw those rocks, I am not free to escape the just consequences of my actions. Plotinus expresses the eminently scientific notion that the overarching principle of cause and effect applies to the living and non-living alike. We humans are not exempt from providence just because we can think to ourselves, "I am free." Even that seemingly insignificant thought, says Plotinus, is within the province of providence. That is, it seems that I am not even free to decide whether I'm free.

> For one must not think that some things are contained in the order, while others are let loose for the operation of free will. [IV-3-16]

Now, many people consider free will to be a central (or even essential) aspect of being human. "If we are not free," they say, "then what differentiates us from animals?" Plotinus probably would answer in this fashion: "The wise soul does not seek freedom of action but freedom from action. Presently you act in order to attain something that you believe will bring well-being. But when you come to possess the ultimate Good, there will be no further desire, and hence no action to be willed."

In other words, when the soul returns to the unity of the One it has no separate will, free or otherwise. And there can be no actions when there is only One, for an action requires an independent actor and something separate to be acted upon. True, we are not yet enjoying union with the One, existing as we do in the realm of separateness. But even while here on Earth we should recognize and respect the interwovenness of all things. The mystic philosopher, says Plotinus, knows that in truth he lives as a part of the whole, not just as a part.

> *So then living things are all conformed to the complete pattern of the All, both the ones in heaven and the rest which have been made parts in the whole, and no part, even if it is a great one, has power to bring about a complete change in the patterns or the things which happen according to the patterns.* [II-3-13]

Isn't it interesting that miracles are, by nature, so rare and miraculous? Well-documented miracles are few and far between (skeptics would say non-existent). Even purported miracles are so much an exception to the general run of worldly predictability that they receive widespread and avid attention in both holy books and impious tabloids. If great souls have lived on Earth, and I believe they have, then why hasn't a miracle been performed that is so grand, so out-of-the-ordinary, so impossible to disregard, that believers and unbelievers alike are left awestruck at this display of other-worldly power?

For example, adding another full-sized moon to the night sky would be the sort of thing that would grab everyone's attention. Emblazoning a message on the newly-created celestial body—"Believe!"—would be a nice additional touch.

Some may consider these thoughts blasphemous, but it isn't irreligious to point out the supremacy of providence. As Plotinus noted above, even "the ones in heaven" are "conformed to the complete pattern of the All." No soul has the power to bring about much of a change in the pattern of creation, for the whole necessarily prevails over the parts. And if a partial soul returns to the One, then it is barely qualifiable as a part, having almost completely united with the whole. At that point, where is there any capacity, or desire, to act contrary to providence?

From Plotinus's perspective, even something we would call miraculous is a result of the eminently lawful interconnectedness of the cosmos. J.M. Rist says, "It is because of the 'sympathy' of the various parts of the cosmos that both prayers can be answered and magic effective. . . . Prayer, like magic, is a quasi-scientific means of harnessing certain powers in the cosmos to the service of man. These powers are predictable and can be understood by 'scientific' laws."[3]

Providence, says Plotinus, is akin to a general who commands not only his own troops but the enemy as well. How is it possible to battle against such a commander? Your resistance is under his control.

> *The universe is ordered by the generalship of providence. . . . But if it was possible for him* [the general] *to command the enemy force as well, if he was truly "the great leader" to whom all things are subject, what would be unordered, what would not be fitted into his plan?* [III-3-2]

Self-willed actions seemingly would be part of the enemy force Plotinus speaks of above, for if I could truly choose to do whatever I wanted whenever I wanted to do it, I'd be outside the command of providence. And this indeed is how many people consider themselves: independent, bound to obey no one unless they want to, free to blaze their own path through life.

However, what if our choices spring from a source, providence, beyond our awareness? Then there would be no difference between what I choose, and what providence has in store for me.

> *Suppose you say "I have power to choose this or that"? But the things that you will choose are included in the universal order.* [III-3-3]

In other words, choice too is covered by the all-encompassing span of providence, or destiny. We may believe that we are able to wield our own itty-bitty looms of thought and action that are separate from the grand weaving of the Soul of the All, but Plotinus teaches that we are mistaken. What we weave in our lives is part of an overall design. The threads of our thinking and our doing are interwoven with the fabric of the entire cosmos. Pull here and something moves there because all is connected by providence.

Good and evil are both integral aspects of this universe, just as white and black threads each contribute to the design of a fabric. Evil, says Plotinus, isn't produced by providence. Rather, providence includes evil.

Now the universal rational principle includes both good and evil things; evil things are parts of it too. It is not that the universal rational principle produces them but that it is the universal principle with them included. [III-3-1]

Since presently we have only a partial vision of reality, we are not able to see how things seemingly at odds actually are complementary aspects of a broader unity. Good cannot exist without evil just as light would be invisible if it could not stand out against a darker background ("light is transparent to light," we read earlier). Similarly, we are aware of the bits and pieces of pleasure and pain that come our way but are ignorant of the universal law of providence, cause and effect, which controls the flow of our well-being.

"What goes around, comes around," is a popular saying in the United States. This is a pithy, but entirely accurate, synopsis of Plotinus's teachings about providence. What we give to others we will eventually get. What we take from others will one day be taken from us.

Plotinus recognizes that everyone is seeking the well-being that only union with the One can provide. As we spoke of earlier, most of us necessarily must be content with substitutes: the world's myriad mental and physical pleasures that promise but fail to provide true happiness. Our longing for the Good is transmuted into desires for lesser goods we try to acquire by means fair and foul.

Notwithstanding our underlying (and usually unconscious) spiritual motivation, providence assures that we must pay the price for the harm we do to others.

The cause of the wrongs men do to one another might be their effort towards the Good. . . . But the wrongdoers pay the penalty, being corrupted in their souls by their works of wickedness, and are set in a lower place. [III-2-4]

Providence doesn't need to use miraculous means to enforce divine justice, because the sympathy, or interconnectedness, of the cosmos assures that the fitting consequence for every action is right at hand. Plotinus's teachings about providence are far removed from earlier Greek conceptions of the gods personally intervening in human affairs. In the *Enneads,* providence appears as a universal natural law (quite similar to the principle of karma in Eastern thought) that operates automatically, not by fiat.

This means that it is impossible to evade the lawful consequences of our willful thoughts and actions. Yet the connection between what we do and what happens to us isn't always obvious because of the frequent time lag between a cause and an observable effect. For example, a sudden city-shattering earthquake is the result of slight slippages in the earth's crust that build up unnoticeably over many years.

So life often appears unfair to us since we lack the intelligent vision of providence that sees the complete picture, all the cause and effect linkages that combine to produce the show of "Our Life." But the universal law knows my just deserts and implants within me the desire for whatever tasty thought or action will lead me to my proper place at the table of providence.

Along these lines, most of us have had the disconcerting experience of setting out to avoid some problem and finding that our intentions led us right into the maw of what we were trying to escape. I'm stuck in traffic, worried that I will be fifteen minutes late to an important meeting, and impulsively take a shortcut that I think will save me time. Then I end up driving around lost for an hour.

> *He too who is to suffer punishment is carried unknowing to what he has to suffer; on his unsteady course he is tossed about everywhere in his wanderings, and in the end, as if utterly weary, by his very efforts at resistance he falls into the place which suits him, having that which he did not will for his punishment as a result of the course which he willed.*
> [IV-3-24]

So, says Plotinus, providence returns to us the unwilled effects of freely-willed (or quasi-freely-willed) actions. This makes life interesting, to say the least, and unpredictable. We never know for sure what is going to happen to us next because we are not improvisational actors each in our own one-man shows. Rather, each of us is but a single player in a cast of billions that is putting on a well-scripted production. My freely-spoken lines may begin a scene: "You are a dastardly demon, Dudley!" Yet the fistfight that ensues was not part of my original creative vision, and sets me off on a different dramatic course.

What we really want is more than a providence that simply keeps on providing, for this takes us nowhere but around in circles: actions and consequences forever following one upon the other. Plotinus teaches that, fortunately, providence provides not only rewards and punishments but also a means of escaping from the rule of justice that prevails in the physical universe. In the spiritual world there is no such law because all is bound by a higher unity than cause and effect. The quotation above ends with this promise of liberation, return to the One:

> *But it is stated in the law how much and how long he must suffer, and again there come together the release from punishment and the ability to escape up from these regions by the power of the harmony which holds the universe together.* [IV-3-24]

However, we have not yet reached that point in these pages. Before a return, a departure. A descent precedes the climb back up.

Section III

The One

And Many—

SOUL'S DESCENT,

And Return

Psyche Is a Pilgrim

OUR SOUL, or *psyche*, has been called "the wanderer of the metaphysical world."[1]

Recall the central elements in Plato's parable of the cave. There is the light of the One shining eternally beyond the cave opening. There are the forms of spirit moving back and forth along a platform within the cave, casting shadows onto the cavern wall. There are the prisoners, chained so that they cannot escape from the cave. Each of these elements is unchanging, or nearly so.

And then there is the escaping prisoner, the human soul who is capable of existing on different levels of reality: imprisoned within the darkness of materiality, moving toward spiritual illumination, or fully enlightened in the radiance of the One. Spirit and the Soul of the All are essentially fixed in place, unceasingly contemplating what lies above them and forever bringing into being what lies below.

The individual soul is the only entity in Plotinus's cosmos that is capable of spanning all domains, akin to an elevator that has access to everything from the lowest level of creation all the way to the highest. A person can go to any floor if he or she learns how to push the right buttons, so to speak, to take the soul's attention from the physical universe to spiritual worlds.

> *It* [soul] *is said to be buried and in a cave, but, when it turns to intelligence, to be freed from its fetters and to ascend, when it is started on the contemplation of reality by recollection. . . . Souls then become, one might say, amphibious, compelled to live by turns the life There and the life here.* [IV-8-4]

Some aspect of the soul, says Plotinus, always is there in the realm of spirit. Currently most of us are conscious only of the aspect that is here in the material world. So to realize one's spiritual nature all that is required is to recollect that forgotten part of one's self. The pilgrims who traveled from England to America in the 1600's necessarily traveled by ship, but the conscious soul traverses an ocean of consciousness and requires no means other than what it already possesses to make its journey.

However, this ease of transport is a two-edged sword. The soul can easily descend, and not-quite-so-easily ascend. While the English pilgrims got off the *Mayflower* and stayed in the New World (most of them, at least), the pilgrimage of the soul has an amphibious nature: here, there, here, there. It is as if the pilgrims went back and forth across the Atlantic, not content to remain in either land.

Until the soul enjoys complete fulfillment by returning to the One it is prone to bounce back and forth between the physical and spiritual worlds. As Pierre Hadot puts it, "If we fall back down, it must be because we could not stand being up above any longer. From now on, however, we won't be able to stand being down here. Henceforth, we don't belong anywhere: we are too terrestrial to be able to keep the divine gift, but have now become too divine to forget it."[2]

Just as amphibians are able to live either on land or in water, so is the soul well-adapted for life on both higher and lower planes of reality. For while spirit is always spiritual, and matter is always material, Plotinus teaches that the soul has a wide-ranging capacity.

This accounts for the amazing variety of human pursuits, interests, inclinations and preoccupations. Some are angelic, some beastly. Some are refined, some crude. Some are uplifting, some degrading. There is nothing we cannot be because the soul is both all that is heavenly and all that is earthly.

> *For the soul is many things, and all things, both the things above and the things below down to the limits of all life, and we are each one of us an intelligible universe. . . . And since it is a thing belonging to the frontier between the worlds, and occupies a corresponding position, it moves in both directions.* [III-4-3, IV-4-3]

The soul is, we might say, footloose and fancy free. Like someone who has dual citizenship in two countries, nothing prevents us from crossing and re-crossing the border that separates the spiritual and material realms.

> *Soul is something separable.* [IV-3-20]

However, this freedom of movement carries with it the danger that we may leave a better place for a worse. From spiritual oneness we descend to physical manyness. Why would we want to do this? Because, says Plotinus, we can.

> *As if it* [soul] *cannot bear its being to be one when it is capable of being all the things that it is.* [VI-2-6]

The soul is pulled in two directions, toward unity, and toward multiplicity. One way takes us closer to the creator, the other closer to creation.

> *The individual souls, certainly, have an intelligent desire consisting in the impulse to return to itself springing from the principle from which they came into being, but they also possess a power directed to the world here below.* [IV-8-4]

Our intelligent desire is to return to spirit and the One. But if a soul is unintelligent, having lost sight of where genuine truth, goodness, and beauty reside, then it will seek what is lesser than itself, materiality, rather than what is greater, spirit and the One. If a soul desires to express its creative capacities and become involved with what has been created, inevitably it will be drawn downward to the physical creation.

> *And we remain with all the rest of our intelligible part above, but by its ultimate fringe we are tied to the world below.* [III-4-3]

Our involvement with worldly affairs has no effect on the part of soul that always remains in touch with the spiritual realm. It is possible, then, to straddle the two worlds, enjoying the lower without totally leaving the higher. In an ideal situation we wouldn't forget that we are permanent denizens of Spirit paying a visit to Matter. The reality, however, generally is quite different.

For most of us consider Earth to be our home. Even though death is inevitable, we still view this universe as a lasting habitation rather than as a place to visit temporarily. This is evidenced by the fact that people generally are much more concerned about the health of their bodies than the well-being of their souls, notwithstanding the lip service that may be paid to religions or spiritual paths. To understand how immersed we are in matter rather than spirit, just consider: What mostly occupies our attention each day?

Recall that creation is contemplation. Whatever soul or spirit pays attention to, that comes into being. The Soul of the All contemplates the forms of the spiritual world and brings the physical universe into existence. But the contemplation of this universal soul leaves it unmoved (which explains why the laws of nature are so dependable and immutable) while the contemplation of lesser souls generally draws them to what has been created.

Plotinus teaches that every soul has a power of illumination. This is what brings life to materiality, for matter is inert, formless, and dead without the energizing intelligence of soul. Because part of the soul always remains in touch with the spiritual world some of this illuminating power brightens "heaven." The rest is directed downward, just as a lantern perched on a ladder casts some of its light upon the ceiling and some upon the floor: the higher the ladder, the lesser the amount of light that reaches ground level.

> *All souls then illuminate the heaven and give it the greatest and first part of themselves, but illuminate the rest of the world with their secondary parts.* [IV-3-17]

The problem is not so much with the illumination itself but with the movement of the soul that is doing the illuminating. Everything would be fine if we would just stay put, high up on the ladder, as the Soul of the All does. Then we could enjoy the spectacle of this physical creation from an elevated state of consciousness. We'd have a better and broader view of things and would remain detached from the messy side of life: all the death, disease, distress, delusion and dissatisfaction that comes from mistaking shadows for substance.

Unfortunately, our presence on Earth is evidence that we have become enthralled by what soul has illumined. We're casting much of our light on the bottom level of the cosmos because we want to be as close as possible to physical creation.

Instead of wisely choosing to return to the One we've made a pilgrimage in the opposite direction to worship at the Shrine of Materiality. The creation, rather than the creator, has captured our love and attention. It's as if a father took his son down into the basement and presented him with a wonderful surprise: a train set that fills the whole room! The boy is overjoyed and exceedingly grateful. He will have so much fun playing with what he's been given. And he does for a while. But then the boy becomes so absorbed in operating the locomotive, switching tracks, coupling and uncoupling train cars, and all the other activities involved in managing his own little rail line that he forgets *this is just a game*.

What was at first carefree fun gradually becomes more and more worrisome. There are mechanical breakdowns. Parts fall off and the child doesn't know where they're supposed to go. His father could get him, let's say, back on track, but the boy is too absorbed in dealing with the trials and tribulations of his make-believe world to call out for help. Besides, it's kind of satisfying to cope with all these problems. He feels important; he's in charge of things, just like Dad.

The vicissitudes of a child's obsessive play are easily rectified. All it takes to break the spell is a parent entering the room: "Johnny, stop playing and wash your hands for dinner." "Okay, Mom. I forgot what time it was." However, most of us human souls have gotten ourselves into more of a morass because we've entered so deeply into creation's play. We've lost sight of what is real and truly worthy of concern, and what isn't.

> *Then as the things which are illuminated* [by souls] *need more care, just as the steersmen of ships in a storm concentrate more and more on the care of their ships and are unaware that they are forgetting themselves, that they are in danger of being dragged down with the wreck of their ships, these souls incline downwards more with what is theirs.* [IV-3-17]

How strange, says Plotinus, that life has been hijacked by what is lifeless. The soul freely creates and then is held hostage by what it has created. Fortunately, those who are dissatisfied with their current dwelling place are not bound to remain where they are.

> *But if you have come by now to dislike the world, you are not compelled to remain a citizen of it.* [II-9-9]

Descent Is Debasement

ARETHA FRANKLIN nicely summed up a basic human desire when she sang about wanting a little respect.

Yes, almost universally we feel that we deserve a little respect. And generally not just a little but a lot. One wants people to respect one's ethnicity; maleness or femaleness; sexual orientation; religion; nationality; and role as parent, boss, breadwinner, coach, teacher, spouse, leader, or whatever. It doesn't matter if we're poor or rich, smart or dumb, tall or short, fat or thin, old or young, slacker or workaholic. Everyone wants to be respected for who they are.

Plotinus agrees that the pure soul deserves respect. But he unabashedly declares that we have willfully descended from the purity of the spiritual world, thereby debasing ourselves by embracing materiality.

So this has the effect of leveling out the earthly playing field where each of us is trying to stand at least equal to, if not a bit higher than, our fellow humans. No matter what our position is, we're on the lowest level of the cosmos and don't have much to be proud about. We've descended from the lofty spiritual heights and surrendered much of the power that comes from being a part of the whole rather than just a part.

> And so this soul, which belongs to the whole intelligible universe and hides its part in the whole, leapt out, we might say, from the whole to a part, and actualizes itself as a part in it, as if a fire able to burn everything was compelled to burn some little thing although it had all its power. [VI-4-16]

Each of us, in other words, is now almost totally concerned with the little bit of reality that immediately surrounds us and that we even consider to *be* us. One sign of how far we have fallen is that the slightest worldly affront or failure can have such a great effect on our self-respect. If we hadn't lost touch with the wholeness of spirit, the solid ground of the true self, we wouldn't have such a need to prop up our self-images with shaky substitutes.

If I believe that I'm a worthy person because I play golf well, then a string of double-bogeys is going to get me down in the dumps. If my main satisfaction in life comes from my job, then getting fired will be a nightmare. If there is nothing more important to me than my spouse, marital separation by divorce or death will throw me into a tailspin. The problem, says Plotinus, is that we're no longer solidly centered in the immovable whole of creation, but have come to believe that we are parts who both support, and are supported by, other parts.

> *But they* [souls] *change from the whole to being a part and belonging to themselves, and, as if they were tired of being together, they each go to their own. . . . And in its separation from the whole it* [a soul] *embarks on one single thing and flies from everything else.* [IV-8-4]

We once stood on the border between the spiritual and physical worlds. One way, toward spirit, led to light, truth, love, life, and union. The other way, toward matter, led to darkness, illusion, discord, death, and separation. Each of us knows which path we chose: if we are consciously aware only of earthly existence, and all that comes with it, then we embarked on the downward course. Now we're solidly established in the shadows of reality, and must seek the forsaken spiritual light.

> *The partial soul, then, is illuminated when it goes towards that which is before it* [spirit and the One]—*for then it meets reality*—*but when it goes towards what comes after it, it goes towards non-existence.* [III-9-3]

So we come to what Pierre Hadot says is the great Plotinian question:

> *Why, then, do we not remain up there?* [VI-9-10][1]

Why would we choose ignorance over wisdom, earth over heaven, shadows over substance, many over the One? If we knew the answer we'd have a clue as to what it takes to move in the opposite direction. It's much as if we found ourselves standing in the middle of a large supermarket but couldn't remember why we entered the store. We can't get rid of a nagging feeling that we came in for something important, so wander the aisles hoping that when we see it we'll know that *this* is what we were looking for. If we could find it, we'd be able to leave the store and head for home.

However, for most of us there is no end to our shopping. Nothing fully satisfies. Every experience, whether pleasurable or unpleasurable, leads to another need, another want, another craving, another walk down another aisle of this earthly bazaar that promises so much more happiness and well-being than it delivers.

Plotinus asks us to look at our situation from a fresh perspective. Maybe, he suggests, we already have what we came for: ourselves.

> *What is it, then, which has made the souls forget their father, God, and be ignorant of themselves and him, even though they are parts which come from his higher world and altogether belong to it? The beginning of evil for them was audacity and coming to birth and the first otherness and the wishing to belong to themselves.* [V-1-1]

So that feeling of "I need something more" doesn't arise because of an unfulfilled desire for something the world has to offer. Rather, our original audacious wish to be a part rather than the whole, to belong to ourselves rather than to spirit and the One, has been granted. Our independence just hasn't turned out to be as satisfying as we expected. We wanted to live apart from our spiritual parents and now we have. The problem is that our separation has made us heartbroken but we can't recall what has made us so sad. All we know is our sorrow, not its cause: homesickness.

We're orphans. We've lost our father, the One, and our mother, spirit. We thought it would be lots of fun to descend from the close-knit familial unity of the spiritual world and live on our own. Well, things haven't worked out so rosily and now we're in a good news/bad news situation.

The good news is that nothing prevents us from returning to our spiritual home. The bad news is that we're no longer just "us," but our true selves and something more. What has been added on to each of us is an ego that is unwilling to give up its separate existence, and considers unconscious material things to be more interesting and important than the conscious soul that is doing the considering.

This is a bizarre state of affairs made all the more bizarre by how natural it seems to most of us. It's merely unfortunate to be abjectly poor, but it's crazy if someone chooses to forget about his vast wealth and live as a pauper all the while wanting to be rich. It would be insane to revere others who are well-off and despise one's own poverty while a forgotten treasure gathers dust in the attic. Yet this is what we are doing.

There is nothing more precious than the pure soul and this is what each of us truly is. Sadly, our inner spiritual wealth remains unnoticed while we chase after worthless material baubles. Every longing for something outside of ourselves is a reflection of how far we have fallen. "That is more worthy than me" is the unspoken declaration that accompanies every worldly desire.

> *Since they* [the souls] *do not any more see their father or themselves* [as pure soul], *they despise themselves through ignorance of their birth and honor other things, admiring everything rather than themselves.* [V-1-1]

Here's an important point: Plotinus makes it clear that earthly things don't debase the soul. The cause of our debasement is giving material things greater honor than they deserve and forgetting our true nature. It isn't the world that draws us away from spirituality but rather our inability to control what is meant to be under our command. Rather than mastering materiality we have become mastered by it.

> *If it* [soul] *escapes quickly it takes no harm by acquiring a knowledge of evil and coming to know the nature of wickedness, and manifesting its powers. . . . But when it wants to direct a part* [of the universe] *it is isolated and comes to be in that part in which it is.* [IV-8-5, IV-7-13]

What should have been a brief visit to this physical plane has turned into a lengthy sojourn. Plotinus says that souls come here to show off, so to speak, what they can do. The Soul of the All provides us with a playground, the universe, and the individual souls are free to romp around within it. A city is built here, a farm springs up there; a painting is created by this soul, a song by that one.

We don't lose anything by simply coming into physical existence, for the soul is eternal and unchangeable. The danger is that something will be added onto us, an inordinate concern for matter rather than spirit. A child happily plays with a doll, but when her mother asks her to put it away a furious tantrum erupts. Pleasure turns into pain. Attachment to a physical object creates emotional distress. Mind is controlled by matter, a reversal of the natural order of the cosmos.

The mystic philosopher, then, treads lightly through the world. He or she is happy to explore this furthest emanation of the One, if only to realize that here is not the best place to be. Light is made manifest by darkness as is truth by falsehood. If we had never ex-perienced what it is to be a part there would not be such a longing to return to the whole. We were free to come and now we are free to go if we so desire.

But if the souls came willingly, why do you blame the universe into which you came of your own free will, when it gives you leave, too, to get out of it, if any of you dislike it? [II-9-8]

Coming into a physical body doesn't necessarily degrade us because it is possible, though rather rare, to live in accord with spirit even while sojourning in matter. Those who are able to do this may be called saints, prophets, or sages. Universally they tell us that, when rightly viewed, earthly existence is the best possible material reflection of spiritual reality and so should be revered.

However, spiritual blindness afflicts us when we lose perspective and worship what has been created rather than the creator. Even worse, says Plotinus, our idolatry becomes focused on just a small slice of creation, the relatively few people, places, and things with which we are immediately concerned. How can we even dream of returning to the One when we are so immersed in caring for bits and pieces of the many?

Evil Is Emptiness

A UNITED STATES Supreme Court justice famously said about pornography, "I know it when I see it." Most of us can say the same about evil or at least what we consider to be evil. For evil, like pornography, is much easier to recognize than to define. That pain, suffering, harm, and hate exist is undeniable. Every person has experienced the undesirable side of life, which is a useful (if general) definition of evil.

But what produces evil? Is it a creation of the mind of man, a purely personal concept that reflects only subjective likes and dislikes? Or is it an objective reality, like gravity or electromagnetism, part and parcel of nature's universal order?

There is no end of answers that have been proposed to such questions. Debates about moral relativism and moral absolutism have raged for millennia, and show no sign of abating.

Unfortunately, in modern times these arguments usually bring out far more rancor, judgment, stridency, rigidity, and holier-than-thou sanctimoniousness than cool reason and calm discourse. So it is refreshing to ponder Plotinus's teachings about evil, for he is much less concerned with laying out a code of conduct than with understanding what such a code should be based on.

As an aid to understanding Plotinus's perspective, consider the difference between saying "It's hot" or "It's cold" and knowing that temperature is a measure of molecules in motion. The temperature of something is objective. It can range from absolute zero to near-infinity, as in the earliest moments of the big bang. However, the interpretation we give to that temperature, hot, warm, cool, cold, is subjective. What a polar bear feels in icy water must be quite different from what a human feels.

Similarly, Plotinus teaches that evil is a name given to the lower range of what might be termed the good scale. This varies from infinity with the One, to essentially zero with undefined matter. Thus Plotinus comes down squarely on the objectivist side of the ethics debate, for he says that ethics is inseparable from reality.

The greatest good is the One, for this is ultimate truth, unchanging and eternal. Whatever is not the One is less than Good. Thus as emanation proceeds—spirit from the One, soul from spirit, materiality from soul—goodness steadily diminishes along with reality (or being), just as the sun's heat is lower in the distant reaches of the solar system.

In general, we must define evil as a falling short of good; and there must be a falling short of good here below, because the good is in something else. [III-2-5]

How simple. Evil is a falling short of good, just as darkness is a falling short of light and cold is a falling short of warmth.

Let's consider how this understanding can liberate us from some unproductive misconceptions. First, we mustn't think that evil stands alone as a substantial reality in its own right, that there is a Devil or force of darkness engaged in some sort of cosmic battle with God or the forces of light. Plotinus teaches that immaterial forms are the foundation of everything that manifests within physical or spiritual creation. And evil isn't one of those forms.

For there is no Form of Evil. . . . But the nature which is opposed to all form is privation. . . . So if there is evil in the soul, it will be the privation in it which will be evil and vice, and nothing outside. [V-9-10, I-8-11]

Everything is good in itself; nothing is evil in itself. If I'm bad it isn't because the Devil made me do it. I'm just insufficiently filled with the Good. Wrongdoing is produced by an internal absence, not an external presence. Nothing is more of a nothing than evil. Absolute zero isn't the presence of something called cold; it is the complete absence of the energy of molecular motion, or heat.

So this brings us to another common misconception: that evil is unnatural and that it is both possible and desirable to eradicate it. If we can pull up weeds from our gardens it might seem that we should be able to rid the earth of evils, especially since Plotinus says that evil is nothing, a privation. How difficult could it be to do away with nothing?

Well, it is so difficult as to be impossible. Evils never can be done away with because anything other than the One will not be the absolute Good. So if there is to be a creation there must be evil, for evil is absence of good. Or, if we wish to speak positively (though less accurately), the presence of less-than-good.

Then are the evils in the All necessary, because they follow on the prior realities? Rather because if they did not exist the All would be imperfect. [II-3-18]

Still, it is difficult to understand why some things exist. I often think after being served some food containing disgusting crimson chunks of gustatory evil, "Wouldn't the world be a nicer place without red peppers?" Of course, I'm not a great lover of spicy food, so I'm biased. Which is precisely Plotinus's point. He reminds us that everything in creation is a useful part of the whole, even what we call evils. If we possessed a broader vision we would see this clearly.

As Pierre Hadot says, "Evil is not extraneous to the order of the universe; rather, it is the result of this order. . . . To accept the universal order is to accept the existence of degrees of goodness, and, thus, indirectly, to accept evil. We must not criticize the order of the world just because there are consequences in it which seem bad to us."[1]

We are like people who know nothing about painting and yet reproach the artist because he did not put pretty colors everywhere, whereas the artist distributed the appropriate color to each and every spot. Cities, too—even those which have a good constitution—are not made up of equal citizens.

It is as if one were to criticize a drama because all the characters in it were not heroes, but it also contained a slave and a foulmouthed hayseed. And yet they make the play complete, and it wouldn't have been any good if you took them away. [III-2-11][2]

If there is to be a beginning, there has to be an end. A start does not exist without a finish. We can rail all we want about the suffering, depravities, ignorance, ugliness, and evils in this world, yet Plotinus's simple logic speaks softly and clearly: after the First must come a last.

Since not only the Good exists, there must be the last end to the process of going out past it, or if one prefers to put it like this, going down or going away: and this last, after which nothing else can come into being, is evil. [I-8-7]

The furthest emanation of the One is matter. So primordial matter is evil in the sense that it is deprived. It is as empty of spiritual form as anything can be. Hence, if we live in the material world we live in a world of evil. Marsilio Ficino says, "Since souls are divine, why do they live such unholy lives? Because they inhabit an unholy house in an unholy land."[3]

But whenever reading the *Enneads* gets us depressed about our miserable, lowly condition, Plotinus kindly offers us a hand up. He is an incurable optimist. Just as every shadow heralds the presence of light, so does the emptiness of evil pronounce the fullness of the One, or God.

> *Moreover, it* [evil] *provides, in and of itself, many useful side effects: it wakes us up, and awakens the spirit and intelligence, as we are forced to stand against the inroads of wrongdoing; and it makes us learn how great a good is virtue, by comparison with the evils which are the lot of wrongdoers.*
>
> *Now, it was not for this purpose that evils came about, but since they have come about, the world makes use of them as appropriate. . . . This is a sign of the greatest power: to be able to make good use even of evils.* [III-2-5][4]

If we were content with our lives here on earth we wouldn't have much desire to seek a greater good. "Absence," it is said, "makes the heart grow fonder." Sometimes closeness breeds a certain contempt, or at least a blasé taken-for-grantedness. Just as a person often enjoys the company of his or her spouse more after being apart for a while so is it possible for the soul to more passionately embrace the better after experiencing the worse.

> *In those whose faculties are too weak for them to be able to know evil by the mere faculty of knowledge, prior to any experience, the experience of evil makes the knowledge of the Good more clear.* [IV-8-7][5]

We don't fully appreciate good health until we get sick. Something negative, an absence, can more clearly define its opposite, a presence. Air is never so precious to a man as when he is hit in the stomach and loses his breath for a few seconds. In like fashion, our longing for the One intensifies when the presence of that Good is feebly felt but deeply desired.

The soul remembers, albeit unconsciously, what it was like to be fully immersed in God. Now, like fish out of water, we lie gasping for goodness on the arid shore of physical existence. This is why matter is absolute evil, for it is absolutely deprived of the Good.

The soul doesn't become evil by simply descending into the physical universe. At that point the soul is merely deficient in spirit, having departed from the incomparable abundance of the world of forms. It is still good, just not as good here as it was there. Materiality, however, provides the opportunity (not the necessity) for the soul to fall into desperate straits, and most of us have done just that.

Evil, being emptiness, is akin to a pit that is ready to receive the unwary. If the soul treads carefully in the world there is no problem. But even a single misstep toward matter and farther away from spirit can have dire consequences. If we're walking along the edge of a deep abyss, losing our balance on a few loose pebbles can take us all the way to the bottom.

> *But living beings which have of themselves a movement under their own control might incline sometimes to what is better, sometimes to what is worse. It is probably not worth enquiring into the reason for this self-caused turning towards the worse; for a deviation which is slight to begin with, as it goes on in this way continually makes the fault wider and graver.* [III-2-4]

So Plotinus's oft-repeated advice is for the soul to remain firmly rooted in higher realms of consciousness. Then there is no danger of falling into evil. We can do this on Earth right now, right here, even though materiality is nothing other than the ultimate emptying of goodness. With the aid of philosophy, the pursuit of wisdom, it is possible to pass through the world like a teetotaler enjoying a stroll in a beer garden. All one needs to do is say, "No thank you," to what is being proffered.

> *We must consider, too, what Plato means when he says "Evils can never be done away with," but exist "of necessity.". . . But when he says "we must take flight from thence" he is no longer referring to life on earth. For "flight," he says, is not going away from earth but being on earth "just and holy with the help of wisdom."* [I-8-6]

Matter Is Malignant

FLY FROM EVILS. That's the advice Plotinus, echoing Plato, just gave us. But this is a spiritual sort of flying that doesn't require wings. For we won't get away from evils by ascending to a mountain top or rocketing off to another planet. What we must fly from is our love affair with matter, particularly the matter that we wrongly believe to be us, our bodies.

> How then is one to escape? Not by movement in place, Plato says, but by winning virtue and separating oneself from the body: for in this way one separates oneself from matter as well, since the man who lives in close connection with the body is also closely connected with matter. [I-8-7]

But why does Plotinus consider matter, and by extension, the body, to be so malignant?

This seems to contradict his assertion that evil is emptiness, a deficiency of good. Matter certainly doesn't seem to be empty. Rather, for most of us it is the bedrock of our lives, what can be relied on when all else fails. If we've had a bad day at work, the chocolate box is loyally waiting to comfort us when we get home. Family and friends may let us down but a walk on the beach or a stroll in the woods reassures us that nature's companionship is never-failing.

To Plotinus, matter is alive and even divine in a certain sense, for it is the body of the Soul of the All. But since physical creation is the lowest manifestation of being there isn't much good to be found in it. The universe is akin to the dregs at the bottom of a cup of coffee, almost totally drained of pleasing flavor.

Recall that the strong, clear essence of reality is spirit, the World of Forms. The spiritual realm is true being where all that could possibly exist does exist perfectly and eternally. Spirit, as we read earlier, "gives to the Soul of the All, and Soul gives from itself to the soul next after it."

This last soul is what we call nature. Its product, the physical universe, may appear beautiful to our eyes but Plotinus cautions us that material reality is twice-removed from ultimate reality. Our world is the residue of the spiritual forms, which are greatly dimmed and weakened in the course of their transformative passage through the Soul of the All and nature.

Its [the last soul's] *product is a living being, but a very imperfect one, and one which finds its own life disgusting since it is the worst of living things, ill-conditioned and savage, made of inferior matter, a sort of sediment of the prior realities, bitter and embittering.* [II-3-17]

These words sound harsh but we need to clearly understand what Plotinus means by matter. He isn't referring to all the objects we sense in the world, such as plants, clouds, rocks, and water, nor is he even talking about the unseen chemical elements that make up everything material. For all of these manifestations of matter possess some form. And since forms come from the spiritual world, the World of Forms, material forms are the manifestation of spirit here on earth.

What is truly malignant to Plotinus is primordial matter, matter completely emptied of form. We can't perceive this variety of matter, for it is devoid of any quality that could be sensed. It is not a body, because a body is matter shaped by form. So matter is immaterial, barely existent.

Hard to believe? Consider these findings of modern science.

The familiar objects of everyday life are almost entirely empty space. If a hydrogen atom could be magnified until its nucleus was the size of a ping-pong ball, then its electron, as small as a grain of dust, would be whirling about some three hundred meters away. In a neutron star, matter is compacted down to its essence. If the sun became a neutron star, its radius would be seventy thousand times smaller than it is now, but its mass would be the same (a cubic inch of a neutron star has a mass of about a billion tons).

Thus when form is removed from physical matter a vanishingly small amount of sheer bulk is all that remains. Astronomer Frank Shu says, "A sugarcube of neutron-star stuff on Earth would weigh as much as all of humanity! This illustrates again how much of humanity is empty space."[1]

For matter has not even being—if it had it would by this means have a share in good. . . . Matter, then, is incorporeal, since body is posterior and a composite, and matter with something else produces body. [I-8-5, III-6-7]

Perhaps this incorporeal undefined matter is what scientists are approaching as they delve ever deeper into the subatomic realm in their quest to discover the essence of physical existence. Atoms are found to be made of electrons, protons, and neutrons. Protons and neutrons are found to be made of quarks. And what are electrons and quarks made of? No one knows. But the answer may be "strings."

According to physicist Brian Greene, string theory posits that the fundamental constituents of the universe are not point particles, but almost infinitely small one-dimensional filaments that vibrate to and fro: "All strings are absolutely identical. Differences between the particles arise because their respective strings undergo different resonant vibrational patterns."[2]

This emphasizes Plotinus's teaching that primordial matter is as near to nothing as anything can be. For string theory holds that the ultimate essence of all sub-atomic particles is identical, a sameness broken only by varying vibrations that produce different patterns (or forms).

To Plotinus the form is what is important, not the medium of matter that transmits a semblance of the incorporeal spiritual forms to the physical realm. It's rather like when I have a grand insight about something, "Ah, now I understand," and then I try to describe my revelation to someone else. To communicate, words are necessary, but inadequate. Once we get beyond the simplest messages, the form of what is said outwardly is always less than the form of what is known inwardly.

This is the pitfall of matter. It diffuses and dims spiritual forms that in reality are unified and bright.

Matter darkens the illumination, the light from that source, by mixture with itself. [I-8-14]

The problem, it seems, is that physical matter is always empty, a void that can be covered over by a semblance of form but never is filled. This is why Plotinus tells us that matter's nature is contrary to form. When form mixes with matter, it isn't truly combined, as when milk and honey are put into a blender and a sweet drink is made. Instead, form and matter are akin to water and oil; they lie next to each other and on the surface seem to be one substance but actually remain separate.

By contrast, Plotinus speaks of divine matter in the spiritual, or intelligible, world that does take on the light and life of forms.

So those who say that matter is substance must be considered to be speaking correctly if they are speaking of matter in the intelligible world. For that which underlies form There is substance, or rather, considered along with the form imposed upon it, it makes a whole which is illuminated substance. [II-4-5]

The danger of descending into materiality is that we will be dazzled by the insubstantial wrappings that cover the deadness of matter. These wrappings, images of the spiritual forms, are undeniably attractive. But they are akin to the reflection in a mirror of a beautiful person. The image may be beguiling, yet when we reach out to it we find there really is nothing that can be grasped, just photons shimmering upon an empty surface.

So it [matter] *is actually a phantasm: so it is actually a falsity.* [II-5-5]

Matter, says Plotinus, is like reflective glass. There is nothing in it but the spiritual forms, which come from elsewhere. Take away these forms and what remains is utter emptiness. This is not the formlessness of the One, for the One is formless because of a surfeit, not a deficiency; since it is all things, it cannot take on the limiting form of any particular thing. No, the formlessness of matter is complete absence of form; since it is no thing, it is capable of reflecting the image of any form.

The fullness of the One reaches its utter contrary in the emptiness of matter. Since the One is absolute Good, matter is absolute non-Good, which is what Plotinus considers evil to be.

Anything which lacks something, but has something else, might perhaps hold a middle position between good and evil, if its lack and its having more or less balance; but that which has nothing because it is in want, or rather is want, must necessarily be evil. [II-4-16]

The soul yearns to reunite with the spiritual forms: virtue, beauty, strength, and so on. However, this is possible only when the soul returns to the immaterial world of spirit, for here on Earth we sense only the shadows of spiritual substance. So long as we are enthralled by material people and things we will remain separate from spirit. As John Dillon explains, "Essentially, matter throws up a screen of attractive illusion, which the soul must see through, and evil is its not being able to do that."[3]

Matter is particularly malignant because, like cancer, it masquerades as something normal, even something good. Just as cancer cells are unrecognized by the body as malevolent and stealthily take over more and more of a person's energy, so does materiality generally capture an increasing share of the soul's care and attention. This happens quietly and naturally, an unnoticed sleight of hand that nevertheless results in the theft of our spirituality.

> But because of the power and nature of good, evil is not only evil; since it must necessarily appear, it is bound in a sort of beautiful fetters, as some prisoners are in chains of gold. [I-8-15]

We need to look beyond the attractive glitter of the physical world and consider what it would be like to be freed from matter entirely. Isn't it true that we spend almost all of our time dealing with problems that wouldn't exist, and desires that wouldn't arise, if our souls weren't connected to bodies?

> But if one considers that things external to the soul are evils, illness or poverty for instance, how will one trace them back to the nature of matter? Illness is defect and excess of material bodies which do not keep order and measure; ugliness is matter not mastered by form; poverty is lack and deprivation of things which we need because of the matter with which we are coupled, whose very nature is to be need. [I-8-5]

If we're ill and want a lasting cure rather than merely symptomatic relief, it's important to properly diagnose the cause of our suffering and get to the root of the problem. That is just what Plotinus does in the intriguing preceding passage, which deserves careful consideration.

Soul, he implies, has no share in evil. Evil is absence of good, and the pure soul has no such deficiency. Being essentially identical with spirit, every soul contains all of the forms that comprise creation. Each of us is a spiritual world and the spiritual world is within each of us. So how is it that we continually feel we are lacking something?

The cause of this perpetual neediness is that whatever is external to the soul will be less than soul. So when we turn to matter we aren't making deposits to our happiness accounts, we're actually making withdrawals.

The soul is never sick. It is the body that falls ill because the order that keeps it healthy is precarious, a house of cards that collapses at the slightest tremor of disease or trauma.

The soul is never ugly. Ugliness is an insufficiency of form, much more a spiritual defect than a physical lack that can be rectified by a plastic surgeon or a cosmetic makeover.

The soul is never poor. Poverty is caused by the soul's descent into materiality, for the physical body needs food, shelter and clothing to survive. Without enough of these so-called material goods we feel impoverished, since we no longer enjoy a carefree and bodiless spiritual life.

Matter is the cause of most, if not all, of our problems. Failing to realize this, we turn to material things and bodily forms in fruitless attempts to resolve those problems. Fruitless because a void cannot be filled by nothingness; hunger cannot be assuaged by an empty plate. Since matter is a barrier, not a bridge, to well-being, it is foolish to expect that the people and objects of this world will bring us any sort of lasting happiness. The cure to our troubles will not be found in what is producing our distressed condition.

We need to separate from matter and cleave to spirit. In that union, not the soul's present marriage with materiality, will be found the peace and bliss we long for.

"This is the life of the gods," without sorrow and blessed; evil is nowhere here. [I-8-2]

Body Is a Bother

LOOKING BACK, it probably was a mistake for me to adopt the critter. I'll tell you, caring for him is exhausting, almost a full-time job.

Morning, noon, and night he's got to be fed. If I forget one of his meals he gets cranky and pesters me until his stomach is full. That keeps him quiet for a while but soon he's bothering me again because he needs to go to the bathroom and get rid of what I just gave him. Okay, I take care of that and finally I figure I've got some time to myself. Wrong!

Now he wants some exercise because he's an energetic animal. So we go off to the park for a jog. Everything is running along smoothly until he notices a female of breeding age. Then I've got all I can do to hold him back from making a nuisance of himself. Thank heavens he's leash-trained. Sometimes he's come close to getting in a fight with another animal and I worry about what might happen if I lost control of him.

To be honest, he's most pleasant to be around when he's sleeping. Other times, it's just one demand after another, an almost constant yapping and whining for something or another: Feed me! Play with me! Groom me! Take me for a walk! Let's go in the car! I need to go potty! And it's not as if he comes free. I pay a lot for the privilege of keeping this nuisance. His food isn't cheap; we've had to take lots of training classes together; his health care is expensive and will get even more costly as the years go by.

You might be wondering why, if he's so difficult to take care of, I don't find another home for him. Well, as bothersome as he is, it's not easy to make a break with someone you've been close to for so long, especially when that someone is yourself—or, more precisely, my own body. It's difficult to separate the two, the bodiless me and the bodily me, so for now we're involved in this strange relationship I've described.

> *For every man is double, one of him is the sort of compound being and one of him is himself. . . . So "we" is used in two senses, either including the beast or referring to that which even in our present life transcends it. The beast is the body which has been given life. But the true man is different, clear of these affections.* [II-3-9, I-1-10]

It sounds strange to have the body called a beast. Yet there is no doubt that we are animals. All of our gross bodily functions and activities—eating, drinking, digesting, defecating and urinating, mating, and so on—are shared by other mammals. However, humans also possess an intelligence other animals lack and it is this quality of the soul that makes it possible for us to be "clear of these affections" if we use our reason and intuition rightly.

It is natural, says Plotinus, for the soul to be the alpha in its relationship with the beast. Soul, whether the Soul of the All or individual souls, should care for the body, not be controlled by the body. Then the soul, so to speak, is top dog and can enjoy the best of both the material and spiritual worlds.

Unfortunately, most of us have fallen into a dysfunctional relationship with our bodies. We've allowed the beast to get the upper hand and even though it seems like we're in control of the creature, the body actually is calling the shots (cat owners, especially, can relate to this).

Just consider how much of our day is devoted to meeting bodily needs. We shop for food, then have to cook and eat it. The body must be cleansed, clothed, groomed, and exercised. Sexual drives lead to dating, marriage, and child raising. We must find the time and money to keep up homes that are basically elaborate dens to comfortably house the beast.

Soul enlivens the body but the body can deaden the soul with all the care it requires. When soul entered into a partnership with body, Plotinus tells us that the advantages accrued to the material partner.

Let us assume, then, that there is a mixture [of soul and body]. *But, if this is so, the worse element, the body, will be improved and the other element, the soul, will be made worse.* [I-1-4]

A person's true self is soul. Soul is the essence of his identity, the core of his consciousness. In its bodiless state, soul is free to enjoy the delights of the spiritual forms or the ineffable wonder of the One. There, soul is united with universal order. It is a drop in an ocean of spirituality, an instrument playing in harmony with the cosmic symphony. This is freedom, the freedom to know and love reality as it truly is, as a part of the whole that lies beyond the illusory divisions of materiality.

When a soul descends into physical existence and attaches itself to a body, it enters the realm of many. Here, far from the One, what remains of primal unity is interconnectedness, lawful relationships, give and take, cause and effect. Natural consequences now constrain the soul's freedom of action. For while we may be free to act, we aren't free to avoid the results of our actions.

> *Now when the soul is without body it is in absolute control of itself and free, and outside the causation of the physical universe; but when it is brought into body it is no longer in all ways in control, as it forms part of an order with other things.* [III-1-8]

Recall Plotinus's teaching that the physical universe is the body of the Soul of the All. Since human bodies are part of the physical universe this means that there is an overlap between the particular body being cared for by an individual soul and the universal body, the universe, being cared for by the Soul of the All. When the locus of control is in doubt the universal triumphs over the individual. Or we might say, "man proposes, and God disposes."

To believe that we can control the world, a small part of the world, or even just our own bodies, is to be ignorant of the interconnectedness and impermanence of physical reality. The mystic philosopher recognizes that the body will be troublesome only if we allow ourselves to be unduly bothered by its desires and cravings, its pleasures and pains, its joys and sorrows. Just as a pet owner isn't hurt if his animal breaks a leg, so should the sage view his own body in a similarly detached manner.

> *For as there are two reasons why the soul's fellowship with body is displeasing, that body becomes a hindrance to thought and that it fills the soul with pleasures, desires, and griefs, neither of these things could happen to a soul which has not sunk into the interior of its body, and is not anyone's property, and does not belong to the body, but the body belongs to it, and is of such a kind as to want nothing and be defective in nothing.* [IV-8-2]

We might do well to imagine that our bodies are wearing collars with ID tags that read: "My name is Matter. I belong to Soul." If we can have the attitude that we possess and control our bodies instead of our bodies possessing and controlling us, then we will go through life much more contentedly. After all, if a person's dog or cat gets sick, runs away, or dies, he or she is able to go on living a human life. Similarly, Plotinus teaches that the immaterial soul is unaffected by material experiences whether these be tribulations or triumphs.

Why, then, is a person's sense of well-being influenced so much by what happens to his or her body? A bad case of the flu leaves us feeling listless; after a relaxing massage, all is right with the world. This is, says Plotinus, a result of being asleep and dreaming that we are our bodies. This waking dream, of course, seems fully real, but so can the dreaming that occurs when our eyes are closed. We've all had terrifying nightmares that were no less scary for being purely a product of our own brains, as well as glorious visions that were both delightful and imaginary.

Those who believe that what the senses tell them is real, says Plotinus, are dreaming. And they will be affected by their dreams, for good or ill, until they are able to wake up from the slumber of physical reality.

> *They act like people dreaming, who think that the things they see as real actually exist, when they are only dreams. For the activity of sense-perception is that of the soul asleep; for it is the part of the soul that is in the body that sleeps; but the true wakening is a true getting up from the body, not with the body.* [III-6-6]

The soul is a unity, formless and without parts, but its powers are many. When soul descends from the spiritual realm to the material world, some of its powers remain above while others are directed below. This creates a division in us. We generally are unconscious of our higher powers because our attention is focused almost entirely on our lower powers, such as sense-perception.

> *It* [soul] *happens to become divided in the sphere of bodies, though it was not affected in this way before it gave itself to bodies.* [IV-1-1]

Spiritual wakening occurs when soul is able to separate from body and be aware of all of its powers, not just those that can be exercised in concert with a physical frame.

We then will realize the true relationship of soul and body, which is poorly understood by even religiously-minded people. Soul commonly is considered to be some sort of mysterious life force that enters the body at birth and leaves it at death. Movies sometimes portray this as a small blob of light descending to or ascending from a person.

There may be some grain of truth in this imagery but Plotinus would challenge it on several counts. First, the soul cannot be seen with physical eyes so any sensory depiction will be misleading. Second, in truth the body is in the soul not the soul in body. Thus it is more accurate to say that the body enters and leaves the soul when we are born and die.

Dominic O'Meara says, "Plotinus asks us to reverse our normal way of thinking. We should not think of soul as being somehow 'in' body. . . . Such is the relation between soul and body that we should try rather to conceive of body as being 'in' soul, in the sense that it depends entirely for its organization and life on soul."[1]

> But if the soul was visible and perceptible, in every way surrounded by life and extending equally to all the extremities [of the body], we should not have said that the soul was in the body, but that the unimportant was in the more important, and what is held together in what holds it together, and that which flows away in that which does not. [IV-3-20]

What a carefree life we would enjoy if we could only take this message to heart. The body that flows away gradually through aging, then suddenly at death, is so much less important than what remains, soul. There really is nothing to worry about when the body falls ill, grows infirm, and loses its youthful vim and vigor.

What is changing and failing is not us. The body is merely a material mirror. It reflects spiritual forms so long as this dreamlike projection is energized by the Soul of the All and the individual soul attached to that body. Why cry and wail when a cinema show is over? Just leave the theatre and do something else.

> For without body the soul is wholly in the intelligible world. [IV-5-1]

Soul's production of "My Life" had a beginning and it will have an end. When the prop of the body is no longer needed it is laid aside. This is cause more for rejoicing than despair since the play of life won't have a happy ending until the soul stops acting its illusory part on this worldly stage.

> The sage will care for his earthly self and put up with it as long as he can, as a musician does with his lyre, as long as it is still serviceable.

When it is not, he will exchange it for another, or else he will abandon his lyre and will give up playing on the lyre altogether, since he now has another task to perform, without a lyre.

He will leave it lying next to him and keep on singing, now without an instrument. Yet it was not in vain that the instrument was given to him in the first place, for he has played on it many a time. [I-4-16][2]

Here is a wonderful encapsulation of Plotinus's attitude toward the physical body, one's earthly self. So long as the body is a useful instrument in our search for truth we should take good care of it. After all, there are some spiritual advantages that come with living on the material plane. Because we are so far from the highest good the soul has an intense longing to return to the One, in much the same fashion as bitter cold makes us desperate to find a warm fire.

When the body wears out or no longer serves its purpose the soul takes one of two directions. It either exchanges one body for another, reincarnation, or it exists without a body, the preferable state of affairs. It is possible, Plotinus tells us, to sing life's song without the accompaniment of a body. Here on Earth we need that physical instrument to be in tune with the crude conditions of materiality. But in the higher realms, the soul sings "a cappella" in harmony with spirit and the One.

Reincarnation Is Reality

REINCARNATION, for Plato and Plotinus, is both real and reasonable. This may surprise those who believe that rebirth into a succession of bodily forms is a peculiarly Eastern doctrine. Actually, reincarnation is a central tenet of a surprising number of otherwise diverse spiritual traditions including early Christianity and Judaic mysticism—plus, of course, Hinduism and Buddhism. And since rebirth makes sense, it fits comfortably into the schema of Plotinus's rational mysticism.

It is certain that bodies are born, live for a time, and then die. What is uncertain is whether some non-bodily essence of a human, or other living being, continues to exist after its body dies. If this doesn't happen then spirituality as we normally conceive it is moot. For even if God or a higher creative power exists our existence ends after a single life, which makes our earthly stay both exceedingly precious and largely meaningless in the grand scheme of things.

Alternatively, if this essence, or soul, lives on after the body dies, then we are led to ask: When did the soul come into being? If the soul is deathless, seemingly it also is birthless. For if the soul was created by a divine power at some time one would think that this same power could uncreate it at another time.

Yet even in the physical realm, science tells us that energy and mass cannot be created or destroyed; they only change form. So does it make sense to hold that a subtle immaterial soul pops into existence within time while comparatively crude material energy and mass are eternal?

In truth, taught Plato and Plotinus, each of us existed before the life we are living now, and we will continue to exist in one form or another until our return to the formless One.

> For Plato says that the souls' choices take place according to their previous lives. . . . The souls, changing their bodies, appear now in one form and now in another, and also, when it can, a soul takes its place outside the process of becoming and is with the universal soul. [IV-3-8, III-2-4]

The passage back to God thus is through a revolving door, which makes the traveling more difficult. For the spiritual path would be much easier to traverse if the journey to higher realms was through a door that could be approached and then opened by a simple act of will. However, one problem among several is that our conscious choice to try to open that door or not is largely determined by tendencies brought with us from previous lives. We may be carrying too much baggage with us to even want to leave this material world.

Death, of course, eventually takes all people on a trip out of the body regardless of whether or not they want to go. But what generally happens at death is that a soul enters the revolving door of reincarnation, catches a fleeting glimpse of inner planes of reality without being able to fully enter them, and then is whisked around back into another earthly body with all memory of the revolving, glimpsing, and whisking having been erased. Only occasionally are souls able to remain with the Soul of the All, and even more rarely with spirit, or the One.

> *Pure souls when they are set free abandon what was plastered on to them at their birth, but the others remain with it for a very long time.* [IV-7-14]

It isn't easy to become a pure soul, fit to remain in the spiritual world at death, because most of us are born with innumerable earthly connections that only grow stronger during the course of our lives. If we just needed to discard the worldly impurities we've accumulated since birth perhaps this cleansing could be accomplished fairly easily. But the darkness that dims the soul, like the ashes covering Pompeii, contains many strata. Each lifetime adds another layer of ignorance and illusion and the soul gradually becomes accustomed to its degraded condition, dirt being attracted to dirt.

> *What was formerly the soul of a man may become the soul of an ox; so that the worse being is justly dealt with. . . . And one must carry back the reckoning to what happened in previous lives, because what happens afterwards depends on that too.* [III-3-4]

The reckoning that can turn a man into a beast, or the reverse, isn't an arbitrary affair, as when someone casually says, "Oh, I reckon I'll have salad instead of soup." Providence assures that each soul receives its just deserts, nothing more and nothing less.

J.M. Rist says, "The soul descends . . . to whatever aspect of the material world it itself resembles. If it is itself humane, it will therefore enter a human body; if it is bestial, it will enter the body of a beast. All evidently still depends on the nature of the soul itself and on its own power to choose its own fortune."[1]

We've already learned that providence is pervasive. The presence of the Soul of the All in every particle of the physical creation results in a universal and inescapable order. No thing and no one stands alone, separate and distinct. What is done by a part affects the All; what is done by the All affects a part. The ceaseless weaving of providence creates ever-changing patterns of causes and effects, a monumental living tapestry, yet each soul is aware of only a few threads, not the entire pattern.

Most people know only about the life being lived now, not what has brought a person to this body, this place, this time. We can, however, take heart in Plotinus's teaching that whatever our present circumstances may be, they are just and well-deserved.

The soul's descent to this world encompasses two sorts of "sins," remembering that, to Plotinus, sin is a distancing from the Good. One is the descent itself, the act of self-will in which soul desired to be part of the many rather than united with the whole. The second variety of sin includes any further embracing of multiplicity and concomitant separating from the One after the soul arrives here on Earth. Each, the descent and what follows it, is within the purview of providence. The soul gets what it deserves.

> *And since the sin of the soul can refer to two things, either to the course of the descent or to doing evil when the soul has arrived here below, the punishment of the first is the very experience of descent, and of the lesser degree of the second the entrance, and a very quick one, into other bodies according to the judgment passed on its deserts.* [IV-8-5]

So the natural consequence of descending from the spiritual world is living in this physical world. That is punishment enough for the soul's *tolma*, or self-assertion, that led to our separation from spirit. Loneliness is what comes from being alone; leaving the warmth of our home takes us into the cold. In such cases cause and effect follow so immediately upon the other as to be virtually indistinguishable.

But once we start acting on the stage of this world, the situation gets murkier. The justice of providence still rules the roost yet the connection between an action and its consequences often lies hidden beneath coverings of time and space. Though the randiness of a rooster leads to the hatching of an egg, it takes a practiced eye to recognize the link between what happens one day in the chicken yard and another day in the henhouse.

If we possessed the clear sight of spiritual wisdom, says Plotinus, we would see that we have become what we've done. The body inhabited now is the just result of actions performed in the past.

> *Those, then, who guarded the man in them, become men again. Those who lived by sense alone become animals. . . . But if they did not even live by sense along with their desires but coupled them with dullness of perception, they even turn into plants.* [III-4-2]

Even if we're mostly acting like humans, rather than plants or other animals, providence assures that there is a wide choice of *Homo sapiens* forms to reincarnate into. Consider how many different sorts of people there are. Two sexes, all kinds of nationalities and ethnic groups, so many varieties of shapes and sizes, wide ranges of intelligence and physical prowess, talents and proclivities beyond counting. All of these characteristics too, not just the species a soul becomes, are formed by the hand of providence.

> *Each soul comes down to a body made ready for it according to its resemblance to the soul's disposition.* [IV-3-12]

Here's the general rule of reincarnation: we become what we do. Those who act divinely become divine. Those who act humanly become human. Those who act beastly become beast. Hence we need to carefully choose our actions as well as thoughts, since thoughts are seeds that bear the fruit of actions. At present it may seem that what I do and think has little effect on what I become. After all, I can fantasize about being as ferocious as a lion for my whole life, and I will never be transformed into a real lion. But after death, who knows?

> *In this city [of the world] virtue is honored and vice has its appropriate dishonor . . . giving to each his fitting portion in changes of lives as a consequence of the deeds he did in previous existences; he who ignores this is one of the rasher sort of humans who deals boorishly with divine things.* [II-9-9]

These are strong words but Plotinus wasn't one to mince a phrase. Many people find it impossible to believe that a person can become a plant, or a bee a buffalo. Fine, there is nothing truer than the truth, as the *Enneads* put it. After each of us dies we may learn, if only momentarily, whether reincarnation is fact or fiction. And Plotinus says that the soul, which is able to remain in the spiritual world for some time after death, will eventually remember previous earthly incarnations.

> *What then would the other soul say when it has been freed and is alone? The soul which drags after it anything at all [from the body] would speak of everything which the man had done or experienced. But as time goes on after death, memories of other things would appear from its former lives, so that it would even abandon with contempt some of these memories [of its immediately past life].* [IV-3-27]

So it is wise to place our present lives in proper perspective. If we knew that after death we would "abandon with contempt" memories of the lives we are living now, perhaps our sufferings and tribulations are not so awful as we currently believe, nor are our pleasures and delights so wonderful.

A belief in reincarnation broadens our horizons. It expands the possibilities open to us. We begin to realize that we're responsible for choosing the course of our lives. We can rise to the most radiant spiritual heights or descend to the darkest material depths. This body that currently covers the soul is not a permanent cloak. It is up to us how finely ethereal, or how crudely physical, we appear.

> *The souls when they have peeped out of the intelligible world go first to heaven, and when they have put on a body there go on by its means to earthier bodies, to the limit to which they extend themselves in length.* [IV-3-15]

Heaven, it seems, is within the domain of the Soul of the All, the region immediately below the spiritual world. Here, says Plotinus, the soul puts on an ethereal body, what other metaphysical traditions speak of as the causal or astral body.

Clothed in this covering, the soul is able to descend further, much as a diver is able to remain below the surface of the sea with a wet suit and breathing apparatus. To go deeper, a stronger shell is needed such as a bathyscaphe or submarine. Similarly, the soul puts on increasingly denser bodies, changing from a body of "air" to one of "fire" to that of "earth," the physical form.

Now there are two ways of soul entering body; one is when a soul is already in a body and changes bodies, or passes from a body of air or fire to one of earth (people do not call this change of body because the body from which entry is made is not apparent); and the other, passage from bodilessness to any kind of body, which would of course be the first communication of soul with body. [IV-3-9]

Clothes cover bodies. When we want to be most intimate with our physical beloved, we take off our clothes and embrace skin to skin.

Bodies cover souls. Plotinus teaches that when we want to be most intimate with our spiritual beloved, God, we take off our bodies and embrace soul to spirit.

To return to the One, we need to get spiritually naked. Completely. Unashamedly. Gloriously. Reincarnation is a re-covering of the soul. Rebirth results in another physical incarnation but this is not the sort of life the mystic philosopher seeks.

Destiny Is Deserved

IMAGINE A HAMMER hitting your thumb, *hard*.

Ouch, it hurts! Physical pain is undeniably real. But what about the mental suffering that almost always accompanies physical injury or illness? This sort of suffering also is real to the sufferer. However, it mostly flows from the subjective meaning we ascribe to our afflictions. Consider these two hammer-hitting scenarios:

Here I am at my workbench fixing a rickety birdhouse. As I'm about to pound in a loose nail, the phone rings, momentarily distracting me. Bam! I hit skin instead of steel. My mental reaction? I'm irritated that I hurt myself but accidents happen. I find a bandage to stop the bleeding and get back to work. The next day, my thumb is still a little sore. Otherwise, the incident is out of mind.

Alternatively, here I am at a restaurant studying the menu. A waiter walks up to my table and asks if I'm ready to order. Yes, I am. He reaches into his apron and instead of bringing forth a pen he brandishes a hammer. Bam! He hits my thumb. My mental reaction? Shock, anger, bewilderment. I have been attacked for no reason. The order of my world has been violated. The next day, my thumb is still sore, and so am I. Visions of lawsuits dance obsessively through my head.

In each case, the physical pain was the same. My suffering, however, was much more extreme when there seemed to be no good reason to explain my aching thumb. It's arbitrary randomness (bolts of lightning striking out of the blue, hammers hitting when we least expect it) that makes us think, "Life is not fair."

Yet, Plotinus taught, it *is*. If we possessed a broader vision, we'd realize that a hidden order underlies the events of life. What seems to arrive unbidden at our doorsteps is, in truth, delivered by providence in response to invitations penned by our own hands.

> *And the injustice which one man does to another is certainly an injustice from the point of view of the doer, and the man who perpetrates it is not free from guilt, but as contained in the universal order it is not unjust in that order, or in relation to the sufferer, but it was ordained that he should so suffer.* [IV-3-16]

While some readers may jump to the conclusion that this is a simplistic blame-the-victim philosophy, rest assured that this isn't what Plotinus is saying. It just takes a bit of study to wend our way through the "buts" in the quotation above and understand the subtleties of his teaching.

Plotinus begins by affirming that there is indeed right and wrong. If we hurt others we are guilty of harming them. The pain they feel isn't illusory, nor is our recognition that we have caused them to suffer. But these understandings are on the individual level, one person's action having an effect on someone (or something) else. Plotinus quickly takes a big jump up to the universal order, a view that encompasses the entire vast tapestry of physical existence, not just the few threads of space and time with which we presently are acquainted.

From this much broader perspective, no action is unjust. All is ordained: good and evil, pleasure and suffering, causes and effects. In Plotinus's cosmos nothing is left to chance.

> We must say that all always have a cause for coming to be; nothing un-caused can be admitted. [III-1-1]

As parts of the whole, it is exceedingly difficult to envision the interconnectedness of all life. If we could truly grasp unity, we assuredly would be unity. This is why Plotinus observes in another quotation that the universal order keeps its reasons hidden. Knowing only that a waiter hammered my thumb instead of taking my order, I conclude that I've experienced an inexplicable absurdity, a miscarriage of justice, a random act of meanness.

Yet what if I could look back upon the countless incarnations in which the waiter and I had existed in various physical forms? Possibly in a life long, long ago I had hurt him in a like degree and the inexorable wheels of justice had turned in such a manner as to bring us together at that moment of dining, with providence having implanted a malevolent intent in my server's mind and a hammer in his apron.

Or let's look into the future after I had left the restaurant in a huff and returned home. Turning on the television, I hear a news announcer say, "A few minutes ago a gas line explosion destroyed a downtown restaurant. Many are feared dead or injured." A close escape. Thank heavens for crazy waiters.

The point is, we don't know what we've done to others in previous lives, or what they've done to us. We also don't know what is good for us or what is bad. But we think we do and confidently cast ourselves and others as victims or victimizers when the truth is considerably more involved.

Plotinus teaches that apparent gross injustices would appear in a different light if we could see what has happened in other incarnations. A murderer in this life may have been the murdered in another life, or a slave owner a slave, a captor a prisoner, an abuser the abused. Providence returns to us the just consequences of what we have done to others even though our memories of the deeds for which we suffer now have been removed by reincarnation.

> *There is certainly no accident in a man's becoming a slave, nor is he taken prisoner in war by chance, nor is outrage done on his body without due cause, but he was once the doer of that which he now suffers.* [III-2-13]

I realize that these sentiments sound harsh. They appear to lack compassion and are decidedly politically incorrect. In the same passage Plotinus goes so far as to say that "one who has raped a woman will be a woman in order to be raped," not a saying likely to adorn the wall of a women's crisis center. But let's try to see things from Plotinus's point of view.

He offers some wonderfully persuasive answers to the vexing questions, "Why do bad things happen to good people? And why do good things happen to bad people?" First, a person can't look only to the events that have occurred since his birth for an explanation of why something is happening to him now. There's a reason for everything but often that reason won't be apparent since someone only knows what he or she has done in this life alone (and even these memories are selective).

Second, Plotinus says that we're jumping the gun if we try to answer these questions without knowing the meaning of good and bad. Armed with that knowledge, the questions may answer themselves. For what we presently think is good and bad flows from a limited understanding of what produces genuine well-being. This leads us to wrongly believe that virtuous people are being unfairly deprived of the opportunity to be happy if they suffer from poverty, ill health, a physical handicap, or the like.

Actually, happiness isn't produced by anything external to us. It is an inward quality of the soul unaffected by what nature gives to us or takes away from us.

But why do things against nature come to the good, and things accord-
ing to nature to the wicked? How can this be right distribution? But if
what is according to nature brings no addition to well-being, nor, cor-
respondingly, does that which is contrary to nature take away anything
of the evil which is in the bad, what does it matter whether it is this
way or that? [III-2-6]

Plotinus begins by asking much the same question as we did above:
"Why do bad things happen to good people?" He replies, in effect,
"What is bad? The pure soul is unaffected by anything material, for
soul is nothing but spirit, eternally immersed in love of the One.
You confuse good with the Good. What most people consider to be
good has nothing to do with true Goodness, which is a quality of
soul, not of sense. So what does it matter if you have wealth, health,
beauty, friends, family, fame, or any other worldly accouterment?
The sage realizes that nothing of this world can provide well-being,
nor can its absence detract from well-being."

In other words, one reason that so many people are skeptical that
destiny is deserved is that they wouldn't know a just desert if it hit
them in the face. Yet the justice of providence is doing precisely
that, so to speak, all the time, twenty-four hours a day, seven days
a week. However, our unreasonable expectations about what we
think we should be getting prevent us from realizing that what we
are getting is perfectly just.

Perplexity about how there can be providence stems from a false
assumption that what the world considers to be good truly leads
to well-being.

But if anyone objects to wealth and poverty and the fact that all have
not an equal share in things of this kind, first, he is ignorant that the
good and wise man does not look for equality in these things, and does
not think that people who have acquired a great deal of them have any
kind of advantage. [II-9-9]

Thinking back to when we were teenagers, most of us can remember times when we were sure that our world had come to an
end because we had experienced something incredibly embarrassing
or disappointing. Yet somehow we survived, often with the help of
counsel from someone more mature, and now can look back upon
those days with bemusement. Plotinus is a wise father in this regard.
He reminds us that while we get what we deserve, we needn't take

too seriously either fortune's slings and arrows or its rewards and delights.

Earthly existence should be considered a play in which we act out scenes written by the Master Playwright. We are not our roles, but it's our duty to play our parts enthusiastically, knowing that real life begins after the curtain call ends.

> *In the true dramatic creation, which is partially imitated by people of a poetical nature, the soul is the actress, and she gets the roles she plays from the poet* [the world-creating Intellect]. *Just as actors in this world do not receive at random their masks, their costumes, their expensive robes, and their ragged clothes, so it is with the soul herself: she does not receive her fortunes at random, but they, too, are in accordance with reason. If the soul adapts them to herself, she becomes harmonious and coordinates herself with the drama, as well as with the whole of reason.* [III-2-17][1]

Each of us is born at a certain time into certain circumstances in a certain part of the world. We are unable to choose this stage setting, nor can we pick our sex, physical features, inbred talents and capacities, or genetic heritage. Throughout our lives we're influenced by innumerable factors that are largely or entirely outside of our control. We're schooled in certain settings, become acculturated in certain milieus, work in certain economic conditions, grow up in a certain geographic environment.

Take away all of these "certain" situations and there aren't that many "perhaps" left. Plotinus says that this play of life is tightly scripted by providence, with just a few lines left open for improvisation. What's within our control isn't our roles but the quality of our acting. Coming on stage at birth, a soul finds that the divine playwright and prop master have already provided everything needed to carry on the dramatic production of "My Life." We supply only the good or bad acting.

> *In this way the soul, coming on the stage in this universal poetic creation and making itself a part of the play, supplies of itself the good or the bad in its acting.* [III-2-17]

Plotinus goes so far as to say that even blasphemy is part of the script.

> *It is just as if a poet in his plays wrote a part for an actor insulting and depreciating the author of the play.* [III-2-16]

So what does it mean to be a good actor? Well, let's consider what distinguishes an accomplished actor of stage or screen. He or she has mastered the craft of acting through a combination of natural talent and dedication to learning technique, a mix of grace and effort, we might say. Of course, a sine qua non of becoming a good actor is knowing that one *is* an actor, good, bad, or indifferent.

This is part of what distinguishes the universal poetic creation of life itself from the particularized dramatic creations so easily recognized as drama. It's obvious that we are playing roles when we hold scripts in our hands. But it's not at all obvious when the script of life is so well hidden and when we have identified completely with our parts, believing that we, not providence, are responsible for directing the play in which we act every day.

> *But it* [the universal order] *keeps its reasons hidden and gives grounds for blame to those who do not know them.* [IV-3-16]

An actor is able to separate himself from his role. He realizes that as the plot takes twists and turns his job is to play his part as naturally and believably as possible, secure in the knowledge that what happens to his character is distinct from what happens to him, the true self outside of the script. If his character dies or suffers some terrible calamity, what of it? Plotinus urges us to cultivate a similar indifference to the tragedies and triumphs, ups and downs, honors and dishonors of this earthly drama.

Dominic O'Meara says, "Although the wicked are responsible for their acts, these acts are integrated into a larger cosmic scheme which is good; the goodness and beauty of this scheme require diversity, differences in perfection, just as a good play must include villains as well as heroes."[2]

> *A bad sound will be beautiful in relation to the whole, and an unnatural sound will be natural for the universe. . . . Just as—to use another image—an evil executioner does not make worse a city governed by good laws; a city has to have its executioner—men such as those are often necessary—and he is in his proper place.* [III-2-17][3]

Most of us fail to see the beauty of the big picture. Each of our consciousnesses is pressed tightly against the minute slice of life immediately in front of each of us, so we fail to see how apparent evils contribute to the overall good. If we could take a few steps back, we'd observe that what looks like a mistake close up actually is a positive contribution to the grand design.

Still, we shouldn't view Plotinus as a fatalistic relativist who preaches an "it's all the same and it's not in our hands" philosophy. For he teaches that it is we who determine the course of our individual destinies. As we read previously,

> *Providence must not be such that it makes nothings out of us. If Providence alone were all there were, it would no longer be Providence, for upon whom would it exert providential action?* [III-2-9][4]

Providence, the hand of destiny, is the loom that weaves together the amazingly variegated and ever changing patterns of material reality. If these patterns are completely predetermined from the moment of creation, if free will is silent and all that can be heard is the mechanical ticking of a clockwork universe then there's no need for providence. Why have rules for a game if the outcome has already been decided?

The freedom of the human soul necessitates providence, since there must be some means of linking up freely willed actions with their natural consequences. Otherwise, we would be isolated islands of capriciousness disconnected from all else in the universe, an impossibility in a cosmos united by the omnipresence of the One.

Choice Is Compulsion

IN THE OLD DAYS, I recall, people went into a café and simply said, "Give me a cup of coffee." And without delay they received a cup of coffee.

Today, in many parts of the United States at least, people walk into a café and become temporarily mesmerized, staring slack-jawed at a large board on the wall that enumerates the dizzying array of choices open to them. Small, regular, tall, or grande? Single shot, double, triple, or heart-stopping? Caffeinated or decaffeinated? Expresso, latte, mocha, cappuccino? Non-fat, low-fat, high-fat? Syrup, chocolate, cinnamon, nutmeg?

Clearly coffee drinkers have many more choices open to them than they did before. They can even defy convention, order a plain cup, and drink it black. The question, though, is whether choice implies freedom or compulsion. Our intuitive response is likely to be: "Freedom, that's obvious."

However, Plotinus argues otherwise. J.M. Rist says, "For Plotinus . . . it is only at the level of *nous* [spirit, or intellect] that absolute freedom can be found. . . . Freedom is in fact a kind of natural inclination or élan, present in *nous*, and directed towards the One."[1]

The soul, then, becomes free when it presses on without hindrance to the Good by means of Intellect. [VI-8-7]

We've learned that the soul has an innate yearning to return to the One. This spiritual pull, the longing that never lessens, is akin to a lighter-than-air balloon tugging at the ropes that keep it earthbound. When these ties are cut, the balloon is free to soar upward and move with the wind. Hot-air balloonists often speak of the freedom of this sort of flying. Yet there are few choices to be made on a balloon (usually, just whether to go up or down). The freedom of ballooning is to let the wind determine one's course, just as Plotinus says that the soul is free only when it is guided by the all-pervading intelligent current of spirit.

But we shall grant voluntary action to one whose doings depend on the activities of Intellect and who is free from bodily affections. [VI-8-3]

The descent of the soul from the spiritual world has gotten us into a strange situation. It was *tolma*, a desire for self-assertion, that made us want to leave the embrace of spirit. There, we enjoyed the freedom of moving harmoniously in unison with the whole like a school of fish that is both a one and many. Here on Earth, we are less free because of our power of choice, admittedly a seeming paradox. But Plotinus explains how this came about.

As we learned in the last chapter, providence doesn't conjure up a destiny for us. Providence simply is the universal power that links up causes and effects so that consequences follow naturally, and rationally, from actions. Since actions flow from choices, the ball of providence gets rolling, so to speak, when the soul makes a choice. Thus Plotinus makes it clear that what we are enjoying or suffering in life is entirely the result of our own choosing, and not the fault of providence.

> One has no proper reason for demanding an account or a reckoning from it [providence], *as one admits that "the blame lies with the chooser."* [III-2-7]

Our primal mistake, the original sin if you like, lay in not realizing that plenitude is power. There in the spiritual world the soul already had within it (and still does, for that matter) all that could possibly be possessed, for every form in creation is contained within the one-many of spirit. And the highest aspect of each individual soul is identical with spirit. So if the soul had wanted to exercise true freedom and true power, it should have stayed above rather than descending to the material world.

> And inability to go to the worse does not indicate the powerlessness of what does not go, but its not going comes from itself and is because of itself. And not going to anything else has in it the extreme of power. [VI-8-10]

If we were with the One or spirit, there would be no need to choose anything at all. When there is only good, the question of moving toward bad cannot arise. By contrast, we souls now have to work hard to be virtuous because the potential of vice is ever-present in matter, where evil is emptiness, the absence of form.

People often take pride in their ability to stick to the straight and narrow. However, Plotinus points out that this isn't a mark of pure virtue, which to him is self-contained and self-controlled, since it's impossible to be good without the option of being bad.

> *For to be capable of the opposites belongs to incapacity to remain with the best. . . . Virtue is always being compelled to do this or that to cope with what turns up.* [VI-8-21, VI-8-5]

A man stuck all by himself on a desert island for a year wouldn't be justified in coming home after being rescued and saying to his wife, "Honey, I was faithful to you all that time. Aren't you proud of me?" Well, she would have been *very* proud if the island had been inhabited by a bevy of beautiful sex-crazed Amazons. Virtue presupposes the capacity of engaging in vice.

This is why Plotinus teaches that it is far better for the soul to be beyond the dualities of good and evil, virtue and vice, freedom and necessity. All our vaunted choosing comes about because we've shunned the One and embraced the many. Just as a doctor can make people healthy only if they're diseased and a soldier can demonstrate his bravery only when there's a war, so is the individual soul able to hold to the right path only because it has entered a realm of reality that contains wrong paths.

> *For certainly if someone gave virtue itself the choice whether it would like in order to be active that there should be wars, that it might be brave, and that there should be injustice that it might define what is just and set things in order, and poverty, that it might display its liberality, or to stay quiet because everything was well, it would choose to rest from its practical activities because nothing needed its curative action, as if a physician, for instance Hippocrates, were to wish that nobody needed his skill.* [VI-8-5]

The Plotinian ideal is for the soul to be completely self-absorbed—in a highly spiritual, not egotistical, sense. What keeps the soul from returning to the One is a fascination with outward reflections rather than inner reality.

Consider men being drawn to a hardware store by their longing for power tools, or women flocking to a mall because of their attraction to shoes. It is the power saws and the high-heeled pumps that really hold the power, not those who desire them. This is, says Plotinus, an unfitting tyranny for the once-free soul.

For that which is in need and necessarily desires to be filled does not have
the mastery over that to which it is simply being led. . . . For that which
desires is led, even if it is led to the good. [VI-8-2, VI-8-4]

To want something and then go get it is for most people a sign
that they are in charge of their lives. Some people want to make a
lot of money, and they do. How wonderful, we think. They set their
sights on a goal and had the determination and skill to attain it. It
does indeed seem that our capacity to consciously choose what to do
in life is an expression of the uniqueness of *Homo sapiens*, seemingly
the only species not driven by blind instinct and desire.

Or are we? Let's see how Plotinus approaches this question: What
does it mean for something to be within our control?

But we must enquire into the following: to what ought we to attribute
this which is referred to us as being in our power? [VI-8-2]

As he so frequently does, Plotinus starts by answering his own
query with a "straw man," an argument that appears superficially
plausible, but is easily refuted. Perhaps, he says, acting on some
impulse or desire shows that we are free to do what we choose,
especially if that desire is accompanied by a calculation of the associated costs and benefits.

One possibility is to attribute it [being in our power] *to impulse and any*
kind of desire, for instance what is done or not done by passion or lust or
calculation of the beneficial accompanied by desire. [VI-8-2]

But, on closer inspection, having a desire doesn't hold up as proof
of our free will because even animals and insane people have lusts
and passions. So unless we want to admit that irrational beings
have the power to freely choose what they do, which pretty much
eliminates any distinction between a man putting away cash in his
brokerage account and a squirrel storing up acorns in a hollow tree
trunk, we have to look deeper than desire for proof that humans
are able to make unconditioned conscious choices.

But if [being in our power is] *by passion or lust, we shall grant that*
something is in the power of children and wild animals and madmen

and those who are beside themselves and caught by drugs or casually
occurring imaginations of which they are not master. [VI-8-2]

Is a drunk chasing after a vision of pink elephants or a psychotic
screaming at demonic voices inside his head, in control of himself?
Not to Plotinus and not according to the laws of the state in which
I live, which allow "guilty except for insanity" pleas. We expect that
a cougar will kill a rabbit but that reasonable people are supposed
to know better than to kill each other. So maybe it is reason, what
Plotinus calls "correct calculation," that separates us from purely
desire-driven creatures and allows us to make choices without
compulsion.

Should we perhaps attribute it [being in our power] *to correct calcula-*
tion accompanied by correct desire? [VI-8-2]

By correct desire, Plotinus probably means the soul's primary desire
for the Good, or One, or at least a secondary desire that supports
this divine yearning. For example, if our human incarnation can
help us return to the One, and staying alive is necessary to remain
human, then a desire for food, drink, and shelter would be a correct
desire. Lloyd Gerson says, "There is for Plotinus no such thing as
discovering or generating in oneself a rational desire for anything
but the good. If the desire is not for the good, it is not rational."[2]

So we've gotten down to correct calculation and correct desire as
possible sources of free will. But now we're faced with a chicken-and-
egg question. Which comes first? Do we calculate that something
will be good for us, which makes us desire that thing, or does a
desire for something lead us to calculate that it is good for us?

Yet even here one might enquire whether the calculation set the desire in
motion or the desire the calculation. [VI-8-2]

This all may sound rather academic, but it gets to the heart of
a question each of us wrestles with, consciously or unconsciously,
every day: Who is in charge here, anyway? Do I rule my desires
or do my desires rule me? Am I in control of my body or does my
body control me? Do I determine what I think about or does my
thinking determine me?

It isn't so important that we understand how Plotinus answers these queries as how we ourselves do. And this requires some serious introspection. Most of us like to believe, "I am freely choosing to do what is in my best interest." Perhaps. But who is the "I" that is doing the choosing? Is it soul, body, or mind?

If we're honest, we probably would have to admit that many, if not most, of the choices we make are compelled by bodily needs. Plotinus points out that our physical bodies generate hunger, thirst, sexual desire, and so many other "imaginations" in our minds. Someone who is starving is going to think and act much differently than will someone who isn't being driven by a powerful desire for food. We can't call this self-directed action, because the self is the soul, not flesh and bone.

> *And we shall not class those who are active according to imaginations of this kind among those whose principle of action is self-determined.* [VI-8-3]

The task of the mystic philosopher is to figure out what is truly in his or her self-interest. Our problem is that the soul has descended into this physical world and incarnated into a succession of physical bodies. Matter, whether of our own form or all the forms that surround us, has captured our attention and now pretty much calls the tune. We dance not to the beat of the soul, which longs only to return to the One, but to the drum of the senses and worldly desire. Since our real good is within, not without, this means that we are, willy-nilly, being led away from what is best for us, and toward the worse.

> *For the involuntary is a leading away from the good and towards the compulsory, if something is carried to that which is not good for it; and that is enslaved which is not master of its going to the Good.* [VI-8-4]

It's much as if we had been lured into the clutches of a used car salesman even though we don't even need a car. We've lost sight of the fact that all the choices he's offering us, "I can give you a good deal on this Ford, and a *great* deal on this Toyota," are spurious. The only choice we should make is to leave the car lot and spend our resources on something that will actually improve our well-being.

This is how Plotinus views earthly existence. Most of us are deeply engrossed in striking the best deal we can here, trying to squeeze as much happiness as possible out of the dry sponge of materiality, while the wisest thing to do would be to simply stop the madness and get off the merry-go-round of action and reaction, cause and effect, incarnation and reincarnation. The best choice we could ever make, he says, is to cease making choices. In the stillness of spirit, or intellect, lies the only freedom we will ever know.

> *And if reason itself makes another desire, we must understand how; but if it puts a stop to the desire and stands still and this is where what is in our power is, this will not be in action, but will stand still in Intellect.* [VI-8-2]

Plotinus says we must understand how our reason, that calculating machine inside our heads, comes up with the never-ending stream of desires that spur us into action so those desires can be fulfilled. From where do all our passions, our urges, our dreams, our earthly yearnings arise? Most of us assume that they are seeds freshly planted by our conscious intention with the planting being guided by a mixture of rational and irrational (is love reasonable?) calculations.

However, these seeds of future actions actually are the harvest of previous incarnations. In other words, providence implants in us the desire, so to speak, for a desire. We are aware of what we long for but are blind to what produced that longing.

Providence is a sort of hypnotist that plants a suggestion in a person's unconscious mind: "You will have a desire to go to this particular place at this particular time." When the destined moment arrives an impulse enters his conscious awareness: "I've got to go there now." And whatever providence has in store for him comes to be, and he fondly considers that he has guided his life in a certain direction.

> *For the universal bears heavily upon the particular, and the law* [of providence] *does not derive from outside the strength for its accomplishment, but is given to be in those themselves who are subject to it, and they bear it about with them. . . . It makes itself a sort of weight in them and implants a longing, a birth pang of desire to come there where the law within them as it were calls them to come.* [IV-3-13]

So what's the wisest way to live? A person should, it seems, strive for a sort of Taoist simplicity, a naturalness in which at every moment he does the only thing to be done. If providence is guiding his course, then he can trust that it will implant a longing to meet his date with destiny. And if he is so fortunate as to have united his soul with spirit, or the One, then the unfailing intelligence behind all other intelligences will free him of the compulsion to choose.

Surely, when we ascend to this and become this alone and let the rest go, what can we say of it except that we are more than free and more than independent? [VI-8-15]

Reason Is Restricted

RIGHT NOW I'm struggling to figure out what to write about reason. Given the subject, I'm trying to be reasonable in how I go about this. I've been staring out the window, scratching my chin, pondering the different ways I could start off this chapter. I've sorted through my collection of Plotinus quotations about reason and have made a few abortive attempts to compose some initial paragraphs, but haven't been happy with what I've come up with so far.

Maybe this beginning will work. Maybe it won't. There's no way I can be sure. For the moment I've just got fragments of ideas running through my mind, lots of disconnected thoughts darting this way and that. Sometimes they meet up to form a coherent cluster of meaning; sometimes they remain isolated roguish renegades, unwilling or unable to arrange themselves into a structure that makes sense.

Reasoning is challenging, that's for sure.

Yet many writers and certainly almost all mathematicians would agree with Plotinus and Plato that reasoning is a searching for what already exists. From this perspective, everything—all that is, all that has been, and all that could possibly be—exists all at once within the spiritual world.

Also, knowledge is a kind of longing for the absent, and like the discovery made by a seeker. [V-3-10]

Mathematicians generally believe that mathematics isn't so much created as discovered. That is, a mathematical truth already exists in the Platonic World of Forms and the faculty of reason within the human mind is able to manifest that truth. Few writers claim to reveal such universal verities. But this writer shares with mathematicians a feeling that the craft is more about revealing than creating.

If the revealing isn't of reality, at least it is of what will be. This chapter will be finished in a few days. What I'm trying to do right here and right now is fit together the pieces of a puzzle that is already assembled in some future corner of the space-time continuum. I'm ignorant of what destiny is about to unfold but, says Plotinus, the ruling principle of the universe is not.

Then if it [the ruling principle] *knows future events—and it would be absurd to say that it did not—why will it not know how they will turn out?* [IV-4-12]

Reason, as we've already learned, is only for those who lack intelligence. Intelligence is knowing; reason is an attempt to know. Hence, those who are reduced to reasoning are crying out to their rationality, "Please help me. I don't understand." To repeat an earlier quotation:

Just as in the crafts reasoning occurs when the craftsmen are in perplexity, but, when there is no difficulty, the craft dominates and does its work. [IV-3-18]

When the soul left the spiritual world and distanced itself from the One, it embraced multiplicity. Now we have lots of thoughts about lots of things, not to mention all the thoughts about our thinking about things. Our reason is endlessly occupied in trying to reconstruct the seamless intuitive understanding of reality that we enjoyed in the spiritual world.

The soul experiences its falling away from being one and is not altogether one when it has reasoned knowledge of anything; for reasoned knowledge is a rational process, and a rational process is many. [VI-9-4]

Reason is a tool for manipulating manyness. Rationality is the tape and glue with which we try to assemble a satisfying conceptual representation of reality. Scientists and philosophers can argue all they want about how well reason describes the world but to Plotinus this really isn't the point. Since ultimate reality is the One, any attempt to know this final truth that involves the many is doomed to failure. How can One be realized by dividing it into two or more?

Reason thus eventually is an obstacle for a soul desiring to return to the One, since reasoning necessarily involves the manipulation of multiple thoughts. In contrast, knowledge of the spiritual world is immediate and intuitive.

This wisdom is not constructed out of theorems; it is complete, and it is a unity. . . . It is enough for one to posit it as holding the first place: it does not derive from anything else, nor is it in anything else. [V-8-5][1]

So it is nonsensical to try to construct an argument that purportedly proves the existence of God. The First is the foundation of creation, the spring from which all else flows. It cannot be proven as a geometric theorem can since the supporting proof is an emanation from the One. This would be like me trying to prove that consciousness is the source of my thought by thinking, "I am conscious." The problem is that I could also think, "I am not conscious," just as atheists are able to find rational arguments that supposedly prove the non-existence of God.

If consciousness exists separate from my thoughts, I can never know this by thinking, regardless of the content of those thoughts. In fact, my divided thinking will prevent me from experiencing my undivided consciousness. Similarly, it isn't possible to fathom the One so long as we are aware of anything other than the One. For then we know two or more, not one.

Simply put, a thought of a thing is not that thing.

> *For in general thought, if it is of the Good, is worse than it. . . . But being clear of thought it is purely what it is, not hindered by the presence of thought from being pure and one.* [VI-7-40]

Here Plotinus illustrates the absurdity of ascribing thinking to the One. If there truly is an ultimate reality that we call the Good (or One), then a thought of the Good cannot be equal to the Good itself. This would be like me thinking "I'm Brian," and having that thought be more me than I am. But, Plotinus says, if a thought of the Good isn't the same as the Good itself, then the Good exists separate from any thought of it.

This is why any attempt to describe or think about the One ultimately doesn't help in knowing the One. In fact, since thoughts are always worse than the Good, in a sense our thinking about spirituality detracts from our actually being spiritual. For the goal of the mystic philosopher is to purify his or her consciousness of all rational thought and physical sensation, thereby making the soul fit to return to the simple unity of the One.

What we truly long for isn't ephemeral knowledge of the ever-changing creation, but the eternal wisdom ever-present in the creator. However useful reason may be in helping us to understand and live comfortably in this physical world, it is terribly restricted in its ability to convey any wisdom of the spiritual world. Virtually useless, in fact.

Consider the case of the eminent theologian Thomas Aquinas. When he was urged to complete his great work, the *Summa Theologica*, he replied: "I can do no more; such things have been revealed to me that all I have written seems as straw, and I now await the end of my life."[2]

God is limitless love. Such love can only find its endpoint, its highest manifestation, in the union of the lover and the beloved. For Plotinus, this is the return of the soul to the One in which a drop of the divine emanation purifies itself of materiality and merges back into the Ocean from which it came. The spiritual path thus entails moving from manyness to oneness, a direction completely opposed to the divisions made by reason.

> *So we also possess the forms in two ways: in our soul, in a manner of speaking unfolded and separated, in Intellect all together.* [I-1-8]

The forms of the spiritual world are perceived all together via an intuitive intelligence far removed from the divisions of reason, all those separate thoughts that we vainly hope will one day coalesce into a satisfying explanation of life.

Such coalescing will never happen. When someone responds to a broken silence with, "You interrupted my train of thought," they are speaking truly. Generally that train keeps on rolling down the track of each person's consciousness almost all of his or her waking hours, spewing out thick plumes of ideas and prodigious sparks of inspiration, a noisy rolling mental thunder that, strangely, never makes much progress in spite of all its frenzied motion.

> *After this they must grasp that there is an Intellect other than that which is called reasoning and reckoning, and that reasonings are already in a kind of separation and motion.* [VI-9-5]

Reason would be a wonderful vehicle if it could get us to our final destination: lasting wisdom and well-being. But the danger, says Plotinus, is that we mistake the movement of all those thoughts in our heads for actual progress. Pierre Hadot says that ratiocination "is only a preliminary exercise, a support and a springboard. Knowledge, for Plotinus, is always experience, or rather it is an inner metamorphosis."[3]

This raising up of ourselves to the spiritual world means leaving behind rationality. Reasoning generally is considered to be the height of humanness, a sign that we have evolved beyond our irrational animal heritage. But Plotinus teaches that reason is a characteristic acquired in the course of the soul's devolution, not evolution. Having lost the intuitive intelligence we enjoyed before our souls took on the company of physical bodies, we're reduced to trying to reason out the mysteries of the cosmos.

All of our mental machinations testify to how little we know about reality, not how much. Someone wealthy doesn't have to dig for gold and someone wise doesn't have to dig for truth.

> *And then too there is no rationality there* [in the spiritual world]: *for here perhaps man is rational but in that world there is the man before reasoning.* [VI-7-9]

In addition to the fact that reason is all about searching rather than finding, the *Enneads* warn of another downside to reasoning. We rationally pursue irrational ends. As we've already seen, Plotinus holds that the only goal in life that really makes sense is to strive to attain a state where there is no more striving, to return to the One. Any other desire is irrational in that it will not lead either to the greatest well-being, or the ultimate truth.

The soul's natural longing for the One gets thrown off course by its unnatural connection with matter and by the senses, which connect it with material things. Like a compass that fails to point toward Earth's true north because it is attracted to a local magnetic field, all too often the soul mistakes lesser goods that are near at hand for the genuine Good.

> *And the needs of the body and the passions make us have continually different opinions.* [IV-4-17]

One of the meanings of "rationalize" is to offer a reasonable but specious explanation of one's behavior. People can conjure up a good reason for anything they want to do. Humans are able to concoct logical justifications for mass murder, slavery, rape, adultery, environmental despoliation, religious persecution, and a host of other destructive behaviors. In addition, those who commit atrocities often are eminently rational in the manner with which they go about their maliciousness. The horror of the Holocaust was magnified, not diminished, by the efficient organization of the death camps.

So Plotinus urges us to pay close attention to who is taking center stage in that mental talk fest inside our heads. Which voice speaks the loudest when we're trying to determine our priorities in life, or decide on the best course of action to achieve some goal? Is it the highest self (pure soul) or one of the passions that is attracted to some ephemeral material delight rather than permanent spiritual bliss? If a person is confused about what he should do, it is a sign that what Plotinus calls his best part is in danger of being out-shouted by some disreputable aspects of his self.

> But is it actually our best part which has different opinions? No, perplexity and variety of opinions belong to the gathering [of our various parts and passions]: from our best part the right account of the matter is given to the common gathering, and is weak because it is in the mixture, not by its own nature.
> But it is as if in the great clamor of an assembly the best of the advisers does not prevail when he speaks, but the worse of those who clamor and shout. [IV-4-17]

Deep down each of us knows exactly what should be done. But we allow ourselves to be talked out of that silent soul intuition by our noisy mental rationalizations. That immediate intuitive sense of "Yes, this is right" or "No, this is wrong" is much more likely to reflect true spiritual intelligence than a long drawn-out course of reasoning in which the worse parts of ourselves have the opportunity to dominate the weaker but wiser best parts.

It's an amazing thing, this late classical Greek understanding of the limitations of reason. Clearly the Greek philosophers, including Plotinus, possessed marvelous intellects and unsurpassed reasoning powers. So for the Greek philosophical experience to culminate in a conclusion that reason is ineffectual in knowing the highest realities is akin to Einstein saying, "Mathematics is a farce," or Mozart cautioning, "Don't listen to music."

A divided consciousness thinks divided thoughts; a unified soul intuits a unified intelligence. The goal of the mystic philosopher is to pass beyond a preoccupation with counting shadows on the cave wall, the role of reason. Truth is realized by turning toward spirit, the sun of reality.

Myself Is Multiple

THE EASIEST THING to know seemingly would be myself.

In the outside world, there always is some gulf between me and what I want to know. My senses tell me only about my immediate surroundings and even this understanding is imperfect. I can't smell as keenly as a dog or see as clearly as a hawk. Over the horizon are lands mostly unknown to me, on a planet circling a sun that is only one of billions of stars existing in billions of galaxies.

Books, magazines, television, and other media allow me to know about things I haven't personally experienced. But my mind doesn't retain everything that I've learned and my understanding of the facts that remain is equally limited.

So if I want to know something completely, it makes sense to turn within, to my self. What barrier could there be between me and me? Obeying the Delphic injunction, "Know yourself," should be as simple as existing. I am what I am. What more is there to this business of self-knowledge?

Unfortunately, a lot, according to Plotinus. Echoing modern understanding of the human unconscious, he says that most people have no idea of who they really are. It's fallacious that I'm a single entity just because I go by one name. What I need to do is become aware of all the different aspects of myself. Then I'll be on the way to sorting out which of those parts is the permanent me and which are temporary add-ons.

> Since also "Know yourself" is said to those who, because of their selves' multiplicity have the business of counting themselves up and learning that they do not know all of the number and kind of things they are, or do not know any one of them, not what their ruling principle is or by what they are themselves. [VI-7-41]

It is indeed a strange business, this counting up of our selves. On the face of it, how could there be anybody but me sitting here typing these words? Count off, all you Brians. "One." That's me speaking. Hearing no other voices, that would be my final answer if Plotinus didn't lead me to dig deeper into the nature of myself. Most obviously, the soul has taken on the company of a body. The body of the Soul of the All is the physical universe; my soul's body is what I see when I look in a mirror.

So this introduces an evident duality in my consciousness. For example, I can be happily writing away and my stomach will say, "Stop. Go get some food." Or my bladder will exclaim, "Let's go to the bathroom." Now, the mental Brian who is doing the writing wants to keep on with what he's doing while the bodily Brian has another agenda. This implies that I must be at least two: immaterial soul, and my present compound condition, a soul enmeshed with a body.

> *For every man is double, one of him is the sort of compound being and one of him is himself.* [II-3-9]

We've learned that the Soul of the All effortlessly manages in a detached manner the affairs of its body, the universe. It isn't driven by bodily needs like we are but remains separate from materiality. We individual souls, on the other hand, have become so attached to our bodies (which nevertheless leave us at the end of every incarnation) that we consider the self and the body to be virtually identical. It behooves us to remember that in the spiritual world we existed without bodies, as we will again when we return to the One.

> *That world has souls without bodies, but this world has the souls which have come to be in bodies and are divided by bodies.* [IV-2]

When Plotinus says that the soul is divided by bodies he doesn't mean that the soul is made up of parts, like the body is. A person can have a tooth extracted, a toe amputated, or an appendix removed, because bodies are composed of many parts, not all of which are needed to stay alive. The pure soul, however, is an undivided whole. It is nothing but consciousness, or spirit. So when Plotinus speaks of the parts of the soul, he is referring to the various powers of our present state of consciousness.

> *And then the soul is many, even the soul which is one, even if it is not composed from parts; for there are very many powers in it, reasoning, desiring, apprehending, which are held together by the one as by a bond.* [VI-9-1]

When the soul enters the physical universe, the realm of many, it becomes similarly divided. Otherwise, the soul couldn't function in this alien environment. To experience materiality a separate body is needed. To live as a separate body a sense of individuality or ego is needed. To be an individual, memories, perceptions, thoughts, emotions, and desires are required. These become a personality, the little bit of the cosmos that has become particularized into you or me.

All that gets added on to the soul—body, ego, personality—eventually becomes so familiar that we can't remember or even imagine being anything else. Yet there was a time when we were not conscious of being many in matter, but single in spirit (intellect).

> *Intellect, then, is always inseparable and indivisible, but soul is inseparable and indivisible There, but it is in its nature to be divided. For its division is departing from Intellect and coming to be in a body.* [IV-2]

So long as my attention is directed to the things of this world, which includes my own body, I will consider myself to be a unique individual who is composed of all the polarized parts that I call "me": my likes and dislikes, my strengths and weaknesses, my loves and hates, my luminous longings and dark desires.

Currently my consciousness is composite, marked by a fragmented sense of self that has been cobbled together from the myriad experiences of countless incarnations since my descent from the spiritual world. Most of us cling to our uniqueness with all our might because it seems to be the life preserver that keeps us from sinking into the oblivion of the Other, the harsh external world which threatens to obliterate our being.

We're sadly mistaken, says Plotinus. What we truly are is something universal, not personal. Wrongly believing in the shadowy insubstantiality of a separate personality, we're prevented from experiencing the solid reality of a spiritual consciousness that is one with all that exists.

It's as if the body and ego are fences that keep us confined within a field of illusion. Because everyone else around us is grazing in the same field, we assume that the barriers that divide us from the larger cosmos, the "All," are impassable. Mystics such as Plotinus come to tell us that we need to expand the boundary of what we consider possible. For, in truth, our souls already enjoy the limitless.

As Pierre Hadot says, "We are always in God. . . . Our 'self' extends from God to matter, since we are up above at the same time as we are down here on earth."[1]

> *Our head strikes the heavens.* [IV-3-12][2]

This is a wonderfully encouraging message: nothing needs to be done to become spiritual. A vast spiritual treasure of well-being lies within us, but, ignorant of this, we're still grubbing about for a few coins of happiness out there in the sensible world. Our preoccupation with matter keeps us unaware of what the higher power of our souls continually contemplate.

It seems that human consciousness is akin to a television set that can receive several stations, each of which is broadcasting continuously, twenty-four hours a day. We can tune in to the Spiritual World or the Physical World. Only one station can appear on the screen of consciousness, so we have a choice as to which to watch. A.H. Armstrong says, "On this direction of attention our whole way of living depends: and it is the function of philosophy to turn us and direct us rightly, upwards."[3]

It is the middle part of *psyche*, then, that mostly concerns us. The higher part is eternally in the spiritual world. The lower part is temporarily involved in caring for the body and sensing the physical world. The middle or rational part is where the balance of power, we might say, resides. If our thoughts and desires are primarily directed downward, to sense pleasures and such, then that is where our conscious attention will be taken. Alternatively, if a person's attention is turned toward spirit, his or her lower part will be drawn upward.

> *One part of the soul is always directed to the intelligible realities, one to the things of this world, and one is in the middle between these; for since the soul is one nature in many powers, sometimes the whole of it is carried along with the best of itself and of real being, sometimes the worse part is dragged down and drags the middle with it; for it is not lawful for it to drag down the whole.*
> *. . . Is this lower part, then, always in body? No; if we turn, this, too, turns with us to the upper world.* [II-9-2, III-4-4]

All of us know what it is like to be obsessed with some passion for the physical: sex, drugs, alcohol, money, sports, gambling, travel, shopping. It's impossible to make this list exhaustive, because virtually everything people do is connected somehow with the bodily side of their compound beings. The higher soul gets short shrift. Even a love of physical nature or a desire to know its secrets (the goal of science) reflects a passion for what is material, not spiritual.

Plotinus asks: What if it was possible to discard our present personalities and passionate dispositions? What would be left of us?

> *What's left is what we truly are, we to whom Nature has granted dominion even over our passions. . . . This is why we must "flee from here," "separate" ourselves from those things that have been added on to us, and no longer be that composite, ensouled body in which the nature of the body is predominant. . . . But it is to the other soul, which is not within the body, that belongs the drive towards the upper regions.* [II-3-9][4]

To return to the One, we have to become one ourselves. Since the soul, a drop of the ocean of universal consciousness, has no parts, it goes where the primary focus of its attention carries it. If three climbers are roped together, they all will fall if one loses his grip, and the others are unable to arrest his descent. This is similar to our earthly condition, since one aspect of us is characterized by the power of rationality, another aspect by sense-perception, and a final aspect by vegetative concerns such as staying alive, growing, and reproducing.

In an ideal situation, says Lloyd Gerson, "The 'whole self' is one with a unity of purpose. It is a life that really makes sense because it has ordered the disjointed desires of the endowed [bodily] self."[5] But most people are pulled in all kinds of different directions by a mixture of spiritual yearnings and physical passions. This results in our living less the life of intelligent souls, and more the life of irrational animals, or even insentient plants.

> *In man, however, the inferior parts are not dominant but they are also present. . . . Therefore we also live like beings characterized by sense-perception, for we, too have sense-organs; and in many ways we live like plants, for we have a body which grows and produces.* [III-4-2]

It turns out, then, that what people think they mostly are, body, actually is what they least are. For body is the separable aspect of the composite self. To Plotinus, the bundle of blood and bones to which each of us gives so much care and attention is nothing more than a tool being temporarily used by the soul. A carpenter wielding a saw doesn't consider the saw to be part of himself. If it gets rusty or dull he fixes it. If it breaks he gets a new one. At the end of the day, the saw is left behind in the toolbox. This is the attitude the mystic philosopher takes toward his or her body: use it; don't let it use you.

Body-consciousness is an awareness of what we are not. If we try to know ourselves by turning to our physical frames, this would be like the carpenter pursuing self-awareness by contemplating his saw.

Body-consciousness introduces a confusing duality into a person's sense of self. It's what leads people to say such things as "I hate the way I look," and "I wish I could stop smoking." It's a sign that something is amiss whenever we use two "I's" in the same sentence. There should be just one of us using the body and thinking thoughts. Who am I talking to inside my head? To whom am I complaining when I berate myself? Who am I trying to impress when I praise myself?

Really, it must be admitted that our situation is more than a little crazy. On face value, we're each one person, but we have some company inside consciousness. Who is this other person? Most importantly, how do I know which is the real "me"?

> Who are "we"? . . . As pure souls, we were Spirit. . . . We were a part of the spiritual world, neither circumscribed nor cut off from it. Even now, we are still not cut off from it. Now, however, another person, who wanted to exist and who has found us . . . has added himself on to the original person. . . . Then we became both: now we are no longer only the one we were, and at times, when the spiritual person is idle and in a certain sense stops being present, we are only the person we have added on to ourselves. [VI-4-14][6]

This is a beautiful quotation. Psychologically perceptive, mystically profound, it cuts to the quick of the human condition. Whenever a person feels split, torn, divided, or pulled in opposite directions, the cause is this division in his consciousness between the pure soul he truly is and the doppelganger, the bodily form that has been added on to him.

Bhagavan Ramana, an Indian sage, says it simply: "If the idea 'I am the body' is accepted, the selves are multiple."[7]

Our return to the One is nothing but a return to ourselves. When a soul becomes a single being rather than many, the One is near. Pierre Hadot says, "Being present to yourself is in fact being present to the universal being, to the totality in which all beings commune. . . . To be present to the self, to be conscious of the real self, is thus to be present to God."[8]

Image Is Illusion

A SOFT DRINK advertisement offers the "real thing." An ad for mustard intones, "Accept no substitutes." If these companies wanted Plotinus's endorsement of their messages (not their products), I'm quite sure he would give it.

For the quest of the mystic philosopher is to know reality as it is, not as it seems to be. He or she cannot be content with anything other than the absolute truth. Just as a material scientist delves ever deeper into physical reality, seeking to lay bare what lies beneath appearances, so does the spiritual scientist.

What differentiates a physicist and a mystic isn't their common search for objective knowledge but the sort of truth being sought. One looks without, one within. Plotinus's inner experiences led him to confirm a central tenet of Greek philosophy: that truth, beauty, and goodness are manifestations of a single ultimate reality that may be called the One, or God, but is far beyond name and form.

Spirit is the first emanation of the One, which makes it ultimate reality once-removed. Soul comes next and so is twice-removed. This physical universe, the lowest aspect of the Soul of the All, thus is a reflection of a reflection. The seamless unity of the One becomes the multitude of forms contained within the one-many of spirit, which then are projected by soul onto the empty reflecting surface of matter.

Here we are, then, hapless humans wandering around the world looking for truth, beauty, goodness, and love in all the wrong places.

> But we, because we are not accustomed to see any of the things within and do not know them, pursue the external and do not know that it is that within which moves us: as if someone looking at his image and not knowing where it came from should pursue it. [V-8-2]

The physical universe is a most imperfect reflection of higher immaterial realities. And we ourselves are part of this illusory materiality, for our bodies are a mixture of insubstantial matter and substantial form. So what I'm able to sense of the physical me is nothing but smoke and mirrors, a falsity made out of falsehood, and the same is true for you.

It is as if, the visible Socrates being a man, his painted picture, being colors and painter's stuff, was called Socrates; in the same way, therefore, since there is a rational form according to which Socrates is, the perceptible Socrates should not rightly be said to be Socrates, but colors and shapes which are representations of those in the form. [VI-3-15]

Practically speaking, of course, I can't go around introducing myself with Plotinian exactitude: "Hello, I'm Brian, a fleshly shape serving, for the moment, as a representation of the true Form of Brian in the spiritual world. Glad to meet you."

Some of my conversations might be more interesting if I did this but most probably would end rather abruptly. After all, it generally isn't socially acceptable to tell people that what we're living isn't really life. Plotinus, though, isn't shy about saying so and within ourselves, even if this isn't expressed without, we should realize the difference between our shadow and our substance.

We all want to be happy and most people also want to be good, to be truthful, to be loving, to be kind. But what a handicap each of us labors under: the physical self is barely being; it hardly *is* at all. So it isn't surprising that we fail to achieve well-being, what with all the attention we give to bodies that are a shadow of being. As was noted before, it's impossible to have genuine well-being without a firm foundation of being.

This is so easy to say but so difficult to take to heart. Philosophical verities and spiritual proverbs spring lightly from our lips while we continue to act as if we believe in the reality of illusion. Plotinus, like many other mystics, isn't out to scare us into living our spirituality with as much vigor as we profess it, but he points out that those who cling to images will have no support, either now or at the time of death.

For if a man runs to the image and wants to seize it as if it was the reality . . . [he will] *sink down into the dark depths where intellect has no delight, and stay blind in Hades, consorting with shadows there and here.* [I-6-8]

Strong words. But those wearing blinders who believe they can see need to be shaken out of their complacency. The problem is that we're immersed so totally in a mirage. Plotinus says that nothing made of matter—nothing—possesses any substantial truth at all. No holy book; no sacred shrine; no revered person; no time-honored ritual.

Matter is merely a mirror that reflects a terribly indistinct image of the spiritual forms and nothing at all of the ineffable One. We should laugh at the pretentiousness of all things physical including our own bodily selves.

> *Whenever announcement it* [matter] *makes, therefore, is a lie, and if it appears great, it is small, if more, it is less; its apparent being is not real, but a sort of fleeting frivolity; hence, the things which seem to come to be in it are frivolities, nothing but phantoms in a phantom, like something in a mirror which really exists in one place but is reflected in another.* [III-6-7]

Spirituality isn't a question of going to the right place of worship or reading the right book or doing the right things. Church or mosque? Bible or Koran? Pray facing in a certain direction or not? For Plotinus, these sorts of outward physical choices amount to deciding which mirage you like best. To a true seeker, that is immaterial because what is sought has nothing to do with matter and everything to do with spirit.

Imagine that you have become mesmerized by your reflection in a mirror and now believe that this image is your true self. On your own or with the help of another person, you could come to realize the nature of the spell, pick up a heavy object, and break the glass. No glass, no reflection. No reflection, no image. Alternatively, you could get up the gumption to simply walk away from the mirror. In either case, when you continued to exist apart from the image, the reflection's unreality would be revealed.

But how do we smash matter? Who has the power to obliterate all of materiality? Further, says Plotinus, we can't even see matter for matter is empty of form. It is merely a nothingness that reflects the images of reality emanating from the Soul of the All. There is no background, so to speak, against which the illusion of the physical universe can be discerned. A mirror, on the other hand, has a frame that delimits the boundaries of the reflection and a visible reflecting surface. It is easy to realize that what is reflected in the mirror exists apart from its image.

By contrast, this earthly illusion is seamlessly complete. Presently all that we are, all that we do, and all that we think about is part of the image, not the reality. We can't see the trickster, matter, because it is nowhere to be seen.

So in this way the images in mirrors are not believed or are less believed to be real, because that in which they are [such as glass] is seen, and it remains but they go away; but in matter, it itself is not seen either when it has the images or without them. [III-6-13]

That said, it bears repeating that Plotinus is unfailingly positive about the physical world, notwithstanding its shadowy status. *Maya,* or illusion, may indeed be a trick played upon us unrealized souls but the Cosmic Magician is utterly good, with not a trace of maliciousness. Our universe is what it is, the final emanation from the One. It is a reflection, not the original.

We don't expect that an image of an orange will be anywhere near as appealing as a real orange (if in a magazine, it will taste like paper, and won't be juicy at all). But a faithful reproduction of reality, as is the material creation, will possess as many qualities of the original as the medium is able to express.

Matter, we might say, does the best it can to reflect the spiritual forms. But a copy impressed upon an imperfect material results in an imperfect image. It's difficult for us to appreciate how utterly insubstantial the medium of matter is. The best analogy, perhaps, is with a mirror made of nothing. Because it is a mirror, forms are reflected in it. Yet because there is nothing for these forms to make an impression on, they leave no trace as they come and go, just like a physical mirror.

But Plato's supposition does at least indicate as clearly as possible the impassibility of matter and the seeming presence in it of a kind of phantasms which are not really present. [III-6-12]

When Plotinus says that matter is impassible he means that matter is incapable of being affected by the spiritual forms that shape it. Everything in our universe is created by the forms that emanate from spirit and are impressed upon matter by soul. The laws of nature, so often capable of expression in precise mathematical form, reflect the unsurpassed intelligence of their source. This wisdom appears in matter much as a reflection appears in a mirror.

However, there is a crucial difference between matter and a mirror: the reflecting surface of a mirror can be sensed because it is made of a combination of matter and form. Thus what is seen in a mirror are material forms appearing in a material form. Matter, on the other hand, isn't one of the spiritual forms. Rather, it is an empty receptacle of form, a nearly-nothing that has the least amount of being of anything that is.

> For if here below you took away the real beings [forms], *none of the things which we now see in the world perceived by the senses would ever at any time appear. Here, certainly, the mirror itself is seen, for it, too, is a form; but in the case of matter, since it is in no way a form, it is not itself seen. . . . So matter itself is not real.* [III-6-13, II-4-16]

Then is the physical world unreal? No, since it exists. But it lacks being.

> *Non-being here does not mean absolute non-being but only something other than being. . . . The whole world of sense is non-existent in this way, and also all sense-experience.* [I-8-3]

There is nothing permanent in the physical world. Everything is constantly becoming, not being. The forms come and go, leaving no trace on matter, like the shadow of a flying bird briefly appearing on the surface of a pond. And lest we think that all is shadows and seeming except for the cherished ideas and beliefs we carry about in our minds, Plotinus reminds us that thoughts also are things that have no substantial reality. They leave the pure consciousness of soul completely unaffected, just as the forms make no impact on matter.

> *But it is like what happens with opinions and mental pictures in the soul, which are not blended with it, but each one goes away again, as being what it is alone, carrying nothing off with it and leaving nothing behind, because it was not mixed with soul.* [III-6-15]

Some people claim that God can be found in the form of nature, or a person, perhaps even in the form of an idea or emotion. Plotinus answers that God, the One, has no form. So whatever can be perceived by either the senses or the mind is of something created, not the source of creation.

> *So then the image of the intelligible is not of its maker but of the things contained in the maker, which include man and every other living being.* [VI-2-22]

Loving God by loving the creation is akin to loving people by loving what they make. It would be senseless for a carpenter's spouse to caress what he or she makes—tables, chairs, and the like—rather than the carpenter. Still, if someone persists in wanting to worship a thing made of matter, Plotinus has a suggestion: Why not revere mirrors? For if what is seen in mirrors is real, then so is what appears in matter. But if reflected images lack the reality of what produces the image, then seek the original.

If, then, there really is something in mirrors, let there really be objects of sense in matter in the same way; but if there is not, but only appears to be something, then we must admit, too, that things only appear on matter, and make the reason for their appearance the existence of the real beings. [III-6-13]

Suffering Is Separation

CLEARLY THERE IS a difference between happiness and suffering. But what produces this difference? Why do we smile when life brings us this and cry when life brings us that? As was noted previously about good and evil, pleasure and pain are easily distinguished but not so easily defined.

Examining everyday language helps us understand Plotinus's philosophical perspective on suffering. In general, when we're pleased we speak words of union. "I'm so happy that it's all coming together." "I'm totally immersed in this book." "I've really gotten into a new hobby." "I feel close to you right now." "This talk narrowed the rift between us."

Pain is almost always described in divisive terms. "I feel like I'm being torn into pieces." "My life is falling apart." "That was a cutting remark." "It bothers me that we're on opposite sides of the fence." "You've broken my heart."

Both pleasure and pain have something to do with physical or psychic distance. When we're close to what we desire or love, we feel good. When we're distant, we feel bad. Thus life is an endless process of moving toward some things and away from others. We're attracted to what brings us closer to what we want and repelled by what distances us from our desires.

The root of both joy and suffering, then, is separation. What is truly one, says Plotinus, is sufficient to itself. It can neither gain by having anything added to it nor lose by having anything taken away.

> *For we must say that experiences of this kind* [pains and pleasures] *do not belong entirely to the soul, but to the qualified body and something common and composite. For when something is one, it is sufficient to itself.* [IV-4-18]

Having descended from the spiritual world, where soul was united with spirit, we now are divided in several respects. First, consciousness is composite. Part of soul's awareness remains in touch with spirit while our conscious attention is occupied with affairs of the physical world. Hence we are split off from our own selves and have an incessant longing to become whole again.

Even our [particular] soul has not come down entirely, but something of it always remains within the Intelligible world. [IV-8-8][1]

So long as a person's conscious attention is directed toward his physical body and the world out there while the unrealized higher part of his soul is subtly communing with spirit in here, his mood is bound to fluctuate. Happiness increases when someone is more one, and decreases when he or she is less one.

H.J. Blumenthal says, "It [the body] has entered into an unstable partnership with the higher. The result is fluctuation between greater and lesser unity. It is in terms of the frustration or realization of this wish for unity that Plotinus explains pain and pleasure."[2]

But when two things aspire to unity, since the unity which they have is an extraneous one, the origin of pain, it is reasonable to expect, lies in their not being permitted to be one. [IV-4-18]

Love, which is nothing other than the pursuit of unity, results in a pain of separation before the bliss of union. When the soul aspires to unite with the One, or spirit, that bliss is fully capable of being realized. Thus the pain is temporary. However, when we love anything other than the One or spirit, it's impossible to consummate our longing for union. For the immaterial soul can never unite with anything material, including thoughts of materiality. So the love we have for things, people, or ideas of this world is doomed to frustration.

Plotinus says that if two entities such as the soul and spirit have the same nature they can become one. Or at least nearly one. But if they have different natures, as is the case with matter and soul, then the better (soul) can only take a trace of the worse (matter). This results, he tells us, in "a communion with the other that is hazardous and insecure, always borne from one extreme to the other."

So it [soul] *swings up and down, and as it comes down it proclaims its pain, and as it goes up its longing for communion.* [IV-4-18]

The ups and downs of life will always be with us if we set our sights on worldly people and objects that can never be ours. Over and over again, we make the same mistake: believing that possessions, relationships, and achievements are what make us happy and pursuing those desires. The chase often is exhilarating. The promise of what awaits us at the end of the hunt keeps our juices flowing. We expend much time and energy to run down our quarry. And in the end? It fails to satisfy.

How could it? The soul longs to return to the One. We mistakenly try to assuage that longing with what is most distant from the One and most unlike the One: matter. Instead of realizing that we're in a cave of illusion where nothing can bring us lasting satisfaction because nothing truly is, we set off on another pursuit of another desire. And then another after that. And another and another.

Try something different, says Plato. Stop chasing shadows.

So long as we are here in this world, we should see human life as it is: shadow people acting out shadow roles on a shadow stage. In his parable of the cave, Plato says that the wall holding the objects that cast shadows is "like the screen which marionette players have in front of them, over which they show the puppets."[3] These "puppets," which represent the immaterial spiritual forms, are not perceived directly in the physical world. We sense only the reflections of the forms that appear in the mirror of matter.

Thus when Plotinus calls us living toys he indicates that we wouldn't take life so seriously if we realized how insubstantial this shadow show really is.

> *There is a Life full of multiplicity in the universe, and it creates and varies all things as it lives, and it cannot bear not to constantly produce beautiful and well-shaped living toys. The arms of men who attack each other—even though they are mortal, they fight in graceful order, as is done for fun in the Pyrrhic dances—go to show that all mankind's serious concerns are only children's games.* [III-2-15][4]

If we believe that we are only physical beings, then naturally we will be terribly concerned about what happens to our bodily selves. When the "toy" is injured or suffers some calamity, it will seem that we're playing a losing game. However, even children can get out their toy soldiers or dolls and have them perform some drama, then put their playthings away, becoming themselves again. Similarly, each of us should try to recognize the difference between the outer roles being acted on this stage of life, and the inner soul that remains serenely detached from these petty goings-on.

Just like on a theater stage, that is how we must consider all murders and rapings and sackings of cities: these are all changes of scenery and costume, acted-out wailings and lamentations. In this world, in each event that happens to us in life, it is not the inner soul, but the outer shadow of a person which laments and grieves. [III-2-15]⁵

We lament and grieve because we are in touch only with the shadow of ourselves. Separated from our true nature, eternal soul, we have come to identify ourselves with what we are not, ephemeral separate bodies and personalities. It's as if the actors in a play had become so immersed in the lives of their characters that they had come to forget they were acting.

"Bang!" Someone is shot and falls dead on the stage. Only crocodile tears are shed by the grieving survivors, for the lamenting is just part of the show. When the scene ends, the actor will return to life in the same way a soul survives the demise of its body. Plotinus doesn't express much sympathy for those who suffer because he teaches that suffering is largely self-imposed. That is, the cause of suffering is forgetting who we truly are. Nothing prevents us from discarding the plaything, body, which is the root of all our pains.

> *Such are the acts* [lamenting and grieving] *of the person who knows only how to live the lower and outer life, and who does not know that in the midst of his tears, even when they are serious, he is playing children's games. Serious matters should be taken seriously only by a person's serious part; the rest of the person is a mere toy.*
> *. . . If you play with them and have a bad experience, at least realize that you have fallen into a children's game, and take off the toy* [the body] *that you are wearing. Even if it is Socrates who is playing, he plays with the outer Socrates.* [III-2-15]⁶

Still, Plotinus recognizes that the suffering that comes with living this lower life can be extreme. Intense physical or emotional pain can't be easily wished away or shunted into a closed-off corner of consciousness. If a person's soul has not yet disentangled itself from body, then the body's experiences will continue to bring him sorrow or joy. Even the sage may become delirious or unconscious, Plotinus says, "as the result of drugs and some kinds of illness." [I-4-5]

But this does not affect his or her well-being, for well-being is "possession of the true good." [I-4-6] The soul that has united with spirit or the One *is* the Good, so can never lose it, no matter what happens to its physical body.

Fortunately, outer happenings have nothing to do with inner happiness. Strong winds of pain and suffering may scatter the embers of bodily consciousness but the inner flame of the soul always burns brightly.

> *As for his [the sage's] own sufferings: when they are intense, he will bear them as long as he is able; but if they become too strong, they will carry him away. Nor will he be pitiable in his suffering, for his inner flame still burns as does the light within a lantern, though outside there rage the fierce winds of a winter storm.* [I-4-8][7]

The light in a lantern remains lit because it is separated from inclement conditions by panes of glass. So there is a difference between the sort of separation that causes suffering and the sort that results in an end to suffering. If someone's attention has sunk deep into the physical world and lost touch with the undescended aspect of his soul that remains serenely in the spiritual realm, then he has separated himself from the source of bliss. This, obviously, leads to suffering.

But if his attention is turned away from the pleasures and pains of earthly life, then he is able to separate himself from matter and this leads to the end of suffering. Like a lantern light that illumines its surroundings but is unaffected by the weather outside, the soul now passes through the drama of life more as a detached spectator than as a passionate participant.

> *In order for the soul to separate herself from the body, perhaps it is necessary for her to gather herself up into herself from what, for her, corresponds to the places she has been in; at any rate, she must remain free of passions. As for inevitable pleasures, she must, in order not to be hindered, turn them into mere sensations: processes of healing and of relief from pain. Pain is to be eliminated, or, if this is impossible, is to be borne with gentleness, and diminished by not suffering along with it.* [I-2-5][8]

Plotinus reminds us that physical pain does not need to result in suffering, nor does physical pleasure need to result in joy. To the mystic philosopher every sort of sensual perception is simply that: a perception. He or she is aware of what the body is experiencing but this awareness isn't converted into psychic distress or elation. It remains, as much as possible, on the bodily level so that the soul is not distracted from its business of returning to the One. For if our attention remains rooted in the physical what chance do we have of realizing the spiritual?

Many people, however, claim that while it might be praiseworthy for a person to have a Stoic attitude toward his own suffering, he should be moved by the suffering of others. Isn't it a mark of humanness to feel someone else's pain? Not to Plotinus.

> *If anyone says that it is our nature to feel pain at the misfortunes of our own people, he should know that this does not apply to everybody, and that it is the business of virtue to raise ordinary nature to a higher level, something better than most people are capable of.* [I-4-8]

Countless people have tried, and continue to try, to make this world a paradise that is free of suffering. None have succeeded and none ever will. A comparatively few people, Plotinus being one of them, have tried to teach humanity how suffering can be eliminated—not by changing the world, but by changing ourselves.

Section IV

The One

And Many—

Soul's Descent,

AND RETURN

Soul Is the Self

WE DESCENDED from the spiritual world.

We fully experienced what earthly existence has to offer.

Now, in every human soul, there is a longing to return to our divine home.

This longing is natural. Our spiritual hunger is ever-present. But we mistake it for a worldly appetite and try to satiate ourselves with matter. Since the immaterial soul can't merge with materiality, a frustrating sense of incompleteness always remains with us. We know we're lacking something but can't quite put our fingers on it.

How could we? The soul has been lost and soul is the true self. What is doing the looking is what has to be found. Our search for happiness takes us everywhere but the only place well-being can be discovered: no place.

> For we should not look for a place in which to put it [soul], *but make it exist outside all place.* [V-1-10]

Here we approach the essence of Plotinus's mystical philosophy. It is wonderfully simple and beautiful. The problem lies not in understanding his teaching but in experiencing it.

Self is the soul is spirit is the source, the One.

This is the formula that transmutes our limited, pained, fragmented consciousness into the omnipresent, ever-blissful, all-knowing principle of the cosmos. Reflecting the perennial message of mysticism, "the macrocosm is the microcosm," Plotinus says that the three grand spheres of reality—the One, spirit, soul—are within each of us, as well as without. I recall a song that proclaims, "We are the world." Yes, but not only the world, *everything.*

So our return to the One is also a return to ourselves. There is no place the spiritual seeker needs to explore other than the depths of his or her own consciousness. The One is overall. It is existence itself. Whatever exists is, at heart, present with the One. This includes us.

> Plato says the One is not outside anything, but is in company with all without their knowing. For they run away outside it, or rather outside

themselves. They cannot then catch the one they have run away from, nor seek for another when they have lost themselves. [VI-9-7]

Rumi, a Persian mystic, speaks of a sage who told a man how to unearth a buried treasure.[1] Paraphrased, the story goes like this: "Stand here," the sage says, "and shoot an arrow in that direction. Where the arrow lands, there the treasure will be found." The man gets a bow and enthusiastically does as instructed, carefully watching the high arc of the arrow as it flies away.

After digging where it landed, he is dismayed at not finding any treasure. "I'll keep trying," he vows. More arrows are shot, and soon the ground is cratered with holes. But still no treasure. Exhausted, he goes back to the sage and complains that all his work has gone for naught.

"I didn't tell you to shoot with all your strength," the sage tells him. "Simply let the arrow drop from your bow." The treasure, it turns out, was right beneath the man's feet.

Similarly, Plotinus says that our spiritual wealth is so close we are unable to find it. What separates us from what we seek isn't physical distance but rather the mistaken notion that we are separated at all. For it is by running outside ourselves that we distance ourselves from the One. A spiritual seeker's first step, then, is to stop moving and realize his or her true self.

The soul is the self. [IV-7-1]

Previously we learned that human consciousness is composite. While the pure soul is formless spirit, consciousness is able to mix with lower manifestations of the One, which include matter in the form of nature, mind in the form of reason, and other mental faculties. These mustn't be confused with their lofty counterparts, the intelligible matter and intuitive intelligence soul experiences in the spiritual world.

Hence, when reading Plotinus we must remember that "soul" can mean different things depending on the context. A translator of the *Enneads*, Stephen MacKenna, says, "The word Soul used of man often conveys, in Plotinus's practice, the idea of the highest in man, what we should be apt to call Spirit; sometimes, where the notion is mainly of intellectual operation, Mind will be the nearest translation; very often 'Life-Principle' is the nearest."[2]

Soul, or *psyche*, has many powers. The quest of the mystic philosopher is to explore the full range of what he or she is capable of,
not being content to act like an animal or even think like a person.
Our beastly and rational sides are indeed parts of our present human
nature but are not the highest aspect of soul.

Reasoning does distinguish us from the unthinking instincts
and growth-principles of lower animals and plants. Rationality
makes us distinctly human but this isn't the same as our true self.
Plotinus explains in the quotation below that spirit is the essence
of soul "when we use it," and spirit isn't ours when we don't use it.
Though his language is rather convoluted, his meaning is simple:
when matter and mind are left behind, soul is spirit.

> *What then prevents pure Intellect [spirit] from being in soul? Nothing, we*
> *shall reply. But ought we to go on to say that it belongs to soul? But we*
> *shall not say that it belongs to soul, but we shall say that it is our intellect,*
> *being different from the reasoning part and having gone up on high. . . .*
> *And it is ours when we use it, but not ours when we do not use it.* [V-3-3]

Spirit cannot belong to soul, or be a part of soul, because spirit
essentially *is* soul, at least when soul has ascended within to the
spiritual world and "gone up on high." However, if a person's consciousness is filled with sensations, memories, and thoughts of the
material world, then he isn't using spirit, for matter is using him.
That is, his consciousness becomes filled with all that he is not and
he loses touch with the purity of what he really is: soul-spirit.

To know himself, he must discard all that has become attached to
him that is not spirit. This means that during inward contemplation
his awareness of just about everything he currently considers himself
to be has to go: his unique body, personality, beliefs, thoughts, emotions, and so on. Gerard J.P. O'Daly says, "First of all, selfhood, for
Plotinus, would be in strict contrast to individuality. . . . [It] is an
ingathering, an elimination of all that is disparate."[3]

> *Yes, we must so know, if we are to know what "self-knowledge" in Intellect*
> *means. A man has certainly become Intellect when he lets all the rest*
> *which belongs to him go and looks at this with this and himself with*
> *himself: that is, it is as Intellect he sees himself.* [V-3-4]

Earlier we learned that creation is contemplation. From the
One's contemplation emanates spirit; from the spirit's contempla-

tion emanates soul; from the soul's contemplation emanates nature, the physical universe. This is how the One becomes many, by the higher force contemplating, and bringing into being what is lower. And contemplation also is how the many become the One. When we turn our attention from what is beneath us, matter, to what is above us, spirit (intellect), the process of emanation is reversed. Now the individual soul begins to return to its source and realize its true nature.

> *Therefore one must become Intellect and entrust one's soul to and set it firmly under Intellect, that it may be awake to receive what that sees, and may by this Intellect behold the One, without adding any sense-perception or receiving anything from sense-perception into that Intellect.* [VI-9-3]

Since the macrocosm is within the microcosm, to know ourselves as soul is to progressively know, or rather become, the levels of the cosmos. What we contemplate, we become. The soul, being form-less, is able to take on the characteristics of what it contemplates. Because the soul isn't made of matter, it has a divine nature. But this nature can be veiled by the soul's association with matter and a longstanding contemplation of material things through countless incarnations in the physical world.

> *Our demonstration that the soul is not a body makes it clear that it is akin to the diviner and to the eternal nature. It certainly does not have a shape or a color, and it is intangible.* [IV-7-10]

Entering the one-many that is the spiritual world, the World of Forms, the formlessness of the individual soul effortlessly imbibes the form of spirit and the two become as united as two can be while still remaining distinct.

> *Intellect therefore makes soul still more divine by being its father and by being present to it; for there is nothing between but the fact that they are different, soul as next in order and as the recipient, Intellect as the form.* [V-1-3]

If the reader doesn't clearly understand the difference between soul and spirit, or intellect, there's no need to despair, for there isn't much that distinguishes them. A.H. Armstrong says, "The boundary between Soul and Intellect is often not very well-defined in the *Enneads*. . . . The unity of the divine, the immediate presence of the higher in the lower, the unbroken continuity of the divine life from its source to its last diffusion were always essential parts of the thought of Plotinus."4

To return to the One it's only necessary to know where spirit can be found, not how spirit can be described. Spirit is found within, as we learned from a previous quotation:

> *As for soul, the part of it directed to Intellect is, so to speak, within, and the part outside Intellect directed to the outside.* [V-3-7]

Within what? Not the body. Recall that Plotinus teaches that the body is within soul, not the other way around. So the spiritual journey doesn't take place within our physical frames, nor, of course, does it involve traveling through any kind of physical space.

Realizing our true self as soul depends on the focus of our attention. When our attention is directed to the outside world, not surprisingly we learn about what is outside of us. When our attention is directed to the interior world, we learn about what is within, ourselves. Even though this "within" can't be delimited by geographical coordinates of up, down, right, left, forward, or back, Plotinus cites an intriguing statement by Plato.

> *And he said obscurely about us that the soul is "on top in the head."* [V-1-10]

This is a reference to a line in Plato's *Timaeus*: "And we should consider that God gave the sovereign part of the human soul to be the divinity of each one, being that part which, as we say, dwells at the top of the body."5 Of course, the intangible soul doesn't actually reside in any particular physical location. But the connection between the matter of body and the consciousness of soul certainly appears to be centered in the head or brain. This is where our thinking, feeling, and perceiving seem to take place.

However, the fact that we say "I think," "I feel," and "I perceive" implies that a person's true self is not the same as all the goings-on in his or her head. There is the "I" that is pure consciousness and then there are the countless thoughts, emotions, and perceptions that each of us is conscious of.

To return to the One, we must become one ourselves, since duality can never experience unity. Presently most of us are fractured. Rather than simply being aware, we are aware of awareness. Instead of simply thinking, we think about thoughts.

This uniquely human splintering of consciousness helps *Homo sapiens* adapt to the complex physical world but it prevents us from experiencing the deeper reality from which the manyness of materiality emanates. From an evolutionary standpoint, a capacity for self-reflection seems to be advantageous. However, the goal of the mystic philosopher is devolution, returning to the source.

Wondrously, self-realization is God-realization. Our real self is reality itself. Spiritual practice thus is exceedingly simple while also exceedingly subtle. Look too far and you miss the immediate presence of what is being sought. Clutch too tightly and you fail to hold onto what has never left your grasp. Move too quickly and you run past the One who steadfastly remains by your side.

Without Is Within

PSYCHOLOGISTS tell us that a mature personality clearly distinguishes between self and other. Newborn babies can't do this. One of the first things an infant must learn is that he or she is an entity separate from the external environment. So, as we grow up, the worlds within and without ourselves become increasingly distinct.

As adults, our personal thoughts and feelings are considered to be separate from both the inner worlds of other people and the outer physical world. While there is communication between these realms of "I—you" and "I—it," there is no true communion. I can know someone or something from the outside but not from the inside. To believe otherwise would, it seems, be a regression to an infantile stage of development in which without is within and within is without.

Yet such a state is what Plotinus urges us to achieve above all else. A Biblical adage, Matthew 18:3, comes to mind: "Truly I tell you, unless you change and become like children, you will never enter the kingdom of heaven." Perhaps the wide-eyed innocent gaze of a newborn baby more truly reflects amazement at what has been lost by coming into the physical world than (as we normally consider) a grateful appreciation of the wondrous sights and sounds of materiality.

> *If we come to be at one with our self, and no longer split ourselves into two, we are simultaneously One and All, together with that God who is noiselessly present, and we stay with him as long as we are willing and able.* [V-8-11][1]

Plotinus says that so long as a person is separated from the self that is his soul, split into two by body-consciousness, he will be separated from both the rest of creation and God. But when we become one ourselves at the same time we become the One that is All, everything that exists. This transformation sounds miraculous and it is. Yet it also is eminently logical.

If God is not a fiction, this power is either present in physical reality or absent. If present, God seemingly would be present everywhere rather than just in certain places. If absent, then spirituality appears to be a lost cause; for then there is no link between God and man, and spiritual endeavor would amount to stumbling around in a material maze with no exit. Plotinus strenuously disagreed with the Gnostics of his time who held that the universe was bereft of God, having been created by an evil maker, and that salvation was promised to only a select few.

As we read before:

> *God is present to all beings, and he is in this world, however we may conceive of this presence; therefore the world participates in God. Or, if God is absent from the world, he is also absent from you, and you can say nothing either about Him or the beings which come after Him.* [II-9-16][2]

In other words, it is the height of arrogance for someone to claim that God is present to him or her but is absent from the rest of us. If God is here in the world, he is in everybody. If he is not in the world, then no one is able to speak with any confidence about divine matters, including those who pretend to proclaim a unique revelation.

Plotinus was a mystic who taught that any person was capable of realizing what he had come to know. In one of Plotinus's few explicit first-person descriptions of his mystical vision, he says that when he was completely within himself he united with the All, the "greater portion."

> *Often I reawaken from my body to myself: I come to be outside other things, and inside myself. What an extraordinarily wonderful beauty I then see! It is then, above all, that I believe I belong to the greater portion. I then realize the best form of life; I become at one with the Divine, and I establish myself in it.* [IV-8-1][3]

How is it possible for a single soul to experience the totality of the spiritual world? Because, as A.H. Armstrong says, "The One is not a God 'outside' the world. Nor is He remote from us, but intimately present in the center of our souls; or rather we are in Him. . . . And just because the One is not any particular thing He is present to all things according to their capacity to receive Him."[4]

Our preoccupation with sensing physical forms and thinking thoughts associated with those forms prevents us from experiencing the presence of the One. When attention is directed without, only what is physical or personal can be perceived. Our senses convey information about materiality; then those sensations become grist for our mental mills, which generate our unique memories and interpretations of physical reality. This keeps us bound to a limited and largely subjective knowledge of the cosmos.

Plotinus says that there is another way of sensing and another way of knowing: rather than bringing inside mere impressions of what is outside, bring the whole shebang (a non-philosophical but entirely apt term) within your consciousness. Don't just sniff the cork if you want to imbibe the essence of ultimate reality, drink the entire bottle. The cautious sobriety of reason and sense perception is incapable of experiencing spirit's intoxicating beauty.

> But those who do not see the whole only acknowledge the external impression, but those who are altogether, we may say, drunk and filled with the nectar, since the beauty has penetrated through the whole of their soul, are not simply spectators. For there is no longer one thing outside and another outside which is looking at it, but the keen sighted has what is seen within. [V-8-10]

Here Plotinus describes, as best he can, the nature of his mystical vision. He did not apprehend spirit and the One in the way we gaze upon an object of this world, as something separate from ourselves. Rather, in the depth of his inner contemplation there was no longer one thing outside, spiritual reality, and "another outside which is looking at it," himself. By uniting his soul-consciousness with universal-consciousness, Plotinus brought within what at first appeared without. Then there was little or no difference between the perceiver and the perceived, soul and spirit, the drop and the ocean.

Someone who becomes spirit comes to know it in the same fashion as he knows his own consciousness: immediately and intuitively.

> If then we have a part in true knowledge, we are those [spiritual realities]. . . . So then, being together with all things, we are those: so then, we are all and one. [VI-5-7]

In this quotation (cited previously), Plotinus assures us that when we are able to raise our consciousnesses to the level of spirit, there is no longer any significant difference between us and the totality of the spiritual world. What a relief! For isn't it true that all of our difficulties here on Earth stem from our separateness?

Our separate bodies must be nourished and protected; our separate egos, the same. This takes time and trouble, and the job doesn't always go so well. We fall ill. Dangers are always present. Disappointments and frustrations dog us. Life as we know it now is a never-ending struggle to preserve our separate existences in the face of onslaughts that threaten the integrity of body, mind, and personality. We look to others for love and support but the Other is also what we fear, for it is not us.

So it's wonderful to hear Plotinus say that in the spiritual world each of us *is* that world. And so is everyone and everything else. All is united in the one-many that is spirit. Thus there is nothing to fear, nothing to crave, nothing to be done except love, know, and enjoy. Here is Plotinus's description of the person who has transcended the illusory separateness of this physical universe and become one with the divine:

> For he will see an intellect which sees nothing perceived by the senses, none of these mortal things, but apprehends the eternal by its eternity, and all the things in the intelligible world, having become itself an intelligible universe full of light, illuminated by the truth from the Good, which radiates truth over all the intelligibles. [IV-7-10]

It isn't possible for a person to know himself as soul, as spirit, or as the One, by observing one part of his self with some other part. Such a dualistic approach would never lead to the unity the mystic philosopher seeks. He or she isn't after the sort of knowledge that comes from dividing reality into pieces, the job of reason and sense-perception, but rather seeks the intuitive intelligence of true being.

Plotinus reassures us: There is nothing to fear in not being yourself. Of course, emptying ourselves of all that is familiar to us now would indeed be frightful if this is all that we are.

If I am merely an individual, then if I take away my individuality—my unique thoughts, perceptions, emotions, and so forth—I am nothing. I face the terror of existential emptiness. What pleasure or goodness could there be in becoming a void? However, if my soul is a drop of the spiritual ocean, then by realizing my deepest self I become everything rather than nothing. Rather than merely being a separate part of existence, I become a part that is also the whole.

> So that a man in this state, by his intuition of himself, and when he actually sees himself, has everything included in this seeing, and by his intuition of everything has himself included. [IV-4-2]

Mystics are often accused of being self-absorbed and world-denying, concerned only with their own salvation or enlightenment. Yet Plotinus says that when a spiritual seeker contemplates himself, his true self, he contemplates everything. Because the essence of us, soul, also is the essence of the universe, spirit, there is nothing more self-less than truly knowing the self.

Detachment Is Delightful

ATTACHMENT AND DETACHMENT, holding on to this and letting go of that, is a basic dynamic of life.

Our lungs absorb oxygen and expel carbon dioxide. Our digestive systems take in nutrients and eliminate waste products. Our attention continually seizes upon certain feelings and thoughts to the exclusion of others. Our eyes move from sight to sight and our ears from sound to sound.

So when Plotinus urges us to attach ourselves to the One and detach ourselves from materiality, the basic process of which he speaks already is familiar to us. We are expert in connecting to one thing while disconnecting from other things. But since our attaching and detaching involves lesser goods, which fail to fully satisfy, we never approach the true Good. Thus if we detach ourselves from everything without, all the people and things that we wrongly believe will bring us lasting happiness, our souls will be able to experience the delight of the One within.

> *The soul must let go of all outward things and turn altogether to what is within, and not be inclined to any outward thing, but ignoring all things (as it did formerly in sense-perception, but then in the realm of Forms), and even ignoring itself, come to be in contemplation of that One.* [VI-9-7]

Here Plotinus describes the scope of the mystic philosopher's detachment. There are three levels of withdrawal from all outward things. First, the spiritual seeker turns away from both sense-perception and any thoughts or memories of the physical world. This leads the soul, now disconnected from materiality, into the spiritual world, the realm of forms.

Next, the ethereal beauty of higher realms also must be left behind. For even though the spiritual world is much more unified than the physical universe, it is still a one-many, not the One. There are sights and sounds and other sensations in the World of Forms. These too must be ignored, says Plotinus, just as physical perceptions were before.

Finally, after casting aside all else, the soul must ignore even itself to truly contemplate the One. This contemplation is so complete that nothing separates the contemplator and the contemplated except the slightest degree of otherness: soul becomes a drop in the spiritual ocean.

A lover, it is said, has eyes only for his or her beloved. Similarly, Plotinus tells us that the realized soul is so happy to have returned to the One that everything else in existence could vanish and the soul would rejoice, since then nothing could possibly interfere with her intimate communion.

> *She* [soul] *is filled with joy, and she is not mistaken, just because she is filled with joy; she does not speak in this way because her body is tickled with pleasure, but because she has become once again what she was before, when she was happy. She says she despises . . . everything which used to give her pleasure.*
>
> *. . . If everything else round her were to be destroyed, that would be just what she wanted, so that she could be close to him* [the One] *in solitude. Such is the joy to which she has acceded.* [VI-7-34][1]

The final destination of the *Enneads*, a travel guide for the soul, may be termed Joy. This is important to remember because if certain quotations are taken out of context, Plotinus can be mistaken for a misanthrope. For example, one of the *Enneads'* most frequently-cited passages is a description of the spiritual journey as "a solitary flight to the Solitary One."

This sounds rather dreary and lonely. The mystic sets forth all alone to return to the heart of aloneness, not exactly the stuff of which spiritual dreams are made. But let's look at the larger passage in which these words are found:

> *When one falls from contemplation, he must reawaken the virtue within him. When he perceives himself as embellished and brought into order by these virtues, he will be made light again, and will proceed, through virtue, to Intellect and wisdom; then, through wisdom, to the One.*
>
> *Such is the life of the gods and of divine and happy men: release from the things down here below, a life which takes no pleasure in earthly things, a solitary flight to the Solitary One.* [VI-9-11][2]

This inward detachment from all down here below is not the act of a world-denier but of a God-affirmer. Through contemplation of higher realities, the spiritual traveler passes through realms of limited pleasure in order to reach the domain of unlimited bliss, the One. The journey is solitary because it takes place within a person's consciousness, not outside in the physical world where others can accompany him or her. And the endpoint is described as the Solitary One because such is the sole foundation of all that exists. As we read before,

> *For from that true universe which is one this universe comes into existence, which is not truly one.* [III-2-2]

Imagine pairs of lovers enjoying a park on a warm summer afternoon. They hold hands, hug and kiss, nestle on a bench, cuddle while lying on the grass. Each of these present attachments flows from a prior detachment. The men and women strolling along with their arms around each other, whispering intimacies, were not always so entwined. A few days, months, or years ago they were apart. And now they are together. If they had not detached from a previous lover, or their own aloneness, they wouldn't presently be attached.

So this is the spirit in which Plotinus's paeans to detachment should be taken: when a person leaves his house to visit a good friend whom he hasn't seen for a long time, it isn't because he hates his home. Rather, he longs to be with his absent companion. In the same fashion, the mystic philosopher doesn't despise this world. Rather, he or she yearns for the One who is beyond this world so much more that, by comparison, nothing on Earth holds any importance.

> *What is there in human affairs so great that it will not be despised by the person who has risen above them, and who is no longer dependent on anything here down below?*
>
> *Such a person will not consider even the greatest strokes of good luck to be of importance, whether they be ruling over kingdoms, power over cities and peoples, or colonizations and foundations of cities, even if he is responsible for them himself. Will such a person, then, think it important if he is thrown out of power, or if he sees his own city razed to the ground?*
>
> *. . . He would no longer be a sage if he considered that wood and stones were important; nor, for that matter, that mortal beings should die!* [I-4-7][3]

Strong stuff. In one fell swoop Plotinus takes away every earthly reason we might have to feel either sad or joyful. He tells us that nothing in human affairs is worth either a tear or a smile. It is all shadows and seeming. Our concern for anything made of matter, including our own bodies, is misplaced.

Those who have reached the spiritual heights realize that everything here comes from there. To a sage, grieving over the loss of something physical is as silly as believing that a person standing in front of a mirror fractures into pieces if the mirror breaks. The true World of Forms is unaffected by what happens to the images of reality cast upon this material world.

Thus it isn't so much that Plotinus is unsympathetic to someone who has suffered a loss as that he doesn't recognize separation from anything physical, even a person's own body at death, as entailing the loss of something valuable. In fact, he goes so far as to consider death a gain.

After all, we say that such a person should believe that death is better than life with the body. [I-4-7][4]

J.M. Rist says, "All this, we should notice, is not intended to represent the wise man as unconcerned with friendship and harsh. . . . On the contrary, his very detachment from the world and its worries will make him the best of friends."[5] Why? Because the sage is able to offer his friends the most precious gift of all: wise understanding of the human condition.

A man of this sort will not be unfriendly or unsympathetic. . . . But he will render to his friends all that he renders to himself, and so will be the best of friends as well as remaining intelligent. [I-4-15]

Just as a sick doctor is handicapped in healing his patients, so is a woman less able to aid a distraught friend if she too is down in the dumps. Hence Plotinus implies that we can be the best of friends only when we have become the companion of the One. Possessing the wisdom that comes from knowing the Good, one is able to offer sound counsel and support to those in need.

Our aim is to emulate the detachment of the Soul of the All as it effortlessly manages the affairs of this universe without being affected in any way by its involvement with materiality.

The soul of the universe is not troubled; it has nothing that it can be troubled by. . . . As we draw near to the completely untroubled state we can imitate the soul of the universe. [II-9-18]

This doesn't mean that we cease to feel painful and pleasurable sensations, for these are undeniable accouterments of human life. But we need to consider what is affected for good or ill by such physical stimuli. Body, soul, or both body and soul? Plotinus teaches that only the lower aspect of soul is entangled with the beast, body. The higher aspect of soul, each person's true self, always is detached from what happens to the beast.

Amazingly, this includes even such extreme suffering as being burned alive in a bronze statue, the "bull of Phalaris" (Phalaris was a Sicilian tyrant who put victims in the statue and, when a fire was lit beneath it, perceived their cries as the bellowing of the lifeless bull).

> As for the activities of the sage relating to contemplation: some, in-deed, might perhaps be hindered [by outside circumstances]. . . . Yet the "greatest lesson" is always near at hand and present for him; all the more so if he were inside the so-called "bull of Phalaris."
>
> It is vain to call such a situation pleasant, whether they repeat it twice or many times, for according to them [the Epicureans], *the person claim-ing "this is pleasant" is the same as the one in a situation of agony.*
>
> For us, however, the person who suffers is one thing, the person speaking is another. Although this other is forced to live with the sufferer, yet he will never leave off the contemplation of the Good in its entirety. [I-4-13][6]

Michael Chase explains that the greatest lesson refers to what Plato calls the Idea of the Good, or of the One. Chase notes that the sage "can, thanks to assiduous exercise, call it to mind at each and every moment, realize the identity of the best part of himself with the Principle of all things, and thereby become indifferent to external circumstances."[7]

By contrast, the Epicurean philosophers believed only in a bodily self that was limited to experiencing physical reality. So Plotinus observes that it would be ridiculous for Epicureans being burned alive to say "this is pleasant," because in their world view the person physically suffering is the same person claiming not to suffer, an obvious contradiction. But if the higher soul is detached from physi-cal sensations, as Plotinus holds, then it is possible to differentiate between the person who is suffering bodily and the person who continues to experience the Good spiritually.

For most of us, life is a never-ending seesaw of ups and downs. One moment we are soaring with delight, the next moment we are cast into despair. The tide of our well-being rises and falls in concert with the moon of outward circumstances. Try as we may to remain level-headed and inwardly balanced, it is exceedingly difficult to remain centered on the fulcrum of consciousness, the higher aspect of soul, and be neither attracted by worldly pleasure nor repelled by worldly pain.

However, such is the state of those whose inner vision is firmly focused on the reality of spirit and the One, not of the ordinary person whose attention is still pulled hither and yon by whatever shadowy material illusion is presented to the physical senses. The sage is detached from what his body experiences. He is aware of physical sensations but inwardly remains almost totally unaffected by them.

> *One must understand that things do not look to the good man as they look to others; none of his experiences penetrate to the inner self, pleasures and pains no more than any of the others.* [I-4-8]

This detached attitude of the mystic philosopher can appear as pathological indifference to those who believe that a person's human-ity is manifested by an empathic sharing of other people's joys and sorrows. But since Plotinus considers physical existence and all that comes with it akin to a dream, it makes no sense to him to share in someone else's fantasy. Even though the vast majority of people spend their lives being either frightened or enthralled by shadows, in no way is this proof of their reality.

> *One must not take weeping and lamenting as evidence of the presence of evils, for children, too, weep and wail over things that are not evils.* [III-2-15]

Lloyd Gerson likens the difference between everyday human emo-tionality and the sage's disengagement from worldly concerns to the difference "between someone who thinks that he is affected directly by an attack on a voodoo doll made in his image and someone who knows that he is not."[8] If we really believe that a stick is a snake, it won't help to mouth the words, "That is not a snake." But when we know without a doubt that it is a stick, a crowd of people could yell "Snake!" and we wouldn't be scared in the slightest.

To Plotinus, everything associated with the body is stickish, not snakeish, even death. So if we're able to maintain a calm composure in the face of what distresses ordinary people, this is an encouraging sign as regards our spiritual intelligence quotient.

> *Even if the death of friends and relations causes grief, it does not grieve him but only that in him which has no intelligence, and he will not allow the distresses of this to move him.* [I-4-4]

It's important that we come to understand the difference between necessities and goods. If we believe that out there in the world is where we'll find the good life, then we will be disturbed when someone or something we're attached to is taken away from us or a material desire isn't fulfilled. But Plotinus teaches that this is an unrealistic attitude. The source of well-being is within, not without.

Divesting Is Divine

TODAY, as I begin writing this chapter, the U.S. stock market experienced its greatest point decline ever. At the moment, many investments are looking a lot more like divestments, so it's an appropriate time to be pondering the message "divesting is divine."

Of course, Plotinus doesn't mean that we become more spiritual by losing money. If that were the case, many people would have turned into saints during the United States' Great Depression. Few mystics teach that financial poverty is associated with godliness even though, throughout the ages, spiritual seekers have been attracted to cloisters, monasteries, deserts, caves, and forests in a hope that forsaking material comforts would lead them closer to divinity.

According to the *Enneads,* they are on the right track. But it isn't our outward connection with material goods that is the problem; it is our inward preoccupation with things made of matter.

If a person gave away all that he had except a coarse cloak and a begging bowl yet worried incessantly about whether his cloak would be stolen or his bowl left unfilled, these two items would be more detrimental to his spiritual progress than would the vast holdings of a king whose serene contemplation of the divine was undisturbed by thoughts of either gain or loss.

No particular physical barrier prevents us from returning to God, for the One is not reached by journeying through time and space. Rather, it is the attention given to anything made of matter that keeps us bound to the cave wall of the material universe, forced to stare at shadows instead of the bright light of reality. A flea is strong enough to hold us here on Earth if we are unable to detach our minds from flea-thoughts and flea-desires.

> *It* [the All] *will not appear to you as long as you are in the midst of other things. It is not the case that it came, in order to be present; rather, if it is not present, it is you who have absented yourself. If you are absent, it is not that you have absented yourself from the All—it continues to be present—but rather that, while still continuing to be present, you have turned towards other things.* [VI-5-12][1]

The One is present in every particle of creation even though the source remains separate and distinct from what has been created.

Thus Plotinus says that the One, or God, never comes and goes, making an appearance here and disappearing there. So if we aren't aware of God's presence, it isn't the divine that has distanced itself. It is we who have chosen to pay attention to the creation instead of the source.

> *Whoever has seen knows what I am saying: when the soul approaches him [God], reaches him, and participates in him, she acquires another life, and when she is in this state, she realizes that the one she is with is the bestower of true life, and that she has no need of anything else; on the contrary, she knows she must reject everything else and rest in him alone.*
>
> *She must become him alone, cutting loose everything else we wear around ourselves. Therefore we hurry to escape from here; we are irritated at the bonds which tie us to other things, so that we may embrace him with the whole of ourselves, and have no part of us which is not in contact with God.* [VI-9-9][2]

The core of Plotinus's mystical philosophy is wondrously simple. God is one, the creation is many. Material multiplicity emanates from spiritual unity. To return to God, we must reverse this creative process. From many we must become one. What has been added on to the soul—matter, and mind mesmerized by matter—must be cast off. We don't need to be filled with spirit, for we already are. To realize this, all a spiritual seeker needs to do is empty his or her consciousness of material images and thoughts and be aware of what is left.

To return to the One, the soul must travel through domains of consciousness that are objectively real. This is the difference between armchair spiritual traveling and actual mystical transport into higher spheres of the cosmos. I can try to conjure up a mental picture of Paris from books and photographs, or memory if I've ever visited the city, but this isn't the same as actually being there. Plotinus's mystic philosophy is aimed at helping us understand what it takes to be in the presence of the One: to truly be with God, not merely with our ideas of God.

Our questioning, "What is God like?" is natural. But does it make sense to believe that we are even capable of asking the right questions about ultimate reality? Plotinus teaches that the framing of a question puts bounds around the answer. Since the One is infinite, omnipresent, and without any divisions, it is meaningless to ask what separate qualities God has. At the moment the question arises, so does the answer. Wrong.

And to inquire into what kind of thing it [the One] *is, is to enquire what attributes it has, which has no attributes. And the question "what is it?" rather makes clear that we must make no enquiry about it, grasping it, if possible, in our minds by learning that it is not right to add anything to it.* [VI-8-11]

Now it might seem that Plotinus contradicts his own message by having written tens of thousands of words in the *Enneads* inquiring into the nature of the One. However, what he points to in this passage is how the soul returns to the One, not how we prepare for the journey. This is akin to the distinction between reading travel brochures and getting on a plane.

A person can think all he or she likes about God before setting forth on the spiritual journey. But during his or her inward contemplation of spirit and the One, the means by which the soul travels homeward, all suppositions about the nature of divinity must be suspended. Otherwise we will find ourselves journeying through an exceedingly confined and almost entirely personal space: imagination. This is where we spend most of our supposedly spiritual time now, but it isn't where we want to be.

Plotinus explains that we generally think about God in a curious fashion. While paying lip service to a belief in a transcendent being who exists in a realm beyond normal mental cognition and sensory perception, we conjure up thoughts and images that are firmly rooted in everyday experiences. Even though we might call these conceptions "divine," actually they are merely material images thinly disguised by a covering of theological abstraction.

We first assume a space and place, a kind of vast emptiness, and then, when the space is already there, we bring this nature [of God] *into the place which has come to be or is in our imagination.* [VI-8-11]

In other words, we first assume that God is an entity like everything else with which we're familiar. Since things and people always occupy a place in space, so must God. This is our first faulty assumption. Building on this shaky foundation, we then go about asking how this divine being got into the place we just imagined for it.

However, it is better to be honest and say "I don't know what the One is like" than to fill our heads with guesses about God. An empty mind can be filled with truth; a mind clogged with false notions cannot.

As long as we're wholly immersed in the creation, how is it possible for us to believe that we can understand anything about the source of all this? Plotinus reminds us that the One existed by itself prior to the emanation of the spiritual and material realms. Can we conceive of anything beyond time and space? No, for our conceptions are products of time and space. These mental abstractions can accurately reflect physical reality (the goal of science) because they are founded on knowledge gained through our physical senses.

Physical reality, physical sensation. Nice match.

Spiritual reality, spiritual sensation. Also a nice match. But where are the spiritual senses that allow us to perceive spiritual realities? They are not part of the body, says Plotinus, because the body is physical. So we have to ignore what the external senses tell us in order to become attuned to the soul's internal senses.

> If there is to be perception of these great faculties within the soul, we must direct the faculty of sensation inwards, and make it concentrate its attention there.
>
> It is as if someone were waiting to hear a long-desired voice; he turns away from all other sounds, and awakens his ear to the best of all audible things, lest it should happen by.
>
> It is the same for us in this world: we must leave behind all sensible hearing, unless it is unavoidable, and keep the soul's power of perception pure and ready to hear the voices from on high. [V-1-12][3]

Between crude earthly existence and the ineffable One lie the grand realms of immaterial soul and spirit. Here there is matter, along with sights, sounds, and other sensations, but all is spiritual, not physical. The bodily senses must be put to sleep in order to awaken what Plotinus calls the soul's great faculties. This is the goal of the mystic philosopher's contemplation: to shift his or her attention from the shadows of Earth to the light of heaven, from the clanging clamor of outward sounds to the melodious music of spirit within.

When we sequester our senses and stop the movements of our minds, Plotinus assures us that we will be filled with the presence of the One since there is nowhere it is not. If we can divest ourselves of all else, God will remain.

If you have come to be within the All, then you will no longer search for anything. Otherwise you will give up, be diverted to something else, and fall; although it was right there, you will not have seen it, because you were looking elsewhere. If, on the other hand, you "no longer search for anything," how will you sense its presence? [VI-5-12][4]

Good question. Usually we conceive of spirituality as seeking for what we lack, the presence of God. If we don't search for God, or the One, then won't we remain in our current discontented condition? Yes, this is true. But Plotinus wants us to engage in a special sort of searching that is unlike any other kind of quest.

If I've lost an object in a dark room, my first thought is to turn on a light. Then I can locate what I'm looking for. This makes sense when my goal is to find something outside of myself. But when the object I've misplaced is my own true self, soul, then a radically different approach is called for.

Consciousness is the light of the soul. Attention is the means by which that light is focused. Plotinus teaches that soul illumines matter, spirit illumines soul, and the One illumines spirit. So what I seek is the source of the very light that is doing the seeking, my consciousness. In a beautiful passage, Plotinus explains that spiritual contemplation aims at uniting the soul's attention so intimately with the light of the One that nothing else is attended to.

> *We must believe that we have seen him when, suddenly, the soul is filled with light, for this light comes from him and is identical with him. . . . Similarly, the soul when she is unilluminated is godless and bereft of him; once she has been illuminated, however, she has what she was looking for.*
>
> *This is the real goal for the soul: to touch and to behold this light itself, by means of itself. She does not wish to see it by means of some other light; what she wants to see is that light by means of which she is able to see. What she must behold is precisely that by which she was illuminated.*
>
> *. . . How, then, could this come about? Eliminate everything [that is not light]!* [V-3-17][5]

As long as there is light, what is lit, and sight, we have three entities, not one. Light and sight, God's universal consciousness and the soul's personal consciousness, must enter into a union. This is accomplished by eliminating the unwanted third party, what is lit, whether this is a material or spiritual entity. If we continue to be conscious of the physical world, we will be aware of physical objects. And even if we come to be conscious of the spiritual world, we still will be aware of spiritual objects.

Thus everything must be left behind if the light of consciousness itself, the One, is to be known in its fullness. The more we let go of, the more we possess, until we have the All.

Forgetting Is Favorable

IMAGINE opening your eyes one morning, and not being able to remember anything that had happened before waking up. You know where you are but not where you've been. You know what you're thinking but not what you've thought. You know what you're feeling but not what you've felt.

Most people would consider this a scary proposition since the security that comes from having a stable sense of self is closely tied to our memories. Remembering that yesterday I was the same person I am today, it seems reasonable to anticipate that tomorrow I still will be me. If my personality had no past, it is difficult to imagine how I could confidently look forward to the future.

On the other hand, the idea of starting fresh has a considerable appeal. It's natural to look back upon the course of my life and wonder wistfully, "If only I had it to do over again." But I can't.

For we are forced into the future by the pressure of the past. Rather than freely choosing the direction we wish to go right now, we find ourselves traveling down habitual avenues of thinking and behaving, driven by a state of consciousness that adores ruts and the motto, "What has been, will be."

Plotinus points us toward another way of being where the wispy chimera of *has been* and *will be* fades away, gloriously supplanted by the solid reality of *is*. This is the life of soul in the spiritual realm, where there is nothing to recall and nothing to anticipate because everything exists all together as a whole.

> And what will the soul remember when it has come to be in the intelligible world, and with that higher reality? . . . It is impossible that there should be a memory there, not only of the things here below, but of anything at all. But each and every thing is present there; so there is no discursive thought or transition from one to the other. [IV-4-1]

Almost everyone has heard the adage, "Be here now," even if few of us are able to practice this wise advice. While physically here (where else could we be?) our minds frequently are far away in some other time or space. Ignoring the immediate presence of the present, we either replay past events that have come and gone or fast forward to an imaginary future. So being fully in touch with even this lower reality entails attending to what is, not what was or may be.

Still, it is understandable that past, present, and future freely intermingle in our earthly consciousness, since we live in a world of time. Time can't be ignored, for it is an undeniable aspect of our current reality. But if we want to experience a higher reality that is beyond time, then memories must be discarded.

Here, time creates divisions of past, present, and future while space divides one material form from another. Since this physical universe is so split up, memories and imagination help to connect one moment with the next and one thing with another. But the spiritual realm is a whole, a one-many of true being outside of time and becoming. In the soul's contemplation of the unchanging World of Forms, where each is in the all and the all is in each, there is no place for memory or thought.

> *If memory is something acquired, either learnt or experienced, then memory will not be present in those realities which are unaffected by experience or those which are in the timeless.* [IV-3-25]

Memories are traces of experiences that no longer exist for us. An experience becomes a memory when something changes. No change, no memory. Consider: throughout your life you have been conscious. Because you've been conscious of lots of different things, you have lots of different memories. But you have no memory of consciousness itself since it has always been with you. Similarly, you have no memory of being without a body because you've always possessed a physical form.

This helps us understand why Plotinus says that the realized soul doesn't remember or think about the One. How could it? That blessed soul essentially has become the One. You don't remember or think about what you are now, a human consciousness in a human body. Rather, you experience this state of being. In like fashion, when a soul returns to spirit and the One it will experience higher states of being, not remember or think about them.

Certainly the prospect of knowing God sounds wonderful. Yet if God is one, how would it be possible to truly know him except by merging with him? This is the genuine meaning of divine love. It isn't a relationship between a lover and a beloved, since this requires two entities. Instead, divine love is a union that is so intimate and natural it isn't even noticed or known. For as long as there is someone around who says, "I know God," the knowing is more accurately called a forgetting.

When a person really is immersed in something—a book, a thought, an activity, an emotion—there isn't enough of him left outside of that experience to know he is immersed in it. Only later does he recollect the experience from the outside, so to speak. Similarly, only when someone leaves God's presence does he or she say, "I was with him."

> *Well, then, will they not remember that they saw God? They always see him; and while they see him it is surely not possible to say that they have seen him: this would be something which would happen to those who have ceased to see.* [IV-4-7]

Of course, most of us would be exceedingly happy to have even a single memory of God. Our problem isn't that we now only remember the One but that we have never known him. So the dilemma faced by a spiritual seeker is how to forget the world without ever having had a remembrance of the divine. I can relax and go to sleep because I've woken up again so many times. But if I didn't know whether the oblivion of dreamless sleep was to last for only a short time or for eternity, it would be much more difficult to leave behind my present waking state.

Only the bold soul is able to traverse the most difficult part of the path that leads to the One: the journey from physical reality to the lower reaches of the spiritual world. As has already been noted, the inner emptiness within my consciousness marks the opening that leads out of the cave of illusion. Yet it isn't easy to turn away from the seeming solidity of all the physical shadows to which I have become accustomed, even if I am intellectually convinced that it is impossible to embrace spirit while clinging to matter.

> *Thus, if someone were to say that the good soul is forgetful, in this sense he would be right: the soul flees from multiplicity, and gathers the many together into one, and abandons the infinite. Thus she is not encumbered by multiplicity, but she is light and by herself. In this world, too, whenever she wishes, even while still in this one, to be in the other world, she abandons everything alien to her.* [IV-3-32][1]

Memories, thoughts, and sensations of multiplicity obviously won't bring the soul closer to the unity of the One. This is why the wise soul would rather be alone by itself than in the company of all this world has to offer. When the mind is empty of matter, it begins to be filled with the Good, even though spirit and the One may not yet be revealed in their fullness.

To rise up, the soul must become light. Material memories, says Plotinus, are like an anvil attached to the leg of those trying to swim in the spiritual, or intelligible, ocean. They drag us down to the bottom and we once again end up stuck in the muck of matter.

> *But if it* [the soul] *comes out of the intelligible world, and cannot endure unity, but embraces its own individuality and wants to be different and so to speak puts its head outside, it thereupon acquires memory. Its memory of what is in the intelligible world still holds it back from falling, but its memory of the things here below carries it down here.* [IV-4-3]

Now it must be admitted that this passage seems to contradict Plotinus's assertion that there is no memory in the spiritual world. But here he seems to be speaking of an in-between state where a soul that has risen to higher realms is no longer fully immersed in spirit, while it hasn't yet sunk all the way back to materiality. Balanced in this precarious condition the soul tilts in the direction of its memories and these are closely linked to its desires.

In an ideal situation, philosophy (the love of wisdom) should be a full-time way of life, not episodic intellectual speculation. Our consciousnesses have to be turned around from their present fascination with material objects and sensual pleasures in order to return to the One. This isn't just a matter of directing attention to the spirit within rather than the matter without. That is necessary, but not sufficient, to break the bonds that keep us earthbound.

As important, if not more so, is what Plotinus calls our general "disposition." This, we might say, is the net effect of all that the soul has experienced in countless incarnations. It's something we don't even know we have since it is so intimately entwined with our present sense of self. Though difficult to define, this global disposition toward heaven or earth is what makes the soul rise or fall.

> *But one must understand memory not only in the sense of a kind of perception that one is remembering, but as existing when the soul is disposed according to what it has previously experienced or contemplated. . . . And this is certainly the experience which makes the soul sink lower.* [IV-4-4]

The anonymous medieval author of *The Cloud of Unknowing* speaks in a similar fashion of what he calls a "filthy and nauseating lump—you do not particularize—between you and God." And what is this horrible barrier that separates us from divinity? The author says, "That lump is yourself. For you are to think of it as being identified with yourself: inseparable from you."[2]

To return to the One a spiritual seeker must first forget the world. Then he must forget his own self, or at least his illusory shadow self. For what presently seems so transparently obvious, that each of us is an ego-encapsulated entity distinct from everyone and everything else, is the densest illusion that must be cast off. What I currently take for granted, the inherent assumption that earthly existence is real as is the "I" experiencing it, must be exhumed from my unconscious and laid on the philosophical examining table for inspection.

Only then will I be able to divide the true me from the false me. As the saying goes, "Reality is that which, when you stop believing in it, doesn't go away." If I cease being aware of worldly sensations and memories and stop paying attention to my own body and personality, what remains? Reality.

Plotinus advises us to use the time-honored mystic approach of the *via negativa*, the negative way, to become aware of what we have forgotten: the unity of the One. By negating a negation, illusory material multiplicity, we arrive at the greatest positive Good. So the soul that longs to return home is happy to forget both the manyness without and the manyness within.

> *The more she hastens towards the upper regions, the greater is her for-getfulness, unless by chance her whole terrestrial life has been such that her memories are only of greater things. Indeed, even in this world, it is good "to be a stranger to human concerns"; necessarily, then, we must also avoid remembrances.* [IV-3-32][3]

This world appears solid and real but actually the eternal forms merely play upon the surface of ever-changing matter, failing to produce anything more than a semblance of true being. All this manyness confounds and depresses the soul, a stranger in a strange land.

So with great joy she turns her attention away from shadows and seeks to embrace her only true love, God. In this world, someone who has been long-separated from a beloved and catches sight of him or her across a crowded room will rush forward, eyes oblivious to everyone but the object of desire. In like fashion, the soul blessed with spiritual passion wants to forget everything but the One so there is no barrier to their divine union.

Purification Is Presence

WITH SO MUCH TALK in the past few chapters of detaching, divesting, emptying, and forgetting, it is important to keep in mind that the purpose of all this purification is presence. Since the One is overall, there is nowhere it is not. But as creation emanates from the One, ultimate reality is masked by increasingly complex spiritual and material forms. Thus Plotinus teaches that God is present when consciousness is purified of everything that is not-God. Returning to the One above means separating from the many below.

> *But the purification of the part subject to affections* [of this world] *is the waking up from inappropriate images and not seeing them, and its separation is effected by not inclining much downwards and not having a mental picture of the things below.* [III-6-5]

The soul's separation and purification happen simultaneously, just as the removal of a dark cover from a light and the consequent illumination are inextricably linked. Because the cosmos is a continuous emanation from the One with no gaps or firm divisions, every movement away from matter is a corresponding step toward spirit. This "turning," of course, doesn't involve any sort of physical motion.

Rather it is the inner attention that must be turned around. There is no problem with perceiving the physical world with our eyes, ears, and other sense organs. That merely involves matter affecting matter—photons, for example, stimulating light-sensitive ocular cells. What pollutes the purity of the soul is a different sort of affection—the mental images and memories that remain in consciousness when the physical sensations they represent are long gone.

It is impossible to contemplate spirit and the One if our attention is directed downward toward the people, objects, and activities of this world. Thus virtue is both the prerequisite and the result of spiritual realization. Pierre Hadot says, "Plotinian virtue is born of contemplation, and brings us back to contemplation."[1] As we read earlier:

> *When one falls from contemplation, he must reawaken the virtue within him.* [VI-9-11][2]

Since the greatest virtue is to turn away from the illusory shadow-shapes of this world and gaze upon immaterial divine light, it follows that Plotinus is much less concerned with what we do here on Earth than with how it is possible to reach heaven. J.M. Rist says, "Plotinus is not particularly concerned to tell us directly what we ought to do. . . . As in Plato, so in Plotinus we are not told what is morally good and what we therefore must (or ought to) choose."[3]

But Rist adds, "Of course, it does not follow that he is unconcerned with what ought to be done or thinks it of little importance. . . . For Plotinus, as for Plato, Aristotle and the Stoics, the good life is a life of virtue and virtue is a state of the soul. Without such a virtuous condition all hope of progress towards God is vain."[4] This is because Plotinian virtue is a simultaneous movement toward holy spirit and away from profane matter. If our consciousnesses are filled to the brim with worldly passions and perceptions, we shouldn't expect that there will be any room for God's presence.

> For it does no good to say, "Look towards God," unless we are taught how to look towards him. . . . What is there to stop us, someone might say, from looking towards God without abstaining from any pleasure, and without suppressing our anger? What is to stop us, let us say, from keeping the name "God" in mind, and yet being kept ensnared by every passion, and not trying to eliminate any of them?
>
> What shows God to us is virtue, as it comes to be in the soul, accompanied by wisdom. Without this genuine virtue, God is only a word. [II-9-15][5]

However, it is important to distinguish between the process of scrubbing the soul, which necessarily begins in our present bodily condition, and what remains when the scrubbing is done.

> But being completely purified is a stripping of everything alien, and the good is different from that. . . . The good will be what is left after purification, not the purification itself. [I-2-4]

As we've already learned, a quintessential Plotinian image is that of a statue encrusted with filth being cleansed until its original gilded beauty shines forth. Gold is different from both filth and cleansing, just as God is different from matter and purification. The One gleams in every particle of creation including every person's soul but is hidden under various material and mental coverings. Hence purification is a "stripping of everything alien," for the Good is what remains when lesser goods have been discarded.

We're reminded here to keep our attention focused on the goal, not the means. Purification, or virtue, is the means by which the soul realizes the One. Just as a destination isn't the same as the path that leads to it, pursuing virtue isn't the same as having attained to God. The soul's cup is cleansed only to be filled.

Our concern, though, is not to be out of sin, but to be god. [I-2-6]

At the end of the road there is no more road. Similarly, virtue is a quality of this lower world, not that higher world. Without virtue we will never be able to rise up spiritually, but when we leave materiality, virtue is left behind as well.

So, then, if we participate in order and arrangement and harmony which come from There, and these constitute virtue here, and if the principles There have no need of harmony or order or arrangement, they will have no need of virtue either, and we shall all the same be made like them by the presence of virtue. [I-2-1]

Plotinus says that virtue does not exist in the spiritual world. How could it? Virtue is the means by which the soul becomes akin to spirit and the One. Since spirit and the One are, obviously, already themselves they have no need of virtue. However, we do, because we are not yet who we truly are, pure soul. Hence it is necessary to put bounds on our otherwise limitless worldly desires. Limitless, because the fulfillment we seek cannot be found in a realm that possesses so little being and thus so little well-being.

But in the spiritual world it is just the opposite. There, what is boundless is the fulfillment of desire, for the World of Forms contains all that does exist, has existed, or could ever possibly exist. The purified soul is able to contemplate these forms so completely as to virtually become them, thereby achieving the wonderfully satisfying confluence of attainment and desire.

What is virtue for the soul? It is what she obtains as a result of her conversion. And what is this? Contemplation. . . . Wisdom and prudence consist in the contemplation of that which exists within the Intellect. . . . The best kind of justice for the soul is when her activity is directed entirely towards the Intellect, while temperance is turning inwards towards the

Intellect. Bravery is impassability, in imitation of that which the soul looks at: the Intellect, which is impassible by nature. [I-2-4, I-2-6][6]

So we see that Plotinian virtue is much more of a quiet turning within than an active doing without. The goal isn't to perform good deeds and stop there but to become the Good. While it certainly is better to act rightly than wrongly, Plotinus espouses a withdrawal from worldly concerns in which even the best external action is still "vulgar" in comparison to the sage's internal union with spirit.

John Dillon puts it nicely: "He [Plotinus] would, of course, observe the vulgar decencies; it is just that they would be subsumed into something higher. One feels of Plotinus that he would have gladly helped an old lady across the road—but he might very well fail to notice her at all. And if she were squashed by a passing wagon, he would remain quite unmoved."[7] While this may sound heartless, to Plotinus such a Stoic attitude actually is divine, for it reflects the impassible nature of spirit and the Soul of the All, which similarly remain unaffected by all the goings-on of the physical universe.

Whether a person lives a good life or a bad life, it is still a bodily life. Thus true virtue entails breaking every sort of attachment to matter and cleaving solely to spirit through inward contemplation.

It could perhaps be said that, in and of itself, life within the body is an evil, but that, thanks to virtue, the soul can come to be within the Good, not by living the life of the composite [of soul and body], but by separating herself from it already in this life. [I-7-3][8]

It is fine to live with a body but not for a body. The mystic philosopher's life isn't centered around bodily needs and desires. Rather, he or she recognizes that the body with which an incarnated soul presently is involved should be the servant of the soul, not the master. After all, who is better able to decide what is right and good: unintelligent matter or intelligent soul?

Since the soul is evil when it is thoroughly mixed with the body and shares its experiences and has all the same opinions, it will be good and possess virtue when it no longer has the same opinions but acts alone. [I-2-3]

Still, all this talk of controlling the body and not sharing in its experiences shouldn't leave us with the impression that Plotinian virtue involves any sort of forceful repression of our natural appetites. Sensual passions and the cruder sort of human desires simply fade away as the sage's attention becomes more firmly rooted in the bliss of a higher consciousness. Hence, virtue isn't something distinct from a person's innermost being, a flimsy façade he presents to the outside world that masks his genuine inclinations.

> *In short, the soul herself will be pure from all these things, and will wish to make her irrational part pure from them as well. In this way she will not be disturbed, or if at all, then not intensely; but the disturbances will be few and easily dissolved by the proximity [of the Spirit].* [I-2-5][9]

Best of all is for the soul to not have any physical desires at all, but to provide for the body almost as a matter of duty. We should eat and drink and have sex to live, not live to eat and drink and have sex.

If we are still attracted to sensual pleasures, they should be simple pleasures. Spending a quiet evening drinking wine with friends is preferable to reveling drunkenly at a Bacchanalian orgy. Unnatural desires that go far beyond fulfilling the body's physical needs and wants are to remain a fantasy, not reality, and should enter a person's imagination only when reason is temporarily helpless.

Bodily needs and sensual desires are part of our physical nature that we share with other animals. Yet the true natural condition of the soul is either not to be tied to a material body, or, if already incarnated, to be as detached as possible from the crude flesh, blood, and bone with which it is temporarily partnered.

> *The true person is something different, pure from contact with the animal part of our nature.* [I-1-10][10]

If our bodies could make us truly happy, not just for a moment but permanently, then this would be unarguable evidence that alcohol, drugs, sex, food, beauty, fame, and money have been given to us for our guilt-free enjoyment. But experience demonstrates that this isn't the case. Every body eventually withers and dies along with the hopes for happiness placed in it. And even while we remain in materiality, the soul remains hungry after every meal of physical sensation, no matter what is served.

Only when the soul is able to enjoy the light of spirit in the World of Forms will it finally begin to enjoy true bliss. The sage no longer seeks solace through outer activities and external sensations because a much greater source of satisfaction has been found within.

> *The illumination which comes from the Intellect gives the soul a clearer, brighter life, but a life which is not generative. On the contrary, it turns the soul back upon herself and does not allow her to become dispersed, but rather makes her satisfied with the splendor within her.* [V-3-8][11]

Since people have an outer life and an inner life, there are two different kinds of virtue. The lower civic virtue is a foundation for the higher purificatory virtue. Basically, civic or social virtue encompasses the qualities and behaviors we normally associate with a good person: prudence, justice, civility, generosity, honesty, kindness, courage, temperance, and so on.

> *The civic virtues . . . do genuinely set us in order and make us better by giving limit and measure to our desires, and putting measure into all our experience.* [I-2-2]

The civic virtues aid in turning our attention away from physical concerns and pleasures, and toward spirit and the One. We might think of them as giving us some wriggle room, loosening the ties that bind us to materiality enough to allow us to turn toward the purificatory virtues that lead fully to spiritual freedom. For Plotinus says that a good man who possesses the lower virtues is not necessarily godly, while a godly man who has the higher virtues will necessarily be good. Thus the lesser comes along with the greater but by itself the lesser does not lead to the greater.

> *Whoever has the greater virtues must necessarily have the lesser ones potentially, but it is not necessary for the possessor of the lesser virtues to have the greater ones.* [I-2-7]

A seed of evil can only sprout when there is some ground to grow in. When the soul has been purified of its inclination toward matter, the battle is over, and the spiritual seeker rests in peace. Pierre Hadot writes: "Thus the purificatory virtues correspond to a complete transformation of inner life, in which one could say that all our spiritual energy flows back inside and upwards. . . . Lower things are no longer of interest; we don't really pay attention to them anymore, and they therefore no longer present a problem. All our activity is turned towards God."[12]

It comes down simply to *presence*. The presence of spirit, the presence of the One, the presence of ourselves as soul—at heart it's all the same presence, the sublime reality that lies beneath appearances. This is the presence we long for, the presence we've been missing since we separated from the spiritual world, the presence we look for and never find in other people and outside things.

Plotinian virtue, says Hadot, "is only a continuous attention to the divine, and a perpetual exercise of God's presence. . . . The Good acts on the Spirit by its mere presence; the Spirit acts on the soul, and the soul on the body; all by their presence alone."[13]

> *The soul receives into herself an outpouring that comes from above. . . .*
> *The Good is gentle, mild, and very delicate, and always at the disposition*
> *of whomever desires it.* [VI-7-22, V-5-12][14]

Simplicity Is Superior

SCIENCE AND MYSTICISM often are at loggerheads, notwithstanding their common interest in knowing the truth about ultimate reality. In large part, this is because the outwardly observable methods of scientists necessarily limit them to investigating the material, while the inward observations of mystics are directed toward the spiritual.

So it is wonderful that science agrees so heartily with a central tenet of Plotinus's mystic philosophy: simplicity is a reliable guide to truth. This principle often is termed Ockham's razor, as William of Ockham (a fourteenth-century scholastic) held that the simplest explanation is the best: "Entities are not to be multiplied beyond necessity."[1] Plotinus echoes this sentiment.

> *For that which generates is always simpler than that which is generated.*
> [III-8-9]

Findings of modern science have confirmed the validity of using Ockham's razor to pare away layers of unnecessary complexity to arrive at a core of primordial simple truth. Physicist James Trefil says, "If I had to pick out a single overall characteristic of the evolution of the universe, it would be the development of complexity from simplicity. The universe seems to get simpler as we move backward in time."[2]

In the beginning, according to current theories about the origin of the universe, there was only a single substance, an unimaginably potent unified energy. Much as a huge banyan tree springs from a single seed, and a person grows from a single cell, the amazing variety of life and non-life now evident in material existence sprouted and branched from one root.

> *For many does not come from many, but this [intelligible] many comes from what is not many.* [V-3-16]

Science accepts that the development of complexity from simplicity occurred on the physical level over time. Plotinus teaches a deeper mystic truth, that simplicity also produces complexity in a metaphysical and timeless sense, since on both the macrocosmic and microcosmic levels what is less unified continuously emanates from what is more unified. Hence, simplicity is superior for those who want to know the source, rather than what flows from the source. Creation is complex, while the creator is simple. It's up to us to decide which way to face.

Returning to the One means embracing an inner simplicity. Presently the ensemble known as "me" comprises three primary entities: body, a lower reasoning and emotional aspect of my consciousness (mind), and a higher spiritual aspect of my consciousness (soul). This is two too many if I seek unity. What has to go is what I am not: the complicated accretions to my simple soul.

Previously we read, "The soul alone may receive him alone." The simplicity of the One can be known only by a soul that is almost equally simple. For what is simple is single, pure, unified, one. Each of these words points to the same undivided reality. Another synonym is self-sufficient, since anything that exists solely and always as itself needs nothing else.

> *And we call it the First in the sense that it is simplest, and the Self-Sufficient, because it is not composed of a number of parts; for if it were, it would be dependent upon the things of which it was composed.* [II-9-1]

Complexity and neediness are linked, since anything that is not a simple unity needs the parts that make it up to preserve its being (which helps explain why the partless One is said to be beyond being). Thus neediness serves as a gauge of our spiritual progress. As the soul becomes purified, it becomes simpler, and thus increasingly self-sufficient. We might consider, then, to what extent we look to the outside world to fulfill us. Are we able to spend a few quiet hours absorbed in spiritual contemplation without feeling that we're missing something?

> *What then is more deficient than the One? That which is not one; it is therefore many.* [V-3-15]

Matter is the most deficient of all that has emanated from the One, because it possesses the least unity, the least being, the least substance. We mustn't be misled by matter's seeming simplicity. For even though its emptiness of all form superficially mimics the formlessness of the One, the inescapable nature of matter is multiplicity, not unity.

This is because the spiritual forms always remain distinct from matter, so the unified reality that lies behind physical appearances never can be known in this world. Reaching out for reality, the senses are limited to grasping a bunch of separate perceptions devoid of true meaning. This existential emptiness is a sort of simplicity but not the kind that satisfies the soul.

A simpleton stays silent because he has nothing to say; a sage abstains from speaking because he possesses a wisdom beyond words. Their silences are outwardly similar but inwardly flow from markedly different states of being.

Likewise, Plotinus teaches that nature's apparent simplicity is more accurately viewed as a last gasp of the One's creative energy. Matter is like a car that has run out of fuel, for it is a completely passive receptacle of the spiritual forms. Its activity is simple—nothing, nothing some more, and then more nothing—because it can't do anything. By contrast, the One's activity is simple—all, still all, always all—because it does everything.

> *For the activity of the last and lowest is simple as coming to a stop, but of the first is all activities.* [VI-7-13]

What the mystic philosopher seeks to contemplate within is not the void of matter, but the fullness of spirit and the One. Yet this true All is unlike anything that we know now. So how is it possible to bridge the seemingly unbridgeable gap between our personal consciousness, currently firmly enmeshed in shadows and illusion, and the light of universal consciousness?

Thankfully, each of us possesses a lifeline that is capable of pulling us back to our divine source, if we are able to attach ourselves to it, and let go of all else.

> *They* [souls] *are linked to the brevity of intellect by that in each of them which is least divided.* [IV-3-5]

"Brevity," Shakespeare tells us, "is the soul of wit."[3] According to Plotinus, brevity also is the soul of the soul, so to speak. The soul, like spirit and the One, is without parts. Thus, whatever can be split off from consciousness isn't soul but something else. Since thoughts, emotions, perceptions, memories, and imaginations continually come and go within consciousness they can't be our link to the unchanging reality of true being.

Spiritual contemplation requires a delicate touch. It is all about simple presence, not complex movement.

It turns out that the source of our wanting is what we truly want. If we could only reverse the flow of attention, tracing our cravings back to the lofty headwaters of desire instead of moving downstream with them into the marshes of materiality, we would find the simple unity from which all else comes.

> *And the All could not any more come into being if the origin did not remain by itself, different from it. Therefore, too, we go back everywhere to one.* [III-8-10]

Soul, like the One, creates. God creates objective reality; our souls create subjective reality. From a spiritual perspective, the contents of these worlds within are much less important than the powers that produce them. The powers of the soul are universal and God-given. How these powers are manifested is largely a matter of individual whim and personal circumstance. Physical desires, for example, differ in various sorts of people, while the power of desire operates the same in all.

Thus it is unfortunate that few people seriously try to trace the creations within consciousnesses back to their source. Most of us remain absorbed in what is showing on the screen of consciousness and never make much of an effort to discern how those images are projected. This keeps us imprisoned in Plato's cave of illusion, absorbed in counting the shadows on the cavern wall and debating among ourselves which comes first and which after, which is most desirable and which least desirable, all the while failing to turn around and learn the source of the light that produces the shadows.

We aren't going to be able to approach the single source of consciousness, the One, so long as we are occupied with its many products. The most basic of these products is a primal division between consciousness and self-consciousness. Somehow *psyche* creates a sense of self along with all the other thoughts, emotions, images, and what-not it brings into being. This duality between our simple awareness and our more complex awareness of being aware is an insidious barrier to the unity we seek. Insidious because self-awareness seems so natural to us it is difficult to imagine existing without it.

For intimate self-consciousness is a consciousness of something which is many: even the name bears witness to this. [V-3-13]

Adhering to the adage "know yourself" means being present to one's self *as* one's true self, not looking upon one's self as if it was an object, something to be perceived or pondered. We can perceive an apple, a galaxy, and a starfish, or ponder truth, justice, and love. We can't perceive or ponder what is at the root of all our diverse perceiving and pondering just as an eye cannot see itself and a finger cannot touch itself.

The goal of spiritual contemplation is to merge the knower, what is known, and the process of knowing into a unified whole. So living daily life un-self-consciously is a preparation for the favorable forgetting of the lower self upon reaching the spiritual world. There, we are drunk with divinity and don't remember who we were before our intoxication.

How does it [the soul] *remember itself? It will not even have the remembrance of itself, or that it is the man himself, Socrates for instance, who is contemplating, or that it is intellect or soul.* [IV-4-2]

In all that the sage does, whether it be in the world without or the world within, he or she seeks to be spontaneously guided by spirit's intuitive intelligence. His or her locus of action becomes increasingly natural and universal, mimicking the effortless activity of the Soul of the All, which always does exactly what needs doing when it needs to be done.

It isn't necessary to go through life as a sort of double image: a me that does things and a largely unnecessary hanger-on inside my head who watches and comments on the doer. The internal mental dialogue most people take for granted is akin to a play-by-play announcer who never stops gabbing about what is happening on the field of our awareness. The problem is that I already know what is going on because I'm directly experiencing it. I should be able to simply wash the dishes without an inner voice telling me the obvious: "I'm washing the dishes."

Indeed, what we do and what we are is clearly separable from our self-awareness of those actions, thoughts, and inner states. This self-consciousness doesn't add to reality but rather runs the risk of diffusing our attention between what is and what we believe "is" to be. Plotinus asks if a good man is still good if he isn't conscious of being a good man. Absolutely, he answers.

> *But if he does not know that he is healthy, he is healthy just the same, and if he does not know that he is handsome, he is handsome just the same. So if he does not know that he is wise, will he be any the less wise?* [I-4-9]

It's a wonderful mystery. By losing ourselves, we find ourselves.

> *The seer . . . cannot then see or distinguish what he sees, nor does he have the impression of two entities [the seer and the object seen]; rather, it is as if he has become someone else, and no longer himself.* [VI-9-10][4]

Stillness Is Sublime

IT'S A JOURNEY like no other, this return to the One. Our progress is most rapid when we move the least. Indeed, we'll arrive at our destination only when we're absolutely still.

If this sounds paradoxical, it's because our experience of reality currently is firmly rooted in the physical. Here on Earth we move from physical place to physical place by transporting our physical bodies through physical space. Even if our movement is from thought to thought or perception to perception, this sort of meandering still takes time, and time is motion.

Thus, presently few of us know what it is like to be truly at rest. Since change is continuous in everyday life, it's understandable that most people's spirituality is based on activity rather than stillness. Prayer. Good works. Worship. Reading of holy books. All this entails motion of body or mind. Where, though, does such movement lead us?

While it is commonplace to speak of being on a spiritual path, Plotinus teaches that most of what we do in the name of God actually leads us farther from divinity rather than closer. Movement is what produces separation from the One, so the notion of an active spirituality contains an inherent contradiction.

For this reason Movement, too, was called Otherness, because Movement and Otherness sprang forth together. [II-4-5]

Everything that is not the One is, obviously, part of the otherness to which Plotinus refers. Spirit, however, remains exceedingly close to the source from which it emanates. Though separate from God, it eternally embraces the highest Good, as intimately connected with what is beyond being as possible. This is our goal: to enjoy, with spirit, the intimate companionship of the One.

Movement, says Plotinus, is what primarily distinguishes soul and spirit. Soul would be essentially the same as spirit if not for its motion. The activity of soul, both of the universal Soul of the All and of individual souls, is directed toward the One, for all things aspire to God. But this lofty aspiration is sidetracked by our sensual and bodily inclinations. Our innate longings for the One become transmuted into desires for the many.

The soul thus becomes bound by matter and keeps on circling within the cage of the physical universe. We know we are missing something, so keep on searching. However, this very movement is what prevents us from experiencing the presence of spirit and the One. We keep on in this fashion, life after life, both out of ignorance and out of a desire to be separate. *Tolma* (self-assertion) makes the soul want to move in manyness rather than rest in oneness.

> *And it* [soul] *is one being, but makes itself many by what we may call its movement. . . . For if it appears as one, it did not think, but is that One.* [VI-2-6]

Separateness, self-consciousness, and movement are all interrelated. Desiring to exist as parts of creation rather than as the whole, we naturally want to know that we are parts. So we as soul contemplate our own selves and thus become conscious of ourselves as distinct entities. This unique capacity of humans to be self-aware allows us not only to think but to think about thinking. Now we can move in directions other animals cannot. Books can be written, cultures created, philosophies developed, sciences structured.

This is wonderful if our goal is to explore and experiment with the creation rather than return to the creator. However, if our goal is the One, then there is a problem with all of this thinking, for that, Plotinus says, "is the cause of its appearing many." [VI-2-6] Intuitive spiritual intelligence is worlds apart from discursive (step by step) mental reasoning. Neither spirit nor God think in the way we do, but they are infinitely wiser.

Any movement of our minds can only take us farther from the calm, pure consciousness that each of us already is, but has covered under layers of sense perception, emotion, and cogitation. Our inner essence is virtually identical with that of spirit. This is why we need to cultivate stillness, for spirit is forever at rest. The more a person contacts the unmoving center of his own being, the closer he comes to the stationary center of universal being. As we read earlier:

> *It* [spirit] *has therefore everything at rest in the same place, and it only is, and its "is" is for ever, and there is no place for the future for then too it is—or for the past—for nothing there has passed away—but all*

things remain stationary for ever, since they are the same, as if they were satisfied with themselves for being so. [V-1-4]

On the face of it, we're caught in a vicious circle. Since we always have a longing for some indefinable "more," some aspect of each of our consciousnesses is in constant motion (with the possible exception of dreamless sleep). This constant motion, however, prevents us from rising up to the spiritual world, the only place where what we long for can be found. So our seeking leads to more seeking, never to finding.

It's no wonder that so many people turn to prayer. For it certainly seems that, unaided, the soul is powerless to extricate itself from this material maze. Blind alleys abound. Running aimlessly leads nowhere. What we know how to do, think, emote, perceive, imagine, remember, won't enable us to reach a realm beyond thought, emotion, perception, imagination, and memory. It's as if we had studied hard for an all-important exam only to find that none of the material on the test was covered in the classes we had attended.

"Help me, God!" is an understandable reaction to this perilous condition. Death awaits us all and though we may feel that we're competent to get through life, the afterlife is *terra incognita*, unknown territory. Faced with the uncertainty of what will happen to us after our last breath, an appeal to a power stronger and wiser than ourselves is entirely in order. However, says Plotinus, there is a proper way to pray. And it doesn't involve words.

Let us speak of it in this way, first invoking God himself, not in spoken words, but stretching ourselves out with our soul into prayer to him, able in this way to pray alone to him alone. [V-1-6]

What, indeed, could we possibly say to God that needs saying? We pray because we believe God is all-knowing and all-powerful. Yet praying in words belies our belief, since this implicitly conveys the message that God is incapable of doing what needs to be done unless we help him out.

"My mother is ailing, Lord. Please take care of her." Thoughts like these imply there is an off-on switch to divine providence that prayer somehow manipulates. Utter a prayer and, click, God comes to life and is in charge of the situation. Stop praying and God goes on a break, uninvolved in earthly affairs until another prayer calls him back to duty.

To Plotinus, this sort of thinking is hopelessly at odds with the true nature of the One, spirit, and soul. Genuine prayer is simple presence, a wordless turning toward the One who is always turned toward us. J.M. Rist says, "Prayer is a means of uniting the One in ourselves with the One in itself. . . . When a man prays 'alone to the Alone', he has come to recognize that the One is always present and that it is up to himself to look towards him if he wishes. . . . The One is always turned towards us; in the highest act of prayer we turn again towards him."[1]

This turning is neither a physical nor a mental action. What we must do is try to merge the unity that is us with the unity that is the cosmos. This can't be accomplished by an act of will, for will involves duality: a doer and a thing to be done. Hence, any fervent effort to become one will prevent us from simply being one. Rather, the sage seeks a state of rest that, nonetheless, carries him away.

> But he was as if carried away or possessed by a god, in a quiet solitude and a state of calm, not turning away anywhere in his being and not busy about himself, altogether at rest and having become a kind of rest. [VI-9-11]

Mountaineers who aspire to reach the lofty heights of Everest or K2 must train mightily to prepare for the rigors they will face. Muscles must be strengthened, climbing skills perfected, endurance expanded, determination deepened. The mystic philosopher must also transform his being into a fit vehicle for ascending to the One, but the training method is considerably different. For a climber needs to perfect his ability to move, while a mystic must become expert at remaining motionless.

> And the soul is so disposed then as even to despise intelligence, which at other times it welcomed, because intelligence is a kind of movement, and the soul does not want to move. . . . It does not even think that it does not think. [VI-7-35]

The intelligence to which Plotinus refers is the ever-moving train of human thought that possesses one object of knowledge after another, not the all-encompassing intuitive intelligence of spirit. When Plotinus wrote the *Enneads*, word by word and sentence by sentence, to some extent he necessarily used a lower power of his consciousness: discursive reason. His moving pen reflected his moving thoughts.

But when Plotinus contemplated the unchanging One, it was with true intelligence, a power of the *psyche* far beyond thinking. God's truth is absorbed by the soul through a spiritual osmosis in which the knower communes so intimately with the known that seeing becomes sight. It is fruitless to expect or force this vision, since the One is utterly unlike anything that we know now, or could possibly imagine knowing.

J.M. Rist says, "If we 'pursue' the One, of course we shall always tend to specify it, to see it under some particular aspect. We must learn instead to be passive, to let it come, as it will come if we take away our own restlessness, that very restlessness which prevents us from being like it."[2]

> *Suddenly, a light bursts forth, pure and alone. We wonder whence it came: from the outside, or from the inside? Once it disappears, we say, "It was inside—and yet, no, it wasn't inside." We must not try to learn whence it comes, for here there is no "whence."*
>
> *The light comes from nowhere, and it goes nowhere; it simply either appears or does not appear. That is why we must not chase after it, but quietly wait for it to appear, preparing ourselves to be spectators, as the eye waits for the rising sun. [V-5-7, V-5-8][3]*

We're reminded of John 3:8. "The wind blows where it chooses, and you hear the sound of it, but you do not know where it comes from or where it goes. So it is with everyone who is born of the Spirit."

Spirit and God are neither outside of us nor inside of us. Spiritual illumination accompanies a change in consciousness, not a shift in space or a traversing of time. When divine light fills the soul, its source is a mystery. Indeed, as Plotinus says, the radiance comes from nowhere and it goes nowhere, for it is the root of all that exists.

The only thing we must do to quietly contemplate the One is to stop actively contemplating the many. The sun appears to rise as the world turns, but actually it is always shining. Similarly, as our attention turns from the multiplicity of matter to the singleness of spirit, illumination *will* occur. But in its own fashion, not ours.

Happiness Is Here

IN THE PRESENT moment, you and I are as happy as we will ever be.

On the face of it, this thoroughly Plotinian sentiment appears both nonsensical and unappealing. Nonsensical because it's obvious that day by day (if not hour by hour or minute by minute) our level of happiness rises and falls, pushed higher or driven lower by external and internal circumstances. Unappealing because belief in the prospect of greater future happiness helps us endure present pain and unpleasantness.

Still, there is undeniable delight in the notion that happiness is here. Here now, here tomorrow, here where I am, here where I will be. Who wouldn't prefer to go through life enjoying the ever-present companionship of happiness rather than always expecting to meet up around the next corner? The older we get the more corners we have turned and the harder it is to believe that the unalloyed happiness we seek ever will be found.

We're right. It won't be found. At least, not so long as we look for the source of happiness anywhere outside of us. Marcus Aurelius, the philosophical second-century Roman emperor (whose Stoic conceptions closely resemble aspects of Plotinus's teachings) says, "Happiness, by derivation, means 'a good god within.' "[1] Such is the meaning of *eudaimonia*, the Greek word for happiness. Thus happiness and spirituality go hand in hand.

> *Being happy pertains only to that which has an excess of life. . . . Perfect, true, and genuine life consists in that intellective nature. . . . That person's life is complete who possesses not only the faculty of sensation, but also rationality and true Spirit. . . . The person who is happy here and now [is] the one who is this form of life in actuality, and has reached the stage of becoming this life itself.* [I-4-3, I-4-4][2]

The sage is always happy because he or she is always turned toward God, the ultimate Good, not the lesser goods offered up by the physical world. As noted before, our attempts to find well-being through interactions with people, places, and things are stymied by the fact that these entities lack true being. So no matter how closely we physically hug them to our breasts or mentally absorb them into our consciousnesses, they fail to satisfy us. What we long for is within so the search for happiness without, in time and space, is bound to be fruitless.

Happiness, or well-being, isn't a will-of-the-wisp that flutters here and there, always escaping our grasp, frustrating us by remaining just out of reach. This is true only of the dim reflection of genuine happiness that is able to manifest in the physical world. Time pushes a present moment of enjoyment into the past, so if our happiness is dependent on the ever-changing circumstances of materiality, our well-being is bound to fluctuate.

The Good, however, is eternally present at the core of all that exists, including our own selves. By inwardly contemplating spirit and the One, the mystic philosopher forges a direct connection between his soul and the wellspring of happiness. No longer dependent on the trickles of physical and mental pleasure that most of us try so assiduously to collect in our cups of consciousness, the sage enjoys a torrent of divine bliss that flows freely and continuously, like an artesian well, in his own soul.

> *He is his own good for himself, thanks to what he possesses. The cause of the Good within him is the transcendent Good. . . . The person in this state no longer seeks anything; for what could he seek? Certainly not for anything inferior to him; and as for what is best, he is with it already.* [I-4-4][3]

We see here how far removed Plotinus's philosophy is from the extreme sense of asceticism, a hatred of the material world. The good man doesn't shun worldly pleasures because he considers them evil, ungodly, sinful, or depraved. Rather, he possesses something better, the Good itself, and so has no need for anything that is less than the best. Happiness, probably better termed "bliss," turns out to be inseparable from being, as in the Hindu description of the highest reality as *sat-chit-ananda*, or truth-consciousness-bliss.

To ask a sage, or realized soul, "How happy are you?" would be as absurd as someone saying to us, "How existent are you?" For just as existence is part and parcel of our present state of being, so is happiness part and parcel of the being of those who have united their soul with spirit. Happiness then is not something that we have, a changeable quality like blood pressure, weight, or body temperature, but an integral aspect of what we are.

This explains why some people, though poor or sick, are happy, while others are miserable notwithstanding their wealth and health.

Well-being is a state of the soul, not of outward circumstances. Plotinus says that each of us has the potential to enjoy unalloyed happiness but generally this remains a possibility, not reality. Thus most people look upon the good life as something separate from themselves, envisioning that it will make an appearance when they retire, move to a nicer climate, strike it rich in the lottery, or get the kids through college.

Rarely does a person consider that happiness is something he or she already possesses but has misplaced under all the myriad thoughts and perceptions that clutter consciousness. Virtue, as Plotinus uses the term, means eliminating from the *psyche* all that is not spirit or the One. What remains will not be anything good in particular, but the Good in itself.

> *If he is virtuous, he has all he needs for well-being and the acquisition of good; for there is no good that he has not got.* [I-4-4]

Feeling unhappy, most people think, "What can I do that would make me happier?" Sometimes this is as simple as going to a movie, walking in a park, reading a book, talking with a friend, or eating chocolate. Sometimes we seek more radical changes: moving to another city, changing jobs, getting a divorce, losing lots of weight. These sorts of actions may assuage our malaise temporarily but they aren't lasting solutions. For happiness doesn't depend on what we do but on what we are.

> *It is one's inner state which produces both well-being and any pleasure that results from it. To place well-being in actions is to locate it in something outside virtue and the soul.* [I-5-10]

Some people work amazingly hard at trying to be happy. For example, they may put in a twelve-hour day on the job to make money that will enable them to buy things or go places that will, they hope, bring them satisfaction.

One problem with this circuitous approach to gaining happiness, in which a person engages in external actions to produce an alteration in his or her internal state of being, is that it is terribly inefficient. The periods in which we rest content are eclipsed by all the time we spend straining and sweating to reach a state of ease. By contrast, through inward contemplation it is possible to tap directly into the soul's source of happiness: spirit and the One. Then well-being is enjoyed continuously, rather than episodically.

This is as it should be, teaches Plotinus, for happiness is like breathing. I can remember that my lungs were filled with air a moment ago but after being punched in the stomach and losing my breath that remembrance is of no use to me. I need air!—not a memory of air. Similarly, all that matters is present happiness, for a memory of prior well-being is like a memory of spent money: it can't buy current satisfaction.

> *And besides, what pleasure is there in the memory of pleasantness—for instance, if someone remembers that yesterday he enjoyed some nice food? And if it was ten years ago that he enjoyed it, he would be even more ridiculous. The same applies to the memory that one was virtuous and intelligent last year. . . . Memory, surely, can play no part in well-being; nor is it a matter of talking, but of being in a particular state.* [I-5-8, I-5-1]

We shouldn't expect that recording a memory of a good or wise act and playing it back inside the mind when we're no longer virtuous or intelligent is a suitable substitute for a live performance in the present moment. A thought of a thing is not that thing. Similarly, remembering or anticipating happiness is not the same as being happy. Nor can imagining union with God be equated with actually returning to the One. Plotinus urges us to realize the actual living presence of what we long for. To be content with anything less is to never truly be content.

> *This is the reason why one would not find acceptable the feeling produced by something one has not got. . . . Nor do I think that those who find the good in bodily satisfaction would feel pleasure as if they were eating when they were not eating or as if they were enjoying sex when they were not with the one they wanted to be with.* [VI-7-26]

Consider three people reading, respectively, a romance novel, a pornographic magazine, and a religious scripture. Each finds enjoyable the feeling of love, broadly speaking, that their reading material produces in them. In one person this love has a romantic tinge, in another a lustful flavor, in the last a sacred sense. But the common element between them is that they are experiencing a feeling that approximates, to some degree, the sensation they would have if they actually possessed the object of their desire.

"Oh, to be swept away by the man of my dreams." "Oh, to make passionate love to the woman of my fantasies." "Oh, to be in the presence of my blessed God." The feelings that accompany such thoughts, says Plotinus, are pleasurable only in a severely limited sense because what we really want are not the feelings that accompany thought, but the feelings that accompany reality.

Ersatz feelings of the sort just described can become an unhealthy substitute for the real thing. It's wonderful if reading stimulates us to find a real man, a real woman, or a real God that can satisfy our longing. But if we remain content with, in Plotinus's words, "the feeling produced by something one has not got," then it can be argued that we are worse off with that false feeling. The danger here is the same sort of danger faced by a seriously dehydrated person who hallucinates that he is drinking water when a well is within his reach.

> Certainly the good which one chooses must be something which is not the feeling one has when one attains it; that is why the one who takes this for good remains empty, because he only has the feeling which one might get from the good. [VI-7-26]

We need to recognize that there is a big difference between (1) the full feeling that accompanies the actual attainment of a good, and (2) the empty feeling that accompanies the imaginary attainment of a good. What we crave is the real thing, not a thought or emotion produced by a conception of that thing. This seems obvious and almost trite when we look at specific examples such as romance novel, pornography, and religious addicts, people who spend their days in a fantastical haze, immersed in a seductive world of subjective imagination that they never try to convert into objective reality.

Plotinus says that anyone who believes happiness can be found in physical pleasure or mental sensation is equally deluded. And this, it must be admitted, includes almost all of us. The purpose of philosophy is to awaken us to the fact that we're grasping after empty external material images even though we possess the fullness of spirit within our own selves.

> And he must have the doctrines of philosophy implanted in him; by these he must be brought to firm confidence in what he possesses without knowing it. [I-3-1]

Pleasure is the image of happiness, as the physical universe is the image of the spiritual world. If someone hasn't realized the happiness within his soul, then he will mistakenly consider that well-being springs from sensual delights. However, every sort of pleasurable physical sensation bears the same relation to genuine happiness as a photograph has to what was photographed, or an imaginary feeling that one possesses something has to the actual immediate presence of it.

This allows Plotinus to argue that the presence or absence of worldly goods has no effect on the well-being, or happiness, of the mystic philosopher.

> *But suppose there were two wise men, one of whom had all of what are called natural goods and the other their opposites, shall we say that they both have well-being equally? Yes, if they are equally wise.* [I-4-15]

One person is healthy, the other sick. One person is wealthy, the other poor. One person is famous, the other not known. One person has many friends, the other has none. Yet if they both have an equal knowledge of the Good, or the One, then they are equally happy.

What most people call pleasure the sage considers mere bodily sensation, irrelevant to his or her inner well-being. For what really derives benefit from eating a tasty meal, engaging in passionate sex, imbibing delicious drink, soaking in scented water, lying on a warm beach, or any other of the physical activities normally valued as pleasurable? It isn't the higher aspect of soul that needs or wants these sorts of feelings. Rather, it is the body and the lower aspect of soul which drive us to fulfill physical desires.

If our desire is directed toward the One, then actions properly aimed at fulfilling this desire will end up satisfying us. But if our longing is misdirected toward the ever-changing and illusory objects of the material world, then we will be continually frustrated. How can people and things that fail to last succeed in bringing us lasting happiness? Plotinus provides a simple and straightforward criterion for determining what is truly good: when we get it, we don't want anything else.

> *But the attainment* [of the Good] *is confirmed when a thing becomes better and has no regrets, and fulfillment comes to it and it remains with the Good and does not seek something else.* [VI-7-26]

We enjoy a good meal but the goodness doesn't stay with us very long. Hunger returns in a few hours. The same is true of every other sort of physical, mental, or emotional pleasure. Here today, gone tomorrow, or even sooner.

By contrast, what the mystic philosopher seeks is something that satisfies so fully there is no more seeking. Hard to conceive of, but wonderful to envision. Jean Stafford said that "Happy people don't have to have fun."[4] Neither does the sage attuned to spirit and the One.

> *This is why the First has no pleasure, not only because it is simple but because it is the acquisition of something needed which is pleasant.* [VI-7-29]

Just as the richest person is someone who has no desire for material wealth, the happiest person has little desire for sensual pleasure. He or she already enjoys the unchanging presence of the Good. A candle does not add to the noonday brilliance of the sun, nor does bodily sensation affect the radiant happiness of the purified soul.

> *But when he* [the sage] *is experiencing pleasures, health, and lack of pain, he will not consider them an addition to his happiness, nor, when he is in the opposite condition, will he consider them a negation or diminution of it. If one condition does not add anything to a subject, how could the opposite condition take anything away from it?* [I-4-14][5]

Fear Is a Fiction

FEAR ARISES when a person feels that his or her well-being is threatened. A hazy future threat may create only a mild sense of concern. A clear and present danger can produce a heart-pounding, adrenaline-pumping, chills-up-the-spine paroxysm of terror. In between these extremes lie the myriad anxieties, frettings, worries, gripes, irritations, and resentments that so frequently course through consciousness.

Like a bird who wants to peacefully enjoy juicy worms on the lawn but is forced to stay on a nervous lookout for cats hidden in the bushes, we rarely are able to relax our vigilance against the threats to happiness that seem to be all around us, and also within us.

Even if we're happy for the moment, a fear lurks not far beneath the surface of our contentment: "Will this moment last?" For anything that comes, can go. So a happiness dependent on external circumstances spawns a fear that what is currently propping up our well-being will eventually let us down. This is a justified fear, for nothing physical is permanent.

The sage, however, carries his own source of happiness around with him, for it *is* him, his purified soul. Knowing the soul to be immortal, an indestructible drop of the divine ocean that is the One, he smiles at the illusory fears that make other people frown. Fear for him is a fiction.

> But we bring our own weakness into it when we are considering whether a man is well off, and regard things as frightening and terrible which the man in a state of well-being would not so regard. [I-4-15]

Plotinus says we project our own weaknesses onto the world, assuming those defects to be immutable truths. Since *we* don't feel happy if we're in great physical distress or in danger of losing our lives, pain and death are considered to be evils, threats to well-being that have to be guarded against.

Much anxious effort on both an individual and societal level is devoted to protecting the fragile crop of happiness each of us is trying to grow in our consciousnesses. It's taken for granted that illness, poverty, crime, discrimination, lack of education, and the like are locusts able to strip our well-being bare, leaving us bereft of the good life.

> *And the activities which are undertaken to avoid suffering have fear as their origin.* [IV-4-44]

Fear is so much a part of most people's lives, as well as the lives of nations, that it is difficult to envision existing without worry. This is, Plotinus teaches, because we can't envision existing without our bodies. When our physical being is considered the end-all of existence, it isn't surprising that the prospect of losing some bodily pleasure, or worse, the body itself, fills us with dread.

> *So too, it will be the body that desires—for it is the body which is going to enjoy the objects of desire—and is afraid for itself—for it is going to miss its pleasures and be destroyed.* [I-1-4]

Fear, then, is as real as the physical form that is afraid of losing some particular bodily sensation while alive, or all sensation after death. More precisely, it is our *psyche's* identification with a body that makes us afraid, since the unconscious matter that comprises our physical forms obviously can't be conscious of anything, including fear.

What happens is that one's wise reason and even wiser spiritual intelligence become overwhelmed by the throng of pseudo-selves inhabiting one's consciousness. Though ultimately illusory and fabricated by the single self that is the soul, these fragmented pieces of our personality—whom we might personify as Lust, Anger, Greed, and the other familiar vices—are like boorish party-crashers. Open the door of your consciousness to them and they burst right in, wrecking the pleasant conviviality of the higher self and spirit.

When a person feels overwhelmed by fear, passion, depression, sadness or any other human frailty, it's important to remember that the "I" who is aware of that sensation is separate from the feeling itself. A child runs up to her father or mother and cries, with tears in her eyes, "A monster is under my bed and wants to *eat* me!" The parent hears the fear but doesn't share it. He or she tells the child that monsters aren't real, then looks under the bed with her. "See, you were just imagining things."

In this fashion, the child begins to absorb the adult's wisdom and way of looking at the world. Children gradually learn that many fears of things unseen are unjustified and that it is the role of reason to distinguish between reality and imagination. Similarly, Plotinus urges us to take firm hold of the frightened aspects of our self and tell them, "There's nothing to be afraid of. Don't bother me any more with your silly woes and worries."

> *If sometimes when he is concerned with other things an involuntary fear comes upon him before he has time to reflect, the wise man [in him] will come and drive it away and quiet the child in him which is stirred to a sort of distress, by threatening or reasoning; the threatening will be unemotional, as if the child was shocked into quietness just by a severe look.* [I-4-15]

Again we come back to the power of presence. As a child can be brought under control by just a stern glance from an authority figure and as a speeding driver slows down at the mere sight of a police car, so is it possible for us to eliminate irrational fears by simply being present to our wiser, higher self. If this doesn't work, then reasoning with our foolish lower self may be necessary. Whatever means are used, the goal of the mystic philosopher is to stop being afraid of fantasies.

> *One must not behave like someone untrained, but stand up to the blows of fortune like a great trained fighter, and know that, though some natures may not like them, one's own can bear them, not as terrors but as children's bogeys.* [I-4-8]

Cowards never will be able to return to the One because the journey back to God means passing through the gates of death, a fearful prospect to most people. Indeed, Plotinus's spiritual practice is directed toward the end of separating soul from body. Inevitably this happens at the moment of physical death, but the sage strives to die before his or her death.

In Plato's *Phaedo*, Socrates speaks with Simmias about this subject.

> And what is purification but the separation of the soul from the body. . . . And this separation and release of the soul from the body is termed death? . . . And the true philosophers, and they only, are

ever seeking to release the soul. Is not the separation and release of the soul from the body their especial study?

. . . And the true philosophers, Simmias, are always occupied in the practice of dying, wherefore also to them least of all men is death terrible. . . . And is not courage, Simmias, a quality which is specially characteristic of the philosopher?[1]

Plotinus echoes these sentiments.

Courage, too, is not being afraid of death. And death is the separation of body and soul; and a man does not fear this if he welcomes the prospect of being alone. [I-6-6]

The mystic philosopher attempts to die a living death through spiritual contemplation. Leaving behind physical sensation and mental cognition, becoming again what he or she once was, pure consciousness, the sage dies to illusion so as to be reborn in truth. This is a happy death, free of fear, a choice to live by the higher principle of spirit rather than the lower principle of the senses.

Most people are afraid of death because it is a leap into the unknown. Even though we may have beliefs about what will happen after our last breath, these are unproven hypotheses rather than experientially verified facts. Actually, says Plotinus, what we are before death is what we will be after death. So we need fear the prospect of dying only if we are afraid to examine the reality of our living.

That is, if a person can honestly say, "I have lived a good life," then it is virtually certain that he or she will enjoy a good death. But if there are things that he or she has done, or is still doing, that are painful to scrutinize, this pain will not lessen after death. So it makes sense to fear death if we haven't preserved the purity of soul that makes for an enjoyable afterlife. Yet, Plotinus points out, in that case it isn't death that we should be worried about, but the lives we'll have to live after dying.

> *If life and the soul exist after death, then death is a good, all the more so in that the soul is better able to carry out her proper activities without the body. If she becomes a part of the universal Soul, what kind of evil could affect her there?*
>
> *In general . . . there is no evil for the soul who has maintained her purity; and if she has not maintained it, then it is not death that is an evil for her, but rather life.* [I-7-3][2]

If our consciousness doesn't continue to exist after death, then we have nothing to fear, for we will be nothing. But if the soul is immortal and indestructible—and the *Enneads*, as do countless other spiritual writings, tell us that it is—then what should concern us isn't death but the living that awaits us after dying. Human life is precious not because it is so rare or brief. Rather, its value lies in the opportunity offered to us to become more than human, to learn to live now the true life of soul unfettered by body.

If the mystic philosopher fears anything, it is not making the best use of his or her time in this physical world. There is a reason each of us is here, and it isn't to make money, have children, get an education, create art, enjoy nature, serve humanity, or any other of the myriad worldly activities that usually consume the bulk of our attention.

Most souls remain caught in an endless cycle of incarnations because their earthly doing prepares them for nothing else than more earthly doing, just as the endpoint of a plant grown to maturity is to bear seeds that make more plants. To Plotinus this is fruitless since what we harvest from the physical branches of the tree of life lacks genuine taste and permanence.

But this world can be a staging ground for leaving it and such is its greatest value. The more spiritual progress someone makes before death, the more elevated will be his or her spiritual position after death. Hence, suicide is not a wise choice since it cuts short the opportunity to further purify the soul. In addition, it is unseemly to be dissatisfied with the course of life that providence has laid out.

And after all, taking drugs to give the soul a way out is not likely to be good for the soul. And if each man has a destined time allotted to him, it is not a good thing to go out before it, unless, as we maintain, it is necessary. [I-9-1]

Fear of misfortune, including a painful or ignominious death, is only for those who have failed to realize that the Good is always present. The sage knows that what he truly is, soul, never can be taken away from him. So it doesn't matter what happens to his body, for even the most extreme sort of physical suffering or bodily degradation is a petty frivolity to anyone who knows that matter is a mirage.

There are thousands of things which, if they do not turn out according to his mind, disturb in no way the final good which he has attained. [I-4-7]

Fear springs from a single presumption: "I can lose something important" (pleasure, wealth, health, life, love, and so on). Plotinus challenges this belief, which is why, for him, fear involves a fiction. A loss is a change but what really exists, true being, is permanent.

So if something presently possessed can be lost it isn't real and isn't worth wanting in the first place. It's a learning experience for a person to feel disillusioned when he doesn't get something he desired or loses something he had. This is the purpose of life: to separate fact from fiction, reality from illusion. In the end, death will be the greatest dis-illusion because the soul will separate permanently from the body that presently seems such a prized possession.

If, then, death is a changing of body, like changing of clothes on the stage, or, for some of us, a putting off of body, like in the theatre the final exit, in that performance, of an actor who will on a later occasion come in again to play, what would there be that is terrible in a change of this kind, of living beings into each other? [III-2-15]

Always, to die is to live. Those still bound to the wheel of reincarnation will revolve into life in another body. Those freed of the ties that bind them to physical existence will live without body. They will make a "final exit" at death, leaving the stage of materiality to return to the company of spirit and the One.

In either case, as Plotinus says, there is nothing terrible in the transformation of life into life. It is all good, wonderfully free of any reason to fear.

Return Is Reunion

EMANATION AND RETURN. These are the two grand currents in the cosmos that carry everything in creation either farther from, or closer to, the One. "Farther and closer" refer, of course, to a spiritual distance that can't be measured in feet and inches. What separates matter, soul, and spirit from the One is their degree of being, or level of consciousness. The more being an entity has the nearer it is to the source of being, even though the One is said to be beyond being.

> But we exist more when we turn to him and our well-being is there, but being far from him is nothing else but existing less. [VI-9-9]

These sentiments are shared by most, if not all, religious traditions. The highest reality, whether called God or some other name, is considered to be a haven in which we are protected from evils and suffering. But Plotinus differs from many spiritual belief systems and theologies in his contention that the soul's turning to God is actually a re-turn. Lloyd Gerson says, "As incarnate individuals, we are separated from our ideal state. To speak of this separation as a decline is to indicate that the ideal state is a state that we did possess."[1]

Do we turn to God or return to God? The presence or absence of two letters, "re," speaks volumes about our view of the cosmos and the means by which the soul is able to know its creator. For if God put us here on earth newly-formed, with no experience of the spiritual world, then it would seem that God also is completely responsible for taking us to him. The gap between our current and ideal state is just too large to be bridged in any other fashion.

But if we once were with the One and indeed still remain in contact with the highest divinity through the undescended aspect of soul, then spirituality becomes an active discovering of what we already are, not a passive prayer that God will make us into what he wishes us to be.

> And when it [the soul] comes to be there it becomes itself and what it was. [VI-9-9]

When the spiritual quest is reduced to its essence, as Plotinus would have us do, we are left with a simple goal: reunion. Once we were with the One. Now we are not. To return to the One is to be reunited with our source, whom it is fitting to call our father.

> *The soul then in her natural state is in love with God and wants to be united with him; it is like the noble love of a girl for her noble father.* [VI-9-9]

Poets and mystics wisely advise us not to try to pin down the nature of love, for whatever love is, it isn't anything that can be described, discussed, calibrated, or created. In fact, to analyze love in any fashion is to pass right by it, for true love is nothing but union. To break love into separate parts is to destroy its nature.

The divine love Plotinus points to isn't an emotion, nor is it a thought, for emotions and thoughts are passing fancies, not unchanging reality. Though the state of the soul he speaks of is somewhat akin to the love of a child for a parent, it also is unlike such familiar worldly love, for here the bond between a lover and his or her beloved never can be complete. Bodies may entwine and minds meet but always a distinction remains between one person and another.

Our current loves thus are shameful, Plotinus says, because we've been lured away from spiritual union by material and mental enticements: sensual pleasures, intellectual attainments, worldly successes, emotional passions. Still, our central longings are worthy, and can be trusted: to be happy, to know things as they are, to live the good life. However, the direction in which our desires generally take us, toward matter rather than spirit, outward rather than inward, is away from the only One who can fulfill those wantings.

Lloyd Gerson says, "The central notion of Plotinus's philosophy of religion is that of return. All creation is disposed by nature to return to the source whence it came, in so far as it is able. It is on this basis, first of all, that Plotinus can make a distinction between phenomenal and real desire. Appearances notwithstanding, what all things really desire is to be united or reunited with the source of their being."[2] As we read before:

> *If anyone sees it, what passion will he feel, what longing in his desire to be united with it, what a shock of delight!* [I-6-7]

The divine father hasn't gone anywhere. He waits for our return where he has always been, ready to embrace us. We, on the other hand, race about hither and yon desperately searching for what will bring us happiness and well-being. The crazy thing, of course, is that all this running around prevents us from realizing that the One we're looking for is right here, for he is the center of our selves.

A child, certainly, who is outside himself in madness will not know his father; but he who has learnt to know himself will know from whence he comes. [VI-9-7]

In this world, people often travel long distances for a family re-union. Traveling is necessary when two or more things have been separated and need to be brought together again. This also is true as regards the soul and God, but with a crucial difference: the One is already here, present as the essence of every person's being.

Thus the distance we must travel to return to God is precisely zero, no distance at all. It is traveling in time and space that takes us away from our source. This is why the mystic path is traversed through stillness, not motion—through inward contemplation, not outward perception.

We human souls have reached the end of the line of divine ema-nation. The emptiness of matter is an impassible blank wall beyond which none can travel farther. It is tempting to run along this wall exploring all that physical existence has to offer, hoping that some-where there is a hidden passageway leading from matter, thoughts about matter, or feelings about matter, to spirit. But there isn't. The wise soul turns inward, returning to the One by reversing the process of emanation that originally brought it outward and downward.

But if it [the soul] *runs the opposite way, it will arrive, not at something else, but at itself. . . . And if one goes on from oneself, as image to original, one has reached "the end of the journey."* [VI-9-11]

To return to the One is purely and simply to return to our own selves. Not our shadowy ego-selves, the personalities that presently absorb almost all of our attention, but our bright soul-selves, the pure consciousness that remains when everything external and extraneous has been eliminated.

Some would say that this is a terribly self-absorbed, solipsistic mystical philosophy. How could it be that you and I are God, the sole reality? Doesn't this make a mockery of divinity, to reduce the highest to the lowest, turning the sacred into the profane?

No. For Plotinus doesn't consider our true selves to bear any resemblance to the people we are now. Lloyd Gerson calls the thoroughly human being who is writing or reading these words the "endowed self," endowed, that is, with an ego and body that foster a sense of particularized individuality. I am me, you are you, and each of us recognizes this difference.

By contrast, the ideal self is what each of us truly is: soul. Gerson says, "Plotinus believes, however, that one's ideal self is eternally real and that it is the same in kind for everyone. . . . Thus return is also discovery. Paradoxically, the idea is of a return to what we are, not a return to what we were. . . . The idea is to recover oneself, but this is not a recovery of the endowed self. It is a recovery of what in one sense we (the endowed self) never were and yet in another sense what we (the ideal self) eternally are."[3]

To consider ourselves to be God isn't blasphemy, teaches Plotinus, but the truth. For what remains after the soul has reunited with the One is nothing, really, but the One. So only God is God, and we can know God by becoming God insofar as it is possible for a drop to become the ocean.

> When the soul has the good fortune to meet him, and he comes to her—rather, once he, already present, makes his presence known—when she turns away from all other things present, having made herself as beautiful as possible, and has achieved resemblance with him—just what these preparations and adornments are is obvious to those who are preparing themselves—then, suddenly, she sees him appear within her; there is no longer anything between them, and they are no longer two, but both are one.
>
> Indeed, as long as he is present, you could not tell the two of them apart; an imitation of this is when, in this world, lovers wish to be united to one another. The soul is no longer conscious of her body nor aware of being within it, and she no longer claims to be anything other than him: neither person nor animal; not individual or even the All. [VI-7-34][4]

In this state of union, the soul makes no claim to be a separate entity, for all sense of individuality has been dissolved. The One appears in the mirror of one's consciousness when the reflection of everything that is not the One, including the lower aspects of one's own self, have been eliminated. Then there is no distinction between subject and object, perceiver and perceived, soul and God, because one's essence has blended with the essence of the cosmos to such an extent that no one can tell them apart.

How do we know we have attained this incomparable state of divine union? When, says Plotinus, there is nothing left to attain, nothing left to desire, nothing left to love, because the soul has become what she has always yearned for. To know ourselves as soul is good; to know ourselves as spirit is better; but to know ourselves as the Good is to finally come to rest in the best.

> *Once, however, a "warmth" from the Good has reached her, she* [the soul] *is strengthened and awakened; she becomes truly "winged," and although she is seized with passion for what is close to her, nevertheless she is lifted up, as if by memory, towards another, better object.*
>
> *As long as there is an object higher up than the current one, she keeps rising, by a natural movement, raised up by the giver of love. She rises up beyond the Spirit, yet she cannot run beyond the Good, since there is nothing lying above it.* [VI-7-22][5]

The soul's memory (albeit largely unconscious) of her long-lost love, the One, keeps her soaring upward through the spiritual planes of consciousness even though the wonders within the World of Forms are more glorious than anything she has experienced in the physical world. Discarding all that can be discarded, including the beauty of spiritual sights and sounds, she reaches the source from which all else has emanated, the Good.

And there, she is satisfied. Fully. Indescribably. Eternally. Pierre Hadot says, "Once the soul has no more possessions, and has stripped herself of all form, she is at one with the object of her love, and becomes the Good. She *is* the Good."[6]

Vision Is Veracity

THE MOST IMPORTANT question to ask about any religion or spiritual teaching can only be: "Is it true?" For while there is room in the world for a wide variety of beliefs about the nature of God, all of these beliefs can't be equally valid.

Why? Because a spiritual reality that changes to fit my conception of it isn't a reality worth wanting. If my idea of divinity can alter the essence of the divine, then I am more powerful than God and have no need to seek anything beyond myself. But since I am unable to make even matter conform to my thoughts, it is highly unlikely that my thinking creates any substantial metaphysical reality.

Science knows that the physical creation is undeniably objective, not subjective. The same laws of nature have been found to operate everywhere. If the creator has gone to such lengths to establish a material reality founded on these all-pervading laws, then it seems reasonable that spiritual reality likewise obeys universal, not personal, principles.

Why is it, then, that after thousands of years of seeking the truth about God, mankind has failed to arrive at any sort of satisfying consensus? Scientists the world over are in close agreement about the nature of physical reality—but randomly select any two people and they will almost certainly argue to some degree about the nature of God.

Understandably, this causes many to wonder whether there is any such nature to discover. Perhaps, they say, religions are simply the product of wishful thinking that refuses to acknowledge the insignificance of life and the finality of death.

Plotinus does not shrink away from such skepticism. He isn't one to deflect a critical questioner of his mystic philosophy with the familiar adage, "Just have faith." Faith is worthless if it is based on an erroneous conception of reality. Many people have lost their money to swindlers in whom they had faith, as others have lost their health to quackish healers. Hence, in spirituality as elsewhere in life claims need to be backed up by something more substantial than a glib "Trust me."

But Plotinus teaches that the means by which we test the veracity of our spiritual convictions has to be in tune with the unique nature of what is hypothesized to lie beyond the reality we know now.

> *In the higher world, then, when our knowledge is most perfectly con-*
> *formed to Intellect, we think we know nothing because we are waiting*
> *for the experience of sense-perception, which says it has not yet seen; and*
> *it certainly has not seen, and never will see things like these.*
>
> *It is sense-perception which disbelieves, but it is the other one who sees;*
> *and for him to disbelieve would be to disbelieve in his own existence: for*
> *he cannot after all put himself outside and make himself visible so as to*
> *look at himself with his bodily eyes.* [V-8-11]

Physical objects can be sensed. Or, if beyond the capacity of the senses to perceive (as is the case with subatomic particles) they can be represented by mathematical equations or other symbols that *can* be perceived. In contrast, according to Plotinus, when the soul is conformed to intellect (spirit) there is nothing to be seen by the physical body. So if you ask the senses, "Is the spiritual world real?" they must answer, "No, we didn't perceive anything."

Spiritual vision is its own veracity. That is, there is no external criterion in the spiritual world by which one can assess the truth or falsity of what is experienced. This is because the World of Forms is a one-many where all the separate forms are in the whole, and the whole is in each form. There is no place in the spiritual world where the soul can stand apart from what is perceived, since each individual soul is also a form.

> *If you have become this, and seen it, and become pure and alone with*
> *yourself, with nothing now preventing you from becoming one in this*
> *way, and have nothing extraneous mixed within your self . . . if you see*
> *that this is what you have become, then you have become vision.*
>
> *Be confident in yourself: you have already ascended here and now,*
> *and no longer need someone to show you the way. Open your eyes and*
> *see.* [I-6-9][1]

Consciousness is its own confirmation. I may be misled about how real something is within my consciousness, since it is possible to see and hear things that exist only within my own mind. But consciousness itself must be accepted as a given, the bedrock on which stands all else I am and do.

This allows Plotinus to move beyond what the Greek Skeptics considered an impassible barrier to knowing absolute truth: the seeming fact, as Richard Tarnas puts it, "that any conflict between two apparent truths could be settled only by appeal to some criterion;

yet that criterion could itself be justified only by appeal to some further criterion, which would thereby require an infinite regress of such criteria, none foundational. 'Nothing is certain, not even that,' said Arcesilaus."[2]

In contrast, Plotinus teaches that the One serves as the immutable foundation of reality. Everything in existence emanates from the One and the human soul is able to return to the One, sharing in a universal consciousness of what is true and eternal.

This is accomplished not by perceiving the One as something separate from ourselves, for then, as the Skeptics argued, we would indeed need some means of determining whether the object within consciousness was real or unreal, and then need some means of determining the reality of that means, and on and on and on it would go, endlessly seeking validation of the highest truth but never finding it. Rather, Plotinus says, when the soul is purified its seeing is identical to what is seen. To disbelieve in the sight of God at that point would be to disbelieve in our very seeing, consciousness itself, an impossibility.

> *For one must come to the sight with a seeing power made akin and like to what is seen.* [I-6-9]

If we want to know God, then all we must do is develop the capacity to know as God knows.

> *There one can see both him* [God] *and oneself as it is right to see: the self glorified, full of intelligible light—but rather itself pure light—weightless, floating free, having become—but rather, being—a god.* [VI-9-9]

The innocent phrase "all we must do" does, of course, point to-ward a lifetime of effort devoted to becoming spiritually purified. To realize one's consciousness as pure light isn't easy or common. The number of souls on Earth who are enlightened always has been an infinitesimal fraction of those who are endarkened. But the potential of enlightenment is open to all.

Everything we need to return to the One is within us and indeed *is* us. The soul already is clear light and divine knowledge, for the essence of each person's consciousness is none other than the essence of the cosmos. Yet most of us are unaware of the wonder that lies at the spiritual center of our being, for our attention is occupied with the physical and mental periphery.

Plotinus tells us that the means by which we now know the creation must become the end we seek. Like a snake that swallows its own tail, the sage turns his attention back upon the consciousness that usually attends to outer things and thoughts. Uniting within himself the knower and the known, the One is revealed as the ground of the sage's own self. We've seen this quotation before but it is well worth repeating:

> *We must believe that we have seen him when, suddenly, the soul is filled with light, for this light comes from him and is identical with him. . . . This is the real goal for the soul: to touch and to behold this light itself, by means of itself. She does not wish to see it by means of some other light; what she wants to see is that light by means of which she is able to see.* [V-3-17][3]

Presently, we try to know external objective reality through physical sensation and mental cognition, perceptions and thoughts. Emotions are a sort of perception of how we subjectively respond to the outer reality. Thus, perceiving, thinking, and feeling (or emoting) may be thought of as lights human consciousness shines upon physical reality in an attempt to reveal its nature. Those who can see material reality more clearly than most we admire as great scientists, artists, philosophers, and moralists.

But it is only the mystics, such as Plotinus, who seriously seek to know the subtle nature of that by which the obvious nature is known. Instead of using the energy of their *psyche* to power flashlights of sensation, cognition, and emotion that are only able to illumine small patches of knowledge about the cosmos, they switch off these limited instruments of knowing. What remains within their consciousness is the powerhouse itself, the One, the light by which all lesser lights are illuminated.

> *If then thinking is light, and light does not seek light, that ray which does not seek light would not seek to think, and will not add thinking to itself; for what will it do with it?* [VI-7-41]

When purified of all connections and concerns with materiality, the soul intuitively knows the reality of spirit and the One. It doesn't even need to think, "I know." Thinking is engaged in only by those who seek intelligence, not by those who have it. Thinking is an eye for blindness, a means of giving partial sight to those who otherwise would be completely in the dark.

The sun, if offered a candle, would refuse it. Why would the source of light need light? The mystic philosopher, during his or her time of inward contemplation, similarly rejects any lesser means of knowing God than direct perception by the soul.

> *This, then, is what the seeing of Intellect is like. . . . When it turns its attention to the nature of the things illuminated, it sees the light less; but if it abandons the things it sees and looks at the medium by which it sees them, it looks at light and the source of light.* [V-5-7]

Almost certainly Plotinus is not speaking metaphorically here. Clearly, he means that when a person turns his attention away from external reality and becomes completely absorbed in what lies within, he will see the light of consciousness itself, a real light, the only true light.

The light by which we see matter, whether some natural illumination or a manmade radiance, is really nothing but darkness, for physical light is itself material. Matter can be illumined by matter but not known by matter. Hence the sage seeks to be united with the medium, pure consciousness, that is the foundation of all knowing.

What we generally see, both within and without ourselves, is not reality as it is, but reality as it is not. The true form of each and every entity in existence can only be realized by reaching the World of Forms, the spiritual realm. There, things are known as they are, not as they seem to be. Every sort of material knowledge is necessarily limited, because matter only is able to reflect a dim image of the spiritual forms.

Presently each of us lives in a realm of duality. There is an individual and there are entities other than that individual. It is extremely difficult to break out of this manner of being, even to merely envision the possibility of existing as simultaneously one with ourselves and one with the cosmos. Thus Plotinus warns us not to assume that spirituality can be confined within the boundaries of what is familiar.

To be spiritual isn't a matter of moving this way or that along the customary dimensions of everyday life: time and space. We can't know God by becoming as small and insignificant as an atom or by becoming as large and momentous as the universe. Spirit and the One do not lie in a particular direction, nor is divinity realized by having more or less of anything possessed now.

Returning to the One means embracing mystery, cultivating another way of seeing, leaving aside visions and becoming sight.

> *Carried off, as it were, by the wave of the Spirit itself, lifted up high by it, as if it were swollen, "he suddenly saw, without seeing how." But the spectacle, filling the eyes with light, did not cause some other object to be seen by its means; rather, what was seen was light itself.*
>
> *It is not that there were two things within it: on the one hand a visible object, and on the other its light, nor was there the Spirit and then what is thought by the Spirit; there is only a dazzling light, which engenders all these things later on.* [VI-7-36][4]

There, in the higher reaches of the spiritual world, the light that dazzles the soul doesn't illuminate anything, for manyness has not yet emanated from oneness. Here, we see things that are separate from the light that makes seeing possible. But when all separateness and multiplicity have been eliminated from the soul, what remains is awareness of the conscious power that produces separateness and multiplicity, spirit, the creative energy of the One.

Such is to be experienced, for it cannot be spoken about. As we read before:

> *For this reason the vision is hard to put into words. For how could one announce that as another when he did not see, there when he had the vision, another, but one with himself?* [VI-9-10]

Those who have been able to realize higher truths, and I am confident that Plotinus is among this exalted company, know what they know. They tell us how to reach the spiritual heights but cannot bring divinity down to our level, for the One is far removed from many.

Becoming the One is the only way of knowing the One.

Wrap-Up

From Forms to the Formless

HAVING COME to the end of our return to the One, in concept if not in reality, it is fitting to revisit a question that has appeared in various guises throughout this book:

Is that all there is?

This question, wonderfully expressed in a song of the same name written by Mike Stoller and Jerry Lieber, lies at the heart of both the human condition and Plotinus's spiritual teachings. For within every human soul there is indeed a longing that never lessens, a searching for satisfaction that constantly eludes us. In the song, a girl is taken by her father to a circus, "the greatest show on earth." But the happiness it provides her isn't so great and she asks, "Is that all there is to a circus?"

In the same vein, the question "Is the physical universe all there is to reality?" was important to Plotinus. No, he emphatically responds. Does the feeling that something is missing in our lives arise because we've lost touch with the spiritual side of existence and our own selves as soul? Yes, says Plotinus, equally emphatically.

Yet at this point I imagine some readers are asking themselves another question: Are Plotinus's teachings all there is to spirituality? Indeed, I would be the first to admit that the journey of the soul described in the *Enneads* seemingly lacks a vehicle. By this I mean that the formless soul's embrace of God's formlessness takes place without the aid of any intervening forms normally associated with spirituality or religion.

As was noted earlier, there is an almost complete absence of any favorable mention of rituals, rites, prayers, invocations, injunctions, commandments, saviors, or the like in the *Enneads*. Further, Plotinus's own spiritual practice is described in generalities rather than specifics. However, the historical record suggests that ancient Greek and Roman schools of philosophy always described spiritual practice in generalities. Pierre Hadot says:

> No systematic treatise codifying the instructions and techniques for spiritual exercises has come down to us. However, allusions to one or the other of such inner activities are very frequent in the writings of the Roman and Hellenistic periods. It thus appears that these exercises

were well known, and that it was enough to allude to them, since they were a part of daily life in the philosophical schools. They took their place within a traditional course of oral instruction.[1]

So it is likely that we will never know the exact means by which Plotinus and his students aimed to accomplish the ends set forth in the *Enneads*. Clearly, however, Plotinus's emphasis is on dematerializing and defragmenting the contents of consciousness. We must become spiritually single, not materially multiple. Contemplation of subtle higher realities belongs to those who cease contemplating this perceptible lower reality, which means shunning not only physical sensations but also thoughts, memories and other mental images of earthly existence.

Today, there are various systems of meditation aimed at achieving a similar state and it would be conjecture to venture a guess as to which, if any, come close to the spiritual exercises of Plotinus and his students. Further, this isn't the most important lesson we can learn from the spiritual school of Plotinus, which made up in profundity what it lacked in numbers, for A.H. Armstrong says it was simply "a small informal group of friends meeting in a private house."[2]

Echoing Marshall McLuhan, the medium by which Plotinus conveyed his teachings is itself a central message. Recall that Plotinus was reluctant to put his oral discourses in written form, and only did so after ten years of lecturing to his students. The fluidity and immediacy of the spoken word is, it seems, more akin to the intuitive intelligence of spirit to which the mystic philosopher aspires than is the rigidity and routine of writing.

Still, as formless as Plotinus tried to keep his teachings, they still possessed some form. Urging his students to surpass the limits of sense perception and discursive reason, he sat with them in his visible bodily form and put forth well-structured arguments in support of his doctrines concerning the soul, spirit, and the One.

I'm reminded of a cartoon I saw recently in which a group of people are sitting cross-legged on the floor in front of a Zen master-like teacher. A man is raising his hand, asking "Exactly what is this 'nothing' I've been hearing so much about?"

The question belies the answer, but is necessary nonetheless. As human beings caught for now in the cave of material illusion, we can't head directly into the bright light of the formless One without some aid, physical or conceptual forms we can lean on until our souls are able to stand on their own in the presence of God.

Plotinus speaks of the mystic philosopher returning to the One, "alone to the Alone." But we have to keep in mind that he studied with his own teacher, Ammonius, for eleven years. And he held public classes for most of the time after he left Ammonius until his death.

So his life and his teachings speak to the desirability of a spiritual guide. For even though the soul of every person is virtually identical with the Absolute, each drop having the same essence as the ocean, we need help in learning how to cleanse ourselves of the impurities that prevent us from realizing our pristine spiritual nature.

Such is the role of the spiritual guide. Pierre Hadot points out that the Greek term for spiritual guide is literally the one who leads, who shows the way. Hadot adds, "It is the function of proof by living example that the authority of the spiritual guide has to fulfill, proof for the soundness of doctrines whose validity the student in the first phase of spiritual guidance—that is, of philosophical instruction—is not yet capable of understanding and judging."[3]

Hence, if after studying the *Enneads* we ask if this is all there is to Plotinus's teachings, the answer must be no. For what is missing is Plotinus himself. If the reader isn't fully persuaded by his words that what he says is true, it is only to be expected. In the Greek tradition, the presence of the spiritual guide served as an exemplar of truth until the student was able to manifest the same sublime wisdom within his or her own *psyche*, or soul.

All the same, Plotinus never implies that he is anything other than a guide to the path that leads to the divine. He points out the way but the way is separate from the pointing. Plotinus urges us to leave behind material and mental forms, including his own, of course, and return to the formless One. His urging is necessarily by means of thoughts and concepts, but these symbols are a bridge to the other side of form, a means instead of an end.

Echoing Plotinus, Huston Smith notes the spiritual limitations of reason: "Reason proceeds discursively, through language, and like a bridge, joins two banks, knower and known, without removing the river between."[4]

God, as ineffable unity, cannot be known or loved as an object, for knowing and loving involve two: a knower and what is known, or a lover and what is loved. There is, then, little essential difference between dualistic spiritual knowledge and dualistic spiritual love. Neither will lead to realization of the ultimate Good, the One beyond all differences. Religious thoughts are an attempt to bridge the gap between us and God, as are religious emotions. Yet so long as the bridge remains, so does the gap.

There is, then, another answer to the question about Plotinus's mystic philosophy: "Is this all there is?" Yes. Going further, we could even say that there is less than what there seems to be. For when we focus on the heart of his spiritual practice, the outlines of which are clear even if the details are indistinct, it is all about burning bridges. The concepts Plotinus uses to intellectually convey his teachings have to be discarded from a person's consciousness if he or she is to experience the reality these concepts point toward.

Even so, it also is true that since each of our consciousnesses presently is spread in so many directions—work, home, family, nature, pets, education, entertainment, sports, politics, science, art, and more besides—our constantly wandering attention must be confined within certain bounds so that we aren't led even farther from God.

Thus rites, rituals, moral codes, and other forms of religious observance have a part to play in spiritual development. Even if these forms aren't capable of taking us across the channel that separates soul and the One, they at least help keep us close to the shoreline from which the spiritual journey begins.

That beachhead lies within consciousness, not without in the world. So the less deeply we venture into the dark cave of materiality, the easier it will be to make our way to the opening that leads to the light of the One. Mental and physical forms thus are akin to a doorframe that draws our attention to an otherwise poorly-marked exit. Though spiritual liberation entails moving beyond forms, forms are able to guide us to the gateway of formlessness.

Huston Smith says, "Forms are to be transcended by fathoming their depths and discerning their universal content, not by circumventing them. One might regard them as doorways to be entered, or rather as windows, for the esoteric doesn't leave them behind, but continues to look through them toward the Absolute. But because the symbolism of the spirit always requires that, in the end, space (distance) be transcended, even this will not do."[5]

This will not do because forms, whether mental or material, eventually cannot help but come between the seeker of God and the divinity with which he or she seeks to unite. The One, teaches Plotinus, is formless. So even though holy books, holy people, holy thoughts, and holy actions can aid in removing the grime from the naked purity of the soul, the cleansing power of what the *Enneads* term civic virtues is insufficient. If our *psyche* is to become truly luminous and bright, the purificatory virtues must be practiced.

These virtues, as we have learned, are a matter of stillness rather than movement; of silence rather than speech; of being rather than becoming; of inner essence rather than outer substance. Hence, Paul Henry says that, for Plotinus:

> Finally, salvation is not to be achieved. It is achieved. For its re-alization it is enough that the individual should become conscious of what he is already in his inmost nature. . . . Man for him is not the center of the universe; it is rather the universe, including the transcendent One, which is the center of man.
>
> He accepts salvation by philosophy, but has no use for a Savior who 'comes *down*' to liberate man, or even for a Supreme Being which would in any way concern itself with man or with the world except by remaining apart as the ultimate goal of man's or the world's desire.[6]

Obviously, then, there are significant differences between Plotinus's mystic philosophy and Christianity. These differences are offshoots of the more fundamental distinction between esoteric and exoteric spirituality.

If religious pursuit is viewed as akin to a trek up a mountain with God at the apex, then the various religions may be conceived as paths that attempt the ascent up different vertical divisions of the mountain.[7] In other words, each religion keeps to its own path of upward ascent and the spiritual climbers of different faiths do not meet each other, for they are on separate courses. This is the exoteric divide that separates religion from religion.

But there also is a horizontal division between the esoteric and exoteric side of spirituality that cuts across all faiths, just as some climbers reach a high elevation, and others do not, regardless of their paths of ascent. This is the esoteric divide that separates those who have attained an elevated state of spiritual consciousness, from those who have not.

Because the exoteric divide is founded on outward differences and the esoteric divide is founded on inward differences, every religion or spiritual philosophy has both an inner and an outer aspect, one that can be conveyed in a mental or material form and one that cannot.

Since there are degrees of esoterism, just as there are degrees of immaterial reality between this physical world and the One, the esoteric convergence toward ultimate truth usually is not complete. Mystics of different faiths do not completely agree with each other. However, they are much more in agreement than the theologians, whose province is the more widely-separated lower realm of the exoteric.

Exoteric religion promises salvation to individual souls because it assumes that souls are individual, separate and distinct from the divinity that saves. Exoteric religions ask us to love God, or an incarnation of God, because it assumes that union with God is an impossibility: the best that can be done is to love as two, not merge as one.

Exoteric religion thus distrusts, and often even actively tries to suppress, those who aspire to know God directly and completely through a knowledge in which there is little or no difference between the knower and the known, the individual soul and the universal spirit.

Meister Eckhart and Mansur al-Hallâj may be offered as two examples, among many, of the antipathy exoteric religion often bears to the mystic vision. Pope John XXII condemned as heresy various articles from the teachings of Eckhart, a thirteenth century Dominican theologian. This was one of the supposedly heretical statements:

> We are fully transformed and converted into God; in the same way as in the sacrament the bread is converted into the body of Christ, so I am converted into Him, so that He converts me into His being as one, not as *like*. By the living God it is true that there is no difference.[8]

In the same vein, Mansur al-Hallâj, a tenth-century Sufi mystic, was tried and executed by Islamic authorities for saying "I am the Truth." But Borhân al-Din, another Sufi, spoke of the difference between a profane and a holy claim to identity with God: "Pharaoh, God's curse upon him, said 'I am your Lord.' His use of the word 'I' was God's curse upon him. Mansur said 'I am God' and his use of the word 'I' was a mercy from God."[9] Franklin Lewis elucidates:

The insistence on duality of subject and object disappears when one has submerged his self in the divine, and this phrase, "I am the Truth," in this state actually reflects the extreme humility of the speaker, whereas to speak of oneself as servant and God as an exterior "thou" merely insists upon one's own existence, and therefore on duality.[10]

Since exoteric religions are based on an I-thou relationship between the individual and God, it is no wonder that they always have been much more popular than the esoteric teachings of mystics such as Eckhart, al-Hallâj and Plotinus. For the exoteric, I-ness isn't a barrier to knowing or loving God, because the separate self is considered to remain both here in the world and hereafter in heaven. But the esoteric strives to attain a formless state of union in which all, or nearly all, distinctions between the soul and God vanish.

To make a sacrifice or pray in a place of worship is possible for anyone. To purify one's consciousness of material images and thoughts so as to be able to merge the soul with spirit is a much more difficult task. Further, it is not even a goal sanctioned by the traditional Judeo-Christian-Islamic theologies, which posit that a large gap remains between man and God even at the height of spiritual attainment. This is why mystics are considered heretics if they aspire to know God more intimately than theological doctrine deems possible.

Yet the flame of mysticism never can be extinguished, despite the efforts of doctrinaire fundamentalists, because it is kept alight by the spark of the divine that burns, recognized or not, within the soul of every person. In the nascent mystic, or esoteric, that formless light has begun to pierce the inner shadows. A longing for enlightenment has taken hold. Reflections of God in religious forms no longer fulfill. The sun of the One has made its presence known, and the soul will not be content until it returns to its source.

Huston Smith says:

So the issue of unity and diversity in religion is converted into one of spiritual types: esoteric and exoteric. The esoteric minority consists of men and women who realize that they have their roots in the Absolute. Either they experience the identification directly or, failing this, they stand within earshot of its claim; something within them senses that the claim is true even if they cannot validate it completely. The exoteric majority is composed of the remainder of mankind for whom this way of talking about religion is sterile if not unintelligible.[11]

Religion typically denies that it is within an individual's power to know God directly, at least while still alive in a human form. Faith in salvation after death thus becomes all-important because solid evidence of the divine presence usually will not occur during one's life. However, faith plays a minor role in Plotinus's philosophy because his emphasis is on the soul's direct contemplation of spirit and the One. For the mystic, inner vision trumps outward belief, just as, for the scientist, experimental results trump conceptual theories.

It will be interesting, then, to conclude our study of Plotinus's teachings by viewing him less as a philosopher and more as a spiritual scientist. With this change in perspective, I hope the legacy of the *Enneads* will be perceived more clearly, as will Plotinus's relevance to the spiritual seeker in our modern, scientifically-advanced culture.

In the following chapter, we will consider the nature of a science of spirituality. We'll find that Plotinus's approach to knowing God and spirit has much in common with the scientific method, and that this goes a long way toward explaining the tension between the message of the *Enneads* and traditional theologies such as those in Christianity.

Toward a Science of Spirituality

WE HAVE COMPUTERS that soon will surpass the human brain's information processing power but science still doesn't know whether consciousness is produced by matter or exists independent of physical reality. We have theories that persuasively explain how the universe was formed in a big bang some fourteen billion years ago but science can only guess about what power was responsible for the creation, and continues to sustain material existence. We have made great strides toward deciphering the human genome but science lacks an understanding of what differentiates life from non-life and how living beings arose on earth.

Indeed, we know more and more about the world around us, but the mysteries of the world within us, the world that *is* us, are almost as unfathomed as in the days of the ancient Greeks. The search for meaning, as opposed to facts, is as elusive today as it was two thousand years ago. Erwin Schrödinger, a pioneering twentieth-century physicist, says:

> I consider science an integrating part of our endeavor to answer the one great philosophical question which embraces all others, the one that Plotinus expressed by his brief: . . . *who are we?* And more than that: I consider this not only one of the tasks, but the task, of science, the only one that really counts.[1]

Given that science has expanded so vastly the boundaries of knowledge about material existence in the past few centuries without producing any indisputable advancement in our comprehension of spiritual existence, it is understandable that many people are deeply skeptical of the dominant role presently played by science and technology. They fear that scientism, an unwarranted faith in the ability of science to reveal the truths of the cosmos, is usurping the proper place of spirituality and religion.

However, there is little doubt that our problems stem not from a surfeit of knowledge about reality but from a deficit. If we could meld science's commitment to a rigorous search for truth with religion's openness to the possibility of realms of reality beyond the physical, the world would be much better off. Science has proven its ability to uncover the secrets of the physical realm. Now it is time to recognize that the scientific method is equally well suited to realizing the truth of spiritual domains.

Mysticism thus can be said to have an affinity of method with science, and an affinity of subject matter with religion. That is, the mystic, like the scientist, seeks to move from hypothesis to certainty (or, at least, near-certainty) by confirming or rejecting a possible truth about existence through careful observation and experimentation. Yet the domain of reality being studied lies beyond the physical, as does religion's realm of interest, so non-material consciousness is both the mystic's means of investigation and field of study. Evelyn Underhill says:

> Normal consciousness sorts out some elements from the mass of experiences beating at our doors and constructs from them a certain order; but this order lacks any deep meaning or true cohesion, because normal consciousness is incapable of apprehending the underlying reality from which these scattered experiences proceed.
>
> The claim of the mystical consciousness is to a closer reading of truth, to an apprehension of the divine unifying principle behind appearance. . . . To know this at first hand—not to guess, believe or accept, but to be certain—is the highest achievement of human consciousness, and the ultimate object of mysticism.[2]

Material science has vastly increased our knowledge of the world without. This should encourage, rather than discourage, comparable efforts to realize the deepest truths of the world within, the domain of soul, spirit, and consciousness. For as we learn more and more about the astounding vastness, complexity, and order of the physical universe, what lies at the root of the marvels of creation becomes more of an enigma, not less.

John Wheeler, a physicist, nicely encapsulates the relation between knowledge and ignorance, which holds true in both the material and the spiritual realms: "We live on an island of knowledge surrounded by a sea of ignorance. As our island of knowledge grows, so does our shore of ignorance."[3] The larger the area that is illuminated, the greater becomes the mystery of what lies unseen in the darkness beyond. Seemingly, we are destined to never stop sailing on the vessel of Inquiry, for more truth always lies over the horizon.

Plotinus, though, taught that there was a way out of the ultimately frustrating circularity of more knowledge leading to more ignorance, a distressing condition clearly diagnosed by the Skeptics and other Greek schools of philosophy. The key to the resolution of this dilemma lies in the mystic premise that without is within. The fundamental essence of the cosmos is also the fundamental essence of *us*. The ocean is contained within each drop.

Thus singularity of consciousness, one-pointedness, is the key to realizing the One that is the foundation of everything in existence. This fundamental spiritual precept, "become one to know the One," is wonderfully simple and rational. It lies at the heart of almost every mystical philosophy, though the manner in which this teaching is expressed has varied in different cultures.

The mystic seeks to know the knower within, pure consciousness, rather than what can be known without. Instead of trying to expand his or her personal island of material and mental knowledge, the goal is to shrink it, at least during the time of contemplation or meditation. For when nothing is known, sensed, felt, or willed, what remains can only be everything—the ineffable divinity Plotinus calls the One.

Spiritual science and material science thus look for truth in opposite directions, in accord with a central tenet of Plotinus's mystic philosophy: there are two grand currents in the cosmos, emanation and return. Broadly speaking, the current of emanation is downward and outward, while the current of return is upward and inward (recognizing that these directions refer to states of consciousness, not spatial dimensions).

A physical scientist focuses his attention on outward forms of matter and energy, while a mystic concentrates on the inner formlessness of his own soul. This means that the mystic aims to realize ultimate truth by following the path of ignorance instead of knowledge. Ignorance, that is, of anything connected with materiality.

For if matter is false and spirit true, then a negation of falsity will produce a positive result: knowledge of what is genuinely and permanently real. As we have already noted, this *via negativa* (the negative way) is the spiritual path favored by most mystics throughout recorded history including Plotinus and medieval Christian mystics such as Meister Eckhart.

Eckhart, who has been called the most Plotinian of all Christian philosophers, spoke in his sermons of the danger of confusing images with reality:

Since it is God's nature not to be *like* anyone, we have to come to
the state of being *nothing* in order to enter in to the same nature that
He is. . . . All that smacks of *likeness* must be ousted that I may be
transplanted into God and become one with Him. . . . Once this
happens there is nothing hidden in God that is not revealed, that is
not mine. . . . But so that nothing may be hidden in God that is not
revealed to me, there must appear to be nothing *like*, no image, for
no image can reveal to us the Godhead or its essence.[4]

Consciousness, in other words, must be cleansed of all material
and mental images so that it returns to its original state: an un-
blemished mirror able to perfectly reflect the mysteries and glory
of God. The human soul thus is the ultimate scientific instrument.
Telescopes, particle detectors, chemical analyzers, and the like convey to a researcher's consciousness information about the world out
there. These are images of physical reality, not reality as it is. The
soul, however, is capable of realizing spiritual truth directly, without
any intermediary. Becoming spirit, it knows spirit.

However, it is much easier to embrace a physical or mental
representation of God with body or mind than to merge formless
soul with the formless One. This probably is the main reason why
a scientifically-inspired spirituality fails to appeal to most people.
Simply put, it requires hard work. To think, feel, and act is easy, so
to think purportedly divine thoughts, feel purportedly divine emotions, and act out purportedly divine actions is within everyone's
current capacity.

But to refrain from thinking, feeling, and acting is the most
difficult job in the world—and the most important. Says Eckhart,
"They must know that the very best and noblest attainment in this
life is to be silent and let God work and speak within. When the
powers have been completely withdrawn from all their works and
images, *then* the Word is spoken."[5]

Since turning off the chatterbox of thoughts that plays almost
continuously in the mind appears to be a Sisyphean task, a mystic
who tells us that this is the only way to hear and know God will
not be received all that enthusiastically. As Huston Smith observed
previously, the majority of people will be drawn to exoteric religions
in which much greater emphasis is placed on outward action than
on inner silence.

But exoterism by itself keeps us stuck in a morass of spiritual complacency. Conjecture becomes a substitute for direct perception. Instead of climbing to the top of the mountain of reality and seeing for ourselves what lies above the mist of appearances, we huddle with other flatland-lovers of a like persuasion and say, "How wonderful that the view from the summit is like this."

No, it isn't, for two reasons. First, only those who have returned to the One know the nature of God. Second, these saints and sages universally say that what they know cannot be expressed. So it is reasonable to conclude that until the soul is reunited with the One, we are all agnostics if not atheists. To hypothesize about God is a far cry from realizing God.

Still, there is persuasive evidence that some people have realized the ultimate divinity and that among this august company are founders of the world's great religions. There also may be people alive today with a comparable realization, modern saints and seers. But if a claim is made that someone, living or dead, has attained the highest truth, that claim deserves the closest scrutiny and must not be accepted at face value.

This is one aspect of the scientific method: anyone who proposes that something is true must be prepared to defend his or her thesis against all comers. Such results in a conceptual survival of the fittest, with only the strongest statements about the nature of reality being able to resist attacks against their validity. As A.H. Armstrong says:

> When claims to possess an exclusive revelation of God or to speak his word are made by human beings (and it is always human beings who make them), they must be examined particularly fiercely and hypercritically for the honor of God, to avoid the blasphemy and sacrilege of deifying a human opinion.
>
> Or, to put it less ferociously, the Hellenic (and, as it seems to me, still proper) answer to "Thus saith the Lord" is "*Does* he?," asked in a distinctly skeptical tone, followed by a courteous but drastic "testing to destruction" of the claims and credentials of the person or persons making this enormous statement.[6]

Further, even if we conclude that we are justified in accepting someone's claim to spiritual truth, this certainly doesn't mean that he or she is the only repository of such knowledge.

Most likely, mathematicians could come to agree, albeit with some difficulty, on what distinguishes a great from a good mathematician and perhaps they could even come to a consensus on who the greatest mathematician of all time was. But this wouldn't preclude someone else from being just a little bit less great than that person, or even equal. And it certainly wouldn't obviate the possibility of an even greater mathematician living in the future, or having lived unrecognized in the past.

After all, there is every reason to believe that both the material and spiritual laws of nature are unchanging. So these laws are capable of being discovered or realized by anyone at any time, if the investigator engages in the proper experimental method. Indeed, scientists have confirmed that there is no trace of arbitrariness in the physical laws of nature (even probabilistic events, as in the quantum realm, are governed by well-defined laws of probability). Likewise, Plotinus taught that unalloyed contingency, caprice, or chance are similarly absent from the higher realms of soul and spirit.

In part this is because individuality as we know it ends early on in Plotinus's cosmology. Here on Earth, souls have taken on coverings of many different physical and mental forms. There in the spiritual world, those veils are removed and each soul is found to contain the All, just as the All contains each soul. True intelligence—an immediate, intuitive, universal and unerring knowing—replaces the limited knowledge to which we are privy now, so shakily founded on fallible reason and sense perception.

Hence, upon the possibility of separating one's consciousness from matter and the lower realms of mind rests Plotinus's claim to a scientific status for his metaphysics. Granted, he doesn't make such a claim explicitly, but this is because both the ancient and the classic Greek philosophers made no distinction between science and religion or physics and metaphysics. So Plotinus took it for granted that mystic philosophy was science and science was mystic philosophy.

Plotinus terms the essential nature of all things the One. Hence, if we want to know God most completely, we are advised to seek for the divine within—or, more accurately, *as*—one's own self. Porphyry, echoing Plotinus, tells us that "Indeed, when one is present to oneself, he possesses the existence that is present everywhere; when one departs from himself, he also departs from it."[7] Thus the universal is to be found in the personal, which admittedly is a seeming paradox.

However, the paradoxes in the *Enneads* are more accurately viewed as reflections of the unfathomable unity that lies beneath appearances. For example, in addition to saying that the universal is the most personal, Plotinus also tells us that detaching from people and things leads to the greatest intimacy; in the formless is found true substance; the highest wisdom comes from embracing ignorance; and God is found by traveling nowhere.

In each apparent paradox (and more could be given) a circle is closed. Just as a man walking along a looping path initially moves away from his starting point, only to find that he eventually returns to that beginning place from the opposite direction, so did Plotinus teach that soul will return to God by moving in an unexpected fashion.

The spiritual path follows a course opposite to worldly ways. It means doing what comes unnaturally: shutting down the senses, turning away from thoughts, distancing from desires, abjuring actions, ignoring I-ness.

And then, seeing what happens. Wondrously, our own seeing will, with practice, become the divine happening that we seek so deeply with all our heart. Meister Eckhart speaks of this great mystic truth: "The eye with which I see God is exactly the same eye with which God sees me. My eye and God's eye are one eye, one seeing, one knowledge and one love."[8]

Neoplatonism and Christianity

WE NOW HAVE to ask how it is that two mystics, the "pagan" Plotinus and the Catholic Eckhart, can agree so closely about the nature of God and spirituality, while the perspectives of Neoplatonism and traditional Christianity are not nearly as compatible.

To begin with a little history, Plotinus's mystical philosophy, as part of the broader current of Neoplatonism that co-existed with Christianity in the initial centuries of the first millennium, never penetrated into the mainstream of Mediterranean beliefs. Though his ideas were highly influential among the educated and philosophically inclined, they failed to take root among the masses.

Christianity, on the other hand, did, spreading with remarkable rapidity throughout the Greco-Roman world. In the fourth century a Roman emperor, Constantine, was converted to this relatively new religion and thereafter used his considerable imperial power to propagate Christianity.

The ascendancy of Christianity did not come without a struggle, however. One skirmish in this battle for the soul of Western culture was fought by Porphyry, the student of Plotinus who edited the treatises in the *Enneads* into their present form after Plotinus's death in 270. Porphyry was a noted philosopher in his own right, and had an expert knowledge of Hebrew.

R. Joseph Hoffman says that Porphyry developed an intense dislike for popular religion and regarded Christianity as a pernicious disease that was infecting the Roman empire.[1] He wrote fifteen books that came to be known as *Kata Christianon* (*Against the Christians*). In 311, the church ordered all existing copies to be burned.

Presently all that is known about *Against the Christians* comes from fragments of Porphyry's words preserved in refutations written by Christian faithful, which one can expect do little justice to the scope and persuasiveness of Porphyry's arguments.

Unwittingly, the Christian authorities validated one of the central objections Porphyry almost certainly raised to Christianity: its elevation of blind faith over enlightened reason. Hoffman says, "From the standpoint of Socratic method, the Christian style was distinctly un-Socratic, consisting of injunctions to have faith and *believe* rather than ask questions. The Christian concept of truth consisted of revealed propositions in search of philosophical legitimation; it was doctrinaire where Platonism was dynamic."[2]

In writing *Against the Christians*, Porphyry was engaging in the same sort of exercise by which he came to be persuaded of the truth of Plotinus's teachings. Recall that, after beginning to attend Plotinus's school, Porphyry raised an objection to a central issue. He was asked to explain the basis of his objection and another student then responded to his response. And so it went, ideas playing against ideas until Porphyry realized the emptiness of his argument.

Christianity, however, considered that there was room for only one person, Jesus, on the platform where divinity is revealed. Since in this view there is only one perfect incarnation of God and one perfect revelation, debate is senseless. If scripture and revelation are the sole repositories of divine truth, no purpose is served in respectfully considering the perspective of a Greek philosopher who held differing views.

By burning *Against the Christians*, the church authorities acted in a manner that would be unthinkable in the scientific community. It's difficult to conceive of a scientist responding to an article critical of his or her theory by destroying every copy of the offending publication. Unfortunately, even today it is all too common to find religious advocates attempting to repress or belittle beliefs that are at odds with their own instead of debating the nature of spiritual truth in an open forum.

Further, it is a fundamental premise of science that it takes effort to reveal the hidden mysteries of the cosmos. After all, if the deepest truths of existence were lying around in the open, they wouldn't need to be searched for. Thus Porphyry objected both to the Christian belief that Jesus possessed a knowledge of divinity unavailable to other men and women, and to the Christian premise that faith alone was sufficient to unlock the gates of heaven.

In a letter to his wife Marcella, Porphyry wrote, "We must have faith that our only salvation is in turning to God. And having faith, we must strive with all our might to know the truth about God. And when we know this, we must love Him we do know."[3]

Here we see the nature of Plotinian faith, which perhaps is more accurately described as a working hypothesis, so long as the zeal and passion the mystic philosopher brings to his or her spiritual experiment are not lost in the translation. For Porphyry says that faith in the possibility of salvation, which for him is the soul's return to the One, must be followed by mighty striving to know God. Mere belief is not enough.

Once God is known, truly and fully known, love follows naturally. This makes sense. How is it possible to love anyone or anything that isn't known to us? Even if we believe we love that person or entity, we really don't love them as they are but as we envision or imagine them to be.

So Plotinus and Porphyry certainly wouldn't have disagreed with the emphasis Christianity (and Jesus) placed on love. But they viewed love more as the result of contemplation upon spirit and the One, than as a prerequisite for such contemplation. They also would have been ready to admit the possibility that Jesus was divine, perhaps even possessing unsurpassed divinity. However, the caveat would have been that Jesus's spiritual attainment was not different in kind from the godly knowledge of others who both preceded and followed him.

John N. Findlay says that in Plotinus's Platonism, there can be a human who participates more fully in the Absolute than any other human. But this will be a matter of degree, not of kind. Further, says Findlay, even if the divine *Logos* fully incarnates as a person, it "may have other sheep that are not of a given fold, and may shepherd many who have never heard of or acknowledged his Christian manifestations."[4]

The Christian doctrine that God became man one time and one time only clearly was at odds with Plotinus's teaching that divinity could be manifested in every purified human soul. R. T. Wallis says that "it was well-nigh impossible for Hellenic thinkers to accept a unique once-for-all incarnation of divinity," and so they "found the new religion's claim to a unique revelation especially distasteful."[5]

The Christian idea of a suffering god also was anathema to Porphyry and other Neoplatonic philosophers, who considered that all who become godlike imbibe the qualities of God, including a serene detachment from the illusory pleasures and pains of physical existence. Wallis says, "To the Hellenic sage all suffering is a matter of indifference; hence, Jesus's lamentations before his death attracted particularly unfavorable comment."[6]

Still, despite the many conflicts between Plotinus's mystical philosophy and Christianity, it is important to recognize that the Platonically-inspired teachings of the *Enneads* and the message of the Gospels have much in common. Richard Tarnas lists some of the Platonic principles evident in the New Testament:

> The existence of a transcendental reality of eternal perfection, the sovereignty of divine wisdom in the cosmos, the primacy of the spiritual over the material, the Socratic focus on the "tending of the soul," the soul's immortality and high moral imperatives, its experience of divine justice after death, the importance of scrupulous self-examination, the admonition to control the passions and appetites in the service of the good and true, the ethical principle that it is better to suffer an injustice than to commit one, the belief in death as a transition to more abundant life, the existence of a prior condition of divine knowledge now obscured in man's limited natural state, the notion of participation in the divine archetype, the progressive assimilation to God as the goal of human aspiration.[7]

But the similarities between the two great worldviews of Platonism and Christianity tended to be overshadowed by the inherent differences between an inward-looking and an outward-looking spirituality. For even though Christianity was esoteric in comparison to the excessively ritualized Judaism of the time, it was decidedly exoteric in comparison to Plato and Plotinus's teachings.

For example, great emphasis was placed in Christianity on the divinity of Jesus, a unique historical personage who was considered to be the exclusive source of truth in the cosmos.

The Christian who sought God thus looked outward to Jesus, for even if man is the image of God (the *Imago Dei* doctrine), Christianity held that the perfection or realization of this image can only take place through the mediation of Christ and within a community of believers. By contrast, a believer in the Plotinian message looked inward to the divine reality of his or her own soul, which could be purified without any intermediary, and thereby returned to its natural state of near-identity with spirit and the One.

In addition, Plotinus never failed to emphasize the universal, whereas Christianity has a decided bias toward the particular. This helps explain why, in contrast to the Gospels, the *Enneads* are almost completely devoid of any reference to individual lives, personal stories, discrete historical events, specific forms of worship, or any other particular way the divine might be reflected in this physical world. Plotinus isn't interested in unique instances; he cares only for what applies always and everywhere.

The Neoplatonist perspective is that while an individual may be honored for pointing humanity toward divinity, we dishonor the absolute by reducing eternity to a particular time, omnipresence to a particular place, omniscience to a particular idea, omnipotence to a particular act.

This is one of the points John N. Findlay makes in an essay (quoted from earlier), "Why Christians Should Be Platonists." He says that in both the Old and New Testaments there is "a considerable element of the arbitrary," such as "the choice of a particular human nature for fusion and transfiguration by the divine, timeless Logos. . . . This large element of the arbitrary, in my view, tarnishes the Absolute's image."[8]

Further, says Findlay, the traditional Christian emphasis on an individual incarnation of God at one time and one place in the universe's history sets into place an unbridgeable gap between us and the Absolute. Though Jesus may have spanned this divide, having one foot on earth and one in heaven, conventional Christian dogma holds that it is heresy to consider that we can do so ourselves by our own efforts.

So Findlay observes that in Christianity, humans are relegated to being puppets of the Absolute because there is an immense gap between the Absolute and its dependents that must be bridged by an individual who incarnates as a unique instance of divinity. By contrast, in Platonism the Absolute is universal, and can communicate what it has, or is, in various degrees to what falls beneath it.[9]

Plato and Plotinus taught that God can be fully known and fully loved by us because the One is not restricted in any fashion. Jesus can know and love God; Plotinus can know and love God; anyone, including you and me, can know and love God. Just as an apple falling from a tree in Argentina does not diminish the force of gravity in Australia, so is the One ever-present to those capable of realizing the power behind all other powers, regardless of who else has attained this realization.

Thus Findlay praises to Christians (and, by implication, those of other faiths) the virtues of what he calls Platonic and Plotinian absolutism.[10] By teaching that the One, spirit, and soul are universal aspects of reality, Plato and Plotinus downplay the importance of individual instances of absolute patterns, such as persons, rites and rituals, books, religious institutions, and so on.

We can only imagine how early Christianity must have appeared at the time to serious students of Neoplatonism who believed so firmly in the unchanging transcendence and ineffability of the One. Living as most of us do in a Christian culture, where "pagan" often is considered to be virtually equivalent to "heathen," it is difficult to appreciate that to Plotinus and his philosophical brethren it was the followers of Jesus who appeared irreligious and disrespectful of God.

To hold that God reveals himself through miraculous manipulations of matter, that the eternal spiritual laws of the cosmos were cast in a new direction with the virgin birth of a carpenter's son in Palestine, that God's plan is for the souls of the faithful to one day be rejoined with their long-dead physical body, that spiritual realization is reserved only for the select who were fortunate enough to live after Jesus's incarnation—all this and more seemed wildly fanciful in comparison to the more transcendent and coherent teachings of Plato and Plotinus.

The Legacy of Plotinus and Plato

INDEED, even the church fathers recognized that the Bible needed to be fleshed out, since its philosophical framework is bare bones. For example, answers to questions concerning the nature of God, spirit, and soul, as well as the relationship between these entities, are difficult (if not impossible) to discern by merely reading scripture.

So St. Augustine and other Christian theologians turned to Greek philosophy. Here, notwithstanding the tensions between Platonic and Christian teachings, they found a ready-made conceptual framework that, with a little manipulation, could be wonderfully supportive of the Gospel. Richard Tarnas says:

> The Christian world view was fundamentally informed by its classical predecessors. . . . So enthusiastic was the Christian integration of the Greek spirit that Socrates and Plato were frequently regarded as divinely inspired pre-Christian saints, early communicators of the divine Logos already present in pagan times—"Christians before Christ," as Justin Martyr claimed.[1]

Augustine, who wrote early in the fifth century, is largely responsible for the form that Christianity took through medieval times. Having been converted after a dual education in the Greek and Roman classics, and the ways of the world, he was well-suited to address both philosophical and moral problems from the new Christian perspective.

In his great work, the *City of God*, Augustine lavishes considerable praise on Plotinus and Plato:

> For we made selection of the Platonists, justly esteemed the noblest of the philosophers, because they had the wit to perceive that the human soul, immortal and rational, or intellectual, as it is, cannot be happy except by partaking of the light of that God by Whom both itself and the world were made; and also that the happy life which all men desire cannot be reached by any who does not cleave with a pure and holy love to that one supreme good, the unchangeable God.
>
> . . . These philosophers, then, whom we see not undeservedly exalted above the rest in fame and glory, have seen that no material body is God, and therefore they have transcended all bodies in seeking for God. They have seen that whatever is changeable is not the

most high God, and therefore they have transcended every soul and all changeable spirits in seeking the supreme.

. . . Plotinus, whose memory is quite recent, enjoys the reputation of having understood Plato better than any other of his disciples. . . . Plotinus, commenting on Plato, repeatedly and strongly asserts that not even the soul which they believe to be the soul of the world derives its blessedness from any other source than we do, viz., from that Light which is distinct from it and created it.[2]

Augustine observes that some of his fellow Christians are amazed when they learn how closely Platonism corresponds to their own faith: "Certain partakers of us in the grace of Christ wonder when they hear and read that Plato had conceptions concerning God, in which they recognize considerable agreement with the truth of our religion."[3]

He considers possible reasons for this, and then concludes that the most likely explanation can be found in Romans 1:20, where Paul says: "Ever since the creation of the world his eternal power and divine nature, invisible though they are, have been understood and seen through the things he has made." In other words, even non-Christians such as Plato and Plotinus are able to comprehend much about the creator through a careful study of the creation.

But Augustine still expresses a disturbing possessiveness toward spiritual truth, which helps to explain how he could be both so fond and so mistrustful of Platonic teachings. In a chapter called "Whatever has been rightly said by the heathen, we must appropriate to our uses," Augustine says that Christians must claim the truths that the Platonists have come to unlawfully possess, and "are perversely and unlawfully prostituting to the worship of devils."[4]

Augustine struggles to try to reconcile how Plato and Plotinus's metaphysics could so closely agree with Christian theology, even though neither Greek philosopher accepted Jesus as savior (Plato died over three hundred years before the birth of Christ, and Plotinus makes no mention of Jesus). This indeed is a significant problem for the Christian faithful. If God became man in the person of Jesus to reveal his hitherto hidden Word, then how is it that these pagan Greeks were able to realize so much of that truth?

This brings us back to a central dispute between Christianity and Platonism: the need for a mediator between God and man. For even though the teachings of these two great spiritual systems differ in other respects (such as reincarnation), they diverge most strongly when it comes to the means by which a common goal, God, is to be attained.

In this regard Plotinus was at odds not only with Christianity but with other contemporaneous philosophies and religions. Émile Bréhier notes that Plotinus's teachings are unique in the almost complete absence of a savior who mediates between man and God: "The very idea of salvation, which implies a mediator sent by God to man, is foreign to him."[5]

Notwithstanding this fact, in one passage Augustine approvingly quotes Plotinus: "We must fly to our beloved fatherland. There is the Father, there our all. What fleet or flight shall convey us thither? Our way is, to become like God."[6]

Thus Augustine wholeheartedly shares Plotinus's goal: to return to the One. And he agrees that the nature of the soul is utterly unlike the "temporal and mutable" things of this world. But whereas Plotinus urges the spiritual seeker to find God by purifying his or her own consciousness of material and sensual preoccupations, Augustine considers that salvation is possible only with Jesus's intercession.

> We need a Mediator Who, being united to us here below by the mortality of His body, should at the same time be able to afford us truly divine help in cleansing and liberating us by means of the immortal righteousness of His spirit, whereby he remained heavenly even while here upon earth. . . . From this hell upon earth there is no escape, save through the grace of the Savior Christ, our God and Lord.[7]

To Plotinus, a spiritual guide (such as his own teacher Ammonius) points toward the truth.

To Augustine, there is only one spiritual guide, Jesus, and he is the truth.

For Plotinus, the fundamental essence of the cosmos is unity, so the soul of the mystic philosopher is fully capable of making the journey from manyness back to oneness: the ocean of God is of a piece and can be traversed by anyone able to cast aside the anchor of matter and catch hold of the omnipresent current of spirit.

For Augustine, creation is marked by a battle between the dualities of good and evil, or God and Satan, and humankind has aligned itself so strongly with the wrong camp that God had to send his own son to set things right: left to our own devices, we can never separate ourselves from the forces of darkness and embrace the light.

In Plotinus's spirituality, each individual must experience the wisdom and love that is God for him- or herself. The path that returns to the One is traveled by each soul independently; hence, great effort is needed to purify each of our consciousnesses of all that is physical or personal so that we may attune ourselves to the immaterial universality of spirit and the One.

In Augustine's spirituality, Jesus incarnated in the world to redeem all sinners. The way to God is through the church and the embrace of a collective Christian identity; thus, great faith in Jesus is all that is required to enjoy, for eternity, God's company after death.

Both Plotinus and Augustine were firmly committed to discovering the ultimate truth that would lay bare the mysteries both within and without every human soul. There was, however, a stark difference in how Platonism and Christianity viewed this divine research.

Plotinus believed that all of the means necessary to discern divine realities already are present in a spiritual seeker's consciousness. If the *psyche* or soul could be restored to its original likeness to spirit and the One, the seeker would intuitively realize the highest truth in a wonderfully simple and direct fashion: by becoming it.

Augustine believed the only truths that really mattered had already been revealed through the loving sacrifice of Christ, who, by his crucifixion, corrected all the errors of humanity and revealed the wisdom of his Father.

Richard Tarnas says, "In contrast to the previous centuries of metaphysical perplexity, Christianity offered a fully worked out solution to the human dilemma. The potentially distressing ambiguities and confusions of a private philosophical search without religious guideposts were now replaced by an absolutely certain cosmology and an institutionally ritualized system of salvation accessible to all."[8]

On the face of it, this sounds great, for who wouldn't be happy to trade confusions for certainties? Picking up an already revealed truth certainly is preferable to having to go through the trouble of discovering it on one's own. Why bother to cook a meal when dinner is waiting on the table?

But the question seems to come down to whether a promise of spiritual sustenance is sufficient to satisfy a hunger for God. For mainstream Christianity, in common with all traditional religions, asks the faithful to wait until after death to enjoy the main course: salvation. Those who are starving for an unequivocal, direct experience of spirit and God are expected to have faith that all will be revealed after the believer's last breath.

Basically, Christians are asked to trust that the desired results of their God-experiment will be produced when soul separates from body. This is a science of sorts, but a science in which promised spiritual effects are separated by the gulf of death from their purported causes—grace, faith, good works, prayer, and so on. When it isn't possible to connect a cause and an effect within the span of a single lifetime, faith becomes all-important. But faith is a promissory note for truth, and there are those who yearn to have God's treasure in hand, *now.*

Plotinus was one such person, as are all true mystics. Through contemplation, they desire to die to this world before their physical death in order to know as soon as possible the truth of what lies beyond life. Lovers are impatient to be united with their love. The mystic philosopher, lover of the wisdom that is God, embraces a death to all that is bodily or physical so that his or her soul may unite fully with the spiritual. Porphyry says:

> Nature releases what nature has bound. The soul releases what the soul has bound. Nature binds the body to the soul, but it is the soul herself that has bound herself to the body. It, therefore, belongs to nature to detach the body from the soul, while it is the soul herself that detaches herself from the body.
>
> There is a double death. One, known by all men, consists in the separation of the body with the soul. The other, characteristic of philosophers, results in the separation of the soul from the body.[9]

Plotinus sought God within himself. So did Augustine, but this search took place in the company of the Gospel of Jesus and the Holy Church, for Augustine believed that the gap between him and the divine could be bridged only by an intercessor who incarnates at the behest of the Lord to redeem souls by faith and grace alone. Richard Tarnas summarizes these different perspectives on spirituality:

> Augustine differed from Plotinus in positing an increased distinction between Creator and creation as well as a more personal relation between God and the individual soul; in stressing God's freedom and purposefulness in the creation; in upholding the human need for grace and revelation; and above all in embracing the doctrine of the Incarnation.[10]

Augustine's personal relationship with God, mediated by Jesus, was founded on a felt distance between humans and the divine that was utterly foreign to Plotinus's experience. Thus it is rather strange that Augustine could feel closer to God by embracing a religion that posited a gulf between him and God, and rejecting a philosophy that placed the One at the very center of his own self.

It seems that by making God into a person, Jesus, Christianity offered Augustine a personal relationship with a separate being. By contrast, Neoplatonism taught that there is, in essence, no difference between the soul and the One, other than the fact that a drop is distinct from the ocean. So it isn't possible to have a relationship with God when, in truth, the soul is God.

As Émile Bréhier says, "Piety, in the usual sense of the word, is almost absent in him [Plotinus]. . . . Prayer never has a personal note. It never expresses an intimate relation of the soul with a higher person. . . . Now the One of Plotinus is neither a thing nor an object. It is the pure, absolute, single subject, without any relation to external objects."[11]

Thus a study of the *Enneads* can lead to a conclusion quite different from what Augustine came to: that there is nothing more personal than realizing God as the essence of our personhood, nor anything more intimate than uniting with spirit and the One. As for the *Logos* (or spirit) becoming flesh, Plotinus teaches that there is a sense in which this happens with every birth. Meister Eckhart echoes this conception in his mystical Christian theology:

> People think that God became human only in the Incarnation, but this is not the case, for God has become human just as surely here and now as he did then, and has become human in order that he might give birth to you as his only begotten Son, and no less.[12]

The difference between a saint and a sinner is thus, in Plotinus's view, a matter of realization, not of capacity. The divine heights Jesus was able to attain could with sufficient effort be scaled by any person. This perspective was uncongenial to the Church, so Christian thinkers were both attracted to and repelled by Plotinus's mystic philosophy.

Since the Church was at best ambivalent toward Platonism and Neoplatonism, it isn't surprising that by medieval times Plotinus's teachings were only indirectly available in the West, though copies of the *Enneads* continued to be studied in the Byzantine and Islamic worlds. Then, in 1492, Marsilio Ficino, an Italian philosopher who was one of the great Renaissance humanists, translated the *Enneads* from Greek to Latin.

Ficino's lifelong devotion to studying and translating the works of Plato and the Neoplatonists was part of what has been called the rebirth of classical humanism. This re-discovery of neglected parts of Greek thought infused new energy and vitality into both Christianity and Western culture in general. Richard Tarnas says:

> In Platonism and Neoplatonism the Humanists discovered a non-Christian spiritual tradition possessing a religious and ethical profundity seemingly comparable to that of Christianity itself. The Neoplatonic corpus implied the existence of a universal religion, of which Christianity was perhaps the ultimate but not the only manifestation.
> . . . The classical Greeks' sense of man's own glory, of man's intellectual powers and capacity for spiritual elevation seemingly uncontaminated by a biblical Original Sin, was now emerging anew in the breast of Western man.[13]

To attempt to describe more fully the influence of Plato and Plotinus on Western religion, science, and art from the fifteenth century onward is beyond both the scope of this book and the author's capacity. The reader is urged toward Richard Tarnas's highly readable overview of the evolution of Western thought, *The Passion of the Western Mind*, a work cited frequently in these pages.

Suffice it to say that the teachings of Platonism and Neoplatonism in general, and Plotinus in particular, are deeply engrained in the Western mindset, though rarely recognized as such by most of us today. These ideas are mediated to us by the great mystics, theologians, scientists, and artists of Renaissance times, who serve as a bridge between the far distant shore of Greek philosophy and the present day.

To read Meister Eckhart, Nicholas of Cusa, the anonymous author of *The Cloud of Unknowing*, Marsilio Ficino, and other like-minded thinkers of that era is to hear the voice of Plotinus, for all who follow the *via negativa* speak of the spiritual path in a similar fashion. This is not so much because they share a common intellectual or theological framework, as that each has experienced, or seeks to experience, a wholly inward divine unity that transcends all outward distinctions.

There can be no more awe-inspiring conception: that the soul is in God. Or, to use more scientific-sounding language: that personal consciousness is in universal consciousness (following Plotinus, we must understand "in" not spatially, but as in the power of). This astoundingly simple idea is enormously profound. It had, and still has, the power to rattle the foundation of both individuals and entire cultures. Indeed, more than rattle—*transform*.

The Platonically-inspired challenges to the prevailing Christian worldview planted the seeds of a mystical revitalization that drew many people toward an inward experience of divinity that supplanted, or at least supplemented, traditional outward modes of worship. Interestingly, the infusion of Platonic and Neoplatonic ideas also prepared the ground for the Western scientific revolution that continues apace today.

For if it was considered that man could form his consciousness into a means of knowing the secrets of God that lie within, it followed that the same consciousness could be fashioned into an instrument for knowing the mysteries of creation that lie without. The medieval Church discouraged scientific inquiry (witness Galileo's fate) because, as Richard Tarnas says, "The truths of Christian faith were supernatural, and needed to be safeguarded against the insinuations of a naturalistic rationalism."[14]

But if the One and spirit are immanent in the creation, then the study of nature becomes, in a certain sense, the study of God. And since Plotinus and other Neoplatonists held that creation is taking place continuously in the present moment, a view shared by Meister Eckhart, then coming to understand how the laws of nature function is tantamount to gaining a vision, however veiled, of spirit's transcendent creative intelligence.

In contrast to the Church's focus on God's power to perform unique and almost capricious miracles, Plotinus and Plato emphasized the universality and regularity of the divine design. Thus Platonism harmonized nicely with scientific inquiry, which focuses more on learning the causes of recurring patterns in the cosmos rather than what creates irreproducible unique instances.

Hence, says Tarnas, "The scientific ramifications of the Platonic revival were no less significant than the religious. . . . Neoplatonist mathematics, added to the rationalism and nascent empiricism of the late Scholastics, provided one of the final components necessary for the emergence of the Scientific Revolution."[15]

Our Great Experiment with Truth

IT SEEMS, THEN, entirely fitting to close with some final observations about the scientific character of Plotinus's mystical philosophy. For what he urges us to pursue, above all other priorities, is the study of our own selves as soul. And this investigation takes place nowhere else but in the laboratory of our individual consciousness which, when purified of all that is physical or personal, will be found to be virtually identical with the universal consciousness of spirit and the One.

There is so much to admire in this conception of spirituality. It hews to the original root meaning of "religion," *religare*, to bind back to God. Yet it avoids the divisiveness and rancor of what so often falsely passes for religion in the world today. By teaching that the pursuit of spirituality involves an inward transformation of the *psyche*, or soul, rather than any sort of outward action of body or mind, Plotinus asks us to focus on the only relationship that really counts, the connection between us and divinity.

That connection is established by contemplating higher spiritual realities, not the lower reaches of matter in which we find ourselves firmly planted now. The mystic philosopher detaches from everything connected with this world so that he or she may become attached to the wisdom, beauty, and truth of the spiritual world. To forsake things and thoughts is to embrace spirit and the One.

So each of us might do well to examine our commitment to spirituality or religion from this perspective: Assuming we want to try to know God now, before we die, what do we take with us into the laboratory of spirit where, in whatever fashion we choose, we attempt to perform this great experiment with truth? What instruments, if any, are needed there? What thoughts and actions, if any, are essential to our work, and what thoughts and actions must be left outside the laboratory of consciousness to avoid contaminating the experiment?

I would suggest that Plotinus, in common with all great mystics, asks us to carefully differentiate between what might be aptly termed the laboratory, lecture hall, and university of spirit. The laboratory is where our experiment with truth is actually carried out. Thus it is essential to keep this place, our innermost consciousness, empty of confounding elements during the time of contemplation in which we seek to know God. For the *Enneads* proclaim that the radiance of spirit and the One is reflected in the soul only when consciousness is still and clear.

Hence, in this laboratory we can't even take our notes from the lecture hall, where spiritual books are read, teachers of spiritual science speak, and spiritual discussions are held. These are great aids to learning how to conduct our experiment, to be sure. But what transpires in the lecture hall—physical sights and sounds, mental thoughts and emotions—cannot be brought into the laboratory without ruining our experiment with pure truth.

This is why Plotinus tells us, over and over again, in so many different ways, that the One is ineffable and beyond conception. He wants us to understand why the break between what might be called the theory and the practice of spirituality has to be complete. An accomplished teacher of spiritual science can tell us how to properly conduct the experiment within our consciousnesses. But the telling must not be confused with the experiment, which, unfortunately, happens all too often.

That is, we wrongly believe that we have gained some knowledge of spirituality after hearing or reading an explanation of how this knowledge is to be realized and what that mystic realization generally consists of. In fact, we know nothing. And, as the mystics of the *via negativa* (the negative way) tell us, it is only by entering into the nothing we truly are that we will ever know anything of spiritual matters.

Even worse is to believe that merely being enrolled in a university leads to any sort of spiritual understanding. If we look upon spirituality as a science, as I am suggesting Plotinus would have us do, then aligning ourselves with a specific source of instruction, Christianity, Islam, Buddhism, whatever, is akin to enrolling at Harvard, Yale, Oxford, wherever. It seems unarguable that some schools are a better fit for certain students than other schools, but it also is unarguable that a place of study mustn't be confused with what one learns there.

Material scientists are considerably wiser in this regard. They identify to some extent with their school or university but have a much stronger identification with their field of study, such as physics, chemistry, or geology. And most scientists realize that their chosen field is set off from the much larger expanse of human knowledge by largely arbitrary distinctions. The line between physics and chemistry, for example, is blurry.

But the situation is much different in spirituality. Ask someone about God, and you are much more likely to hear, "I'm a Catholic" or "I'm a Buddhist" than "I'm a seeker of the divine." Wouldn't it be strange to have a physicist say, throughout his career, "I'm a Harvard man," when queried about his profession? So Plotinus's non-sectarian and universal approach to metaphysics is to be emulated even by those who profess allegiance to some particular spiritual school.

It isn't the school that is important. It isn't the professors that are important. It isn't the books, readings, and discussions in the lecture hall that are important. What's important is the *experiment*, our great experiment with truth. For in the laboratory of our elevated consciousness the mystery will be revealed of what lies beyond the cave of illusion in which we presently reside.

Death also will bring us to the edge of discovery, but there is no guarantee that we will be able to permanently remain with truth after the falsehoods of this world are dispelled. Reincarnation, says Plotinus, is reality, at least for those who have not been able to return to the One.

Mystics such as Plotinus urge us to live life with one goal in mind: that we die well. May we be inspired by what Plotinus told a disciple in his last moments:

> *I am trying to make what is most divine in me rise back up to what is divine in the universe.*[1]

The body of this book ends with some thoughts from Meister Eckhart, the Christian mystic who melded so wonderfully the spiritual teachings of Jesus and Plotinus. We can ask for no clearer summary of the ageless *via negativa* that transcends every distinction of creed or religion.

> Now take note of what we must have if we are to dwell in him, that is in God. There are three things we must have. The first is that we should take leave of ourselves and of all things and be attached to nothing external which acts upon the senses within, and also that we should not remain in any creature which is either in time or in eternity.
>
> The second is that we should not love this or that good thing but rather goodness as such from which all good things flow, for things are only desirable and delightful in so far as God is in them.

. . . The third is that we should not take God as he is good or just, but should take him in the pure and clear substance in which he possesses himself. For goodness and justice are a garment of God, since they enfold him.

Strip away from God therefore everything which clothes him and take him in his dressing room where he is naked and bare in himself. Thus you will remain in him.[2]

Conclusion

WE EXIST. All that exists emanates from the One. So the soul, the enduring spiritual aspect of us, has an inherent inclination to return to the source, somewhat as drops of water in a river naturally flow downhill until they merge in the ocean.

However, the unfortunate difference between this metaphor and reality is that spiritual realization generally takes a lot of work, leaving aside the few fortunate souls who are reported either to have been born with knowledge of God, or able to acquire this wisdom without much effort. They are the exceptions, not the rule, as evidenced by the mystics who, throughout the ages, engaged in great exterior and interior struggles to reveal the mystery of hidden divinity.

Thus returning to the One is more like climbing a mountain than floating down a stream. This is almost universally true, at least, of the early stages of spiritual ascent, for here we have to fight against the considerable pulling power of the myriad attractions of matter and mind, much as a rocket straining to escape the earth's gravity expends most of its fuel shortly after liftoff when the forces trying to keep it earthbound are at their strongest.

When I considered how my study of Plotinus's teachings had affected my attitude toward spirituality and my spiritual practice, this image came to mind: I have been comfortably camping at Lake Partway, enjoying only the lowest reaches of Mount Spirit, still far from the summit of One. Then Plotinus came along and jolted me out of my complacency. He raised the bar, set a higher standard, challenged me to play the spiritual game as well as I can talk about it.

The following fable builds on this image, and is my attempt to convey something of what Plotinus has come to mean to me. He is a guide to regions of reality that are rarely explored. I'm sure that he is not the only guide, and he may not be the best guide, but this is not for me to judge. I'm simply grateful that mystics such as Plotinus are willing to give us even a veiled description of the spiritual heights to which they have ascended, and, more importantly, offer to show us the path that leads to the summit so we can see for ourselves.

This tale necessarily has a personal flavor because it reflects my own impression of Plotinus and his teachings. Yet it also serves as a rough and ready reflection of the general thrust of those teachings themselves. After reading *Return to the One*, you should be able to recognize how the central elements of this tale relate to Plotinus's philosophy. If this isn't the case, just take the story as it strikes you.

Stuck at Lake Partway

MOST SPIRITUAL SEEKERS, and the author includes himself in this group, are akin to campers at Lake Partway. We're pleased that we have escaped the dirty and crowded city of Godless Materialism. We've piled what we consider to be the basic necessities of life into our present vehicles of spirituality, and have driven with considerable ease to the lakeshore campground, nestled at the base of Mount Spirit, where now we are comfortably settled in.

Ah, how pleasant it is to be among like-minded people. Here we are, the spiritually blessed, enjoying the refreshing breezes that blow down from the mountain while so many other poor souls suffer through an endless hot summer in the miasmic streets of Godless Materialism.

We sing devotional songs around the campfire at night. We read holy books during the day. Brief explorations of the surrounding territory give us a little exercise without wearing us out. The food is tasty, there are just a few mosquitoes, and a battery-powered TV can pick up stations from the city (we sure don't want to miss out on news and entertainment while camping).

Still, things could be better. Lake Partway is shallow and clogged with weeds. The many vehicles going in and out of the campground are noisy and stir up clouds of dust. Often there are arguments over who gets an appealing campsite. The air is smoggy, though not as bad as in the valley below. And after we've sung all the songs, read all the books, and hiked all the nearby trails, there isn't that much new to do.

Childish voices keep echoing in our brains: "We're bored! There's nothing to do here! When are we going back to the city?" And though we've been able to put them off one way or another—"Don't you just *love* camping at Lake Partway, kids? Maybe we'll roast marshmallows tonight!"—a hidden concern lurks beneath the surface of our outward enthusiasm: maybe trading the excitement of Godless Materialism for the blandness of Lake Partway wasn't such a good idea.

Then a stranger appears. Tall, exceedingly fit, bronzed by the sun, eyes with a depth that comes only from gazing on the unimaginable. He is spotted striding boldly down the mountain path that no one ever takes because it is too steep and rocky. Where did he come from? Someone invites him to stay for dinner, and afterward, over coffee, he is asked where he's been camping.

"Nowhere. I live here. Well, not right here, up *there*." He gestures over his shoulder into the darkness. "It's a pleasant place. It fits me."

"Tell us about it. Is it better than Lake Partway?"

"Oh, yes. It's better than every place. There's nothing like it. That's why I stopped camping here like you, and settled into One."

"One what?"

"Just One. If it was anything else, any thing at all, it wouldn't be One. Don't you see?"

Actually, we don't. But this conversation is a stimulating change of pace, since the stranger, who just wants to be called "Guide" (he's forgotten his old name, he says with a wink), has an engaging, if decidedly eccentric, manner about him.

"Guide, can you tell us more about this wonderful place you call One?"

"Sorry, I can't. Really, it's indescribable," says Guide. "All I can say is that if you saw it, you'd like it so much better than Lake Partway. It's the place you were wanting to find when you left that terrible city, Godless Materialism. You just stopped too soon once you got a little way up the slope of Mount Spirit. This campground is all right, compared to what you left behind, but nothing like what lies at the top of the mountain. I can show you how to get to One, if you like."

"What road do we take? And how long a journey is it?"

"There isn't any road. The vehicles that got you here can't take you any farther. From here on the path is narrow and not clearly marked. As to how long you'll be walking, well, it depends. Some people make it a quick trip. Others meander more. This mountain is much vaster than you can begin to imagine. There are folks who have been wandering around up there for an awfully long time. That's why you'd be smart to let me show you the way."

As captivating as Guide is, he's starting to lose some of his audience. A fair number of campers left when they heard they couldn't take their vehicles to One. "I'd like to see this place," they explain, "It sounds wonderful, but no way am I going to walk there. I'll wait until they put in a road."

A few of us, however, have grown so tired of Lake Partway, and so enthralled by Guide's cryptic praise of One, that we take him up on his offer. We're told, "Meet me at the bottom of the path at dawn. And come prepared for a tough hike."

We do just that. There we are, right on time, the first rays of the sun hitting our expectant faces, everyone carrying large knapsacks filled with water bottles, peanut butter sandwiches, cameras, toilet paper, sunscreen, extra clothes, first aid kits. We're ready to go, Guide!

He takes a quick glance at us and says, gruffly, "Leave all of that here."

"Are you kidding?"

"I said, leave it here. You won't need any of that stuff where we're heading. It'll just slow you down. Anything we have to have, we'll find along the way."

Guide didn't have many aspiring travelers to One to begin with, and he just lost a good share of the group that had gathered at the trailhead. The malcontents shake their heads and return to their campsites, talking among themselves: "That guy is crazy. We were smart not to follow him. You can't climb a high mountain without supplies, especially food and water."

A small band, though, follows Guide's orders and we take off our knapsacks.

"All right, then, here we go," he says. "Straight up!"

It's a hard climb. The path is amazingly steep, and doesn't have any switchbacks. We just put one foot in front of another and slog our way up the side of Mount Spirit the best we can. Soon we've stopped talking among ourselves, saving our breath for climbing.

But when Guide calls for a stop and we turn around, the view makes us forget how tired we are. Lake Partway now looks like a pond, we've climbed so high. The air is much cleaner. Just as Guide promised, without moving far from the trail we drink from a creek flowing with crystal-clear water and feast on delicious berries. Our exhaustion gives way to a second wind. We jump up eagerly when told it's time to move on.

Guide points out sights along the way. There are lots of side trails where, he says, explorers of Mount Spirit have gone off and never bothered to return to the main path. "They like where they are," Guide adds, "but I wish they had kept climbing. It's so beautiful at the very top."

Those words bring a little more spring to our legs, which now are back to being wearied, matching the condition of our spirit. Our enthusiasm is starting to fade along with the scenery. Once we passed timberline, the terrain turned barren. No more creeks and berry bushes, just craggy rocks and tufts of hardy vegetation. The food and water we enjoyed at the overlook are a distant memory. Now we're darn hungry and thirsty.

Some people turn back, notwithstanding Guide's attempts to encourage them: "It's just a bit farther, don't give up."

"Yeah, that's what you've been telling us since we started," they say disgustedly, setting off at a lope down the mountain, eager to get back to the comparative comforts of Lake Partway.

The handful of us who are left have a strong urge to follow in their footsteps, but something keeps us moving uphill, struggling to keep pace with our indefatigable companion, who isn't even breathing hard. He seems very much at home on Mount Spirit. Part of the reason, we note enviously, is that Guide isn't carrying an extra ounce anywhere on his lean and muscular form. The same definitely can't be said for us, over-fed and under-exercised as we had become at Lake Partway.

"Well, here we are," Guide finally says to his bedraggled party. We look up, mouths devilishly dry, sweat pouring from our foreheads, feet blistered, stomachs growling from hunger.

A cry goes out in unison. "What?!" All this, for *that*? A sheer cliff rises before us, the height of which can't be measured, as the top is hidden in clouds. There's no way around the cliff, for deep chasms fall off on each side of the narrow ridge on which we're standing. There doesn't seem to be any way up, either. The rock wall is almost perfectly smooth, and we don't have either the energy or the skill to even hazard an attempt to climb it.

"Is this the One?" we ask, not sure what answer we want to hear. For even though it would be dismaying if this was what we'd been working so hard to reach, being told that this was the end of the path would mean that the rough climb was over.

"No," says Guide with a grin, "but we're close. The way is through here." He points to a small hole in the cliff that we had failed to notice before. "Let's get moving. Don't want to dawdle now."

"You want us to go in there? You can't be serious." It's a narrow, pitch-black tunnel. We can't see more than a few feet inside. There doesn't seem to be any room to turn around if you got stuck. And then there is a final blow to our already shaky confidence. Guide tells us: "Oh, I forgot to mention that you need to take off all your clothes. It's a tight fit, and even a small button or zipper could be enough to hang you up."

Well, that does it. We followed Guide this far because he spoke so enthusiastically to us about the wonders of One. And even though the path up Mount Spirit was more challenging than any of us had imagined, at least we could always see where our next step was taking us. Up to this point we also had the option of turning back, which made it easier to move forward.

Now Guide is asking us to embrace an act of reckless abandon: crawl into a lightless tunnel that leads god-knows-where, with no food, no water, no clothes, no illumination, nothing at all.

Still, we've come this far. And if Guide made it in and out, safe and sound, we should be able to do the same. Yet again, why take a chance? Maybe Guide is a beguiling psychopath who lures trusting victims into a deathtrap. But Lake Partway has lost its appeal and we certainly don't want to go all the way back to Godless Materialism. Who knows, though, whether the uncertain promise of what the One offers warrants risking all that we have in hand now?

So we stand in front of the mysterious passageway, unable to decide whether we are on the brink of making the most marvelous discovery imaginable or if we are about to lose our lives in addition to everything that Guide had made us discard already.

We gaze at Guide, trying to decide. Is he a saint? Or is he insane?

"It's up to you," he says, as if he knows what we are thinking. "Alone to the alone, that's the way to the One. Each must decide for himself. I'll see you on the other side, or maybe not."

Then, we glimpse a gentler side of Guide that hadn't been much in evidence before. With a smile he comes up to each of us in turn, holding our hands in his, looking into our eyes. No words are exchanged but we understand Guide's silent message: I once stood where you are standing; I once questioned as you are questioning; I once hesitated as you are hesitating; we are the same, One.

Guide's final words mirror his unspoken sentiments. "You can know what I know if you do what I do." With incredible alacrity he turns on his heel, tearing off his clothes in a single motion, and dives headfirst into the tunnel. He's gone.

We're alone. It's unbearable. Tearfully, we turn to each other. What do we do now? The full course of our lives has brought us to this question, this cliff, this passageway, this choice. To move any closer to the One means stripping ourselves naked, maybe even abandoning our very existence. To return to the shores of Lake

Partway means never knowing what wonders, or perhaps terrors, are at the pinnacle of Mount Spirit.

Tearfully, we turn away from each other, realizing that Guide was right: it is up to each of us alone to decide what path to take. Indeed, I already know what I must do. It just will take some time—an instant, or an eternity—to tell myself.

> *And the attainment of it* [the One] *is for those who go up to the higher world and are converted and strip off what we put on in our descent. . . . until, passing in the ascent all that is alien to the God, one sees with one's self alone That alone, simple, single and pure, from which all depends and to which all look and are and live and think: for it is cause of life and mind and being.* [I-6-7]

Suggestions for Further Reading

Listed below are books recommended to readers who desire to explore Plotinus's teachings in greater depth. They are organized into five categories: (1) *Translations,* (2) *Non-scholarly overviews,* (3) *Scholarly yet accessible books,* (4) *Seriously scholarly treatises,* and (5) *Related works.*

1. Translations

Those who want to read the *Enneads* in English have a choice of translations by Stephen MacKenna and A.H. Armstrong. Each is, to put it frankly, pretty heavy-going. Only the most dedicated scholar, or student of philosophy, will delight in reading Plotinus's writings cover to cover. But it's unarguable: there is no substitute for the source.

Plotinus: In Seven Volumes, translated by A.H. Armstrong, Harvard University Press (Loeb Classical Library), 1966-88. This is the clearest and most reliable translation of the *Enneads.* Armstrong's translation faces the authoritative critical edition of the Greek text published by Henry and Schwyzer so it is the translation to use if you know Greek, or want to locate a quotation by line number (i.e. IV-3-9, 36-44, where 36-44 refers to lines in the critical edition). Helpful "Introductory Notes" precede each main section of the *Enneads,* and Armstrong elucidates many passages with footnotes.

Plotinus: The Enneads, translated by Stephen MacKenna, Penguin Books, 1991. Whereas Armstrong's translation includes all fifty-four chapters in the *Enneads,* this publication abridges MacKenna's circa 1921 translation to only thirty-three chapters. However, for most readers this is a plus, since they won't have to wade through the densest examples of Plotinus's abstruse prose. Further, MacKenna is more literary, though less literal, in his translation, making for easier reading. Prefatory writings by Paul Henry and John Dillon add to the value of this book. An unabridged edition of MacKenna's translation is available from Larson Publications.

2. NON-SCHOLARLY OVERVIEWS

There aren't many books in this category, which naturally includes the work in hand, *Return to the One*. However, several titles can be recommended to those who want to learn more about Plotinus's philosophy, but aren't interested in wading through scholarly dissertations. Each of these books is clear and well-written.

Plotinus: An Introduction to the Enneads, by Dominic J. O'Meara, Clarendon Press, 1995. Seemingly aimed at undergraduate students, this book pithily describes the essence of the *Enneads* in just 119 pages. The back cover correctly observes that "no knowledge of Greek is needed, nor is expertise in ancient or modern philosophy presupposed." This is a good place to start a further exploration of Plotinus.

Plotinus or The Simplicity of Vision, by Pierre Hadot, translated by Michael Chase, The University of Chicago Press, 1993. Better than anyone else, Hadot captures the spirit as well as the substance of Plotinus's philosophy. After painting a word-portrait of Plotinus, the author organizes his chapters in a refreshingly non-scholarly manner: "Presence," "Love," "Virtues," "Gentleness," "Solitude." Chase's original translations of passages from the *Enneads* (many of which have been included in this book) complement Hadot's equally sensitive prose.

The Philosophy of Plotinus, by Émile Bréhier, translated by Joseph Thomas, University of Chicago Press, 1971. Since this book is composed of lectures given by Bréhier at the Sorbonne in 1921-22, it reflects both the vitality of speech and the clarity that one would expect from a noted French translator of the *Enneads*. The author has limited his study of Plotinus to the "intelligible," the realms of soul, intellect (spirit), and the One, omitting discussion of the sensible world, nature, matter, and evil in relation to matter. Still, this is a fine introduction to Plotinus's philosophy.

The Passion of the Western Mind, by Richard Tarnas, Ballantine Books, 1993. This marvelous book is an overview of the entire history of Western thought, so Plotinus and Neoplatonism necessarily occupy only a few pages. Nevertheless, it is highly recommended because Tarnas not only cogently explains classical Greek philosophy, but also (in the words of reviewers) "allows readers to grasp the big picture of Western culture as if for the first time . . . unfolding the great drama of the evolution of the Western mind act by act, scene by scene in precise and scholarly detail . . . a work of genius." High praise, but richly deserved.

3. SCHOLARLY YET ACCESSIBLE BOOKS

In this category are books that are more scholarly than the preceding, yet are, by and large, accessible to the general reader who is motivated to delve more deeply into the philosophy of Plotinus.

Nature, Contemplation, and the One, by John N. Deck, Larson Publications, 1991. Deck focuses on only one of the fifty-four enneads, Ennead III-8, which is titled "On Nature and Contemplation." Yet because Plotinus's entire philosophy generally is reflected in every part of his writings, the central chapters of this book cover the gamut of his thought: "The One," "The Nous," "Soul," "Logos," "Nature," "Matter." This is a valuable resource for those who want to more clearly understand what Plotinus means by contemplation.

The Cambridge Companion to Plotinus, edited by Lloyd P. Gerson, Cambridge University Press, 1996. These sixteen essays on various aspects of Plotinus's philosophy will serve to flesh out the *Enneads* for those who have already grasped the skeleton of his thought. The essays by Dillon and Rist, "An ethic for the late antique sage" and "Plotinus and Christian philosophy," are particularly recommended, along with the introductory "Plotinus: The Platonic tradition and the foundation of Neoplatonism."

Classical Mediterranean Spirituality: Egyptian, Greek, Roman, edited by A.H. Armstrong, Crossroad Publishing Company, 1986. Even though only two of the twenty-one essays in this book focus on Neoplatonist spirituality, there are broader insights to be had into the spiritual tenor of the times in classical Mediterranean culture. In "The Spiritual Guide," Ilsetraut Hadot describes the role of mystic philosophers such as Plotinus in the Hellenistic period. In "The Spiritual Importance of not Knowing," R.T. Wallis takes up the subject of how one experiences a divinity that is beyond the reach of knowledge.

Philosophy as a Way of Life, by Pierre Hadot, edited by Arnold
Davidson, translated by Michael Chase, Blackwell Publishers Ltd.,
1995. This collection of essays by Hadot is subtitled "Spiritual Exercises
from Socrates to Foucault," indicating the breadth of the author's
philosophical vision. A central theme is that philosophy in antiquity
was a spiritual exercise, and not merely intellectual speculation. But,
says Hadot, "in modern university philosophy, philosophy is obviously no longer a way of life, a kind of life, unless it is the kind of
life of the professor of philosophy." Nicely put.

Porphyry's Against the Christians: The Literary Remains, edited
and translated by R. Joseph Hoffman, Prometheus Books, 1994. No
copies of Porphyry's scathing attack on Christianity have survived to
the present time, but Hoffman is among those scholars who believe
that the "pagan critic" cited in the Apocriticus of Macarius Magnes
is actually Porphyry (Plotinus's most noted student). Hoffman
extracts these pagan criticisms and organizes them into categories,
such as "The Attack on Paul the Apostle," "The Christian Doctrine
of God," and "Critique of the Resurrection of the Flesh." He also
contributes his own commentary on Porphyry's arguments, and
provides a historical overview of the tension between Greek thought
and early Christianity.

Porphyry: On Abstinence from Animal Food, translated by Thomas
Taylor, edited and introduced by Esme Wynne-Tyson, Centaur
Press Ltd., 1965. This apparently is the most extensive of Porphyry's
surviving writings, and indicates the importance he and Plotinus
placed on adhering to a vegetarian diet, even though the subject is
never mentioned explicitly in the *Enneads*. Porphyry's arguments
against killing animals for food are cogent, convincing, and almost
as relevant today as two thousand years ago. A newer translation
(*Porphyry: On Abstinence from Killing Animals*) by Gillian Clark is
available through Cornell University Press.

Reading Neoplatonism: Non-discursive Thinking in the Texts
of Plotinus, Proclus, and Damascius, by Sara Rappe, Cambridge
University Press, 2000. A fascinating discussion of how one goes
about reading a philosophy, Neoplatonism, which "insisted that
wisdom could be located only outside all texts and outside all language." Rappe examines various Plotinian thought exercises from

this perspective, arguing that Plotinus aims to transform the reader's entire manner of perceiving reality, as contrasted to merely affecting his or her rational understanding.

Mystical Languages of Unsaying, Michael Sells, The University of Chicago Press, 1994. If mystics want to tell us that the divine is beyond words, how do they say this in words? Such is the subject of Sells's intriguing book, which has chapters on Plotinus, Eriugena, Ibn 'Arabi, Marguerite Porete, and Meister Eckhart. It turns out that the manner in which mystics speak conveys a large part of their message. That is, Sells's thesis is that when a mystic speaks apophatically—unsaying what has been said to affirm the ultimate ineffability of the transcendent—he or she aims to produce a "meaning event" in the reader or listener which is the semantic analogue of mystical union. More simply put, if your mind is blown by a mystic's words, that's the point.

4. SERIOUSLY SCHOLARLY TREATISES

Don't be scared away from the books in this category. Even though they are not light reading and some presume that the reader has a fairly extensive knowledge of the Greek language or Greek philosophy, the serious student of Plotinus's teachings will find insights in these volumes that can't be discovered elsewhere.

Neoplatonism and Christian Thought, edited by Dominic J. O'Meara, State University of New York Press, 1982.

Neoplatonism and Indian Thought, edited by R. Baine Harris, State University of New York Press, 1982.

Neoplatonism and Islamic Thought, edited by Parviz Morewedge, State University of New York Press, 1992.

Neoplatonism and Jewish Thought, edited by Lenn E. Goodman, State University of New York Press, 1992.

Each of these books contains essays in which some aspect of Neoplatonism is compared to some aspect of a traditional religion: Christianity, Hinduism, Islam, or Judaism. Samples: "The

Neoplatonism of Saint Augustine," "Plotinus and the Upanisads," "The Neoplatonic Structure of Some Islamic Mystical Doctrines," and "Utterance and Ineffability in Jewish Neoplatonism." It is striking that Neoplatonism in general, and Plotinus's teachings in particular, are found to lie so close to the core of the world's enduring religious traditions. If there is such a thing as a universal metaphysics, it way well be Neoplatonism.

Neoplatonism, by R.T. Wallis, Gerald Duckworth & Co. Ltd., 1995. Lauded in a foreword as the "most comprehensive and reliable introduction to the subject in English," this book indeed covers all the bases. Beginning with a discussion of the aims and sources of Neoplatonism, Wallis turns successively to Plotinus, then to Porphyry and Iamblichus, then to the Athenian School, and finally to the influence of Neoplatonism. Clearly written and well-referenced.

Plotinus: The Road to Reality, by J.M. Rist, Cambridge at the University Press, 1967. The author notes that his book isn't meant to be an overview of Plotinus's philosophy, but rather is intended "for those who are interested in a more detailed discussion of certain problems in Plotinus's thought which have not always received the attention they deserve at the hands of either classicists or philosophers." Rist presumes a knowledge of Greek, but the book still can be read and enjoyed by skipping the foreign terms.

Plotinus, by Lloyd P. Gerson, Routledge, 1994. This is a serious and comprehensive analysis of the *Enneads* which examines Plotinus's teachings from a somewhat broader perspective than other scholarly books, as evidenced by some of the chapter titles: "An Argument for the Existence of a First Principle of All," "Truth and the Forms," "Human Psychology," "Some Epistemological Questions," "Conquering Virtue," "Philosophy of Religion." The author admits in a conclusion, "This is a difficult book." True, yet still well worth studying.

From Word to Silence: The Rise and Fall of Logos, by Raoul Mortley, Hanstein, 1986. The author says that this two-volume work "seeks to situate the development of negative theology within the context of the whole Greek concept of thought. . . . We know the Greeks as rationalists: others have noted their irrationalism; it also seems worthwhile to investigate their developing opposition to reason and language." Even though only a single chapter of Vol. 2 focuses on Plotinus ("Plotinus and abstraction"), it is fascinating to trace the history of the *via negativa*, or negative way, from the earliest days of Greek thought through medieval times. Highly recommended for serious students of mystical philosophy.

The Cambridge History of Later Greek and Early Medieval Philosophy, edited by A.H. Armstrong, Cambridge at the University Press, 1967. In a single volume, eight scholars have contributed substantial essays on such wide-ranging subjects as "Greek Philosophy from Plato to Plotinus," "Philo and the Beginnings of Christian Thought," "The Greek Christian Platonist Tradition," and "Early Islamic Philosophy." Armstrong's essay, "Plotinus," clearly describes the essence of the philosopher's life and thought in only seventy-three pages.

Plotinus: The Experience of Unity, by Gary M. Gurtler, Peter Lang, 1988. This book focuses on Plotinus's psychology: his teachings about consciousness, soul, perception, reason, intellection, being. The philosophical arguments are quite dense, though important. Gurtler often includes both the English and Greek words for key terms in quotations from the *Enneads*—a helpful aid for the reader who doesn't know Greek, but wants a greater understanding of Greek terms. Here's an example: "For in general thought [*to noein*] seems to be an intimate consciousness [*synaisthesis*] of the whole when many parts come together in the same thing."

Plotinus's Philosophy of the Self, by Gerard J.P. O'Daly, Barnes and Noble Import Division, 1973. Even though this is simply a published version of the author's doctoral dissertation, it is quite well-written and clear. One of the interesting questions O'Daly examines is in what manner the individual self continues to exist in the Plotinian mystical union. As scholarly books often do, the text bounces back and forth between English, Greek, French, and German, but the bulk (thankfully) is in English.

Plotinus's Psychology: His Doctrines of the Embodied Soul, by H.J. Blumenthal, Martinus Nijhoff, 1971. This is another published doctoral dissertation that focuses on the less-mystical side of Plotinus: his teachings concerning the nature of the soul that is still earth-

and body-bound. Blumenthal discusses the relation between soul and body, the faculties of the soul, sense-perception, memory and imagination, reason, and the limits of individuality.

Mystical Monotheism, by John Peter Kenney, Brown University Press, 1991. Subtitled "A Study in Ancient Platonic Theology," this is an interesting examination of the roots of the modern Western religions. As Kenney says, "Each of the Western monotheistic religions has engaged in a prolonged process of philosophical self-definition, and for each this endeavor has been rooted in ancient Greek metaphysics." Approximately a third of the book is devoted to the mystical monotheism of Plotinus.

Monopsychism, Mysticism, Metaconsciousness, by Philip Merlan, Martinus Nijhoff, 1963. As befits a book based in part on a lecture course given at the University of Oxford, Merlan's treatise is heavy going for the non-scholar. But he addresses intriguing questions concerning the nature of mystical experience and higher states of consciousness.

The Significance of Neoplatonism, edited by R. Baine Harris, State University of New York Press, 1976. In this collection of essays, Harris contributes a clear and comprehensive historical survey of Neoplatonism, ranging up to the Neoplatonic notions of Berkeley, Blake, Bergson and other quasi-modern thinkers. Other interesting essays include Armstrong's "The Apprehension of Divinity in Plotinus," Mamo's "Is Plotinian Mysticism Monistic?" and Rist's "Plotinus and Moral Obligation."

Advaita and Neoplatonism: A Critical Study in Comparative Philosophy, by J.F. Staal, University of Madras, 1961. This is a published doctoral dissertation that compares two great philosophical systems of East and West. Staal begins by asking how one goes about the business of comparative philosophy, an intriguing question in itself (for example, is a third normative system needed as a basis to judge the others?). He then moves to a discussion of the metaphysics of Advaita, and concludes by comparing Advaita and Neoplatonism. An interesting work, though filled with abstruse Indian and Greek terms.

5. RELATED WORKS

It is impossible to delimit those works that bear a close relation to Plotinus's teachings, since Neoplatonic thought permeates Western philosophy and religion so extensively. Nevertheless, here are some books that are personal favorites of mine both because of their innate value, and also because each echoes, in its own unique fashion, the sublime spiritual message of Plotinus. I end the list with a single selection from the vast corpus of Eastern philosophy, just to remind us that the One at the center of all transcends distinctions of West and East.

Marcus Aurelius: Meditations, translated by Maxwell Staniforth, Penguin Books, 1964. Aurelius was a Roman Emperor who lived about a hundred years before Plotinus, and shared his Stoic inclinations. Apart from the philosophical value of Aurelius's pithy musings and maxims (written during his martial campaigns), they are wonderfully applicable in everyday life. I took this book with me when I had to have a root canal, and these words comforted me in the dentist's chair: "The substance of us all is doomed to decay. . . . Why must you agitate yourself so? Nothing unprecedented is happening; so what is it that disturbs you?" For a deeper understanding of Aurelius's writings and his Stoic philosophy, read *The Inner Citadel* by Pierre Hadot, translated by Michael Chase.

Meditations on the Soul: Selected Letters of Marsilio Ficino, translated by members of the Language Department of the School of Economic Science (London), Inner Traditions International, 1997. Ficino was the leader of the Platonic Academy in fifteenth-century Florence. Even though he generally is termed a humanist, his humanism is of the deeply spiritual Neoplatonic variety. From the back cover: "Ficino was utterly fearless in expressing what he knew to be true. This collection of letters between Ficino and some of the most influential figures in European history, including Lorenzo de' Medici, Cosimo de' Medici, and Pope Sixtus IV, covers the widest range of topics, mixing philosophy and humor, compassion and advice."

Pseudo-Dionysius: The Complete Works, translated by Colm Luibheid, Paulist Press, 1987. No one knows the real identity of the fifth or sixth-century person who wrote under the pseudonym of

Dionysius the Areopagite. And what the Pseudo-Dionysius taught is deeply mystical and often almost incomprehensible. Still, his Neoplatonic emphasis that God can be known only by an "unknowing" that transcends reason, mind, and even being itself had a great influence on later Christian mystics. His short essay, "The Mystical Theology," beautifully captures the essence of the *via negativa*, the negative way.

Nicholas of Cusa: Selected Spiritual Writings, translated by H. Lawrence Bond, Paulist Press, 1997. Cusa has been called "the outstanding intellectual figure of the fifteenth century as well as the principal gatekeeper between medieval and modern philosophy." Echoing Plotinus and the Pseudo-Dionysius, he speaks of the importance of what he calls learned ignorance. For example, in his wonderful "Dialogue on the Hidden God" he deflates those who intellectualize their spirituality: "One knows that which one thinks one knows less than that which one knows one does not know." If you like to ponder such thoughts, you'll love Nicholas of Cusa.

The Cloud of Unknowing and Other Works, translated into modern English by Clifton Wolters, Penguin Books, 1987. These writings by an anonymous fourteenth century English parson are a much easier read than those of Pseudo-Dionysius and Nicholas of Cusa, yet reflect to as great a degree, if not more so, a Neoplatonic approach to Christianity. "Our work," says the author, "is a spiritual work, and not physical; nor is it achieved in a physical fashion. . . . Everything physical is external to your soul, and inferior to it in the natural order." This is one of my favorite books, well worth reading and then re-reading.

Meister Eckhart: Selected Writings, selected and translated by Oliver Davies, Penguin Books, 1994. There are many books about Meister Eckhart, the German Dominican of the late thirteenth and early fourteenth centuries who boldly melded Greek thought and Christian theology. This volume contains some interesting Eckhart sermons that are not easily found elsewhere, and a clear introduction to Eckhart's mystical thought. Meister Eckhart demonstrates that Neoplatonism is fully compatible with a mystically-inspired Christianity.

Open Mind, Open Heart, Thomas Keating, Continuum Publishing Company, 2001. Keating is one of the leaders of the modern Christian "centering prayer" movement, which, he says, "is an effort to renew the teaching of the Christian tradition on contemplative prayer." Keating notes that the Greek Fathers borrowed the term *theoria* (contemplation) from the Neoplatonists, and I had the feeling, while reading this book, that whatever form of mystical contemplation Plotinus practiced, it must have borne a close resemblance to centering prayer. "Divine union," says Keating, "is the goal for all Christians," as for Plotinus.

Nature Loves to Hide: Quantum Physics and the Nature of Reality, a Western Perspective, by Shimon Malin, Oxford University Press, 2001. This book should make Classics department faculty stand taller when they run into their Physics colleagues. Malin, a professor of physics, explains the intricacies and mysteries of quantum physics in a highly readable manner. Then, in the final chapters, he shows that the philosophy of Plato and Plotinus (and Alfred North Whitehead, a modern philosopher) is entirely commensurate with what physics has come to know of quantum reality. Malin writes: "For the individual, therefore, the quest for the experience of Oneness is the quest for the experience of his or her deepest identity, as well as the experience of the nature of reality."

Mysticism, Mind, Consciousness, by Robert K.C. Forman, State University of New York Press, 1999. Forman argues persuasively, on the basis of both philosophical insight and his own mystical experience, that "pure consciousness events" are real, and can't be explained away as an artifact of a mystic's belief system or personal expectations. He also describes the nature of a "dualistic mystical state" in which the no-thought of pure consciousness can co-exist with everyday worldly living. Though this book contains no mention of Greek philosophy, per se, reflections of Plotinus's teachings are on every page. For example, Forman speaks of knowledge by identity, where "the subject knows something by virtue of being it." That's pure Plotinus.

Talks with Ramana Maharshi: On Realizing Abiding Peace and Happiness, Inner Directions Publishing, 2000. If you want to put a label on Ramana, a twentieth-century Indian sage, he could be called a teacher of advaita—which simply means "not two," or we might say, one. But Ramana, like Plotinus, transcends labels. He never traveled, gave formal talks, or wrote books. He spontaneously answered questions posed by visitors, and these conversations form the basis of this captivating book. Echoes of Plotinus can be heard throughout the book, just as Ramana's voice speaks in the *Enneads*. At heart, every pure mystic says the same thing, albeit in distinctive styles of saying.

Notes

Introduction

1. Hadot, *Plotinus or The Simplicity of Vision*, p. 54.
2. Underhill, p. 13.
3. Huxley, p. vii.
4. Tarnas, p. 441.
5. Tarnas, pp. 442-43.
6. Tarnas, p. 2.
7. Gatti, p. 24.
8. Tarnas, p. 103.
9. Ward, p. 113.
10. Rappe, p. 33.
11. Rappe, p. 3.
12. Meagher, p. 3.
13. Meagher, p. 5.

Plotinus, a Rational Mystic

1. Luce, pp. 152, 153.
2. Hadot, *Plotinus or The Simplicity of Vision*, p. 74.
3. Hadot, *Plotinus or The Simplicity of Vision*, p. 20.
4. Harward, pp. 809, 810.
5. Hadot, *Plotinus or The Simplicity of Vision*, p. 82.
6. Hadot, *Plotinus or The Simplicity of Vision*, p. 88.
7. Hadot, *Plotinus or The Simplicity of Vision*, p. 88.
8. Hadot, *Plotinus or The Simplicity of Vision*, pp. 83, 84.
9. Hadot, *Plotinus or The Simplicity of Vision*, p. 88.
10. Hadot, *Philosophy as a Way of Life*, p. 64.
11. Harris, p. 2.
12. Hadot, *Plotinus or The Simplicity of Vision*, p. 85.
13. Hadot, *Plotinus or The Simplicity of Vision*, pp. 91, 93.
14. Hadot, *Plotinus or The Simplicity of Vision*, p. 93.
15. Jowett, p. 427.
16. Hadot, *Plotinus or The Simplicity of Vision*, p. 84.
17. Hadot, *Plotinus or The Simplicity of Vision*, p. 17.

Philosophy as a Way of Life

1. McGinn, p. 46.
2. Hadot, *Philosophy as a Way of Life*, pp. 271, 272.
3. Hadot, *Philosophy as a Way of Life*, p. 265.
4. Hadot, *Plotinus or The Simplicity of Vision*, p. 30.

5. Hadot, *Philosophy as a Way of Life*, pp. 267, 268.
6. Hadot, *Philosophy as a Way of Life*, p. 272.
7. Hadot, *Plotinus or The Simplicity of Vision*, p. 34.

Making a Leap of Faith

1. Malin, p. 7.
2. Hadot, *Plotinus or The Simplicity of Vision*, p. 46.
3. Sells, p. 31.
4. Sells, p. 32.
5. Kavanaugh, pp. 81, 107.
6. Kavanaugh, pp. 67.
7. Benoit, p. xiv.
8. Hadot, *Plotinus or The Simplicity of Vision*, p. 19.
9. Hadot, *Plotinus or The Simplicity of Vision*, p. 19.
10. Kavanaugh, p. 67.
11. Jowett, p. 202.

Reading the Writings of Plotinus

1. Rappe, pp. 64, 85.
2. Sells, pp. 9, 216.
3. Rappe, p. 238.
4. Rappe, p. 20.
5. Yun, p. 141.
6. MacKenna, p. xxii.

THE ONE

God Is the Goal

1. Hadot, *Plotinus or The Simplicity of Vision*, p. 58.
2. Gerson, p. 187.
3. Gerson, p. 187.

One Is Overall

1. Kenney, p. 154.
2. Hadot, *Plotinus or The Simplicity of Vision*, p. 44.

First Is Formless

1. Hadot, *Plotinus or The Simplicity of Vision*, p. 57.
2. Hatab, p. 28.
3. Hadot, *Plotinus or The Simplicity of Vision*, p. 58.
4. Hadot, *Plotinus or The Simplicity of Vision*, p. 58.

5. Hadot, *Plotinus or The Simplicity of Vision*, p. 57.

Love Is Limitless

1. Hadot, *Plotinus or The Simplicity of Vision*, p. 59.
2. Hadot, *Plotinus or The Simplicity of Vision*, p. 54.
3. Mencken, p. 723.
4. Hadot, *Plotinus or The Simplicity of Vision*, p. 52.

Infinity Is Ineffable

1. Sells, p. 5.

Beauty Is Beyond

1. Armstrong, *Plotinus I*, p. 69.
2. Hadot, *Plotinus or The Simplicity of Vision*, p. 49.
3. Hadot, *Philosophy as a Way of Life*, p. 102.
4. Hadot, *Plotinus or The Simplicity of Vision*, p. 21.
5. Hadot, *Plotinus or The Simplicity of Vision*, p. 43.

Universe Is a Unity

1. Hadot, *Plotinus or The Simplicity of Vision*, p. 38.
2. Hadot, *Plotinus or The Simplicity of Vision*, p. 45.

AND MANY

Spirit Is Substance

1. Casti, p. 27.

Above Is Astonishment

1. Hadot, *Plotinus or The Simplicity of Vision*, p. 37.
2. Hadot, *Plotinus or The Simplicity of Vision*, p. 44.

All Is Alive

1. Hadot, *Plotinus or The Simplicity of Vision*, p. 46.
2. Hadot, *Plotinus or The Simplicity of Vision*, p. 37.
3. Hadot, *Plotinus or The Simplicity of Vision*, p. 37.
4. Hadot, *Plotinus or The Simplicity of Vision*, p. 37.
5. Malin, p.141.
6. Rist, *The Road to Reality*, p. 205.

Creation Is Contemplation

1. Hadot, *Plotinus or The Simplicity of Vision*, p. 22.
2. Deck, pp. 102-103.
3. Hadot, *Plotinus or The Simplicity of Vision*, p. 42.
4. Hadot, *Plotinus or The Simplicity of Vision*, p. 42.
5. Hadot, *Plotinus or The Simplicity of Vision*, p. 38.
6. Deck, p. 124.
7. Hadot, *Plotinus or The Simplicity of Vision*, p. 43.

Truth Is Transparent

1. Hadot, *Plotinus or The Simplicity of Vision*, p. 37.
2. Eddington, p. 174.
3. O'Meara, p. 39.
4. Hadot, *Plotinus or The Simplicity of Vision*, p. 33.
5. Hadot, *Plotinus or The Simplicity of Vision*, p. 92.

Form Is Foundation

1. Hadot, *Plotinus or The Simplicity of Vision*, p. 37.
2. Rist, *The Road to Reality*, p. 22.

Intelligence Is Intuitive

1. Hadot, *Plotinus or The Simplicity of Vision*, p. 40.
2. Mortley, p. 61.
3. Hadot, *Plotinus or The Simplicity of Vision*, p. 44.
4. Hadot, *Plotinus or The Simplicity of Vision*, p. 33.

Time Is Temporary

1. Armstrong, "From Intellect to Matter: The Return to the One," in *The Cambridge History of Later Greek and Early Medieval Philosophy*, p. 251.
2. Hawking, pp. 8, 9.
3. *Meditations on the Soul: Selected Letters of Marsilio Ficino*, p. 31.

World-Soul Is a Weaver

1. Armstrong, *Plotinus IV*, p. 27.
2. Gerson, pp. 62-63.
3. O'Meara, p. 26.
4. Hadot, *Plotinus or The Simplicity of Vision*, p. 94.
5. Hadot, *Plotinus or The Simplicity of Vision*, p. 35.
6. Hadot, *Plotinus or The Simplicity of Vision*, p. 94.

Providence Is Pervasive

1. Hadot, *Plotinus or The Simplicity of Vision*, p. 104.
2. Wallis, p. 68.
3. Rist, *The Road to Reality*, pp. 204, 206.

SOUL'S DESCENT

Psyche Is a Pilgrim

1. Blumenthal, p. 2.
2. Hadot, *Plotinus or The Simplicity of Vision*, p. 64.

Descent Is Debasement

1. Hadot, *Plotinus or The Simplicity of Vision*, p. 64.

Evil Is Emptiness

1. Hadot, *Plotinus or The Simplicity of Vision*, p. 103.
2. Hadot, *Plotinus or The Simplicity of Vision*, p. 103.
3. *Meditations on the Soul: Selected Letters of Marsilio Ficino*, p. 138.
4. Hadot, *Plotinus or The Simplicity of Vision*, p. 104.
5. Hadot, *Plotinus or The Simplicity of Vision*, p. 104.

Matter Is Malignant

1. NASA High Energy Astrophysics Science Archive Research Center: http://heasarc.gsfc.nasa.gov/docs/objects/binaries/neutron_star_structure.html
2. Greene, p. 146.
3. Dillon, p. 329.

Body Is a Bother

1. O'Meara, p. 27.
2. Hadot, *Plotinus or The Simplicity of Vision*, p. 102.

Reincarnation Is Reality

1. Rist, *The Road to Reality*, p. 125.

Destiny Is Deserved

1. Hadot, *Plotinus or The Simplicity of Vision*, p. 105.
2. O'Meara, p. 87.
3. Hadot, *Plotinus or The Simplicity of Vision*, p. 106.
4. Hadot, *Plotinus or The Simplicity of Vision*, p. 104.

Choice Is Compulsion

1. Rist, *The Road to Reality*, p. 136.
2. Gerson, p. 161.

Reason Is Restricted

1. Hadot, *Plotinus or The Simplicity of Vision*, p. 40.
2. *Great Books of the Western World, Thomas Aquinas I, Vol. 19*, p. vi.
3. Hadot, *Plotinus or The Simplicity of Vision*, p. 48.

Myself Is Multiple

1. Hadot, *Plotinus or The Simplicity of Vision*, p. 27.
2. Hadot, *Plotinus or The Simplicity of Vision*, p. 27.
3. Armstrong, "Man and reality," in *The Cambridge History of Later Greek and Early Medieval Philosophy*, p. 226.
4. Hadot, *Plotinus or The Simplicity of Vision*, p. 107.
5. Gerson, p. 217.
6. Hadot, *Plotinus or The Simplicity of Vision*, p. 28.
7. Ramana, p. 157.
8. Hadot, "Neoplatonist Spirituality," in *Classical Mediterranean Spirituality: Egyptian, Greek, Roman*, pp. 232, 233.

Suffering Is Separation

1. Hadot, *Plotinus or The Simplicity of Vision*, p. 27.
2. Blumenthal, p. 59.
3. Jowett, p. 388.
4. Hadot, *Plotinus or The Simplicity of Vision*, p. 105.
5. Hadot, *Plotinus or The Simplicity of Vision*, p. 105.
6. Hadot, *Plotinus or The Simplicity of Vision*, p. 105.
7. Hadot, *Plotinus or The Simplicity of Vision*, p. 102.
8. Hadot, *Plotinus or The Simplicity of Vision*, p. 94.

AND RETURN

Soul Is the Self

1. Nicholson, pp. 366-67, 389.
2. MacKenna, p. xxxi.
3. O'Daly, p. 91.
4. Armstrong, *Plotinus VI*, pp. 270, 271.
5. Jowett, p. 476.

Without Is Within

1. Hadot, *Plotinus or The Simplicity of Vision*, p. 34.
2. Hadot, *Plotinus or The Simplicity of Vision*, p. 44.
3. Hadot, *Plotinus or The Simplicity of Vision*, p. 25.
4. Armstrong, *Plotinus I*, p. xvii.

Detachment Is Delightful

1. Hadot, *Plotinus or The Simplicity of Vision*, p. 59.
2. Hadot, *Plotinus or The Simplicity of Vision*, p. 67.
3. Hadot, *Plotinus or The Simplicity of Vision*, p. 101.
4. Hadot, *Plotinus or The Simplicity of Vision*, p. 102.
5. Rist, *The Road to Reality*, p. 161.
6. Hadot, *Plotinus or The Simplicity of Vision*, p. 71.
7. Hadot, *Plotinus or The Simplicity of Vision*, p. 72.
8. Gerson, p. 151.

Divesting Is Divine

1. Hadot, *Plotinus or The Simplicity of Vision*, p. 47.
2. Hadot, *Plotinus or The Simplicity of Vision*, p. 59.
3. Hadot, *Plotinus or The Simplicity of Vision*, p. 31.
4. Hadot, *Plotinus or The Simplicity of Vision*, p. 46.
5. Hadot, *Plotinus or The Simplicity of Vision*, p. 63.

Forgetting Is Favorable

1. Hadot, *Plotinus or The Simplicity of Vision*, p. 31.
2. Wolters, p. 111.
3. Hadot, *Plotinus or The Simplicity of Vision*, p. 31.

Purification Is Presence

1. Hadot, *Plotinus or The Simplicity of Vision*, p. 67.
2. Hadot, *Plotinus or The Simplicity of Vision*, p. 67.
3. Rist, "Plotinus and Moral Obligation," in *Significance of Neoplatonism*, pp. 218, 228.
4. Rist, "Plotinus and Moral Obligation," in *Significance of Neoplatonism*, p. 218.
5. Hadot, *Plotinus or The Simplicity of Vision*, p. 66.
6. Hadot, *Plotinus or The Simplicity of Vision*, pp. 71, 70.
7. Dillon, p. 324.
8. Hadot, *Plotinus or The Simplicity of Vision*, p. 108.
9. Hadot, *Plotinus or The Simplicity of Vision*, p. 94.
10. Hadot, *Plotinus or The Simplicity of Vision*, p. 70.
11. Hadot, *Plotinus or The Simplicity of Vision*, p. 69.
12. Hadot, *Plotinus or The Simplicity of Vision*, p. 70.

13. Hadot, *Plotinus or The Simplicity of Vision*, pp. 71, 95.
14. Hadot, *Plotinus or The Simplicity of Vision*, pp. 69, 74.

Simplicity Is Superior

1. *Encyclopedia Britannica 99 (multimedia edition)*, "Ockham's razor"
2. Trefil, p. 198.
3. Mencken, p. 127.
4. Hadot, *Plotinus or The Simplicity of Vision*, p. 58.

Stillness Is Sublime

1. Rist, p. 212.
2. Rist, p. 225.
3. Hadot, *Plotinus or The Simplicity of Vision*, p. 61.

Happiness Is Here

1. Staniforth, p. 108.
2. Hadot, *Plotinus or The Simplicity of Vision*, p. 101.
3. Hadot, *Plotinus or The Simplicity of Vision*, p. 101.
4. James Atlas, "The Fall of Fun," *The New Yorker*, November 18, 1996, p. 71.
5. Hadot, *Plotinus or The Simplicity of Vision*, p. 81.

Fear Is a Fiction

1. Jowett, p. 225.
2. Hadot, *Plotinus or The Simplicity of Vision*, p. 108.

Return Is Reunion

1. Gerson, p. 210.
2. Gerson, p. 203.
3. Gerson, pp. 141, 209, 210.
4. Hadot, *Plotinus or The Simplicity of Vision*, p. 57.
5. Hadot, *Plotinus or The Simplicity of Vision*, p. 52.
6. Hadot, *Plotinus or The Simplicity of Vision*, p. 57.

Vision Is Veracity

1. Hadot, *Plotinus or The Simplicity of Vision*, p. 21.
2. Tarnas, p. 77.
3. Hadot, *Plotinus or The Simplicity of Vision*, p. 63.
4. Hadot, *Plotinus or The Simplicity of Vision*, p. 62.

Wrap-Up

From Forms to the Formless

1. Hadot, *Philosophy as a Way of Life*, p. 83.
2. Armstrong, "Introduction," in *Classical Mediterranean Spirituality: Egyptian, Greek, Roman*, p. xiv.
3. Hadot, "The Spiritual Guide," in *Classical Mediterranean Spirituality: Egyptian, Greek, Roman*, pp. 445, 449.
4. Smith, p. xiv.
5. Smith, p. xxv.
6. Henry, pp. xxxix, lviii.
7. Smith, p. xii.
8. Walshe, p. xlviii.
9. Lewis, p. 101.
10. Lewis, p. 101.
11. Smith, p. xv.

Toward a Science of Spirituality

1. Malin, p. 230.
2. Underhill, p. 14.
3. Pereira, p. 143.
4. Walshe, p. 66.
5. Walshe, p. 6.
6. Armstrong, "Negative Theology, Myth, and Incarnation," in *Neoplatonism and Christian Thought*, p. 214.
7. Guthrie, p. 67.
8. Davies, p. 179.

Neoplatonism and Christianity

1. Hoffman, p. 17.
2. Hoffman, p. 158.
3. Zimmern, p. 53.
4. Findlay, p. 229.
5. Wallis, p. 104.
6. Wallis, p. 104.
7. Tarnas, pp. 101-102.
8. Findlay, p. 227.
9. Findlay, p. 228.
10. Findlay, p. 229.

The Legacy of Plotinus and Plato

1. Tarnas, pp. 100, 103.
2. Dods, pp. 298, 268, 291, 299.

3. Dods, p. 271.
4. Shaw, p. 655.
5. Bréhier, p. 112.
6. Dods, p. 295.
7. Dods, pp. 295, 608.
8. Tarnas, p. 117.
9. Guthrie, p. 33.
10. Tarnas, p. 475.
11. Bréhier, pp. 113, 189.
12. Davies, p. 124.
13. Tarnas, pp. 213, 215.
14. Tarnas, p. 192.
15. Tarnas, p. 218.

Our Great Experiment with Truth

1. Hadot, *Plotinus or The Simplicity of Vision*, p. 45.
2. Davies, pp. 148, 149.

Bibliography

Armstrong, A.H., translator. *Plotinus I-VII.* Seven volumes published by Loeb Classical Library. Cambridge: Harvard University Press, 1966-1988.

_____"Introduction." In A.H. Armstrong, editor, *Classical Mediterranean Spirituality: Egyptian, Greek, Roman.* New York: Crossroad Publishing Co., 1986.

_____"Negative Theology, Myth, and Incarnation." In Dominic J. O'Meara, editor, *Neoplatonism and Christian Thought.* Norfolk, VA: International Society for Neoplatonic Studies, 1982.

_____"From Intellect to Matter: The Return to the One." In A.H. Armstrong, editor, *The Cambridge History of Later Greek and Early Medieval Philosophy.* Cambridge: Cambridge University Press, 1967.

_____"Man and Reality." In A.H. Armstrong, editor, *The Cambridge History of Later Greek and Early Medieval Philosophy.* Cambridge: Cambridge University Press, 1967.

Benoit, Hubert. *The Supreme Doctrine.* New York: Viking Press, 1967.

Blumenthal, H.J. *Plotinus' Psychology.* The Hague: Martinus Nijhoff, 1971.

Bréhier, Émile. *The Philosophy of Plotinus.* Chicago: The University of Chicago Press, 1958.

Casti, John L. "The Outer Limits: In Search of the 'Unknowable' in Science." In John L. Casti and Anders Karlqvist, editors, *Boundaries and Barriers.* New York: Addison-Wesley Publishing Co., 1996.

Davies, Oliver, translator. *Meister Eckhart: Selected Writings.* London: Penguin Books, 1994.

Deck, John N. *Nature, Contemplation, and the One.* Burdett, NY: Larson Publications, 1991.

Dillon, John M. "An Ethic for the Late Antique Sage." In Lloyd Gerson, editor, *The Cambridge Companion to Plotinus.* Cambridge: Cambridge University Press, 1996.

Dods, Marcus, translator. "The City of God." In *Great Books of the Western World, Augustine, Vol. 18.* Chicago: Encyclopedia Britannica, Inc., 1952.

Eddington, Arthur. "Beyond the Veil of Physics." In Ken Wilber, editor, *Quantum Questions.* Boston: Shambhala Publications, 1985.

Findlay, John N. "Why Christians Should Be Platonists." In Dominic J. O'Meara, editor, *Neoplatonism and Christian Thought*. Norfolk, VA: International Society for Neoplatonic Studies, 1982.

Gatti, Maria Luisa. "Plotinus: The Platonic tradition and the foundation of Neoplatonism." In Lloyd Gerson, editor, *The Cambridge Companion to Plotinus*. Cambridge: Cambridge University Press, 1996.

Gerson, Lloyd P. *Plotinus*. New York: Routledge, 1994.

Great Books of the Western World, Thomas Aquinas I, Vol. 19. "Biographical Note." Chicago: Encyclopedia Britannica Inc., 1952.

Greene, Brian. *The Elegant Universe*. New York: W.W. Norton & Co., 1999.

Guthrie, Kenneth, translator. *Porphyry's Launching Points to the Realm of Mind*. Grand Rapids, MI: Phanes Press, 1988.

Hadot, Pierre. *Philosophy as a Way of Life*. Translated by Michael Chase. Cambridge: Blackwell Publishers Inc., 1995.

_____*Plotinus or The Simplicity of Vision*. Translated by Michael Chase. Chicago: The University of Chicago Press, 1993.

_____"Neoplatonist Spirituality" and "The Spiritual Guide." In A.H. Armstrong, editor, *Classical Mediterranean Spirituality: Egyptian, Greek, Roman*. New York: Crossroad Publishing Co., 1986.

Harris, R. Baine. "A Brief Description of Neoplatonism." In R. Baine Harris, editor, *The Significance of Neoplatonism*. Albany: State University of New York Press, 1976.

Harward, J., translator. "The Seventh Letter." In *Great Books of the Western World, Plato, Vol. 7*. Chicago: Encyclopedia Britannica, Inc., 1952.

Hatab, Lawrence J. "Plotinus and the Upanisads." In R. Baine Harris, editor, *Neoplatonism and Indian Thought*. Norfolk, VA: International Society for Neoplatonic Studies, 1982.

Hawking, Stephen W. *A Brief History of Time*. New York: Bantam Books, 1988.

Henry, Paul. "Introduction: The Place of Plotinus in the History of Thought." In Stephen MacKenna, translator, *Plotinus: The Enneads* (London: Faber and Faber Limited, 1966.

Hoffman, R. Joseph. *Porphyry's Against the Christians: The Literary Remains*. Amherst, NY: Prometheus Books, 1994.

Huxley, Aldous. *The Perennial Philosophy*. New York: Harper & Row, 1970.

Jowett, Benjamin, translator. "The Dialogues of Plato." In *Great Books of the Western World, Plato, Vol. 7*. Chicago: Encyclopedia Britannica, Inc., 1952.

Kavanaugh, Kieran, editor and translator. *John of the Cross: Selected Writings* New York: Paulist Press, 1987.

Kenney, John Peter. *Mystical Monotheism*. Hanover, NH: Brown University Press, 1991.

Lewis, Franklin D. *Rumi: Past and Present, East and West*. Oxford: Oneworld Publications, 2000.

Luce, J.V. *Introduction to Greek Philosophy*. London: Thames and Hudson, 1992.

MacKenna, Stephen, translator. *Plotinus: The Enneads*. London: Faber and Faber Limited, 1966.

Malin, Shimon. *Nature Loves to Hide*. New York: Oxford University Press, 2001.

McGinn, Bernard. *The Foundations of Mysticism*. New York: The Crossroad Publishing Company, 1995.

Meagher, Robert. *Augustine: An Introduction*. New York: Harper & Row, 1979.

Meditations on the Soul: Selected Letters of Marsilio Ficino. Translated by members of the Language Department of the School of Economic Science, London. Rochester, VT: Inner Traditions International, 1997.

Mencken, H.L. editor. *A New Dictionary of Quotations*. New York: Alfred A. Knopf, 1960.

Mortley, Raoul. *From Word to Silence I: The Rise and Fall of Logos*. Bonn: Hanstein, 1986.

Nicholson, Reynold A., editor and translator. *The Mathnawi of Jalalu'ddin Rumi: V & VI*. Cambridge: Trustees of the "E.J.W. Gibb Memorial," 1990.

O'Daly, Gerard J.P. *Plotinus' Philosophy of the Self*. New York: Barnes and Noble Books, 1973.

O'Meara, Dominic J. *Plotinus: An Introduction to the Enneads*. Oxford: Oxford University Press, 1995.

Pereira, Lancelot. *The Enchanted Darkness*. Gujarat, India: Gujarat Sahitya Prakash, 1995.

Ramana, Bhagavan. *Absolute Consciousness*. Bangalore: Ramana Maharshi Centre for Learning, 1997.

Rappe, Sara. *Reading Neoplatonism*. Cambridge: Cambridge University Press, 2000.

Rist, J.M. *Plotinus: The Road to Reality*. Cambridge: Cambridge University Press, 1967.

_____ "Plotinus and Moral Obligation." In R. Baine Harris, editor, *The Significance of Neoplatonism*. Albany: State University of New York Press, 1976.

Sells, Michael A. *Mystical Languages of Unsaying*. Chicago: The University of Chicago Press, 1996.

Shaw, J.F., translator. "On Christian Doctrine." In *Great Books of the Western World, Augustine, Vol. 18.* Chicago: Encyclopedia Britannica, Inc., 1952.

Smith, Huston. "Introduction to the Revised Edition." In Frithjof Schuon, *The Transcendent Unity of Religions.* Wheaton, IL: The Theosophical Publishing House, 1993.

Staniforth, Maxwell, translator. *Marcus Aurelius: Meditations.* London: Penguin Books, 1964.

Tarnas, Richard. *The Passion of the Western Mind.* New York: Ballantine Books, 1993.

Trefil, James. *Reading the Mind of God.* New York: Anchor Books, 1990.

Underhill, Evelyn. *The Essentials of Mysticism & Other Essays.* Oxford: Oneworld Publications, 1995.

Wallis, R.T. *Neoplatonism.* London: Gerald Duckworth & Co., 1995.

Ward, Keith. *God: A Guide for the Perplexed.* Oxford: Oneworld Publications, 2002.

Walshe, M.O'C., translator. *Meister Eckhart: Sermons and Treatises, Volume 1.* Shaftesbury, Dorset: Element Books, 1987.

Wolters, Clifton, translator. *The Cloud of Unknowing and Other Works.* New York: Penguin Books, 1987.

Yun, Hsing. *Describing the Indescribable.* Translated by Tom Graham. Boston: Wisdom Publications, 2001.

Zimmern, Alice, translator. *Porphyry's Letter to His Wife Marcella.* Grand Rapids, MI: Phanes Press, 1986.

Index

About the Author

IN ADDITION TO *Return to the One*, Brian Hines is the author of *Life Is Fair* and *God's Whisper, Creation's Thunder*. More information about these books and Brian's current writing projects can be found at **www.brianhines.com**, his website.

A serious student of meditation, metaphysics, and philosophy for over thirty years, Brian has a bachelor's degree in psychology/humanities, a master's degree in social work, and two years of doctoral-level training in systems science.

He has been a research associate at the Oregon Health Sciences University, a manager with Oregon's health planning agency, and executive director of Oregon Health Decisions. Most recently, Brian was the communications director for Eco-Enterprises, Inc.

Printed in the United States
98210LV00007B/134/A

9 781588 321008